ife of
devise
ompre-
Mental
akers,

ryland

ganisa-
as an
ough a
he first

al care
impact
f using
Quality
studies
health
quality

xley is
es was
try and
y at the

Quality of Life and Mental Health Services

Joseph Oliver, Peter Huxley,
Keith Bridges and Hadi Mohamad
Foreword by Anthony Lehman

London and New York

First published 1996
by Routledge
11 New Fetter Lane, London EC4P 4EE

Simultaneously published in the USA and Canada
by Routledge
29 West 35th Street, New York, NY 10001

First published in paperback 1997

Typeset in Times by Pure Tech India Ltd, Pondicherry
Printed on acid-free paper
Printed and bound in Great Britain by
T.J. International Ltd, Padstow, Cornwall

British Library Cataloguing in Publication Data
A catalogue record for this book is available from the British Library

Library of Congress Cataloguing in Publication Data
Quality of life and mental health services/Joseph Oliver ... [et al.]
    p. cm.
  Includes bibliographical references and index.
  1. Mental health services. 2. Quality of life. I. Oliver, J. P.
  J. (Joseph P. J.)
  RA790.Q35   1997
  362.2–dc20   96–44152

ISBN 0–415–16151–7

Contents

Illustrations

FIGURES

TABLES

Foreword

The pursuit of happiness is age-old. Certainly a bulwark of democracy is the premise that all persons have an equal right to this pursuit. The degree to which a society concerns itself with the happiness and well-being of all of its members reflects its humaneness. Despite even the best of intentions, however, all societies have their disadvantaged groups at risk of invisibility and exclusion from the mainstream social agenda. A hallmark of democracies in the latter part of the twentieth century has been the push to ensure that all citizens have access to the fruits of their rights and responsibilities.

Throughout history, persons afflicted with severe and persistent mental disorders have been excluded in a variety of ways from participation in setting their society's agendas. They have been hurled from cliffs, burned at the stake, banished from towns, placed on floating 'ships of fools', chained in cellars and prisons, segregated at remote mental institutions, and simply ignored. It is easy for us to sniff at such inhumanity and to comfort ourselves that we today are much more egalitarian and humane. However, we all know that, at best, many of these persons live marginally in our communities and an alarming number end up homeless or in jail. It is a credit to nations on both sides of the Atlantic that we have elevated in our social agendas concerns about the quality of life afforded to persons with mental disorders. This at least acknowledges their right to the pursuit of happiness and is a step toward giving them the opportunities to sustain a fulfilling existence.

As with many grand ideas, the current emphasis placed on enhancing the quality of life of persons with mental illnesses runs the risk of rhetoric unless we devise ways to monitor and guide progress toward this goal. *Quality of Life and Mental Health Services* chronicles the efforts of a dedicated group of researchers and clinicians in the United Kingdom to translate rhetoric into data and, hence, informed policy. What is unique and immensely valuable about this book is that it presents, in one place, the articulation of one nation's policy to promote the quality of life of persons with mental disorders, a thoughtful and thorough discussion about the conceptual issues faced in defining and assessing the quality of life for these persons, an honest, scientific description of the development of methods to measure quality of life, and the results of implementing these methods in order to inform service evaluations. At the most basic level this accomplishment precludes arguments that quality of life cannot be measured and reduces the risk that the goal of improving the quality of life for these persons will become just a passing bit of political hyperbole or societal face-saving.

The comprehensiveness, clarity and practicality of this volume will be of great assistance to policy decision-makers, researchers, programme evaluators and service providers alike. Policy decision-makers will particularly like the articulation and operationalisation of the concepts, the results of evaluations of current service alternatives and their relevance to the development of social policy. Researchers and programme evaluators will appreciate the care and detail given to measurement development and the examples of applications of the methodology to actual programme evaluations. Clinicians and other service providers will find highly relevant the application of the quality of life assessments to individual patients and to programmes; these, in particular, illustrate the utility and relevance of quality of life assessment to work at the front line.

There is, of course, a potential downside to asking questions about quality of life for persons with severe and persistent mental disorders. The answers may challenge our preconceptions about what patients want and may cast unexpected light upon the effects of the services that we provide. Indeed, my own interest in studying quality of life arose from clinical experiences in which it was clear that the patient's perspective on a situation differed substantially from my own. But that is the point. If we are sincere in our intent to enhance the quality of life of those whose voices are often not heard or who are disregarded, then we must be prepared to hear the unexpected and to struggle with the need for new solutions. Oliver and colleagues show us in this book that it can be done.

Anthony F. Lehman, MD, MSPH
Professor of Psychiatry
University of Maryland
Baltimore, Maryland
1 July 1994

Acknowledgements

While the authors accept fully the responsibility for all that is written herein, few projects of this magnitude and complexity could have been undertaken and progressed without the approval and support of many individuals and agencies. The authors wish to thank the following for their cooperation at various stages of the development work.

We acknowledge the considerable support from our departmental colleagues during our work on quality of life in the UK and abroad. In particular, we would like to thank the Psychiatric Social Work Department and the heads of the School of Psychiatry and Behavioural Sciences, David Goldberg and Francis Creed, for their encouragement. The University of Manchester provided the basic, but essential, resources of time and academic facilities. The Social Services Departments in Bolton, Bury, Cheshire, Clwyd, Lancashire, Manchester, Rochdale, Salford, Stockport, Tameside and Trafford supported the Mental Health Social Work Research Unit work, of which the quality of life project has been an integral part. In particular, we wish to thank the directors representing the North-West Association of Directors of Social Services on the Advisory Group, Val Scerri and Bob Lewis.

We have had the benefit of first-rate administrative and secretarial services from Dianne Price, Chris Williams, Beryl Fielding, Esther Toye and Sue Carmichael.

We have had encouragement, constructive criticism and wonderful hospitality from our colleagues in Europe: Wilma Boevink, Bertie Gersons, Chijs van Nieuwenhuizen and Aart Schene (Amsterdam); Judith Wolf (Utrecht); Mirella Ruggeri and Michele Tansella (Verona); Tom Sorenson, Katy North and Sven Friis (Oslo); and Stefan Priebe (Berlin).

Lancashire County Council Social Services Department provided a variety of opportunities for us, and we should like to thank the many social workers and community support workers who have completed forms and allowed their services to be evaluated, as well as the administrative and secretarial staff there who have helped in coding questionnaires and keying in data. We are grateful to Paul d'Ambrosio, Steve

Newton and Steve Barrow for their help in writing various internal reports drawn upon in the book. Chapters 6 and 7 are based on reports which were written for Lancashire Social Services Department. Mr P. d'Ambrosio, Mr N. Crichton, Mr S. Newton and Miss C. Fallows assisted and are thanked for their efforts. Thanks also go to the Lancashire Administrative Support Group, who were most helpful in the coding of questionnaires and keying in results. We wish particularly to acknowledge the assistance given by the support teams, their management and staff in completing the quality of life interviews upon which the study is based; and, of course, the clients for their cooperation and interest in telling us about their quality of life.

The director (David Lyne), staff and residents of the independent-sector organisation (Making Space and Warrington Community Care) cooperated enthusiastically in the project. Paul Robinshaw and Margaret Huxley were the quality of life interviewers, and Paul Robinshaw assisted in the data-analysis and report production. Moos kindly gave permission and assistance in the use of the SCES.

The American research would not have been possible without the active support of Richard Warner and his colleagues and clients of the Boulder Mental Health services. Dr Warner co-authored the research reports from the projects, and his contribution to the chapters in the present book are gratefully acknowledged; as are the continuing opportunities for research made available (to PH in particular) by him and Phoebe Norton, the Director of the Mental Health Center of Boulder County. We thank the members of the Chinook Clubhouse for their participation in quality of life assessment; Laura Systra and the Maslin House team for insights into case management and gourmet cooking; and, especially, an anonymous client of the Boulder case managers at Maslin House who refused to participate in the follow-up interview because he had had no feedback from the first assessment. Thanks are due also to Margaret Huxley for the quality of life interviews at the People's Clinic, Boulder, the cooperation of which is gratefully acknowledged.

We wish to thank David Whiting and Diana Birch for their permission to quote freely from materials previously published in the *Social Work and Social Sciences Review: An International Journal of Applied Research*, which is published by Whiting and Birch Ltd, London.

We might not have embarked on this work without the encouragement of Anthony Lehman's seminal works and his help at the outset and at the end of this enterprise. Finally, we thank the LQOLP users, who have adopted the instrument and made helpful suggestions and had creative ideas about its use in practice.

Introduction

This is a book about the lives of psychiatric patients, especially those with severe and enduring conditions. In particular, it is about the health and social care services provided to help them and how one goes about examining the impact which the services make upon them.

National governments, research institutes, the World Health Organisation (WHO) and others are all now using the concept of 'quality of life' as an indicator of the success of health and welfare programmes. A number of books have been published on quality of life but almost all of these are 'generic' and cover every conceivable disorder. No specific text exists on quality of life and mental illness. As well as raising issues of academic interest, such as the discussion of concepts of quality of life, this book reports upon the application of measures of quality of life as part of outcome measurement in service evaluation. The UK Health of the Nation and the US health reforms both place emphasis upon the role of relevant outcome measures. In the UK, the Department of Health has commissioned work on brief Health of the Nation outcome scales in mental illness, and these scales have only one question about quality of life. In contrast, recent scientific seminars have confirmed the importance and popularity of the notion of quality of life in service research (NATO 1993; AEP 1994; ENMESH 1994).

National governments, policy makers, service purchasers and providers are all looking for means to evaluate mental health services. Nurses, occupational therapists, psychiatrists and social workers want operational measures which they can use with people with severe mental illness in community settings, which reflect the realities of the clients' experiences. Clients want feedback about their progress and to be involved in rating their own experiences. Managers want evidence of the effectiveness of mental health programmes, and service purchasers are looking for means of comparing the performance of different providers. Quality of life has a part to play in all of these evaluation efforts and, while it can rarely stand alone as a measure, it does have the intuitive appeal and heuristic value (according to clients and quality of life users) which is missing from other measures. This book will show how one such measure, the Lancashire Quality of Life Profile (LQOLP), has been developed and applied in service evaluation, and it will raise critical issues about the application of operational measures of outcome in service contexts.

Since we began development of the LQOLP in 1988 it has been used in many studies and in many locations. Each of these applications represents an attempt to conduct mental health service evaluation. The LQOLP has been designed deliberately as an operational rather than a research tool. Brevity and economy have been necessary guiding principles in all evaluative work with this particular client group, whose care is so universally characterised by a paucity of resources. Also, its application in other countries in mental health service evaluation appears to be successful. We receive many requests each year for details of the instrument and our research using it. We have sent out copies of the Profile in response to over 200 requests in seventeen countries. At present, there is no direct alternative which contains the wealth of empirical data gathered in service evaluations in the mental health field, with the possible exception of Lehman's data-set in the USA (Lehman, personal communication).

The book aims to provide practitioners from all backgrounds, managers and academic students of all disciplines with valuable normative data, insights and ideas about the role of quality of life in service evaluation. The Profile itself, along with instructions and normative tables, is published as appendices. This, we trust, will make the book of even greater practical value to those struggling with the evaluation of their services, whether these people are clinicians, managers, other providers or purchasers.

BACKGROUND

The closure of psychiatric hospitals, which have housed patients since the Middle Ages but more generally since the beginning of the nineteenth century, is now an international phenomenon. This process of "deinstitutionalisation", greeted with great optimism during the later part of the twentieth century, has arisen from a number of factors. The development of community care, both in other countries such as the USA and here in the UK, sprang from the debate on institutionalisation during the latter part of the 1950s. As we know, deinstitutionalisation came about as a result of professional and public concern over issues which were eventually reflected in legislation. The apparent therapeutic effectiveness of major tranquilisers and psychosocially based treatments on the rates of admission, discharge and readmission for severely disturbed patients (frequently cared for on a more or less perpetual basis within asylums) strongly influenced practice in this country towards short-term, informal admission. The perennial tension of societal interest over the rights of individuals (i.e. civil liberties issues) versus the rights of the general community (i.e. criminal and civil issues) began an extended period of swing in favour of the former, calling into question the 'morality' of indefinite asylum detention. The concern of 'progressives' about the dehumanising effects of long-term hospital care and of the stigmatising effects of 'labelling' a person insane led to the promulgation of social and community psychiatry ideology and eventually to the mental health movement. A suspicion that alternative care for the mentally disabled might be more cost effective than continued hospitalisation found favour with legislators concerned about the rising costs of health care (Krauss and Slavinsky 1982).

Hence, there has been a growing concern for those patients with chronic conditions for whom medical solutions have provided only limited satisfaction and a desire, where possible, to see them cared for within the general community (Lehman *et al.* 1982; Anderson *et al.* 1993). These concerns eventually led to the rundown of the large hospitals, a process which continues in many countries. Those of us who live and work in the north-west region of England can see four large long-stay hospitals being run down 'on our own doorstep'. Like many academic clinical departments, our intellectual interests may be universal but our immediate professional concerns begin, at least, locally with the individuals and families whom we treat, the professionals with whom we work and the agencies who employ us.

Clearly, however, this process of resettling hospital residents and the rundown of traditional facilities is not to be undertaken without considerable thought as to the possible consequences. There has been a recognition that long-term care for these people should imply a broader concern than simply treatment response or the measured level of psychopathology. There is a need to look at issues such as role functioning, community integration and personal adjustment and to take these into account as part of programme evaluation (Lehman 1983a; Anderson *et al.* 1993). The new era of community care and the new ethos (in the UK) of a mixed economy of service provisions create both opportunities and challenges (Cooper 1988a, 1988b). Our concern has been that whatever new services evolve, they should represent real improvements over our existing efforts. Quality of life evaluations fit well into these aspirations.

In recent years, UK government policy documents, including the discussion paper *Community Care: Agenda for Action* (Griffiths 1988), the subsequent 'White Paper' *Caring for People* (DHSS 1989), recent legislation in the form of the *National Health Service and Community Care Act 1990* (DHSS 1990) and the new policy paper *Health of the Nation* (DOH 1993), have outlined the agenda for the community care of several groups, including mentally ill people. Taken together, they constitute a mandate for health and local authority social service departments respectively to take the lead in ensuring the provision of the two central components of community care, i.e. health and 'social care'. Social care is intended for individuals 'whose needs extend beyond health care' (DHSS 1989:18), and has been defined as including 'the provision of help with personal and domestic tasks ... disablement equipment, transport, budgeting, and other aspects of daily living, good quality housing, day services and respite care, leisure facilities and educational opportunities' (DHSS 1989:9).

Among many things, the new legislation has the effect of requiring local authority social service departments to 'assess the community care needs of their locality, ... identify and assess individuals' needs, taking full account of personal preference ... [and] arrange the delivery of packages of care to individuals' (DHSS 1990:1). In practice, local authorities' use of the concept of need received a serious setback when it was realised that to identify a need and then not meet it would lay authorities open to criticism. At the time of writing, a debate is underway in local authorities as to whether, in the face of scarce resources, their services are to be based on needs assessment or eligibility determination. In addition, in moving from the 'welfare state' style of provision to introducing the 'mixed economy of care', the government has emphasised the necessity of utilising and developing networks of services and carers, including both voluntary and private providers (Cooper 1988a; Cooper 1988b; Corden 1990).

In accepting the necessity for considering a range of issues wider than treatment response or symptom levels (Lehman 1983a), quality of life has been cited as the principal outcome measure for the new services. For instance, it is said that social care 'will improve the quality of life enjoyed by a person with care needs' (DHSS 1989:10), with social services departments being required to test and promote ways of 'improving the quality of life for people in residential care' (DHSS 1989:44). The government has concluded that 'where it is effectively implemented, the new style of service will offer a much higher quality of life for people with mental illness and a service more appreciated by their families than is possible in the traditional and often remote mental hospital' (DHSS 1989:55).

To ensure that quality of life is enhanced, the government will require service providers to operate systems for evaluating their own performances (DHSS 1989:27), including the publication and review of community care plans (DHSS 1990:55). Thus, in arranging for such services, local authorities will be required to both assess individual need and monitor service outcomes (DHSS 1989:43). This is integral to a philosophy devoted ultimately to replacing centralised planning with client-centred systems informed by individual needs assessments (DHSS 1990:56). To have any chance of achieving this, it will be necessary to develop some system for monitoring the progress of those individuals currently being helped by health and social services agencies as well as for identifying potential users of the service. The addition of quality of life to service evaluation presents the means of achieving this shift by aiding in the identification of needs of individuals and groups, by providing a means of monitoring overall health and welfare and by setting criteria for programme evaluation.

QUALITY OF LIFE: AN IDEA WHOSE TIME HAS COME?

There is little doubt that ideas, like clothes and pop groups, come and go with fashion. The introduction of a therapeutic or scientific technique is very much governed by the *Zeitgeist* of the age in which it appears. The unfortunate mistress of convention, an idea can be overlooked or even shunned in one era and then fully embraced in another. This would appear to be the time and place for life quality studies to emerge in the UK. As will be discussed later, the strength of the term 'quality of life' is that it has a global and intuitive appeal. By 'quality' one refers to the level, standard or degree of excellence of something and this is contrasted with a notion relevant to quality simply as a characteristic. With 'life' one can encompass the entire state of functional activity of a person, including behaviour, development, pleasures, fortunes or misfortunes and overall manner of existence. Thus, with 'quality of life' there is a ready concept which can refer 'to the sense of well being and satisfaction experienced by people under their current life conditions' (Lehman 1983b:143).

Because of its universal appeal, it is easily understood by professionals of various disciplines involved in the diagnosis, treatment and after-care of mentally ill people. It is a popular notion with service users and carers alike. Not surprisingly, the term appears regularly in policy documents relating to psychiatric patients and in other policy statements. A couple of examples follow:

> The only justification for deinstitutionalisation and its accompanying upheaval is that the potential and actual quality of life enjoyed by the mentally ill person is significantly improved by moving out of hospital into the local service.
>
> (MIND/WFMH 1985:22)

> Quality of life is seen as a balance between stressors, life events, environmental/social factors and resources (knowledge, sense of competency, security, coping skills, a stable value and belief system, a support system) and thus these programmes (i.e. public health) should aim to increase/expand resources and reduce stressors.
>
> (MIND/WFMH 1985:22)

Throughout the UK, quality of life is being translated into local policy. In 1985, the North-West Region Health Authority (UK) strategic document relating to the closure of long-stay hospitals and the resettlement of patients into the community said: 'transfers (from hospital) can only take place if there is every expectation that the quality of life for each individual will be improved' (NWRHA 1985:8); while, on the other hand, it proposed that 'patients remaining in the large hospitals during the run-down years should not suffer from a poorer quality of life, and where possible should benefit from improvements' (NWRHA 1985:9).

Hence, quality of life is of central philosophical and practical importance, appearing as both an ideal and an operational condition in policy papers. That it is a matter of shared concern among mental health professionals is laudable. The problem rests with the fact that there may well not be a universally shared definition or an accepted means of measuring it. The nature of quality of life is inherently complex and, in some ways, contradictory. This complexity is enhanced when we try and apply the concept to subjects who are suffering, or have in the past suffered, from a mental disorder, either an illness or handicap. This is because the concept itself relates to the well-being of the subject. Consequently, anything which disturbs that well-being is bound to affect the quality of life. This, of course, would include the symptoms of a psychiatric disorder itself.

As can be seen above and will be shown immediately, the concept of quality of life itself is far from being unified. It is composed of many constituent parts, the actual content of many being open to debate and interpretation. Which elements in fact need to be included and which do not is uncertain. Which of many factors is the most important and which the least would seem to vary greatly according to place, time of life and past life experience of the subject.

The term 'quality of life' is one which springs easily to the lips as a means of quantifying one's overall standard of well-being. Methods of monitoring the general well-being of 'resettled' people are almost certainly bound to be influenced in some way or another by the idea. Already it is beginning to be used commonly whenever professionals talk about resettlement. Nevertheless, it is not an idea which has been widely investigated in respect of mentally disordered people. Indeed it would appear that few people are in fact able to define precisely what they mean by the term. To date it has most traditionally been applied to economic studies of large communities. Because of this, few instruments exist which are directly relevant to the needs of health and social services professionals. However, it would not appear to be beyond our capacity to produce some. The experiences of others do give us some indications as to where we should begin. The rest of this book dwells on the results of our first efforts at developing a means of measuring the quality of life of mentally disordered people, and on seeing the measure implemented in practice.

CONTENTS OF THIS BOOK

This book, like Caesar's Gaul, is divided into three parts. The first deals with some theoretical concepts relevant to understanding quality of life as an idea. The second, and principal section, presents many practical examples of service developments and how quality of life measures were used in their evaluation. The final chapter of the book deals with issues arising from the implementation of quality of life evaluations in mental health services. The sections which follow are designed to review for readers some of the main points of interest in the current state of the art in quality of life research. Special emphasis is given to how policy, research and agency practice converge in respect of work with mentally ill client groups.

Part I: Concepts and theory

1 Definitions and conceptual issues concerning quality of life

While quality of life has become more familiar in the evaluation of services, it remains poorly defined. This chapter begins by comparing various definitions of quality of life and exploring common themes. Means employed currently in measuring quality of life with the mentally ill are reviewed. Ideas relevant to the contents of quality of life instruments are explored, including objective and subjective well-being, mental health and measures of the 'self'. The method of quality of life measurement with mentally ill people, including the influence of psychopathology in self-report, are discussed. The chapter concludes with suggestions as to what might conventionally be accepted as contents of quality of life measures and means of employing them in practice.

2 The development of a quality of life profile for operational use

As a consequence of the new directives to monitor and evaluate outcomes for community care of the mentally ill, a new interest has been shown in the development of relevant quality of life measures. In particular, a brief but comprehensive instrument, called the Lancashire Quality of Life Profile (LQOLP) has been developed. Drawing on work done previously in the USA by Anthony Lehman and work attempted in the UK, the Lancashire Profile incorporates traditional measures into a means of assessing quality of life. This chapter describes the development of the Profile, outlining the aims, objectives and results of various phases of research. It also describes the contents of the most recent version.

3 Psychometric properties: reliability and validity

In the course of developing a profile for evaluating services, considerable effort has been expended in considering methodological aspects of questionnaire design. This chapter describes the results of various trials. While the task of questionnaire design is still incomplete, the chapter reports on progress to date. This information is vital to those investigators who will require such knowledge as a basis on which to judge between this profile and others prior to initiating their own research. Included are available data on test–retest reliability, inter-observer reliability, reliability of scale scores as well as content, construct and criterion validity.

4 Quality of life in the mental health service context

The development of interest in and measurement of quality of life has not taken place in a vacuum. The system of care for mentally ill people, particularly for those who have severe and persistent illnesses, is complicated. Their needs are wide ranging and have to be addressed by many different service providers, not simply by the health service. Indeed, it is this complexity of provision, and the failures of coordination between the constituent parts, which has been held responsible for recent tragic events in which such a patient, with complex care needs, was poorly served and committed a murder (House of Commons 1994b). Chapter 4 provides a framework for reviewing the service context under the headings: biological factors; social disabilities; environmental factors; psychological factors; and premorbid personal factors. It concludes by examining the target groups of patients for whom the LQOLP is considered a suitable method of assessment.

Part II: Service applications

One of the strengths of the Lancashire Profile is the range of facilities and services to which it can be applied. This section compiles detailed reports on its application to services, providing not only models of how it can be employed but a range of empirical findings which readers should find useful in informing their own efforts. These are the kind of data about which we receive many informal enquiries.

5 The quality of care and the quality of life in independent-sector residential homes

This chapter is based on a survey of all twelve residential homes of a large, independent-sector organisation covering the north of England. One hundred and sixty-nine residents were assessed using the LQOLP, while the quality of care in the homes was assessed using the scales developed by Moos (Moos and Lemke 1984). The quality of life and quality of care are described, and the quality of life results related to other studies in the same location. These results are somewhat controversial because they show that both the subjective well-being of residents and some of their objective QOL ratings are better than comparable patients in orthodox community services. We emphasise the point, therefore, that community services for discharged patients cannot be assumed to provide a better QOL than residential care; that community integration and safety can be greater in residential settings; and that a range of residential facilities needs to be provided to meet client needs adequately. The quality of care in the homes was found to be superior, on the Moos scales, to similar homes in the USA and to homes in the UK for disabled elderly people.

6 Quality of life of clients of a social services department

Social services departments are specifically charged with the responsibility for ensuring the availability of social care for chronically mentally ill community residents. However, few studies have looked at a social services department's caseload. This chapter reports the systematic study of the caseload of an entire English shire county. Four hundred and twenty-two chronically mentally ill clients were interviewed by more than ninety different social workers. This represents the largest and most comprehensive study undertaken to date in the UK. The results will serve to inform practices for the future, providing public social care agencies with interesting information about a carefully sampled agency's caseload against which to consider their own.

7 Community-based support and community mental health support teams

The 'new look' community services have not only employed traditional forms of support but have produced innovations. One such example of the latter is the introduction of home care support schemes for chronically ill clients. One English shire county has devoted a substantial proportion of its operating revenue to development and maintenance. Twelve such teams are now in existence within the county and the Lancashire Profile has been used to evaluate their performance throughout their development. More than 233 clients being cared for by the service have been interviewed. The analysis shows the performance of quality of life measures employed in a longitudinal fashion, with repeated measures. This chapter presents examples both of the new model of services as well as how to employ quality of life measurement in evaluating them.

8 Activity-based services

Chapter 8 is concerned with people with chronic psychiatric illnesses and severe social disabilities supported by a variety of activity-based services in the community. It describes some of the clinical and social charac-teristics of these patients and illustrates the function of two particular services in central Manchester which use imaginative ways of involving patients in meaningful forms of occupation. Our work stresses the importance of a 'long-term' model of care and multi-agency and multi-professional teamwork in the care planning process. In addition, we provide information on the use of the LQOLP in the assessment of changes in the quality of life of some patients involved.

9 Client subjective well-being in a case management service

This chapter reports on two applications of the LQOLP in the case management services in Boulder County in Colorado, USA, which can be described as an assertive outreach model of clinical case management. The results show that the quality of life of patients is high and that for forty-four of the original eighty-one clients (from 1989) who were reassessed two years later, their quality of life had remained high. This confirms the importance of being able to show that programmes such as this can maintain the quality of life of some of the most disabled mentally ill people. It also shows how individual graphic feedback might be used as part of a goal-attainment procedure in clinical practice, while at the same time permitting aggregated data about the programme to be collected.

10 Individual case studies using quality of life assessment in routine practice

While group studies predominate in the evaluation literature, single case studies have long been regarded by practitioners as a useful tool in understanding clinical phenomena. This is particularly true of difficult to measure phenomena, where the patient's condition occurs infrequently or is very singular and difficult to compare with another group, or where treatment or evaluation techniques are unproven and require exploratory work prior to group study. Several examples of single case studies have now been undertaken using the Lancashire Profile and two of these cases are reported.

11 The quality of life of clubhouse users

In 1993 a project using clubhouse users as quality of life evaluators was instituted. A group of six members was trained to use the LQOLP and interviewed two groups of service users (fifty-three in each group). The first group were clubhouse members and the second a matched comparison group in a neighbouring area who were not clubhouse users. There were some significant differences in subjective well-being between the groups, but the main advantage to the clubhouse members was in their more extensive and supportive social relationships.

12 Long-stay patients and quality of life

Within the spectrum of individuals who have chronic mental illnesses are those members of a 'high dependency group' who continue to require, among other things, services with a high staff compliment, access to highly skilled multi-disciplinary teams, and ongoing care and support. The care and treatment of such people present special challenges to both hospital services management and researchers seeking appropriate methods of quality of life measurement. This chapter reviews the issues involved and provides case examples both of individuals and specialist facilities which exist for them, such as 'hostel wards'. The chapter makes the case for dedicated mental health services as a means of improving their life quality.

Part III: Issues arising from application in services

13 Lessons learned from the operational use of quality of life

The purpose of the research has been to introduce quality of life measurements into the everyday operations of social and health care providers. This utilitarian approach to linking research to operations has met with many obstacles, including resistance from managers, professionals and 'users' representatives' alike. A great number of technical problems have had to be overcome to produce a measure which is suitable for everyday operational purposes such as routine monitoring and periodic review. This concluding chapter explores the many problems encountered, the solutions tried, including those which failed as well as those which have proved successful. It pulls themes from the disparate but related series of studies reported and gives suggestions for future directions in research and evaluation of mental health services.

Appendices

During the course of our work we have been in regular contact with many professionals, managers and academics. One question which is asked regularly concerns the instrument itself and relevant norms. Consequently, we include a set of appendices which house copies of the Lancashire Profile and various tables containing normative data.

Part I

Concepts and theory

Chapter 1

Definitions and conceptual issues concerning quality of life

INTRODUCTION

In 1985, our UK research began into the quality of life of clients on the caseloads of social and health care agencies in the north-west of England (Oliver 1991a). At that time, the term had only recently been applied to chronically mentally ill people, with most research until then concentrating on the 'adverse effects of the treatment and indirect effects of the illness' (Tantam 1988:243). Arguably, the most striking work existing in respect of the quality of life of long-term mentally disordered people had appeared in papers by Baker and Intagliata (1982) and Lehman (Lehman *et al.* 1982; Lehman 1983a). Stimulated by these studies, our research began as an attempt to incorporate this research into the UK context.

RATIONALE FOR EMPLOYING QUALITY OF LIFE MEASURES

Before going on to look at the various stages and products of our endeavours, we wish to review briefly some basic elements of life quality research, particularly as they apply to mentally ill people. These have very much influenced our thinking as we have progressed. Those readers who are well versed in this subject will find the following discussion largely familiar.

Various writers have discussed the reasons for making life quality a focal point for mental health evaluation. Some of the reasons are simply negative, dwelling on all the things which are incorrect in the way that we conceptualise mental disorders and treat people with them; others are more positive, focusing on potential gains to the client, the helping professions and the general community of focusing on life quality issues. It is safe to say that while the overwhelming majority of readers will prefer the latter, most will accept that both types of reasons are legitimate. Hence, we begin with a consideration of why quality of life has come to assume an increasingly important place in the evaluation of services for mentally disordered people. While the list of reasons which we offer is by no means meant to be exhaustive, its length serves to give some justification for our concentration on this subject, as well as its growing popularity.

Baker and Intagliata (1982) have suggested the following reasons (1–5):

1 *Comfort not cure.* As most severely disabled psychiatric patients cannot realistically be expected to regain full levels of functioning, treatment and rehabilitation should have more modest goals. Traditional measures of the effects of illness have focused on 'traditional medical outcomes: mortality and symptom severity' (Tantam 1988:243). However, in mental disorders, 'not only is the mortality low, but the disability produced by identical impairments varies from person to person depending on their own appraisal of them and on the presence or absence of counter-acting social factors' (Tantam 1988:243). Maintaining a satisfactory quality of life is a realistic goal for service providers and one which is acceptable to patients.

2 *Complex programmes require complex outcome measures.* Psychiatric patients and their conditions are complex and so are their treatments. Broad-based concepts and multi-dimensional scales to operationalise outcomes are more likely to be valid than less complex ones. Quality of life is one such broad-based concept which frequently results in a multi-dimensional set of measurements (Fillenbaum 1985).

   Another related point is that traditional measures of effectiveness do not presume unwanted negative side-effects of the treatment intervention. In the case of certain drugs used for schizophrenia, and other illnesses such as some forms of cancer, the magnitude of the unwanted side-effects of the treatment are of the same magnitude as the symptoms themselves. Therefore there has been recognition of the need to widen the assessment of benefit to include these indirect effects of illness and treatment (Goldberg and Jones 1980). Under such conditions, 'as far as quality of life is concerned, it is less important to know whether a treatment is effective, than whether it is desirable' (Tantam 1988:244).

3 *Keeping the customer happy.* In an era of increased accountability and consumer involvement, service providers must be seen to address individual needs. Life quality measures ensure that the focuses of treatment and other service provisions remain on individualised improvements following exposure to interventions.

4 *Re-emergence of the holistic perspective.* There is a gradual turning away from narrow views of the patient's life predicaments in favour of seeing them in their 'person-situation configuration'. Also there is movement away from concentration on narrow pathology levels and types and towards health promotion, a much wider idea implying a

'state of complete physical, mental and social well-being' (WHO 1991:5). The scientific challenge is one of describing adequately the totality of a patient's existence, not simply part of it, thus producing a holistic, comprehensive model. Hence, 'the patient's existential situation is the outcome criterion' (Malm *et al.* 1981:478).

5 *Quality of life is good politics.* In the USA, the emphasis on the 'pursuit of happiness' is enshrined in the Constitution. The 'feel-good factor' is a recognised motivation in voting patterns. 'Quality time' has become a sought-after element of family life. A range of life quality dimensions are becoming the legitimate aspirations of citizens, to be pursued by politicians on their behalf. This suggestion has been mirrored by Zautra and Goodheart (1979), who emphasised that people are interested in knowing about this subject in an attempt to increase the quality of their own life.

Our own research (Oliver 1991a) has produced a number of further reasons for employing quality of life measurements. Three more (6–8) are:

6 *Acceptance by patients and relatives.* In order to succeed, the implementation of any system of evaluation requires the consent and cooperation of patients and their relatives. Life quality measures are positively regarded, and compliance rates with interviews, and especially re-interviews, are high. Importantly, many clients find such interviews intrinsically therapeutic and empowering (because they focus on areas which are of central importance to them).

7 *A common basis for multi-disciplinary work.* Many mental conditions are the result of multiple causative factors (overdetermined), with treatment involving a variety of professionals with divergent, sometimes opposing, views. Under such circumstances, the means of evaluation can easily become controversial, providing a focus for disagreements and professional rivalries. Quality of life measurements are sufficiently wide to encompass many perspectives, proving acceptable to a range of different practitioners and thus encouraging teamwork.

8 *Economical measurements for underfunded targets.* In both health and social care settings, mental illness services are universally regarded as low priority and are, hence, underfunded. Among these, the chronic services are lower priority than the acute. Evaluation is lower priority than service delivery. In fact, neither money nor time is readily made available for such tasks. Brief quality of life measures can be employed without adding appreciably to the agency wage bill, thus overcoming worker and management resistance to doing evaluative work.

Closely related to this is the fact that in a time of diminishing financial resources, services are increasingly called upon to justify costs. However, in the health field, gains cannot always be expressed in monetary terms and concern the quality of life of carers as well as patients. In cost-effectiveness analysis these less tangible benefits can be quantified in terms of the cost of the interventions which are required to demonstrate change. In order to demonstrate change, standardised scales should be employed; this makes possible the comparison of different interventions and services.

In our reading we have encountered many other authors who have also suggested reasons for including quality of life measures such as:

9   *Technical advances in data processing have made studies of communities, individuals and even nations more feasible.* This is especially true when powerful statistical packages and the computers on which to process vast amounts of data rapidly are available to clinical practitioners and local service managers (Zautra and Goodheart 1979).

10   *Studying quality of life helps planners to avoid mistakes made previously.* Social and behavioural research has confirmed that the social environment has a major influence on the causes, courses and outcomes of illness (Cochrane 1983). This is especially important when one is considering the lives of more vulnerable groups, such as mentally ill people (Zautra and Goodheart 1979).

11   *Quality of life data is useful in planning the location and evaluation of community mental health services* (Zautra and Goodheart 1979). Accessibility and acceptablity are key principles in the implementation of community care. Socio-demographic factors heavily influence these (Huxley *et al.* 1990).

12   *Empirical measures associated with theory.* 'The combination of data and conceptual framework can be used in making decisions about the delivery of mental health services' (Bigelow *et al.* 1982:34), only if they are closely linked together. This is a scientific point with very important practical consequences for people who wish to see the techniques of social sciences being employed by direct service providers. Many writers have presented models of quality of life (e.g. Lehman *et al.* 1982; Baker and Intagliata 1982; Franklin *et al.* 1986) which might be employed to facilitate the making of these links.

13   *Satisfaction and role performance are central.* This point is really about accountability. The problems of defining models of life quality are perennial. Each of the main contributors to the debate has eventually got around to proposing some model of quality of life in mental health. Whatever models are proposed, no matter how complex their operation or broad or narrow their content, two features remain central. These are satisfaction and role performance. Satisfaction can be the opposite of dissatisfaction or the absence of distress or symptomatology; role performance is essentially about social adaptation and adjustment (Bigelow *et al.* 1982).

As practitioners as well as academics, we particularly endorse this last point. Whatever we, as professionals, may think that we are doing or may wish to do in community mental health programmes, we are certain that the public, including the patients and their families, expect us to be centrally concerned with fostering satisfaction and enhancing role performance. Consequently, come what may, our reality as social and health care professionals is to be held accountable in these areas and we believe that our evaluations should reflect this reality.

THE EVOLUTION OF THE CONCEPT OF QUALITY OF LIFE

According to Flanagan (1982), efforts to measure life quality began in the USA during the decade of the 1950s, with the Eisenhower Commission on National Goals, which noted a variety of social and environmental influences (President's Commission on National Goals 1960:56). This was followed by a number of national government initiatives, which have since become part and parcel of the work of governments. The purpose of this research initiative was to 'chart the social progress of the nation and to develop a regular system of social reporting' to inform efforts to plan and evaluate social policy (Dann 1984:2–3). In 1960, the study by Gurin and colleagues 'explored the psychologic disturbances, physical symptoms, professional help sought and the individual's present happiness. This survey provided reports on sources of happiness and unhappiness, things causing worries and estimates of probable happiness in the future' (Gurin et al. 1960:56).

However, concern about the nature of human welfare, happiness and quality of life are not new, though some of the terms themselves may be contemporary. Indeed, the ideas which underpin these are likely to be found in among the very essential notions of human community, family, social and economic life. Concern for the state of one's self, family, friends, village, town, city and nation are inherent in one's consciousness about human behaviour itself.

Considerations of what constitutes well-being have traditionally been more the province of philosophers and theologians than scientists. Systematic consideration of 'happiness' certainly existed among the classical Greek philosophers who have influenced Western thought. For example, in *Ethics* (see Ross 1947) Aristotle considered the nature of human conduct. He identified the desired (i.e. ethical) human behavioural goal as lying with mankind's pursuit of good. This goal he identified as the condition of *eudaemonia,* literally 'a favourable providence', or well-being. Aristotle maintained that the most virtuous path along which human conduct could travel (i.e. our highest aspiration) was the individual's pursuit of a well-being which resided in the achievement of physical and moral excellence – in his instance, through living a rational life. This is not dissimilar to a quest in order to realise one's true potential (or a process of 'self-actualisation').

In contrast to this meaning, *eudaemonia* has been translated into the modern idiom as 'happiness' and understood, in the Epicurian sense, as a desired state to be achieved by an individual through obtaining excesses of pleasure over pain in one's economic, social and psychological life. This latter, 'hedonistic', view of well-being has been integrated into Western thought by the utilitarian philosophers and writers, commencing with Bentham, Mill and Ricardo. Of course, Sigmund Freud's influential early theoretical writings in psychology also postulate human motivation as being closely linked to this 'pleasure principle'.

The point has been made that had the translation of *eudaemonia* concentrated on the pursuit of excellence or virtue rather than pleasure/happiness, the studies of psychological well-being of the past decades (and our subsequent review) would have been quite different and concentrated on the former rather than the latter (Waterman [1984] cited in Ryff 1989).

Rescher (1972) used the terms 'hedonic' and 'aristic' to describe this division of objectives. He equates 'hedonic' to well-being in terms of happiness or satisfaction (experienced subjectively) while 'aristic', derived from the Greek work *aristos,* which means the best, most noble or excellent, he equates to quality. In using these terms it is important to acknowledge that judgements made regarding the quality of the external, 'public', material world are capable of being shared with others who may agree or disagree. These may be more or less easily quantified with the reliability of such judgements compared against more 'objective' criteria. Those judgements made of the internal worlds of the human psyche are of a substantively different type, being, by nature, 'private' and subjective. Put another way, the 'aristic' is concerned with the welfare of the individual while the 'hedonic' is concerned with their personal well-being – welfare 'refers to the needs of an individual within society', while wellbeing refers to the personal experience of life (Osborne 1992:442). Consequently, according to Rescher, we are always the best judge of our own subjective satisfactions and feelings but we are not always the best judge of what may be in our best interest, our welfare, the objective dimensions of our lives.

EVOLUTION OF DIFFERENT WAYS TO MEASURE QUALITY OF LIFE

Having considered some of the roots of our concerns for 'happiness', we next consider the lineage of attempts to measure it. According to the psychologist Angus Campbell (1976), Western nations have been employing statistics for centuries to ascertain both the levels of welfare of their citizenry and the means of meeting their needs. These statistics have related principally to the economic dimensions of life, including levels of income, expenditures and savings, the production and sales of goods and services and commercial activities. While Campbell suggests that the main reason for concentrating on economic measures is the ease with which information relating to these activities is gathered, others propose different reasons for their emergence.

Economic indicators

Hankiss (1983) maintains that the use of *economic indicators* originated with the concerns of early mercantilists, who assumed the existence of a direct relationship between various commercial activities, such as trade, employment and production, and the general 'commonweal' of a nation. According to this train of thought, well-being is governed by levels of economic activity and, hence, it is axiomatic that evidence of economic growth within a nation implies also growth in welfare or well-being for the nation. Though there has been substantial diversity of opinion among different schools of economic thought regarding the potential value, content and function of economic indicators, various measures have been employed regularly by governments 'to monitor economic progress. They are based on data supplied by institutions such as banks, firms, customs offices, fiscal institutions, ministries, market research institutes, etc. They serve to analyze the economic conditions of social welfare' (Hankiss 1983:15). Traditionally, estimates of well-being have been based upon these statistics and their influence is markedly apparent in the social policy decisions of the current UK government.

Nevertheless, monetary measures alone have proved to be inadequate reflections of the quality or goodness of the life or level of happiness of a nation. As evidence, Campbell (1976; 1981) has cited the post-war years. Considering the previous decades of the Great Depression and the Second World War, the post-war years were a period during which the USA enjoyed a dramatic increase in the average standard of living. However, at the same time, that nation also experienced a decline in other essential aspects of personal, social and political life, such as levels of personal safety, family solidarity and general confidence in government due to crime, drug abuse, presidential assassination and political miscon-duct. This lack of direct association between economic prosperity and happiness gave rise to an exploration for other, non-monetary, measures by which to quantify happiness in the general population. This is to say that economic indicators alone failed in the task of detecting change when it had obviously occurred. The general conclusion was that economic indicators alone neither described nor predicted completely the manner in which societies progress.

Social indicators

To compensate for this shortcoming, the measures adopted from the 1960s have been called *social indicators*. These measures, focusing on many previously excluded areas of life, are thought to be more sensitive to change. By way of example, in their classic work *Indicators of Social Change: Concepts and Measurements* (1968), Sheldon and Moore reviewed the entire field of social indicators, pulling together writings by many of the outstanding social scientists of the period. In addition to economic indicators, the topics covered included: demographic and population trends; labour force and employment trends; the state of knowledge and technology; the nature and levels of political activities of government and citizens; changes in family life; trends in religious participation; distributive features of leisure, health status and schooling; social stratification; and the measurement of welfare. A change in quality of life was implied in a change in quantity. The research methodologies employed have tended to move from cross-sectional studies and correlational associations toward employing time-series data and the analysis of trends. The development of contemporary health indices and profiles begins with this work.

Certainly, social indicators do vary somewhat from one national context to another both in the manner in which they are gathered and in their contents. While some nations such as Germany appear not to gather this data, the study of social indicators of well-being is far from being the exclusive preoccupation of the Americans. The UK has a long and distinguished tradition of economic and social studies into community well-being. Eighteenth-century writers such as Sir Francis Eden and Patrick Colquhoon wrote on the state of the poor. Of local interest to us as writers from a university situated in Manchester was the influential treatise by Sir James Philip Kay-Shuttleworth in 1836 on *The Moral and Physical Conditions of the Working Classes in the Cotton Industry in Manchester* (cited in Dann 1984). This century commenced with Seebohm Rowntree's classic study of the workers of York in England (Rowntree 1901). Spurred on often by an interest (which outsiders might perceive as verging on the obsessive) in the stratified nature of the British social structure, there has continued to be a very active effort to look at social indicators here. For example, the effects of inequality in income distribution on poverty, health and education, in terms of both absolute and relative poverty (Abel-Smith and Townsend 1965; Townsend 1979), have been the focus of research work by an entire generation of British social scientists. Also in the UK, standard means of assessing the social and economic well-being of the population exist in the forms of the General Household Survey (GHS) and the Family Expenditure Survey (FES). The categories under which data are gathered are fixed for the FES but vary for the GHS and include similar measures to those employed in America. The effects of these studies have been felt through pieces of social and economic policy (in turn influencing professional practices in many fields, including both social work and psychiatry) enacted by successive governments of various political complexions. The increasingly refined analyses of the data from these national surveys, and from other sources, continues unabated, linking the study of social indicators firmly into the contemporary quality of life debate (see, for example, Hutton 1990).

The familiar categories under which the study of these social indicators are usually grouped are commonly called life 'domains'. The parameters of domains have been determined either deductively or inductively, *viz* by consensual validation based on a set of theories or values and tested subsequently or discovered empirically and then related to theory.

In respect of the first approach, it is convenient to think of external or material realities as being seen or perceived in the context of some value system or understood in respect of a particular theory. These provide the structures of language and ideas for the construction of concepts which describe, categorise or quantify these realities. It is the instrumentalisation of these concepts which leads to their measurement. Value systems, of course, are highly culturally specific, varying greatly from one epoch, geographical place and national group to another, depending on religious creeds, political and social ideologies and various cultural traditions (Hankiss 1983). In *Adventure for Happiness* (1935), Dr S. Parkes Cadman, a prominent Christian Anglo-American minister of the day, explored 'happiness' in respect of such life dimensions as health, civil government, work and wages, love, domestic life, friendship, imagination, music, literature, art, social service and religion.

Employing the empirical approach, Flanagan developed a comprehensive list of life domains based on an empirical survey of the behaviour and experience of adult Americans. The method employed was the 'critical incident technique'. 'About 6,500 critical incidents were collected each reporting a time when something was actually observed to have significant effect either positively or negatively on the overall quality of life of either the person reporting or a companion' (Flanagan 1982:57). Their classification led to the development of a set of fifteen factors collapsed into five life domains: physical and material well-being; relations with other people; social, community and civic activities; personal development and fulfilment; recreation. Other writers (for example, Lehman *et al.* 1982; Thapa and Rowland 1989; Simpson *et al.* 1989; Oliver 1991a; Huxley and Warner 1992) incline towards using greater numbers of life domains: living arrangements, family relations, social relations, leisure, work, law and safety, health, finances, religion, sense of hope and purpose (Lawton 1984). Yet other writers prefer to use even fewer, such as Kedenburg, who suggested employing only three: i.e. people, helping and providing (Kedenburg 1980:605).

The differences between authors arise from cultural differences, theoretical or value differences and differences in empirical findings. For example, Nagpal and Sell (1985), reporting on a study of quality of life in India, identified a factor which they called 'transcendence', which was associated with a sense of 'being part of mankind' and included 'moments of intense happiness such as ecstasy or bliss, and having deep religious fulfilment in life' and which was identified with the theoretical construct of 'rootedness' (Nagpal and Sell 1985:29). Such a factor is not reported in studies of Western populations, which frequently omit any spirituality dimension (Cox et al. 1992).

The matter of how to generate additional domains through ongoing research is very relevant, not only to cross-cultural studies but also to groups with particular problems such as disabilities. Importantly, Flanagan suggested various adaptations to quality of life research for people with disabilities. He suggested the inclusion of specific critical incidence questions to be gathered in surveys of a thousand-plus disabled people and analysed. This procedure should be repeated until no new factors emerge (Flanagan 1982:59). The questions cited have been employed in modified form in the Lancashire Quality of Life Profile, as shown in later chapters.

Zautra and Goodheart (1979) have produced one of the most authoritative, often-cited reviews. They support the utility of employing quality of life measures for studying community settings, since the quality of the 'good life' is so influenced by social norms, laws and the provision of means by which people achieve and maintain this. They review two research approaches: studies of community settings (employing social indicators) and assessments of individuals (employing psychological indicators) which they define as 'the ways in which individual behaviour, aspirations and also discontent affect well-being and guide the creation, maintenance and evolution of community settings' (Campbell et al. 1976; Zautra and Goodheart 1979:3).

Social indicators are defined as 'those social forces that guide individual behaviour' (see also Zautra and Simons 1978) or 'statistics, statistical series and all other forms of evidence that enable us to assess where we stand and where we are going with respect to our values and goals, and to evaluate specific programs and determine their impact' (Zautra and Goodheart 1979:3; see also Bauer 1966). They also give a more technical definition of social indicators related closely to the measurement of change as:

a statistic of direct normative interest which facilitates concise, comprehensive and balanced judgements about the condition of a major aspect of society; it is, in all cases, a direct measure of welfare . . . If it changes in the right direction. . .things have gotten better, or people are 'better off'.

(see USDHEW 1969:97)

Zautra and Goodheart remind us that the number of potential social indicators is 'virtually unlimited' and that they have either unquestioned face validity (i.e. murder rate) or consensual validation as to what will constitute or change to a 'good society'. These indicators may be very culturally specific in both their value as a measure of change and their manner of computation. In fact, social indicators now have developed a fairly long and rather chequered career. One cynic describes the use of social indicators in social policy as 'fig-leaf government'. He says:

> The procedure is simple and well-known. When you are threatened by some unpleasant development, do a statistical appraisal of the situation. Unless you are extremely unlucky you will be able to get some figures which will justify you in doing what you were going to do anyway – often nothing. . . .There is a further point. Even if the figures don't come out the way you would have preferred, by having 'done research' you have shown a concern with the subject. You can rely on a few people assuming that research is a prelude to action and then forgetting about the whole thing. You can forget it too.

(Brand 1978:239)

Brand subdivides social indicators into: a set of statistics organised in such a way that information is provided for policy makers; a set of measures of the operation of a policy, its success or failure; and information about the total impact of a policy, not simply its intended consequences. The classic and often-quoted example of the last of these is the attempt by the US government to assess the impact of the space programme on American society (Bauer 1966). One of the present authors (Huxley 1986) reviewed the decline of the use of objective indicators and argued that the decline was partly attributable to the futility of attempts to aggregate, in a meaningful way, different objective measures. The subjective social indicator movement began as a response to this failure (Abrams 1973). Brand argues that one must be clear about the purpose of collecting social indicators – i.e. what goals they are to serve – and that indicators become useful only if they form part of a conceptual model.

This new set of social statistics shares the common characteristic that nearly all 'are reported through governmental institutions of one sort or another and do not depend upon the individual's description of his own life. They are what might be called *objective* indicators' (Campbell 1976:118). While social indicators clearly represent an improvement over much cruder economic indicators as measures of quality of life, it has been argued that they are inadequate in that they appear to 'describe the conditions of life that might be assumed to influence life experience but do not assess that experience directly' (Campbell 1976:118). This is to say that they are, at best, surrogate measures for the actual experiences of individuals. Similarly Milbrath (1978, 1979) has distinguished between environmental *quality* as a subjective judgement and environmental *conditions* that may be measured objectively and this distinction has been mirrored by researchers investigating people with long-term mental illnesses (Malm *et al.* 1981; Skantze *et al.* 1992).

Disquiet with objective indicators, like the disquiet with economic indicators before them, is fuelled by the fact that changes in the levels of material well-being, inequalities in the distribution of the economic or social aspects of life, do not necessarily correspond with changes in the way people actually perceive their lives. Individuals, groups, communities or nations may be less satisfied, less happy or less mentally healthy despite or even because of rises in the levels of material comfort and vice versa. The poor association between 'objective' or material conditions and the way in which they are perceived is well established (Bowling 1991). At least one paper (Skantze *et al.* 1992), while reporting findings from a study of sixty-one subjects, has gone so far as to conclude that objective well-being (in this case defined as 'living standards') is quite independent of one's perceptions of it.

Admittedly, while the associations are unclear and sometimes found to be weak, at the level of 'common sense', however, it is difficult to maintain that the two are without any association. Nagpal and Sell (1985), writing about subjective well-being, remind us of Mr Micawber's admonition in Charles Dickens' *David Copperfield*: 'Annual income twenty pounds, annual expenditure nineteen and six, result happiness. Annual income twenty pounds, annual expenditure twenty pounds ought and six, result misery'. Empirical research does support this observation, and the nature and extent of the association will be considered in more detail directly. It would seem that as distinct from our consideration of the characterisation of the external environment through 'objective' measures, in order to describe and quantify more fully an individual's experience of well-being one needs to employ the more refined and psychological set of measures which have come to be called *subjective indicators*.

SUBJECTIVE WELL-BEING INDICATORS

A very substantial body of knowledge is now emerging concerning subjective well-being and indicators with which to measure it. This includes seminal studies by Gurin *et al.* (1960); Cantril (1965); Bradburn (1969); Campbell *et al.* (1976) and Andrews and Withey (1976). Taken together, these studies have explored various aspects of subjective well-being in clinical and normal populations. So many studies now exist that a decade ago one author concluded that they could 'no longer be reviewed in a single article' (Diener 1984:542). The situation has become even more difficult now. A recent WHO review (1993) interrogated Medline database and found 1,520 publications with 'quality of life' keyword references for 1992 and 1,570 for 1993.

Some years ago, in a comprehensive review of subjective well-being theory and empirical findings, Diener (1984) divided definitions of happiness (which he equated with subjective well-being) into three categories: normative definitions, like 'happiness' as virtue or *eudaemonia,* in which the subject's state is compared against external, objective standards; life-satisfaction, in which the individual defines 'happiness' as what constitutes the good life according to his own chosen standards or criteria; and 'happiness' as a preponderance of positive affect over negative affect. Considerations of subjective well-being typically exclude external, material life conditions but include global self-assessments of well-being and substitute positive measures such as health in place of negative ones such as illness (Diener 1984:543–4). These divisions correspond closely to those suggested by Andrews and Withey (1976) in their study of subjective well-being: judgements about life-satisfaction; and positive and negative affect (Bradburn and Caplovitz 1965; Bradburn 1969). It has been suggested that satisfaction has some specific utility as a concept over other measures such as happiness. Campbell *et al.* (1976) observed that it was more relevant to speak of satisfaction with some objective aspects of life than happiness with them. Likewise, satisfaction seems to relate more specifically to the cognitive aspect of psychological life than the affective aspects. Finally, satisfaction can have ramifications for the acceptance or rejection of public policy that are not associated with other concepts such as happiness.

The distinction between the subjective terms 'happiness' and 'satisfaction' are supported empirically by research, which has shown them to vary inversely according to the age of subjects (Campbell *et al.* 1976) and probably their stages of psychosocial development (Krauss and Slavinsky 1982; Ryff 1989). A variety of single and multi-item measures exist to assess these concepts, although the research evidence points to the fact that no one measure is either an exact test of its concept nor do any groupings of the many possible measures exactly cover the required dimensions without at least some overlap or omission; certain degrees of internal invalidity and measurement error seem endemic to the enterprise.

Lawton (1984) defines two important components of subjective well-being as 'perceived quality of life' and 'psychological well being'.

Between them they account for many of the most potent concepts currently afield in this area. 'Perceived quality of life' is a measure of satisfaction and can be described as the 'set of evaluations that a person makes about each major domain of his or her life' (Lawton 1984:68). The second, 'psychological well-being', 'is more global and less clearly tied to the separate domains of everyday life than is perceived quality of life. Psychological well-being is a subjective sense of overall satisfaction and positive mental health that is commonly thought to be the best indicator of unobservable constructs such as self-esteem and ego strength' (Lawton 1984:69).

Having accepted that subjective well-being can be equated to some standard or level of a combination of mental experiences such as satisfactions, thinking, feeling, willing, perceptions and experiences of happiness, the question arises as to its influences or determinants. Does subjective well-being stand alone or does it depend upon other factors, strongly anchored in the external environment, for definition? Diener reviews in depth the associations between subjective well-being and indicators of objective well-being for various domains. Even given that the review is now ten years old, the following findings appear to hold true, substantiated by many empirical studies before and since (for example, readers may wish to see Strack et al. 1991 for a more recent review or are referred to the original work by Diener [1984]).

The associations between demographic variables such as age (Stock et al. 1983), sex (Andrews and Withey 1976) and race (Campbell et al. 1976) and subjective well-being are weak or very confounded. There is a strong, positive relationship between subjective well-being and several objective well-being measures (often even after the effects of other intervening variables have been controlled for), including: income levels (Larson 1978); unemployment (Bradburn 1969; Campbell et al. 1976); social contacts, both of friendship (Rhodes 1980) and of love (Anderson 1977); and, of course, self-reported health (Campbell et al. 1976; Larson 1978; Moum 1992). Other objective well-being variables show significant, if less pronounced influences, or their effects are more intertwined with those of other confounding variables: education (Campbell 1981) and religion (McClure and Loden 1982). Subjective well-being is also strongly associated with many psychological variables such as self-esteem (Campbell et al. 1976, Anderson 1977) and locus of control (Anderson 1977).

Interestingly enough, recent research has cast some light on the nature of the presumption that there is a 'weak' or non-existent association between objective and subjective measures. Cunningham (1985) has established that in larger, more homogeneous samples, the association between social indicators and the way that individuals perceive their lives is quite high, with social indicators accounting for 40 to 50 per cent of the variance of measures of the latter, a finding mirrored by our own research (see Chapter 3). It is possible that some of these confusions occur as an artefact of examining widely heterogeneous, small, clinically derived samples; a point which we have sought to bear in mind when interpreting our own research. Diener concluded that despite limitations in the methodologies of many studies, 'it seems likely that subjective well-being will not be accounted for by a handful of potent variables, because of the immense number of factors that can influence it' (Diener 1984:561). Nevertheless it would be unwise to ignore the wealth of empirical findings when constructing a suitable definition of quality of life.

DEFINITIONS OF QUALITY OF LIFE

In the UK government's new social care directives, the meaning of 'quality of life' has been left open to debate. One author has observed that 'it is indeed rather surprising – at times even annoying – to see how reluctant many researchers are to state explicitly what they consider to be the connotative meaning of "quality of life". However, most practitioners tend to reveal their definitional preferences in their empirical work' (Hankiss 1983:161). This is unfortunate!

Quality of life is certainly a broad concept which incorporates all aspects of an individual's existence (Torrance 1987), including both an individual's success in obtaining certain prerequisite circumstances, states or conditions (McCall 1975) as well as 'the sense of well-being and satisfaction experienced by people under their current life conditions' (Lehman 1983a:143). At its simplest, most literal level, 'quality' can be said to refer to the level or standard or degree of goodness or excellence possessed by someone or something; or it can simply represent a summation of a thing's attributes (Schmandt and Bloomberg 1969). 'Life', on the other hand, includes the entire state of functional activity of a person, including one's behaviour, development, sources of pleasure and displeasure and overall manner of existence. In short, life is composed of everything which characterises any organism's existence between birth and death. Of course, 'life' also refers to everything which is living and also to the process of living and the features of the environment necessary to support it.

One is tempted to speculate that the intuitive and global appeal which 'quality of life' appears to enjoy derives exactly from this inexactitude. The term's vagueness allows it to be understood by practitioners and politicians alike, perhaps each imbuing it with the fine nuances of his or her own understanding and, hence, promoting apparent agreement. One precedent for this process must be in the employment of psychoanalytic terminology wherein so many words with vague technical meanings are happily misused in the vernacular by so many people. Several problems underlie this difficulty in definition. One is the *focus* of the definition.

Most notably, when we speak of quality of life are we speaking of the quality of a person's life or of the state of life, or the meaning of life in general? If one comments that 'Life quality is poor!' is this a statement analogous to 'I feel dreadful!' or 'This country is going to the dogs!' or 'The world is in a dreadful state!'? This dilemma lies at the heart of the distinctions between objective and subjective approaches to life quality research outlined above and is the one which tends most to divide researchers and theoreticians.

However, it is not the only divisive question about quality of life. Another dilemma concerns what we may refer to as the *agency* through which a higher quality of life is to be achieved. Who is responsible for improving life's quality? Does the responsibility lie with the individual to increase life quality through his or her own efforts or with the workings of the 'rational' market economy or with the interventionist efforts of government? And there is the matter of *criteria*. What constitutes a good life anyway? Is it wealth, power, beauty, intellect? Is its highest form of expression to be found in Barchester, in Wall Street dealings, in an afternoon with the famous Liverpool F.C. 'kop' or in life in a hippie commune? Or there is the question of *goals* and how these are to be defined. Does quality of life lie in attaining perfection or pleasure? If it lies in perfection, who defines that 'goodness'? Is it the Church, through doctrine, or God, acting directly through revelation? Is it the government, acting in the 'public good' through the law? Is it the ruling class, who set the standard for the 'good life' (as described by novelists such as Austen and Trollope) to which everyone, especially 'the lower orders' should aspire? Is it the commercial media selling of a quality lifestyle? If it lies in pleasure, what are the infinite number of points on the scale between pleasure and pain? Where on the continuum does eating fish and chips lie for someone who doesn't like fish? Is 'good quality of life' attainable or simply the fanciful description of a place such as Sir Thomas More's (1516) *Utopia*, an imaginary island with an ideal political and social system. One typology, proposed by Gerson (1976), of approaches to quality of life, seems useful. He distinguishes between the 'individualist' approach, where an individual's goals are fulfilled; the 'transcendentalist' approach, which emphasises the community or group's aspirations; and the 'interactionist or phenomenological' approach, where quality of life is focused around a series of negotiated outcomes (Dann 1984:11).

As we have seen, 'quality of life' is a term, coined at a particular time in Western history, which has captured within its parameters a broad range of human concerns which have themselves, at various stages of human history, been known under other names, from *eudaemonia* to welfare. As the essential reality which the term is trying to capture may be disunified, an ad hoc collection of ideas, so it, itself, may be incapable of valid (i.e. internally consistent) definition. Not surprisingly, the definitions rendered to date for 'quality of life' are many and varied. We include a list, drawn from our reading, which is far from conclusive but which gives a sufficiently wide flavour of what people think to enable us to discuss contents.

Some authors render definitions of life quality which are broad but inexact, offering less guidance to the possible contents of quality of life measurement. For example, Liu (1976) said: 'There are as many quality of life definitions as there are people.' Likewise, Torrance (1987) said: 'Quality of life is a broad concept which incorporates all aspects of an individual's existence.' Alas, our own meagre efforts appear to have fallen into this category, having once defined it thus: 'In a modern epoch, quality of life is total health and welfare, ideas which are comprehended and largely accepted by people generally' (Oliver 1991a). Those definitions which focus on the objective well-being side of the divide sound like that offered by McCall (1976): 'Quality of life consists in obtaining the necessary conditions for happiness in a given region or society.' Some writers centre on subjective well-being, favouring measurement of the experience of well-being but not necessarily the conditions which determine it. 'Quality of life means a person's sense of well-being, satisfaction or dissatisfaction with life, or happiness or unhappiness' (Dalkey and Rourke 1972) is one example.

Others have defined quality of life either as a sense of well-being, closely linked to its situational context, or as some other combination of objective and subjective well-being. 'Quality of life is an abstraction which integrates and summarises all those features of our lives that we find more or less desirable and satisfying (Bigelow et al. 1982); 'Quality of life is a state of well-being that is reflected by life conditions, satisfactions with life conditions and adaptation to life conditions' (Franklin et al. 1986). Lehman (1983a) saw quality of life as 'the sense of well-being experienced by people under their current life conditions'. Zautra and Goodheart (1979) concluded that 'essentially quality of life pertains to the goodness of life. . .which resides in the quality of life experiences, both as subjectively evaluated and as objectively determined by an assessment of external conditions'. Recently the World Health Organisation has said:

> [Q]uality of life is defined as an individual's perception of their position in life in the context of the culture and value systems in which they live and in relation to their goals, expectations, standards and concerns. It is a broad ranging concept incorporating in a complex way the person's physical health, psychological state, level of independence, social relationships, personal beliefs and the relationship to salient features of the environment.
>
> (WHO 1993)

One immediate observation is that due to the diversity of opinion regarding the definition of quality of life, there are bound to be subsequent disagreements concerning the contents of anything purporting to measure it. Obviously, quality of life is, and will probably remain, multi-dimensional. Hope, sounding rather cynical about the enterprise, supports this latter view in respect of problems in the measurement of social indicators:

> These problems, which call for the construction of schedules, inventories, assessment procedures and tests of many different kinds, are considered less interesting and of lower stature than broader questions of sociological theory and analysis, though as a matter of fact nothing is better calculated to force the sociologist to define, rectify, analyze and tighten up his concepts than an attempt to construct a means of measuring them.

> (Hope 1978:246)

Certainly, some influential authors now go so far as to support an identification of quality of life with subjective well-being (for example, Dalkey and Rourke 1972). At a recent conference of the Association of European Psychiatrists (1994, Vienna, Austria) one speaker exclaimed excitedly that 'subjective well-being *is* quality of life'. In our opinion, in the present state of knowledge, this is only as helpful as statements by those who have advocated the exclusive use of objective well-being measures for quality of life, maintaining conversely that the inclusion of psychological measures to quality of life investigation has served only to illustrate the inadequacies of the research in this area (Bunge 1975).

We have endorsed the notion of retaining both objective and subjective quality of life measures for reasons which have been supported by many other writers, and we would find little to disagree with the definitions suggested above which incorporate both. For, like Malm *et al.* (1981), we do not accept the assertion 'that the only defensible definition of quality of life is a general feeling of happiness' but feel rather that there may be a number of very fundamental drawbacks to defining it in purely subjective terms.

First, such a definition 'ignores mental abnormality by a tacit assumption that happiness and dissatisfaction are never pathological' (Malm *et al.* 1981:477). In respect of this point, the association between psychopathology and life quality assessments is vexed and the data less than conclusive. Henderson *et al.* (1981) found that the onset of neurosis was more likely to be associated with a personality trait than an actual lack of satisfaction with support in social relations. The question which remains, however, is whether the amount of distortion caused by mental illnesses in observers is of such a degree as to invalidate the assessment. Lehman (1983b) investigated this. His conclusion was that while symptoms certainly influenced subjective well-being they did not determine it. Much of global well-being was determined by factors other than mental illness. Therefore, quality of life is not mental illness; quality of life measures are not simply mental illness measures; and services required to support or improve quality of life for this client group are not purely medical services.

Second, ignoring the environmental dimensions of life quality 'may lead to failure to distinguish the privileged from the disadvantaged and so prove a convenient excuse for inaction' (Malm *et al.* 1981:477). It is now becoming a well-established fact that life satisfaction is frequently improved upon discharge from psychiatric hospital (Simpson *et al.* 1989). An indirect measure of life satisfaction in the domain of living situation is the desire to return to hospital. Such studies of community care indicate that few of those patients discharged actually wish to return (Kinard 1981).

In fact, the ability of community care to improve patients' life conditions and life functioning has been challenged (Rosenfield 1987:48; Huxley *et al.* 1990) for various reasons, including:

1   Many ex-long-stay patients receiving aftercare drop out.
2   Many ex-long-stay patients receive little or no treatment in the community.
3   Fragmented services are difficult for ex-patients to negotiate.
4   Programmes avoid chronic patients, who are seen as unlikely to improve and are unattractive.
5   Hence, readmission rates rise as hospital populations decline.
6   In some areas between 35 and 50 per cent of discharged patients are re-admitted within one year.

Practically, in the actual task of monitoring community care there remains a need to identify not only the individual's experience of community care but what objective reality he/she is in fact experiencing. Service organisations and planners need to know not only what a person's mental state is but what are the current social and economic determinants of that state. It is our concern that, irrespective of their motivations and logic, mentally disordered people would be poorly served by social and behavioural scientists who allowed the commonweal to drift into some fuzzy mind-set which concluded that it is suitable for mentally ill people to be left to sleep in cardboard boxes under a bridge in mid-winter London, or elsewhere, because they are, after all, 'happy enough' doing it.

Third, while their use may have fallen somewhat from favour, social and economic indicators are hardly irrelevant. The fact that additional dimensions have been added to the investigation of life quality must represent progress. However, the fact that objective measures are shown

to be insufficient as measures in and of themselves does not mean
that subjective measures of and by themselves will be sufficient. Empirical evidence from various studies including our own (Lehman *et al.*
1982; Oliver 1991a) shows clearly that objective factors explain significant and substantial amounts of variation in subjective global well-
being variables, even though the same studies should be held to demonstrate, equally, the important contribution to the understanding of
quality of life which the addition of subjective measures has made
(Cunningham 1985). This is perfectly sensible, as a judgement which a
person makes about his or her life may well be a subjective judgement
but it is based upon an appraisal of both the subjective and objective
aspects of life.

Clearly, psychological indicators have their limitations, despite the fact
that they provide, unquestionably, the most direct assessment of people's
levels of happiness. Zautra and Goodheart (1979) urge investigators to
remember that attempts to measure satisfactions, moods and the like are
regularly found to have been influenced by social desirability effects.
Also, there is an inevitable difficulty in controlling for the idiosyncratic
nature of self-report, particularly in feeling states. In fact there is a wisely
held opinion that 'none of the existing indicator systems – neither the
economic, the social, nor the QOL [i.e. by this the author meant
subjective well-being] indicator systems – is able, in itself to give an
adequate picture of people's life quality' (Hankiss 1983:25).

CONTENTS OF MEASURES

Considering the value-laden nature of the subject and surveying the truly
gigantic volume of literature which now exists, leads us to surmise that
really extreme views about quality of life are surprisingly rare. In fact, in
spite of the disagreement as to an exact definition of life quality there is
emerging some agreement as to what should be included in a quality of
life assessment. Before moving on, we provide Table 1.1, a simplified
breakdown of the main categories of quality of life and their contents. It
has been compiled from various sources, including one particularly
useful practical analysis by Lawton in 1984, which has formed a basis for
our own work.

One conclusion to be drawn on the basis of this exercise is that in
seeking elements to include into an assessment of quality of life one
should consider a more *inclusive* rather than *exclusive* approach – i.e.
including indicators drawn from across the range of demographic,
objective or environmental and subjective characteristics. Obviously,
quality of life is an important but overdetermined concept and it is
possible that no single, direct measure of life quality exists, or perhaps
will ever exist. Instead, we can *infer* life quality through its constituent

influences. This is to say that life quality is best regarded as a sum total of its determinants or causes as understood in any particular time and cultural context. Rather, as in Plato's allegory of the cave, with life quality we seem to be left viewing not an entity itself but merely its shadow. This is a very pragmatic definition, certainly implicit in much work, which allows us to proceed from a basis of some certainty to the tasks of either selecting quality of life measures from the many possibilities which currently exist or creating new ones.

Table 1.1 Categories of commonly acknowledged life quality determinants and examples of their contents

Category	Contents
Personal characteristics	Demographic variables e.g. age, gender, ethnicity, socio-economic status
Objective quality of life	Social/economic indicators e.g. social contact, income, housing, employment, etc. Behavioural competence/role performance measures e.g. social skills, functional ability, life events and activities Biological factors e.g. physical health status and mental state (psychopathology – signs)
Subjective quality of life	Subjective satisfaction e.g. perceived quality of life (satisfaction with social indicators in life domains) and general satisfaction (congruence between desired and attained goals) Mental health e.g. positive affect, negative affect (psychopathology – symptoms), affect balance, stress Happiness and morale Personality e.g. self-concept, locus of control, extroversion/introversion Adjustment, social adaptation and personal growth e.g. mastery, independence, values

QUALITY OF LIFE MEASURES FOR HEALTH CARE

Having described the background to life quality interest and its definition, we move the discussion on to a consideration of quality of life's application to health matters. Here, we are only able to offer a general overview, focusing on some areas of general interest. However, readers are reminded that each chapter in this present volume will deal with the literature that is relevant to the specific topic under consideration as required.

To begin with, it is obvious that the many studies cited in this review have not measured quality of life in the same way. In fact, a bewildering array of health indicators, profiles, indices and scales was employed. Some were validated with given sets of reliabilities and validities but many others were not. The need for a variety of such types of measuring instruments to be available to both providers and purchasers of health and social care services is now quite apparent. Recently, Dr Rachel Jenkins (1990) undertook a careful investigation of these data requirements on behalf of the UK Department of Health. Her persuasive review focused on indicators (i.e. summary measures of phenomena). While the evaluation of health services requires mortality and morbidity measures, many of the indicators which she identified as being essential to proper service evaluation were, in fact, life quality measures as discussed above. She concluded that at the time 'the ability to define and measure quality in mental health services is not well developed' (Jenkins 1990:500).

Various bibliographies or reviews of instruments which are currently being used as 'quality of life' measures within health care research have become available recently (see WHO 1993). For those pursuing research into mental health services, several seem promising, including McDowell and Newell 1987 and Bowling 1991. Nevertheless, some aspects of measures and some specific measures are worth a brief introduction, for no other reason than that they will be encountered by the reader subsequently in our own work.

INTEGRATING HEALTH STATUS WITH LIFE QUALITY

One rather disquieting trend is to overly identify well-being or quality of life with health status itself. While it is reasonable to wish to target quality of life measures on areas of health which medicine is most likely to be able to treat effectively, such a narrow focus may do a disservice to services designed for chronic patients whose needs can be seen to range more widely than their health status alone. The tendency to equate well-being with health has sometimes led to the unwarranted conclusion that any health status measure (i.e. usually considered to be the degree of illness or deviation from health) is a quality of life measure and that, conversely, quality of life need be measured only by health status measures.

In reality, this easy association does not exist. As one can observe from the previous discussion, quality of life measures are of a rather different order than health status measures, which have been designed frequently to measure the effects of health outputs (i.e. activity levels). Actual attempts to incorporate quality of life measures into health are in their infancy. Bowling (1991) recently reviewed this entire area. She has concluded that up to now most of the work done in integrating life quality measures had been done in the USA, that what had been produced was usually unwieldy and time consuming and that a great degree of conceptual confusion continues to exist concerning the use of the various concepts. Certainly, health clinicians and policy makers alike tend to employ measures which neglect aspects of quality of life such as subjective well-being, life satisfaction and general welfare, as measured through the range of social indicators. Also, there is the matter of who should make a quality of life assessment. Certainly, there tends to be a wide discrepancy between professionals' views and those of patients (Skantze *et al.* 1992). One certain implication of this is 'that measures of outcome should take account of individuals' self-assessments', as it is the patient's perception of changes in performance which are 'largely responsible for predicting whether the individuals seek care, accept treatment and consider themselves to be well and "recovered" ' (Bowling 1991:10).

A good example of this conundrum is the Nottingham Health Profile which, according to these terms, might be described as a quality of life measure. That instrument, a two-part, self-administered questionnaire, has many of the characteristics which one wishes to see in a quality of life measure. It is cheap to administer, brief, easy to score, valid and reliable, sensitive to changes and specific enough to be used on various health groups (McEwen 1983). It is, however, very narrow in its scope of concerns and really relates not so much to quality of life as to the evaluation of the level of impairment and disability, and the degree to which a person estimates his/her condition causes him/her functional problems in various aspects of life. It is based on six dimensions of health: physical mobility, pain, sleep, energy, social isolation and emotional reactions. It is recommended overenthusiastically for a broad range of uses in evaluation of medical and social interventions, surveys, outcome measures and the like, for the purposes of identifying needs, developing social policy for the allocation of resources, etc. In fact, as can be seen, its contents have really very little to do with most of the concerns discussed throughout the present review. It does not relate to most life domains and it is not a measure of perceived life satisfaction but of satisfaction only with health. This point should be carefully considered before its use as a life quality measure in service evaluations (see also Bowling 1991:11, who has criticised it, and other health status measures, for the same reasons).

QUALITY ADJUSTED LIFE YEARS (QALYs)

One of the effects of the application of Utilitarian theories to health services evaluation has been the emergent notion that health service outcomes are best measured in terms of their economic benefits. Such a measurement, it is argued, is desirable because it will bring about a more rational allocation of health service resources. The study of Quality Adjusted Life Years (QALYs) is the approach most prominently used for this purpose.

Essentially, QALYs research has sought to integrate two concepts, life expectancy and life quality, with QALYs being an arithmetic product of the former with some adjustment for the 'quality of the remaining life years gained' (Kind *et al.* 1990). The concept has been investigated both in the UK and abroad, in the USA, though in slightly different ways. In the UK, the basic research of Rosser and Watts (1972) was concerned with quantifying hospital output. They surveyed consumer and professional opinion regarding objective disability and subjective distress. They employed econometric scaling techniques and careful testing methodologies to produce a system of weighted values for various illness states. These values, in turn, can be applied to health outcomes in order to provide a cost-benefit-based means of allocating NHS resources. This initial work has been elaborated on by subsequent writers.

Although the fundamentals of health economics which lay behind QALYs are beyond the scope of this review, some points concerning them are usefully made here. QALYs represent a valiant attempt to solve head-on some of the difficult methodological problems inherent in the development of life quality scales. In particular, QALYs researchers are producing scales which have a strong numerical basis. Because the scaling derives literally from first principles rather than applying scales pre-established for other purposes, there is likely to be a great degree of unity among the new measures produced. Thus, the measures should be more accurate and statistically powerful, with less overlap (Kind 1990). Also the researchers' works have highlighted the difficulties in aggregating a range of life quality information into a single global measure, which is one goal of QALYs. In the process of this they have contributed to our understanding of how such a feat might be attempted. They have also worked on the assumption that there is a need to aggregate both subjective and objective information about a patient. Limited as are the assumptions about human nature upon which this work is based, it is none the less very valuable. Finally, they have attempted to reinforce the importance of the contribution of economics as a social science discipline working within medicine, a useful and necessary achievement.

There are several reasons, however, for doubting that QALYs are the best solution to quality of life measurement for our client group, at least at this point in time, and these have led us away from employing (or reviewing) them.

First, as shown above, the economic approach, at least by itself, to quality of life research has been regarded as somewhat discredited. QALYs are based on the economic principle that an individual is necessarily the best judge of his or her own welfare. We have already shown above that this may not hold true, even in the general population (Rescher 1972). In the case of those with continuing, severe mental disorders to cloud their judgements, this premise is almost certainly untrue at times.

Second, at the time of the commencement of this research, the QALYs approach had yet to be applied sufficiently to the mentally disordered to ensure its usefulness. Throughout, we have been eager to find measures which already had proven validity and for which there were some existing norms. Also, there are reasons to doubt whether the original calculations made by Rosser and Watts (1972) would have been applicable to our client group.

Third, it was not our intention to focus on the cost benefit side of the service. Important as this must be, it would not justify being the central issue in community care of the chronic mentally disordered (Goldberg 1983). Economic well-being is not quality of life but is, like many other things, one quality of life. It is very difficult to justify the continuing care needed for such people when comparing their outcomes against people whose conditions will obviously show more improvement for the same unit of expenditure. As will be shown, we sought to use quality of life measures to move the concerns for this client group to the centre of the service, not to provide a rationale which, no matter how well meaning, might only serve to marginalise them further. The obvious ethical dilemmas posed by the employment of QALYs to ration the health care for patient groups such as the one about which we write have proved serious enough to produce an EC-funded initiative, entitled 'the ethical QALY', which is working to address these concerns (Jenkins 1994).

LIFE QUALITY STUDIES IN MEDICINE

Medicine sometimes operates in areas where the boundaries between strictly medical matters and those which are the proper concerns of other academic and professional disciplines are unclear. For instance, the influence of social and economic factors on the production of ill health, including inequalities in the distribution of income, are very well documented (Black *et al.* 1982; Townsend *et al.* 1988). Recent reports in the UK (*Guardian*, 25 May 1994) show clearly how the decline in living standards during the past decade has led directly to increases in levels of many diseases and to an increased mortality rate among the poorer segments of society while, conversely, the better off have enjoyed an increase in their own standards of health and living.

The difference between an illness and normality is sometimes uncertain and, in the case of psychiatry, frequently depends heavily on cultural definition. Henry Maudsley said that 'it seems proper to emphasise the fact that insanity is really a social phenomenon, and to insist that it cannot be investigated satisfactorily and apprehended rightly except it be studied from a social point of view' (Maudsley [1879] cited in Shepherd 1983:121). Such a view certainly includes the possibility that information gathered from sources such as social indicators could be of great use in the understanding of psychiatric disorder.

Likewise, it is sometimes difficult to separate medical from moral and philosophical issues. Compulsory detention in hospital of mentally disordered people is one good example. The irreversible effects of some forms of treatment are others. The 'right to life' is yet another. In areas of concern such as these, quality of life considerations some-times compete with clinical ones in decision making and the literature is full of examples. One typical example lies in the area of suicide, where prevention and control services interface with cultural values, civil liberties, other branches of medicine and mental illnesses. Not surprisingly, suicide services have been considered in respect of life quality criteria (Mayo 1983), including coercive suicide prevention (Sartorius 1983).

This 'blurring of boundaries' or widening of interests concerning the parameters of health care have certainly directed health service investi-gators towards consideration of non-clinical, social outcomes. This is particularly true in social psychiatry, concerned as it traditionally has been with rehabilitative outcomes such as reduction or mitigation of the disabling effects of serious disorders, return of the patient to the community and reduction of the burden of care experienced by families (Shepherd 1983).

Increased emphasis on accountability in health care and an emphasis on understanding the cost-benefit ratios of various forms of interventions has also been influential. Gradually, the locus of concern of health service evaluators has begun to move away from the preoccupation with 'hard' measures, such as mortality, towards 'soft' outcomes, such as increased quality of life. This is especially apparent in areas of medicine which deal with chronic disorders, such as psychiatry, but it applies to other specialisms dealing with gastro-intestinal, coronary, hypertensive and respiratory disorders (Stewart et al. 1989), or chronic pain and arthritis (Marnell 1987). In our specialism there is a justifiable fear that overconcentration of the economic benefits of medicine alone will lead to a transfer of resources to:

[H]ighly treatable disorders such as acute depression in those with high earning ability, and away from chronic deteriorating disorders and those who are unemployed or unemployable. The attempt to express all the output of a service in economic terms makes for a result which is easy to interpret, but prevents us from considering important aspects of a service which have no economic consequences.

(Goldberg 1983:70).

As these trends have taken place, a very considerable body of quality of life research has emerged in respect of the range of health matters and medical specialisms. In order to give the reader a flavour of these, we will review some studies from non-psychiatric medical conditions as well as studies from both mental handicap and mental illness sources.

Non-psychiatric conditions

For what has now been a considerable period of time, non-psychiatric medical services have been devoting attention to quality of life issues. Many medical conditions have now been considered in association with life quality dimensions and we offer the following conditions by way of example.

Quality of life is a well-established area of study in chronic medicine, with both clinical and methodological studies having been reported. Harper *et al.* (1986) have published a cross-sectional survey of the quality of life of 301 multiple sclerosis patients. Gill (1984) wrote on the development of an instrument for measuring subjective well-being in the chronically and terminally ill. Boyer (1985) investigated the effects of haemodialysis on the quality of life of patients with end-stage renal disease. Scheibmer (1986) investigated the quality of life of individuals with insulin-dependent diabetes mellitus. Currently, Ostrow *et al.* (1991) have looked at the social support dimension of life quality for men with HIV infections.

Neurosurgical studies exist which have related quality of life concerns implicitly or explicitly to patients' clinical outcomes. Ljunggren *et al.* (1985) investigated psychological impairments and social adjustment following aneurysmal surgery. Jan *et al.* (1986) reported a retrospective study of 161 patients who had been operated upon for intracranial meningiomas. In addition to seizures, these patients frequently had psychiatric symptoms. Cagnoni *et al.* (1986) reported on a series of ninety operations for non-tumoral aqueductal stenosis. Klonoff (1984) investigated patients with closed head injury, comparing patients with and without frontal lobe damage.

Other non-neurosurgical procedures have been investigated in respect of quality of life outcomes. Sandberg *et al.* (1985) compared the effect of hysterectomy and oophorectomy procedures against other medical management. They found a gain in both quality of life and life expectancy for women in the 30–65 age group who underwent surgery for a variety of conditions. Jurmann (1986) investigated quality of life improvement following coronary-artery bypass surgery and Packa (1986) investigated changes in life quality following heart transplant.

Drug trials have used quality of life as an outcome measure. Bulpitt and Fletcher (1985) did this in a single-blind controlled study of anti-hypertensive treatments. Likewise included among medical services evaluated with quality of life measures are services for pulmonary heart disease (Heaton *et al.* 1983; Sandhu 1986) and those for cardiopulmonary resuscitation (CPR) (Roewer *et al.* 1985). One of the most exhaustively reported of the medical specialisms has been that of cancer treatment and research. Many studies have been reported as interest has began to move beyond consideration merely of issues of mortality and survival rates towards various aspects of social and psychological well-being as these related to service outcomes (Priestman and Bauum 1976; Fayers and Jones 1983; Ware 1984), including rehabilitation (Blinov *et al.* 1991).

Another medical specialism which has shown considerable interest in life quality issues has been that of gerontology. Here, quality of life issues are relevant to many aspects of medical services for this group, such as considerations of prevention and treatment of senile dementia (Musella 1984). Reported quality of life studies for the ageing have included the development of relevant instrumentation (Chang and Dodder 1983). These studies sometimes focus on the well-being, including mental health, of ethnic minorities (Johnson *et al.* 1986). As with many patient groups, the ramifications of deinstitutionalisation on life quality have been a source of concern (Markson 1985), and quality of life dimensions are, of course, intrinsic to multi-disciplinary assessments in this client group (Mold *et al.* 1987). Such studies of aged people have frequently been linked with demographic conditions, such as urban residence (O'Brien 1973; Onyenwoke 1983).

Quality of life has been used in association with the study of the mental health of aged people in the general population. For example, Hoeffer (1987) examined the association between quality of life and marital state – that is, the degree to which personal and social factors differentiated between older women of various marital states. An analysis of a sub-sample of 815 taken from the USA 1975 National Survey of the Aged showed that women who had never married were healthier, better educated and had a more positive attitude towards life than those who had been widowed.

Also, quality of life has been determined to be relevant to a range of physical disorders with psychiatric appearances and/or consequences. For example, a review by Tarter *et al.* (1984) mentions the quality of life consequences, especially those relating to cognitive and affective functioning, of chronic, low-grade PSE (portal-systemic encephalopathy, a condition affecting individuals with liver dysfunction).

Learning disabilities

Even within the field of mental disorder, mental health services have not been the first services to apply quality of life. Probably more marked for their earlier use of quality of life assessments have been those services for those individuals known variously as mentally retarded, mentally handicapped or as having learning disabilities. Assessment of the quality of life is regarded as important for this group (Brimblecombe 1985) and many relevant concepts, such as adaptation (Edgerton 1984), have been explored in respect of them.

Clearly, given the preceding discussion, being human implies some appreciation of life quality. What constitutes a reasonable quality of life is rapidly becoming a fundamental moral issue, when 'right to life', involuntary euthanasia (Powell and Hecimovic 1985; Lusthaus 1985) and access to surgery for infants (Simms 1985) are all under consideration. In a related fashion, Kaunitz et al. (1986) have argued that hysterectomy, albeit a controversial intervention, may benefit selected women with severe mental retardation. They cite a possible improvement in quality of life as one justification.

Quality of life has been linked to the evaluation of services for individuals with learning disability, services such as respite care (Joyce et al. 1983), community services for the ageing learning disabled (Edgerton et al. 1984), and type and circumstances of community placement (Heal and Chadsey-Rusch 1985). Examples of model services based on principles of 'normalisation' exist whose purpose is to improve life quality for community residents (Schalock and Konig 1987).

Where improved hospital care has been the goal, quality of life has served as a measure for improvement of inpatient life. For example, studies (Arnold 1986; Marshall 1986) show associations between hospital activities such as creative therapy and education and improved quality of life for this group. As a result of a one-year experiment in institutional reform, enhanced quality of life for care staff (e.g. increased staff influence in decision making) has been identified as a crucial element in the promotion of institutional reform for this group (MacEachron et al. 1985).

The effectiveness of deinstitutionalisation and community resettlement has been considered for this group as well (Vitello 1986). Quality of life measures are thought to add very important dimensions to deinstitutionalisation research, measures which are otherwise lacking or inadequate (Emerson 1985), such as the service consumer's perspective. This includes their satisfaction with elements of the subsequent placement like residence, community setting and services provided (Heal and Chadsey-Rusch 1985). Public attitudes are found to play an essential role in the success of resettlement and quality of life enjoyed by learning-disabled ex-inpatients (Cnaan et al. 1986). A follow-up study of eighty-five people who had been placed into independent housing and competitive employment eight to ten years earlier showed quality of life significantly associated with family involvement, income, number of disabilities and age. People successfully placed had higher assessed quality of life than those who had been unsuccessful (Schalock and Lilley 1986).

Mental illness

Prior to the early 1970s, few studies existed which concentrated specifically on determining the quality of life of mentally ill people. It is also fair to say that published work in this area has taken a considerably longer period to appear in the UK. Gradually, that situation has changed, and recently many more studies have emerged linking quality of life to the concerns of this client group. By 1979, Zautra and Goodheart were able to review a number of studies outlining social indicators for community mental health. At that time, census data was most often used to describe life quality. Various papers which they described focused on factors such as presence or absence of white social rank/ethnicity, family life-cycle, urbanisation, economic state, socio-economic influence, social disequilibrium, social affluence and social isolation. Poverty was shown to be a good predictor of high levels of service request.

Given the nature of our book, this review centres on the concerns of those mentally disordered people with serious and enduring conditions. Of course, serious chronic mental disorders are not the only types of conditions which have been studied using quality of life assessment. Bloom *et al.* (1985) described a preventative programme for newly separated people which used quality of life as an evaluation tool. In the follow-up of a controlled trial of a six-month combined modality therapy programme, the authors reported on thirty-month and four-year follow-ups. Quality of life measures, along with other measures such as level of adjustment, were improved by the intervention and remained improved throughout, although the outcome differences noted initially between the control and experimental groups had lessened over time.

Of all the many things which have attracted the attention of mental illness investigators with an interest in quality of life, hospital closure and the process of deinstitutionalisation are certainly two very important ones. Quality of life has become an important consideration in an appraisal of the consequences of hospital closure programmes and government policies in respect of these (Freedman and Moran 1984; Wallot 1985). Indeed, some would maintain, and we would endorse the motion, that 'the quality of life lived by the patient is the final criterion by which services must be judged' (Wing 1978b:254), including the deinstitutionalisation process. Maintaining quality of life for deinstitutionalised people has been considered against the background of loss of sanctuary provisions. The effectiveness of new community services in replacing these has been found to be related to adherence to various planning principles, such as functional equivalence, cultural relevance and potential trade-offs (Bachrach 1984). Certainly, as studies have begun to appear in the UK they have often taken as their theme hospital closure programmes and resettlement (Simpson *et al.* 1989; Oliver 1991a; Barry *et al.* 1993).

Along with hospital closure, improvement in the patient's clinical condition and quality of life through the processes of resettlement and integration into the community are goals central to the theme of deinstitutionalisation (Rosenfield 1987) (see also Bachrach 1975; Stein and Test 1978; Linn *et al.* 1980; Lamb 1981; Beiser *et al.* 1985; and Levine 1987). MacDonald *et al.* (1988) looked at the quality of life of 104 patients within a British long-stay hospital. One of the findings which has remained consistent is that the quality of life of resettled ex-patients (for whom specific funded programmes have been introduced) tends to increase immediately after resettlement. In the USA, Okin *et al.* (1983) reported the study of thirty-one patients resettled into community residences. Employing a repeated measures design, patients were re-evaluated at three successive eight-month intervals. Significant, positive changes in quality of life measures were found and no patients needed re-admission. Similar pictures of quality of life have characterised UK follow-up studies of English (Simpson *et al.* 1989) and Scottish groups (MacGilip 1991).

As a consequence, community services which actually impact positively on the quality of life of their users are to be valued. Many 'model programmes' are defined in terms of this outcome. Published examples of successful 'model programmes' have been reviewed by Rosenfield (1987) and include The Training in Community Living Programme, Madison, Wisconsin (Stein and Test 1980), a replication of it in Sydney, Australia (New South Wales Department of Health 1983; Hoult 1990), the Vancouver Community Programme (Beiser *et al.* 1985), Fountain House (Beard 1978; Beard *et al.* 1982), the controversial Soteria Programme (Mosher and Menn 1978), a home treatment programme in Philadelphia (Weinman and Kleiner 1978) and the Fairweather Lodge (Fairweather 1978).

Lehman was one of the first to make these links with his studies of resettlement in the Los Angeles area (Lehman *et al.* 1982; Lehman 1983a; 1983b; Lehman *et al.* 1986). Lehman *et al.* (1982) surveyed 278 residents of thirty large board and care residences in the Los Angeles area. They described the circumstances of these discharged patients in terms of their quality of life according to the domains described above. Comparing their results against a national sample, ex-patients were shown to be very much less satisfied than the general population with life conditions in most life areas. These differences were particularly marked in respect of certain domains: finances, legal and safety matters, family relationships, unemployment and social relations. This piece of research and the others associated with it have been the most influential reports on this subject. They highlighted the need for more energetic, higher-standard community social care programmes for this client group, who were found to be more similar in their life patterns to some underprivileged minority groups than to the general population. The authors were also able to provide a useful model of quality of life. Lehman (1983b) also looked at the vexed question of the potential impact of mental symptomatology on perceptions. Does the fact that one has a severe mental illness invalidate one's judgements about life satisfactions? Lehman produced crucial evidence to substantiate the validity of informants' perceptions, thus calling into question the reservations which many investigators and policy makers had held previously.

Baker and Intagliata (1982) studied the quality of life of 118 discharged chronic psychiatric patients in receipt of two community support services (CSS) in New York State, USA, one voluntary and one state funded. Data were gathered by interviews and case managers' ratings. In their investigation they extended the more traditional model of quality of life employed by Lehman to include 'mental health' and a mental health measure. To do this they employed the Affect Balance Scale (Bradburn 1969) which was widely used previously (Berkman 1971; Baier 1974; Andrews and Withey 1976). At a time when quality of life was yet to be widely used in respect of the mentally ill, this study supported the feasibility and warranting of quality of life usage in evaluation. The authors concluded, wisely, that:

> [G]iven the unavailability of norms to provide a standard by which to judge such programmes, perhaps the best strategy will be to focus on changes in the perceptions of clients receiving the services of a CSS programme and those who are in other programmes or not receiving this type of aftercare service.

> (Baker and Intagliata 1982:78)

Also at this time, Bigelow *et al.* (1982) described a 'program impact monitoring system (PIMS)' which was employed for three years in Oregon, and which used quality of life as an outcome assessment tool for the evaluation of the performance of community mental health support service delivery. An instrument was described and pre- and post-treatment data analysed with that from community groups for evidence of programme effectiveness. They tried to integrate quality of life and role theory, focusing on social adaptation. They chose to include a measure of self-esteem – i.e Rosenberg (1965). This is a complex idea, which adds a dimension to service evaluation which we also included in our research.

Malm *et al*. linked quality of life to the task of therapeutic planning. They emphasised the importance of knowing 'which features of quality of life are particularly important to the patient and to the natural raters, that is the persons who in real life make judgements that can have a significant impact on the patient' (Malm *et al*. 1981:478). We found this concept of a *natural rater* to be an important one, justifying the inclusion of an independent measure of the patient's objective state (in our case, by the worker conducting the interview). Such independent assessors may be taken as important people representative of teams, key workers in the care programme approach, etc., who add a supplementary dimension to quality of life assessment.

In circumstances such as this it is important to state specifically what is being measured and by whom. Diener (1984) usefully distinguished between different definitions of subjective well-being and reminded us that under certain conditions, *eudaemonia*, or happiness, is not to be considered in the sense of an affect but as the possession of a quality, hence judged from a particular value framework. The criterion for happiness of this type is not the actor's subjective judgement but the value framework of the observer, 'rather analogous to success, which is also judged against some external standard' (Diener 1984:543). In this respect, well-being can be judged normatively against external standards. Thus, such decisions by professionals who know the patient/client are valid observations about quality of life and fall into this category.

SUMMARY

The assessment of quality of life is emerging as a main criterion against which to judge service performance. Its historical antecedents lie in philosophical debates which have influenced Western thought from at least the 'classical' Greeks to the present. Much of this debate centres around distinctions being made between the external environment (i.e. objective reality) and the individual's subjective perceptions of it. Though there is a tendency for it to be regarded conceptually as a 'rag-bag', many of the underlying concepts are well researched (if not always clearly defined). The most useful definition is one which does not exclude any necessary dimensions arbitrarily or precipitously.

Substantial bodies of research now exist into the various determinants of life quality. The term has been widely used, if not always appropriately, within both social and health care research. Various aspects of the lives and conditions of mentally ill people have now been investigated, justifying the central premise of this book, which is that quality of life, as seen from the perspective of a seriously mentally disordered person, is a relevant consideration in the evaluation of mental health services for individuals with such conditions.

Chapter 2

The development of a quality of life profile for operational use

INTRODUCTION

At the time that this research began into the quality of life of clients on the caseloads of UK social and health care agencies (Oliver 1991a), the term had only recently been applied to chronically mentally ill people. Most research until then concentrated on the 'adverse effects of the treatment and indirect effects of the illness' (Tantam 1988:243). As revealed in Chapter 1, the most striking work then existing in respect of the quality of life of the chronic mentally disordered had appeared in papers by Baker and Intagliata (1982) and Lehman (Lehman *et al.* 1982; Lehman 1983a). Stimulated by these studies, our research began as an attempt to incorporate this research into the UK context.

Initial assumptions about the usefulness of quality of life research as a means of monitoring and assessing client well-being have evolved gradually into an ongoing programme of questionnaire development and research. The programme has involved various health and social care agencies and their managers and clinical professional staff as well as academics. Indeed, the impetus and most of the finance have come about through a network of long-standing joint associations between university academics and their professional colleagues working in operational environments. The programme of research has had two main purposes: first, to describe the quality of life of chronically mentally disordered people; and, second, to develop a research tool for standard operational use in a multi-disciplinary community setting. Success would be judged by achieving an integrated instrument drawn from pre-existing scales which provides a broad, if necessarily selective, picture of the client's current state of well-being across relevant life areas.

THE PROGRAMME OF DEVELOPMENT AND IMPLEMENTATION OF QUALITY OF LIFE MEASURES

While results from developmental phases will be reported in detail in subsequent chapters, by way of presenting the reader with a more coherent overview of our research we would like to outline the general course of the project, along with some of the steps which have been taken in developing an evaluative tool. To date, the developmental work has been characterised by six distinct stages (referred to hereafter as 'phases'). Each has had its own rationale and the results of earlier phases have influenced the direction of subsequent phases. Table 2.1 lists the various phases of the questionnaire's development to date.

Table 2.1 LQOLP development: phases (dates), objectives/settings and sample sizes[2] of research undertaken to date[1]

Phases (dates)	Objectives/settings	Sample size[2] (time 1)[3]	Sample size[2] (time 2)[3]
I	Test PSSRU (University of Kent) interviews		
(2/86–5/86)	Residential homes survey	75	—
II	Test Lehman quality of life interview		
(10/86–1/87)	Residential economic sector study	61	—
III	Test LQOLP		
a (4/87–10/87)	County social services pilot survey	45	—
b (3/88–9/89)	District health authority day-care service	35	25
IV	Test shortened LQOLP		
a (5/89–7/89)	Physical disability survey	27	—
b (8/89–12/89)	Community mental health centre	30	27
c (9/89–9/91)	Community mental health centre (USA)	81	44
d (9/89–12/89)	General health centre (USA)	15	—
V	Full operational test		
(6/90–3/91)	County social services department survey	422	—
VI	Full service implementation		
a (6/91-present)	Mental health support teams	374	98
b (1992–93)	Support team comparison group	50	50
c (1992)	Independent residential homes survey	140	—
d (1992–present)	Yorkshire resettlement survey	241	—
e (1992–present)	Welsh cohort study	100	—
f (1992–present)	Cheshire case management study	17	—
g (1992–present)	Schizophrenia development study	50	—
h (1993–present)	Clubhouse study (USA)	76	—

[1] Excludes joint European research and use by other investigators.
[2] Sample size refers to the number of quality of life interviews recorded.
[3] Times 1 and 2 refer to first and second applications of LQOLP in longitudinal research.

Our work has very much followed the evolving situation of the field, tracking and, occasionally, leading events in the changing patterns of community care. Like the operations of the agencies which it has investigated, the programme has remained flexible, adjusting to changing circumstances and strategic and operational concerns as these have unfolded. We hope that while operating within the short-term considerations which strongly determine social and health care agencies, it retained a long-term vision of what it sought to achieve.

Admittedly, given all of the many studies undertaken, it has not always been possible to adhere to a 'classic' research strategy of identifying problems, developing hypotheses and methodologies, seeking funds, setting plans, conducting research and producing reports. However, our work pattern has had some important advantages. First, there has been the academic gratification of having produced something which has been adjudged relevant by those individuals directly involved in designing and delivering services. Only this adjudged relevance enables academic findings to be understood, valued and subsequently translated readily into practice and planning. This transition from theory to application is not easily achieved by research in the social and behavioural sciences. Second, the close association with operational bodies allows investigators a degree of freedom frequently not easily achievable by those whose work is tied to more structured, government-funded research. This includes access to subjects and services as well as considerable administrative, personnel and some financial support in the conducting of the research.

Viewing our work as a case study of the development of evaluative instrumentation and translating this from an academic context into the work environment, the saga of the Lancashire Quality of Life Profile's emergence will have definite heuristic value for others undertaking similar tasks. As one would suppose, progress can hardly be described as having been 'onward and upward' but more frequently a matter of taking 'two steps forward and one back'. As will become apparent, many changes have been made in both the structure and contents of the questionnaire, from initial inception through to operational product. One area of development has been in the structure of the interview, to do with length of interview and number of questions. The gradual pattern of improvements to do with these characteristics is outlined in Table 2.2.

Table 2.2 Changes in quality of life profile during the first 5 piloting phases

Pilot phase	Number of forms	Number of pages	Number of items	Length of interview	Percentage of interviews completed in one session
I	10	45	354	180	unknown
II	1	38	269	54.5	95%
III	1	38	289	72.2	91%
IV	1	8	105	27.3	100%
V	1	8	105	36.6	99%

Phase I

We began our work by reviewing and piloting existing instrumentation. Anticipating changes in community care, during 1985/6 the first of our quality of life studies surveyed the lives of seventy-five chronically mentally disordered individuals who were drawn from two health districts and who were living in community residential care. The research was undertaken as a response to planning needs. 'New look' community provisions were being introduced into local mental health services. This research attempted to survey existing provisions in order to better understand what the 'standard' services were already providing, lest they be replaced in a wave of understandable but misguided enthusiasm for the novel. Most clients studied had been discharged from one or more large psychiatric hospitals then being run down (mean length of long-stay, psychiatric hospitalisation was 19.5 years) though a smaller proportion (about one in eight) were part of the 'new chronic' population beginning to accumulate in care. The sample had an average age of onset of illness of the mid-twenties and most (75 per cent) were in receipt of psychotropic medication.

This initial survey employed a motley collection of instruments, designed in the UK for the evaluation of community care (Hampson *et al.* 1984), which were said to measure elements of quality of life and had been recommended for use in evaluating community care programmes. These instruments proved to be of little operational use due to their length (interviews took approximately three hours and involved completion of nearly a dozen different forms). Few were completed within a single interview and a trained research assistant was required to collect the information. The questionnaires were abandoned subsequently as there was a general feeling that the scale of the research was of such a magnitude as to skew the actual operational functions of the service under investigation. However, the results of this survey highlighted to some of the agency managers and professionals involved the usefulness of quality of life research on resettled groups (Oliver 1991a). The results of the survey also improved our understanding of the rate of 'normalised' services in comparison with 'hospital hostels' in the case of this client group (Oliver 1991b).

Phase II

The second phase sought to redress some of the difficulties identified so clearly in phase I. Continuing to anticipate government policy changes, sixty-one clients were re-interviewed nine months later in the same venues. This time a different quality of life questionnaire was used (Lehman *et al.* 1982), in conjunction with the General Health Questionnaire (Goldberg 1972). By this time the UK government's commitment to a 'mixed economy of care' in the public services was becoming quite clear. The purpose of this research was to test out new quality of life measures and to investigate the differences made variously by public, private and voluntary economic sector control of provisions on quality of life (Oliver and Mohamad 1992). In this sense, it was research with both methodological (academic) and marketing (managerial) aims.

The single American questionnaire piloted was better received than the multiple UK questionnaires from phase I but was still too long (i.e. thirty-eight pages) and convoluted (269 questions) for regular operational use.

Phase III

When the phase II questionnaire also proved to be operationally unwieldy, phase III research attempted to combine the merits of both the British and the American instruments. As a means of discriminating between questions and scales, data from phases I and II were analysed using stepwise ordinary least squares regression for objective and subjective measures respectively within each domain. Various global well-being measures were examined systematically as dependent variables, a methodology employed previously elsewhere (Lehman *et al.* 1982; Andrews and Withy 1976).

The pilot study was linked to two local operational settings: an experimental psychiatric day service and an interdepartmental project, sponsored by the North-West Regional Association of Directors of Social Services (ADSS), to promote quality of life initiatives in local agencies. In the case of the former, thirty-five outpatients from a psychiatric local service were interviewed and twenty-five were then re-interviewed a year later by a research assistant, employed and trained specially for the task. In the case of the latter, the project aimed at involving managers and practitioners in originating ideas for introducing quality of life outcome measures into services and was given an award by the ADSS. Here, forty-five social care clients were selected from the caseloads of three social services teams and were interviewed by their social workers.

While successfully incorporating the various desirable elements of both styles, this version unfortunately succeeded in being neither briefer nor more 'user friendly' to operational staff. In fact, it was something of a disaster. As can be seen in Table 2.2, it had more questions than the phase II instrument (289), took longer to complete (the mean was 72.2 minutes) and fewer respondents completed it in a single session (91 per cent). This version was quite unpopular with both operational managers and their social work staff.

Phase IV

The lesson from phase III was clearly that briefer quality of life profiles needed to emerge to meet the needs of professionals working in operational settings. A new questionnaire was drawn from the results of the previous pilot studies. However, this time a 'minimalist' approach was taken. Questions were *included in* rather than *excluded from* the new interview. Decisions were taken on theoretical, professional and statistical criteria. Theoretically, a closer link to well-being than we had demanded previously was sought with each measure. Professionally, we sought questions which were likely to be useful or operationally plausible. Statistically, strict criteria were employed and items were included only if they contributed a significant increase in the amount of variance explained, i.e. where F values of questions consistently met or exceeded $<.05$ probability levels. Questions were scrutinised carefully for repetition. Scales were discarded when they had lost their integrity by having several of their items deleted.

The final product combined the advantages of several instruments but was much more well integrated and less cumbersome. It was reduced to eight pages, had 105 items and took less than half the time to administer (27.3 minutes).

Results drawn from its usage were much simpler to interpret than the various individual questionnaires and scales upon which it was based. Prior to its employment in a large-scale service evaluation exercise, it was 'fine tuned' for comparison in several work settings, sometimes by operational staff (i.e. doctors, nurses and social workers). The work settings are listed below:

1 In a UK community mental health centre as an outcome measure, i.e. thirty-five patients were interviewed and twenty-five re-interviewed.
2 For comparison, in a UK social services team, to assess the global well-being of twenty-seven physically disabled individuals.
3 In the community mental health centre of Boulder, Colorado, USA, where it was piloted (by PH) on eighty-one service users during the summer and autumn of 1989. This study also included a small comparison group (n=15) drawn from a general health centre. The service evaluation was repeated subsequently on forty-four of the centre users (see Huxley and Warner 1992).
4 The Mental Welfare Commissioners of Scotland used the profile as a means of aiding them in the task of interviewing clients and making quality judgements about services during their hospital visits. This was an unanticipated use of quality of life interviewing and its warm reception by the Commission increased our confidence in it.

Phase V

By 1989, the shortened quality of life profile was ready for use in the field. A full-scale survey of the long-term mental health clients on the caseload of the social services department (SSD) was undertaken. A randomised quota sample was drawn from the caseloads of specialist mental health social workers (between one and sixteen cases per worker). Of more than one thousand clients selected for possible interview, 422 clients were finally interviewed by ninety-one social workers from twenty-two area and hospital social work teams. No interviews were duplicated.

Confirming the questionnaire's robustness and usefulness in operational settings, application in phase V averaged only 36.6 minutes (S.D. = 15.7), with 92.6 per cent of interviews having required one hour or less to complete.

Phase VI

The programme had now moved into a sixth stage, characterised by the use of quality of life measures in routine operations. This is exemplified by the studies of community mental health support teams presented below and of many other services which employ the measure regularly to monitor and evaluate their services (see Table 2.1). This has been supplemented by the development of CPASS, a computerised information system employed in the care programme approach, within which quality of life plays an important part (see Chapter 12).

Up to the present, 1,985 quality of life interviews have been conducted. The first three developmental and piloting phases interviewed 241 people utilising a variety of different instruments. The fourth through sixth phases have seen the questionnaire move from unwieldy instrument into something more operationally useful, and 1,744 people have been interviewed using this version. For the benefit of readers, we include, in Appendix 2, a selection of norms calculated on a sub-set (1,575) of these.

THE CONTENTS OF THE QUALITY OF LIFE PROFILE

General principles covering selection, measurement and utilisation

As reviewed in Chapter 1, there now exists a range of social, economic and health indicators and measures which may be employed in quality of life investigations. The question of how and what to select is a perplexing one, even for the experienced investigator. Various principles may be drawn from our experiences which could prove helpful in guiding the production of quality of life measures. These principles were not all followed rigorously in the case of this work for the simple reason that they were not available at the time when the work was being undertaken. They are appearing now, as more attention is being given to the subject. While the list is not exhaustive, we offer the following selection drawn from our own experiences and from those of others.

One must accept that at this stage one is operating in an area of only limited certainty. As we have seen, no absolute agreement exists over the definition of quality of life. Nevertheless, there is emerging agreement as to what constitutes valid content. There is every reason to accept this consensus, as we have done, as a starting point.

There is a perpetual debate as to the relative merits of health and welfare in quality of life. Traditional approaches to measuring outcomes have focused almost exclusively on changes in clinical condition. Nevertheless, there is a growing consensus that quality of life is more than measured levels of psychopathology. This also means that instruments which principally measure health status are, at best, insufficient for measuring quality of life and, at worst, very misleading.

At the end of the day, economic factors govern content at least to a considerable degree, if not as much as scientific ones do. While one might like to believe that what determines the actual content of an operational instrument is the same as what might govern an academic one, such a simple assumption would be misleading. In fact, possession of a very large research grant with which to hire paid researchers and the like may actually prove a hindrance to producing a good operational measure. Research instruments and procedures which evolve from practice are strongly influenced, understandably, by these conditions – perhaps 'leaner and fitter', to use the contemporary parlance.

Little empirical research actually exists on identifying what makes life and survival valuable (Bowling 1991). Certain accepted values concerning the essential value of life as a 'good thing' in and by itself are inherent in any such approach. These values will vary widely, and that fact will influence content selection and research methodologies. Emphasising the centrality of context in choice of instrumentation, Cox et al. identify four which have drawn particular attention from health researchers. They are 'measuring the health of populations, assessing the benefit of alternative uses of resources, comparing two or more interventions in a clinical trial and making a decision on treatment for an individual patient (Cox et al. 1992:353). Certainly, in choosing a measure to reflect service outcomes correctly, one must be particularly careful to choose one which is focused on the area where change is likely to occur.

The following points made by Bowling (1991) concerning measurement selection are well supported, if retrospectively, by our own experiences and they may be regarded as good working rules of thumb by which to proceed:

1   *There are no 'gold standards' for quality of life measurements, no absolute standards against which to calibrate and compare.* Internal consistency, logical coherence and utility are good guides in the absence of an absolute standard.

2   *No single study can establish validity to such an overdetermined, multi-dimensional phenomenon.* Research plans must avoid being over-optimistic. Operation managers, under pressure to deliver services, tend to want immediate solutions; this is very understandable. However, those wishing to develop their own instrument must be warned to prepare for a very long process in doing so, with no guarantee of a usable result at the end.

3   *Weighting of scales and scores seems to make little difference in practice.* Scales which can be scored by simple integer are sufficient for most applications and are much easier for the innumerate to understand. This simple fact doubtless will not, and indeed should not, deter psychometricians from investigating the relative influences of various dimensions on outcomes and developing appropriate methods of reflecting these. Statistical procedures, such as factor analysis, exist to refine scoring for computing weightings. In view of the lack of a well-established weighting scheme for life quality, one can only recommend that a variety of weighting approaches are tried before any particular one is chosen. (For further discussion of this topic, readers are referred to Cox *et al.* 1992.)

4   *The optimal strategy, and the one most likely to produce success, is to employ various different approaches simultaneously.* Of course, as with any research in its earlier stages, the cause of progress is best served by not rejecting notions prematurely in advance of reasonable evidence.

Additionally, our own observations show that:

5   *Reliability is usually neither complete nor absolute.* On the contrary, it is ephemeral and must be re-confirmed in each study. Multi-dimensional scales tend to reduce the effect of error if they are not so complex as, paradoxically, to cause error.

6   *Crucially, operational situations often require some compromise in measurement techniques.* Accurate results may only be achieved at the expense of ease of use of an instrument. Sacrificing validity in the form of completeness may be the only practical means of achieving compliance. We have had examples of both. One good example existed in the area of sex. Original questions about sexual activity were eventually excluded from the UK version for the simple reason that fieldworkers, even with training, would not ask the questions, no matter how delicately or indirectly phased. International pilots have reinstated the questions in what may be argued to be less-inhibited cultures (i.e. Italy, Netherlands and Germany).

7   *When developing an instrument, the means of measurement must be strongly influenced by the conditions under which it will be employed as well as by what it is expected to achieve.* The level of sophistication of those who will administer the scales is paramount. In situations where untrained or non-research-minded staff are expected to administer scales with little or no training or support, everything must be kept simple and must be accompanied by clear, concise instructions.

8   *Certainly, it is a good rule to presume that individual perceptions and satisfactions strongly predict outcomes in mental health services, though whether, as Bowling maintains, they predict them 'best', is quite another matter.* Admittedly, in some instances, individuals may not be able to respond coherently to even the most appropriate measurement tool. However, measurement methods which centre on the client and his/her perceptions are generally to be preferred to those which are geared to an independent rater's assessment. We are mindful of research which, although conducted many years ago, has yet to be seriously challenged. Meehl (1954) was unable to find a single instance in which a clinical prediction of patient outcome was superior to an actuarial prediction. Around the same time, a study by Blenker (1954) gave a group of social workers the unenviable distinction of predicting 'movement' (improvement) in clients with an accuracy of 'nil'. Later, Strauss and Carpenter (1972; see also 1977) showed that the best predictors of different outcome functions were the same functions measured at time 1. Huxley *et al.* (1979) found that clinical factors in cases of common mental disorders were no better than and in many cases inferior to, social factors as predictors of outcome. Meehl's work, in particular, alerts us to the fact that independent 'clinical' judgements are frequently prone to error, some of which is unsystematic – personal and idiosyncratic – reducing the capacity of clinical prediction to account for the variance in outcome measures.

9   *Most importantly, there is the condition of the subjects themselves to consider.* Many individuals with severe and continuing mental disorders may well not respond well to certain investigative approaches due to their clinical condition. This problem has been often highlighted by the occasionally heated debate over whether to employ open-ended or closed questions. Those who favour open-ended questions do so for a variety of reasons, including a feeling that the complexity and range of relevant issues cannot be covered adequately by closed questions. This approach, in our opinion, must be tried judiciously. The profile's current content has few such open-ended questions, focusing on structured, brief and very specific question sets. Aside from the obvious problems of reliability which accompany such open-ended formats, we would maintain that structured, closed questions have less chance, clinically, of exacerbating the symptoms

of people with long-term, severe mental illnesses (and causing them to become florid). This could be a most unpleasant and dangerous consequence of employing a valid methodology in entirely the wrong set of circumstances. Also, shorter, less complex question sets are less likely to fatigue already unwell individuals. It is vital, if at all possible, not to burden people with the investigative process.

Again, in our experience, the development of suitable measurement techniques has necessitated the making of choices, frequently between the real and the ideal. We have tried to strike a balance, 'maximising utility' wherever possible. Provided that basic theoretical, scientific and clinical conditions are met, choices may be guided by what is useful. Along these lines, we suggest that the following principles may be considered as guides to utilisation:

1 *Quality of life interviewing is more popular with patients than staff.* This has several correlates, most important of which is that procedures should include opportunities to determine the satisfaction of clients themselves with the interview process. It also indicates that additional work may have to be done with staff to ensure cooperation.

2 *Quality of life interviews have a therapeutic benefit.* As with any interview undertaken by a therapist with a client, there is frequently some benefit from the interview itself. For clinical people, struggling as they are to make improvements, this should be regarded not as an unwanted source of measurement error to be eliminated but as a therapeutic gain to be encouraged. However, as with any treatment element strong enough to have a benefit, there are occasionally people who react badly. Unwanted side-effects must be accounted for, and their presence has been empirically established by our own research, as reported in Chapter 3.

3 *Quality of life measures are exceptionally robust.* They work well under a variety of conditions and are suitable for routine use.

4 *Many quality of life measures appear to be heavily influenced by relatively immutable social and psychological determinants.* This means that the measures are stable over time. Plans for utilisation must take this into account. For example, to ensure both stability and sensitivity, one might like to consider employing techniques such as mixing more stable, personality-influenced measures with less stable, mood-related measures.

5 *Contents will need to vary according to the sample demography and clinical state of the population under study.* Indeed, issues such as age, sex and social class or educational attainment influence strongly the style of question phraseology as well as content. The same caveats apply to variations in quality of life according to the type of treatment or care setting being studied.

Current contents of the LQOLP and their origins

Taking into account the principles of content selection, as can be seen in Table 2.3, the questionnaire has incorporated a selection of well-accepted measures taken from well-regarded research.

Table 2.3 LQOLP: contents, original author(s) and source(s).

Item of content	Original author(s)	Source(s)
Objective well-being		
Life domains	e.g. Strauss and Carpenter (1972)	Lehman (1983a) Bigelow *et al.* (1982)
Social indicators	Campbell *et al.* (1976)	Lehman (1983)
Quality of life uniscale	Spitzer *et al.* (1981)	Spitzer *et al.* (1981)
Subjective well-being		
Cantril's ladder	Cantril (1965)	Lehman (1983a)
Delighted–terrible scale	Andrews and Withey (1976)	Lehman (1983a)
Affect balance scale	Bradburn (1969)	Baker *et al.* (1982)
Critical incidents	Flanagan (1982)	Flanagan (1982)
Disability adaptation	Flanagan (1982)	Flanagan (1982)
Self-esteem scale	Rosenberg (1965)	Franklin *et al.* (1982)
Happiness scale	Bradburn (1969)	Bradburn (1969)

Source: General questionnaire structure from Lehman 1983

Anthony Lehman considered 'how to assess chronic patients' well-being and the possibility that eliciting information on patients' subjective quality of life might enhance our understanding and service needs (Lehman 1983a:370). In his survey of 278 residents of board and lodgings homes in the Los Angeles area, data were collected in one-hour interviews. Four types of information were gathered, based on several other studies of both mentally ill people and the general population:

1   Personal characteristics;
2   Objective quality of life indicators for eight life domains;
3   Subjective quality of life indicators for eight life domains;
4   Global well-being measures.

In turn, the contents of his questionnaire were heavily drawn from well-tested sources such as Andrews and Withey (1976). Besides the general appearance of the questionnaire, also retained were the format of eight life domains – i.e. living situation, family, social relations, leisure activities, religion, work/education, finances, personal safety and health – and a ninth – religion (not mentioned in his papers but investigated) – and some administrative details, enabling the interviewer to record essential details of the data gathering operation (Fillenbaum 1985:57).

Global well-being measures included Cantril's ladder (Cantril 1965). In our work, this scale has been altered from a nine-point categorical scale to a 100-point continuous or analog-type scale. If one chooses to employ subjective global well-being measures as criterion variables it is better if they can act as independent variables for regression analysis. Also, for small samples, it is best to select a means of measurement which does not produce too large a grouping of subjects exactly on the scale midpoint. Objective well-being (for all patients and non-patients) is composed largely of social and economic indicators. These have remained unchanged from Lehman's suggestions, though such measures may need to be altered according to the fashion in which statistical data of this sort are gathered nationally to ensure ready bases of comparison.

Perceived quality of life can be taken as the sum total of subjective assessments of life satisfaction made by individuals regarding their life domains. Lehman used a seven-point version of the 'delighted–terrible scale' (Campbell et al. 1976; Andrews and Withey 1976) to measure this as well as to measure overall well-being. Lehman's questions have been retained but reduced considerably in number. His suggestions were generally followed that at least two were necessary in order to produce a mean score. Also, the delighted–terrible scale was changed to 'couldn't be better'–'couldn't be worse'. This is because there is a mis-translation of the terms 'delighted' and 'terrible' into standard English from American English. New terms were piloted and found to work. The scales were renamed the 'life satisfactions scales' (LSS). In fact, throughout this research, changes in language have been made with caution and only where the original wording would have caused confusion or inaccuracy or brought the interview into disrepute.

Baker and Intagliata (1982) also investigated the well-being of mentally ill people. Their survey concentrated on the lives of 118 clients of the New York State Community Support Scheme. In order to investigate their view of quality of life, which was somewhat more expanded than Lehman's, as well as life satisfaction measures, they also included direct measures of mental health. These are essential for evaluating mental health services. They included the 'affect balance scale' (Bradburn 1969), which was developed as a measure of psychological well-being. It consists of ten questions in the form of a brief self-report measure. Concentrating on the respondents' recent experiences, the positive affect scale is said to measure adaptiveness (being closely associated with two measures of social participation – sociability and novelty, defined as the willingness to try new things). The negative affect scale is said to approximate symptomatology or mental illness. An 'affect balance scale', denoting ego strength or mental health, can be computed from the two, though many investigators find it more useful to keep the scales separate. We also chose to include this. In most applications of these scales, in order to avoid response bias, positive and negative affect questions are mixed. However, following piloting they were separated and are better understood in this way by individuals with very concrete thought processes. Also, in his own research, Bradburn included the 'happiness scale' (Gurin *et al.* 1960), which touches an important dimension of general well-being that is related to satisfaction and mental health but not identical to them. We have also included this.

Franklin *et al.* (1986), during the course of interviewing 220 individuals who had been discharged from mental hospitals into the community, produced a more sophisticated model of quality of life assessment for the mentally disordered. In particular, they found reason to include measures of adaptation but extended the range of measures to a 'self esteem-scale' (Rosenberg 1965) in addition to the Bradburn affect scales (1969). The former consists of five questions which describe high self-esteem and five which describe low self-esteem. The answers are supposed to range on a five-point continuum of strongly agree to strongly disagree. Following piloting, these were abbreviated to simple yes/no choices. This change was made to avoid the confusion which was being generated in patients by the question set, presumed at the time to be an artefact of their negative psychiatric symptoms.

There is a frequently reported problem with the inclusion of objective information. It was a continuous occurrence that the professionals interviewing the clients expressedly wished to be able to make their own assessment of the client's quality of life. To resolve these problems we have included a single quality of life measure, the 'quality of life uniscale' (Spitzer and Dobson 1981). Initial analysis suggests that it adds substantially to the explanatory power of 'objective well-being' measures, even when regressed against subjective, global well-being criterion variables.

Flanagan (1982) and his colleagues at the American Institute for Research in the Behavioral Sciences at Palo Alto in California, employed the critical incident technique to determine the existence of life domains among the normal population. They subsequently suggested that in order to compose quality of life measures for disabled individuals, persons should be asked questions focused on the problems created for them by the impairment. In particular, they have suggested two additional types of questions:

> (1) How well their needs and wants are being met and what specifically is interfering with these needs and wants being met and (2) what changes, whether possible or not, would produce the greatest improvement in their quality of life.
>
> (Flanagan 1982:59)

Both of these have been taken on board. Sets of questions relating to quality of life inhibition for each domain were designed and tested. Sadly, not all proved to be predictive in pilots, but those which did have been retained. In addition, a single question pertaining to quality of life enhancers (factors whose presence is likely to increase life quality) has been likewise created, tested and retained.

EXCLUSION OF MEASURES

It could be argued that a good indication of the quality of what is contained within an instrument can be found in what is not contained in it. As has been seen throughout, one of the major tasks has not been finding measures to include but trying to decide on what grounds to exclude them. Andrews and Withey (1976) tested fourteen global well-being measures! As observed above, our decisions about what to include or leave out were sometimes pragmatic. One way this was done was by using statistics to 'let the data speak for itself' – i.e. the particular element had weak explanatory power. Another was by tailoring the length of the interview to what operational managers were prepared to instruct their staff to complete. 'Sometimes', however, does not mean 'exclusively'. In such early days of research, pure pragmatism alone as a means of distinguishing between items would not have been sufficient. Ultimately, we have made decisions on both *theoretical* and *practical* grounds, often both together.

For example, throughout every phase of this research, regular research discussions have been held with operational teams and their managers. These discussions helped to set research agendas, clarify issues, feedback observations from the workers, review papers and the like. During such discussions very early in this work, it was agreed that quality of life was conceptually separate and distinct from satisfaction with services. While the two were both related to the task of programme performance review, one – consumer satisfaction – was related to service volume or output, while the second – quality of life – was related to service impact or outcome. This point seems obvious now but at the time the argument was much less clear. Great pressure was being exerted, chiefly by service providers and purchasers whom we were advising (but also by other academics and people with political intentions), who incessantly wanted to confuse the two.

Table 2.4 Discarded measures: abandoned scales and reasons (all scales were fully piloted)

Measure	Author	Reason
Adjective checklist	Andrews and Withey (1976)	Unnecessary replication of global well-being
Sheltered care environment checklist	Moos and Lemke (1984)	Lacked explanatory power and was unnecessarily long
The faces scale for life satisfaction	Andrews and Withey (1976)	Less useful than the delighted–terrible scale
General Health Questionnaire (GHQ)	Goldberg (1972)	Too long and shortening destroyed the structure
Skills and performance checklist	Hampson *et al.* (1984)	Too long for routine administration
Psychosocial functioning inventory	Hampson *et al.* (1984)	Essential ingredients contained in affect balance scale

For this reason, and because to do otherwise would have produced serious dangers of bias, two different sets of measures were developed. One author (JO) focussed on quality of life scale development and another (PH) on client satisfaction, developing a General Satisfaction Questionnaire (Huxley 1988; 1990), which is now being used to assess satisfaction with services.

Many ideas and measures have been tried and rejected along the way. During early pilots of Lehman's questionnaire and the PSSRU questionnaires, various measures were tried and subsequently discarded. Table 2.4 shows a few of these and the reasons why they were discarded.

1 The adjective checklist was discarded because it produced unnecessary replication. This was a series of semantic differential measures on seven-point scales which are meant to provide information on global well-being (Andrews and Withey 1976; Campbell et al. 1976). The adjective checklist requires opinions on seven pairs of contrasting, polar opposite adjectives, staggered in order to avoid response bias: boring–interesting; enjoyable–miserable; useless–worthwhile; full–empty; discouraging–hopeful; disappointing–rewarding; brings out the best in me–doesn't give me much chance. Cantril's ladder and the LSS global well-being scores did the same thing adequately, although the adjective checklist was conceptually linked to psychiatric symptomatology as well.

2 Another measure was discarded in the attempt to shorten the questionnaire because, given its length, it did not add sufficiently to the explanatory power of the interview. Lehman employed a thirty-six-question sub-set of the sheltered care environment checklist (Moos and Lemke 1984), a larger set of scales meant to evaluate specific elements of residential life. However, in our studies many clients were not living in residential settings. Also, for those who did, living situation was not the strongest predictor of global well-being. The area of sheltered care was reduced to a few satisfaction questions, relating to specific aspects such as comfort or influence within the living conditions domain.

3 Some types of measurement were less effective than others. Take, for example, the 'faces' scale employed by Andrews and Withey (1976) to measure satisfaction with life domains. These were also employed by Lehman. However, as they made no real improvement on the worded version of the delighted–terrible scale, they were also discarded from use (on Lehman's recommendation but after we had briefly piloted them ourselves).

4 Additionally, some early attempts to find suitable supplementary measures were discarded. An early pilot with the twenty-eight-question version of the General Health Questionnaire (GHQ) was tried (Goldberg 1972). Analysis of the results proved disappointing and the

use was discontinued. While many parts of the GHQ were well correlated to some aspects of global well-being, shortening it proved impossible without the GHQ losing all of its structure. In this regard its utility was lost, as results could no longer have been readily compared with other studies.

5   One measure was simply irrelevant. Education as a life domain was originally included in the American version. Following piloting here in the UK, it was excluded because none of the clients had been involved in adult education.

CONCLUSIONS

In addition to describing the various stages through which the research has progressed, we have attempted to highlight some principles which might serve as guidance to other workers. These are drawn as much from our own experience as from that of others. In addition, the contents of the questionnaire which we currently employ have been discussed in detail as have the various quality of life measures which we have employed but rejected and the reasons why. The presentation of the work as a case study is designed to ensure that the knowledge gained through the experiences is not lost. Of course, they are our own observations and may well not hold true in all circumstances. Time will tell.

Chapter 3

Psychometric properties: reliability and validity

INTRODUCTION

In this chapter we make an attempt to describe some of the psychometric properties of our quality of life instrument. While we have not analysed all of the studies described within this book, data from preliminary phases described in Chapter 2, particularly phases IV and V, have been analysed, employing SPSS/PC+V2.0 (Norusis 1988), in an attempt to illuminate selected methodological issues in the progress of questionnaire development. It must be noted, however, that the following points are meant to be regarded as indicative rather than definitive. This work represents initial stages in research and much more work is being undertaken at the time of writing.

RELIABILITY

Cox and his colleagues define reliability in a quality of life instrument as 'a measure of its ability to yield the same results on repeated trials under the same conditions' (Cox *et al.* 1992:356). The realities of applying such an instrument are that precisely identical conditions seldom, if ever, exist in trials undertaken in various operational settings. In research such as this, the possible sources of bias are many and may come from the very method of investigation proposed, particularly under conditions such as in-house assessments of chronically mentally disordered people. Among these conditions are the large differences in the power or influence between the interviewer and the respondent, and those instances when it may be in the best interest of the interviewer to produce a particular pattern of results. Also crucial are the mental state of the clients, the design and construction of multi-dimensional instruments, and the number and training of interviewers employed. Such threats to validity often appear in the form of unreliable information (i.e. where the results cannot be duplicated by a second investigator or substantiated by a second observer). Programmes inevitably vary according to local conditions. Not surprisingly, reliability can vary from one application of a questionnaire to another and must be checked regularly. Reliability testing is made difficult, generally, by the obvious fact that, as an abstraction, quality of life cannot be directly observed and, further, by degrees of variation in question interpretation within and across cultures (Poortinga and Van de Vijver 1987; Poortinga 1989).

Test–retest reliability

In such circumstances, establishing survey reliability through test–retest procedures presents several problems. One recognises the need to define with certainty the limits of test–retest. To do this it is most likely that one will be required either somehow to build the element into service evaluation designs or to conduct one or more separate, perhaps more academic, exercises. However, while developing our instrumentation under routine operational conditions, we have been obliged to concede the total impracticality of convincing agency managers and professionals of the necessity to interview vulnerable clients twice in a short space of time and to recognise the financial, operational and clinical reasons for this limitation. As a compromise, as part of the quality of life interview, the seven-point life satisfaction scale is administered in respect of global well-being, both pre- and post-interview. Analysed results may be regarded as indicative of general reliability trends for client information.

Typically, the data, which is derived from this test–retest of a subjective quality of life measure and which is gathered both by academic researchers and practitioners in many work settings, has proved stable, revealing little systematic bias. The interviews, for example, from phase IV (see Table 3.1) demonstrated similar stability to that found previously in phases II and III of four other trials, the surveys of a community mental health centre (CMHC) and physically disabled individuals (PD) in a district council in the United Kingdom and a CMHC and a general health centre (GHC) in the USA. The test–retest correlations from these data sets were strong (Pearson r=.60 to .78), with no evidence of systematic bias displayed through mean score pre/post-interview differences (t=1.7 to -1.7, p=N.S.)

Subsequently, though, in the larger (n=422) phase V (SSD) survey sample, a much lower, though significant, test–retest correlation (r=.49, p=.001) was obtained, while a significant difference in pre/post-interview LSS mean scores was evident (t=3.11, p=.002). The changes have been computed for all studies for which we currently have data. These show the overall correlation between pre- and post-interview measurements to be very strong (r=.577, p=.001) but that there is evidence of some degree of systematic decrease in global satisfaction (t=2.4; p=.017).

Table 3.1 Test–retest reliability pre- and post-LSS interview scores for: t-test and Pearson's r for phases IV, V and all studies combined

	SSD (UK)[1]	CMHC (UK)[2]	PD (UK)[3]	CMHC (USA)[2]	GHC (USA)[4]	ALL STUDIES
Total sample	422	25	27	70	15	1430
Valid cases	390	24	27	68	15	1393
Pre-interview						
Average	4.06	4.08	4.19	4.26	5.2	4.18
Standard deviation	1.56	1.68	1.59	1.64	1.27	1.53
Post-interview						
Average	3.79	3.63	4.63	4.47	5.27	4.27
Standard deviation	1.87	1.74	1.36	1.52	1.39	1.5
t	3.11	1.7	−1.72	−1.25	−0.029	2.4
p (2 tail)	0.002	0.102	0.097	0.215	0.774	0.017
r (p= .001)	0.49	0.71	0.6	0.63	0.78	0.58

Notes: 1 SSD = social services department
2 CMHC = community mental health centre
3 PD = physical disability survey
4 GHC = general health centre

While this difference is not substantial, it is important to try and isolate the source of error. As these sources may vary from one study to another we have looked more closely, by way of example, at the changes perceived in our phase V survey (see Oliver 1991a for full details). Changes in global well-being scores are computed differences between LSS scores at the beginning and end of the interviews, the distributions of which are shown in Figure 3.1. The mean amount of change per client interviewed was − .27 (standard deviation = 1.75). As can be seen, change approaches a normal distribution, with the largest single group of clients (n=163) being those who remained completely unchanged. However, thirty-one clients' scores altered significantly (i.e. more than two standard deviations) and of those, twenty-three (74 per cent) adjusted their global well-being self-appraisals downward (i.e. a negative ['−'] score).

Direct associations were sought between test–retest instability and interviewers. The very much larger size of the interviewer force presents many possibilities for error, especially in view of the fact that there was no specific training introduced prior to the survey and there was, in some areas, worker resistance to its undertaking. As stated above, workers interviewed between one and sixteen clients, so it was possible to compute a mean change (error) score for each worker's interviews.

Figure 3.1 also represents the distribution of error of interviewers' clients' responses (rounded off to the nearest whole number). The average amount of error per interviewer was − .48, with forty-two

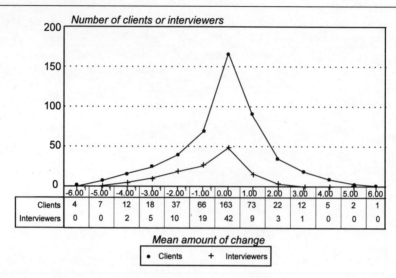

Figure 3.1 Mean changes in LSS scores: distributions of mean LSS changes
per client and per interviewer
Note: 1 A minus score = decreased satisfaction

interviewers manifesting no such change among clients. In fact, the work
of only eight interviewers (8.78 per cent) fell outside the normal distribution for the group (i.e. above or below 2.54), seven to the negative side.
However, recalling that the confidence interval (p< 0.05) for global well-
being scale changes cited above was +/– 3.5, only two interviewers
(having undertaken a total of three interviews) had mean change scores
at or beyond that limit. Therefore, it is unlikely that interviewer bias
alone was responsible for the changes.

The questionnaire contains, as an independent measure of error,
professional opinion about the client's reliability. Adjusting the data for
those clients identified as both 'reliable' and 'very reliable' (t=2.96,
p=.003; r=.54) or for those identified as 'very reliable' alone (t=2.78,
p=.006; r=.57), produced only marginal improvements. Apparently, little
additional enlightenment concerning the accuracy or otherwise of test–
retest correlation is gained by including such measures of professional
opinion. The source of the inaccuracy does not appear to reside simply
in the responses of clients identified by interviewers as unreliable.

Both the questionnaire and interviewing process were investigated. The
length of interview and the willingness of the client to be interviewed
again should indicate client difficulties with interview completion. Test–
retest variation proved to be independent of both measures. Indeed, an
analysis of all questionnaire items and variables computed from them
revealed small but significant associations with test instability in only
two areas, both of which were health related: negative affect, i.e.

symptomatology (r=.13, p=.01); and subjective well-being in the health domain (r= − .17 ; p=.01). The specific items significantly associated with test–retest variation are satisfaction with physical health (r= − .16), boredom (r=.13) and loneliness (r=.13).

In view of the pattern of changes, a likely interpretation of the above is that of a selective reactivity – i.e. changes induced in client well-being levels as a result of having measured them previously. Carmines and Zeller (1978:39) say that such reactivity 'leads to deflated estimates' in test–retest reliability levels. This is consistent with a picture of some individuals becoming sensitised by the interview to their unsatisfactory health, boredom and loneliness and, as a consequence, reconsidering their general well-being estimates less optimistically as an interview progresses. It is also substantiated by interviewer reports that, in a very few instances, interviews had to be terminated as they were upsetting the client.

According to Fillenbaum, scale sensitivity is generally 'assumed rather than measured. One way in which it has been examined is by seeing whether the assessment discriminates between persons expected to differ on functional status' (Fillenbaum 1985:66). Data from 200 clients interviewed during a phase VI project (Community Mental Health Support Teams) also had details taken of chart diagnosis (i.e. as described in case record) in a separate research exercise. As the results are described in detail in Chapter 7 they are not repeated here.

Nevertheless, several subjective well-being variables taken from the Lancashire Quality of Life Profile are shown to discriminate successfully among three main diagnostic groups: schizophrenia, manic-depressive illness and psychotic depression. This ability to identify systematic variations among relevant clinical groups through significant differences in scale scores is evidence supportive of the fact that various of the life quality elements employed are sensitive.

Inter-observer reliability

During phase V, selective inter-observer reliability testing was undertaken of quality of life uniscale scores as this scale requires an independent judgement. From a list of the chronic mentally disordered clients of a psychiatric hospital social work team taking part in the survey, seventeen were well known currently to two qualified social workers from the team. None of these clients had been interviewed previously using quality of life techniques and blind ratings were done by each social worker on the quality of life uniscale only. The results revealed acceptable agreement (Cohen's Kappa =.53) with, however, considerable differences between the two workers' adjudged mean ratings (Rater A= 39.9; Rater B = 62.1; t=5.44; p=.004). This finding highlights the difficulties in basing quality of life assessments on ratings made only by professionals (see also Haberman 1969).

Reliability of scale scores

The chronically mentally disordered clients were examined on three multi-item scales: perceived quality of life (Andrews and Withey 1976), affect balance or mental health (Bradburn 1969), and self-esteem (Rosenberg 1965). Reliability was tested by means of internal consistency and split-half methods, and results are presented for phases IV and V as well as for an amalgamation of all available studies ('All' in Table 3.2).

Table 3.2 Inter-item reliability for three multi-item subjective well-being scales: perceived quality of life, affect balance (negative and positive affect) and self-esteem (negative and positive self-esteem) in phases IV, V, and all surveys from phases IV to VI combined.

Scale	Inter-item mean correlations			Standardised item alpha			Guttman split-half		
	IV	V	All	IV	V	All	IV	V	All
Perceived quality of life	.19	.16	.21	.86	.84	.75	.82	.73	.75
Negative affect	.29	.32	.27	.68	.70	.67	.57	.64	.59
Positive affect	.37	.33	.35	.75	.71	.75	.70	.61	.66
Negative self	.45	.39	.34	.80	.76	.73	.76	.73	.67
Positive self	.53	.38	.36	.85	.75	.76	.85	.67	.72

Perceived quality of life, the twenty-six items rated on the LSS scale, produced convincingly stable results across phase IV and V. While these may be subdivided into sub-scales, the reduced number of items in each sub-scale means that, typically, sub-scales are made up of two items. Hence we have not chosen to present the reliability coefficients for each sub-scale, rather presenting all perceived quality of life measures together. Although the mean inter-item correlations were low (.19/.16), Cronbach's alphas (.86/.84) and Guttman split-half coefficients (.82/.73) showed acceptable levels of reliability. Considering the very different questions being asked, this lowered inter-item correlation is not unexpected. When 'All' available studies were combined, perceived quality of life coefficients remained very stable across the three reliability measures (.21/.75/.75). On the grounds of internal consistency and robustness across settings, it is a reliable measure.

The affect balance scale contains two five-item components: negative affect (restlessness, boredom, depression, loneliness and upset) and positive affect (accomplishment, success, pride, interest and high spirits). Negative affect produced the least convincing evidence for reliability of the multi-item scales in the questionnaire. Analysis produced mean inter-item correlations of .29/.32, Cronbach's alphas of between .68/.70 but reduced Guttman split-half coefficients of .57/.64. Positive affect was generally the stronger of the two, with .37/.33 inter-item correlations, alpha coefficients of .75/.71 and split-half coefficients of .70/61. Reliability measures for 'All' studies were approximately consistent with these limits but slightly lowered (.27) for inter-item correlation.

The self-esteem scale also had two five-item scales: positive self-esteem (high self-worth, good qualities, ability, positive attitude and self-satisfaction) and negative self-esteem (failure, lack of pride, lack of self-respect, uselessness and low self-worth). For negative self-esteem, .45/.39 mean inter-item correlations and alpha coefficients of .80/.76 and .76/.73 for split-half coefficients were observed. Also, in every instance the reliability coefficients for 'All' studies were lowered. Finally, positive affect was the scale showing greatest variability among samples: .53/.38 mean inter-item correlation, .85/.75 alpha coefficient and .85/.67 split-half coefficient. This pattern was repeated in the analysis of 'All' samples.

Phase IV results produced slightly more convincing evidence of reliability than phase V. An overall pattern of adequacy emerged among the measures, with internal consistency and split-half measures only infrequently falling below .7 and frequently being above .8. Though weaker, these reliabilities tended to be sustained in an analysis of more than 1,400 cases drawn from all six phases of research. One note of caution emerged with principal components analysis. While separate factors appeared for the sub-scales of both self-esteem and affect balance, in both instances these were oblique approximations, displaying some cross-over among the predicted item contents. This is being examined in greater detail in research currently underway.

VALIDITY

Content validity

It is observed in the literature that there is no definitive composition of a quality of life assessment. Nevertheless, as noted above, there is increasing agreement among authorities as to what the general components should be, and there are certainly many measures which would imply a particular quality or standard of well-being in one or more particular areas (WHO 1991). As can be seen, this questionnaire draws heavily on previously developed questionnaires and measures of concepts linked to quality of life. No information has been included which has not met that standard. Thus, it is argued that, at the least, the approach has face validity and seems to comply with a growing body of informed opinion. Nevertheless, evidence of content validity alone cannot be interpreted as sufficient (Fillenbaum 1985:65) without further empirical validation being made.

In a small-scale investigation into content validity undertaken by Huxley, twenty-five mental health professionals were asked to identify the most important life domains for their personal life satisfaction. The list of life domains was then classified into similar types by independent mental health professionals. No reference to the Lancashire Profile was made to either group prior to the exercise. The cluster of domains produced through this exercise encompassed all of those contained in the Lancashire Profile and, more importantly, did not produce any substantial areas which fell outside the domains used in the Profile (Huxley 1994a).

Finally, the questionnaire has its own internal means of testing for content validity. Respondents are offered the opportunity to identify things which would, in their opinion, improve their quality of life. This takes the form of three consecutive, open-ended questions placed at the conclusion of the interview. In very large samples, content analysis of the responses to this question set offers the researcher two opportunities. First, it helps to determine the degree to which the questions posed by the interview have covered the topic, i.e. tested the range of quality of life dimensions as seen by the respondent. Second, it provides a means of monitoring the completeness of the interview in the face of local variations. This capacity of a measurement tool for self-adjustment is particularly important when the instrument is being used under a variety of cultural and sub-cultural circumstances, or is being employed during periods or under conditions of rapid change where one anticipates that divergent value and perceptual determinants exist. Much like an ongoing opinion poll, such an internal monitoring mechanism provides a very useful means initially of testing for the presence of significant changes in content validity, then of flagging-up new fields of concern or life domains and, ultimately, of systematically generating new question sets to measure them. In this way, the questionnaire is somewhat flexible, even self-generating.

Throughout this research, the responses to these questions have been coded and classified systematically according to the existing domains and scales of the questionnaire. Staff coding questionnaires have been given specific instructions as to the classification of these open-ended responses, and queries over interpretation of responses have been answered. Coding for these questions has been validated routinely by the same external authorities, i.e. the author or an associate for most subjects whose interviews have been included in this analysis.

From 1,575 individuals interviewed from phase IV through phase VI of the research, a total of 4,725 responses have been received. Of these, only 138 (2.9 per cent) responses did not apply clearly to one of the existing domains or scales, hence falling into the 'other' (unclassifiable) category. Furthermore, excluding the 2,400 (50.7 per cent) responses where individuals identified 'nothing' which would change their life quality, where comments were unintelligible or where their writing was indecipherable, the factors which were identified as affecting their lives but also which remained unclassified amounted to only 5.9 per cent. As the number of these unclassifiable comments was small in each study, they have not been systematically examined for similarities. Informal observation is that they were frequently, though possibly not exclusively, the products of either misunderstanding the question posed or the presence of severe thought disorders.

These results appear to provide powerful evidence in support of the content validity of the questionnaire.

Construct validity

To assure ourselves of the correctness of our assumptions concerning quality of life measures, we have examined the pattern of association between a sample of related concepts. As with Lehman (1983) and Andrews and Withey (1976), we have chosen to relate our data to subjective estimates of global well-being. The bi-variate correlations between three subjective global well-being measures (i.e. Cantril's ladder, the average score for the LSS pre- and post-interview and the happiness scale) and two psychological well-being (PWB) items (the affect balance and the self-esteem scales) (Table 3.3) are described for 'All studies'. The correlations are all significant and range in strength from .35 to .57. Excluded from phase I but re-included subsequently in phase V, happiness shows the weakest set of intercorrelations (.35 to.43), possibly due to it being a three-point scale. Nevertheless, it is significantly correlated with all other global well-being measures and its inclusion is justified on these grounds.

Our correlations tend to be similar to those reported for USA normal subjects by Andrews and Withey (1976:85), from two surveys of 1,118 and 1,072 'normal' respondents. For instance, their global well-being thermometer scale was related to the three-point happiness scale at .39 (ours was .35); to a seven-point satisfaction scale at .46 (ours was slightly higher at .57); and to affect balance at .32 (ours was .56).

Table 3.3 Inter-correlations[1] for subjective global well-being measures (Cantril's ladder, LSS average and happiness) and psychological well-being measures (self-esteem and affect balance) for all samples from phases IV-VI combined.

All studies	Global well-being			Psychological well-being	
	Cantril's ladder	LSS average	Happiness	Self-esteem	Affect balance
Cantril	1.0				
LSS average	.57	1.0			
Happiness	.35	.43	1.0		
Self-esteem	.46	.54	.38	1.0	
Affect bal.	.56	.55	.35	.56	1.0

Note: [1] All variables correlated for two-tailed significance at .001

As they are deliberately orientated to social and economic dimensions, the pattern of intercorrelations between 'perceived quality of life' domain scores and other well-being measures is considered separately though, obviously, they are subjective measures.

To gain an impression of validity across settings, the pattern of associations between the perceived quality of life sub-scales and two global well-being measures, LSS average and Cantril's ladder were examined under various conditions, comparing all samples. Correlations of perceived quality of life in specific life domains with LSS averages revealed much variation across client groups and between cultures, with the most consistent set of significant associations coming in the larger phase V (SSD) survey (Table 3.4). Subjective well-being sub-scale scores for some domains (i.e. work, religion, legal/safety and family) were generally weak. A similar pattern is observed with the intercorrelation of the perceived well-being sub-scales and Cantril's ladder. Though only indicative on small samples, the unevenness of these results draws into question analyses carried out on smaller samples and the stability of measures across settings and cultures. Nevertheless, the results for 'All' samples showed uniform significance, if variable strengths of association.

The pattern of intercorrelations among the various perceived quality of life sub-scales is examined in Table 3.5. Construct validity is supported by an overall pattern of generally strong, positive intercorrelations, which is more pronounced in the larger phase V survey and the combination to 'all studies'. Religion remains weakly correlated throughout. In the case of the smaller sample studies of phase IV, it failed to be associated with five out of eight other perceived quality of life sub-scales. Health, on the other hand, is well correlated with everything, save religion.

Table 3.4 Correlations for perceived quality of life and global well-being (measured by LSS average and Cantril's ladder) for phase IV and V samples and all studies from phases IV-VI combined

| | LSS average | | | | | |
| | United Kingdom | | | United States | | All |
Life domain	SSD	CMHC	PD	CMHC	GHC	
Work	$.40^2$	−1.000	—	.17	.47	$.36^2$
Employed	$.53^2$	—	—	—	—	$.38^2$
Unemployed	$.36^2$	—	—	—	—	$.33^2$
Leisure	$.58^2$	$.61^1$	.50	$.43^2$	$.77^2$	$.55^2$
Religion	.11	.21	.30	.10	.46	$.15^2$
Finances	$.29^2$	$.65^2$	$.51^1$	$.50^2$	.54	$.34^2$
Living conditions	$.36^2$	$.76^2$	—	$.55^2$	.27	$.37^2$
Legal/safety	$.32^2$	.45	.40	.02	$.75^2$	$.31^2$
Family	$.37^2$	.41	−.17	.85	.62	$.35^2$
Social	$.42^2$	$.74^2$	.39	$.37^1$	$.69^1$	$.41^2$
Health	$.61^2$	.45	$.53^1$	$.40^2$	$.65^1$	$.57^2$

Life Domain	Cantril's Ladder United Kingdom			United States		All
	SSD	CMHC	PD	CMHC	GHC	
Work	.28[2]	−1.00	—	.06	.14	.27[2]
Employed	.38[2]	—	—	—	—	.28[2]
Unemployed	.25[2]	—	—	—	—	.25[2]
Leisure	.46[2]	.46	.32	.44[2]	.69[1]	.41[2]
Religion	.13[1]	.14	.32	.18	.52	.15[2]
Finances	.20[2]	.39	.57[1]	.40	.40	.24[2]
Living conditions	.29[2]	.45	—	.48[1]	.39	.26[2]
Legal/safety	.22[2]	.06	.03	.03	.73[1]	.18[2]
Family	.29[2]	.40	-.12	-.21	.22	.27[2]
Social	.34[2]	.51	.06	.45[2]	.60	.33[2]
Health	.48[2]	.50	.47	.37[1]	.57	.44[2]

Note: 1 Two-tailed significance – .01
2 Two-tailed significance –.001
—indicates where figures not computed due to an error in the questionnaire

Table 3.5 Bi-variate correlations for perceived quality of life sub-scales from phases IV and VI (mentally ill groups only)

Phase I

Life domain	Work	Leis.	Relig.	Finl	Living conds	Legal/ safety	Fam.	Soc.	Health
Work	1.0								
Leisure	.26[1]	1.0							
Religion	− .12	.20	1.0						
Financial	.30[1]	.49[2]	.02	1.0					
Living contditions	.25[1]	.30[1]	− .10	.34[2]	1.0				
Legal/ safety	.23	.44[2]	.23	.39[2]	.17	1.0			
Family	− .10	.02	− .01	-.07	.18	.07	1.0		
Social	.26[1]	.49[2]	.30[1]	.47[2]	.25[1]	.40[2]	.20	1.0	
Health	.33[2]	.46[2]	.05	.47[2]	.27[1]	.36[2]	− .045	.39[2]	1.0

Phase V

Life domain	Work	Leis.	Relig.	Finl	Living conds	Legal/ safety	Fam.	Soc.	Health
Work	1.0								
Leisure	.27[2]	1.0							
Religion	.10	.05	1.0						
Financial	.31[2]	.21[2]	.11	1.0					
Living conditions	.21[1]	.37[2]	.15[1]	.27[2]	1.0				
Legal/ safety	.16[1]	.27[2]	.09	.20[2]	.37[2]	1.00			
Family	.16[1]	.30[2]	.07	.21[2]	.35[2]	.34[2]	1.0		
Social	.23[2]	.42[2]	.17[2]	.12[1]	.32[2]	.33[2]	.32[2]	1.0	
Health	.29[2]	.39[2]	.18[2]	.24[2]	.32[2]	.40[2]	.34[2]	.42[2]	1.0

Life domain	Work	Leis.	Relig.	Finl	Living conds	Legal/ safety	Fam.	Soc.	Health
	All studies								
Work	1.0								
Leisure	$.32^2$	1.0							
Religion	$.09^1$	$.13^2$	1.0						
Financial	$.37^2$	$.30^2$	$.14^2$	1.0					
Living conditions	$.20^2$	$.36^2$	$.17^2$	$.30^2$	1.0				
Legal/ safety	$.16^2$	$.28^2$	$.14^2$	$.21^2$	$.37^2$	1.00			
Family	$.14^2$	$.31^2$	$.14^2$	$.22^2$	$.33^2$	$.35^2$	1.0		
Social	$.16^2$	$.38^2$	$.19^2$	$.16^2$	$.29^2$	$.30^2$	$.33^2$	1.0	
Health	$.27^2$	$.45^2$	$.18^2$	$.27^2$	$.30^2$	$.35^2$	$.31^2$	$.39^2$	1.0

Note: 1 Two-tailed significance – .01
2 Two-tailed significance – .001

Criterion validity

Typically, in research such as this, there are no external absolute standards against which the measures can be tested for conformity and instruments calibrated or adjusted. Affect balance and self-esteem are just two components of the multi-faceted abstraction 'quality of life' to serve as examples. What behaviour can we say is *necessarily* linked to the possession of self-esteem? What human action is the sole province of a mentally healthy affect balance? For this reason, criterion validity (i.e. concurrent validity and predictive validity) is examined infrequently.

The quality of life uniscale was included in order to assist in criterion testing. In questionnaires which may also be used for clinical purposes it is very important, if possible, to validate against an assessment made concurrently by a professional. Employing data from all mental health trials (phases IV-VI), uniscale scores were correlated against three client self-report measures of global well-being: Cantril's ladder (r=.29), global life satisfaction (r=.39) and happiness (r=.18). In all cases, bi-variate Spearman correlations were weak but significant, at beyond the .001 level. These results further support the validity of the questionnaire. They must be viewed, however, with some caution, as the uniscale was not designed for use on a mentally ill population and possibly requires adjustment in wording before it will be of maximum value for this particular purpose.

Lehman suggested that global well-being serve as an independent criterion measure for other quality of life variables and proposed a model for analysis. To establish the utility of his model, he reported the results of a multiple regression analysis of personal characteristics, objective and subjective quality of life on global well-being measures (Lehman

1983a:372). A duplication of his analysis on our samples gives strikingly similar results. A three-stage, hierarchical regression analysis was performed on our own phase IV (mental health cases) and phase V surveys, utilising one global well-being score (LSS/ delighted–terrible scale scores) common to both US and UK studies as the dependent variable, thus allowing for direct comparison of results. This was repeated on the 'all studies' data. In the first stage of analysis, the dependent variables were regressed against personal characteristics alone. The second step was to enter personal characteristics plus objective well-being variable sets. The final stage was to enter personal characteristics plus objective well-being sets plus subjective well-being sets. To avoid possible multi-colinearity, other global well-being measures were not included.

Table 3.6. Hierarchical regression for phases IV and V mental health samples and Lehman (1983a): personal characteristics, objective well-being and subjective well-being on global well-being (LSS total)

	Phase IV	Phase V	All (UK)	Lehman (1983a)
Personal characteristics				
Multiple r	.19	.06	.11	—
R-square	.04	.00	.01	.04
R-square change	.04	.00	.00	—
F-change	1.11	.32	1.44	—
Signif. F-change	.35	.81	.22	—
Objective well-being				
Multiple r	.72	.57	.58	—
R-square	.51	.33	.34	.23
R-square change	.47	.33	.33	.19
F-change	2.19	4.97	5.03	11.94
Signif. F-change	.01	.00	.00	.00
Subjective well-being				
Multiple r	.83	.79	.78	—
R-square	.69	.62	.61	.58
R-square change	.18	.29	.27	.35
F-change	2.09	15.10	11.64	66.39
Signif. F-change	.00	.00	.00	.00

Note: — Indicates where statistics were not available

Comparing UK and American studies (Table 3.6), personal characteristics account for small amounts of variance as shown in r-square values (0 to 4 per cent). The addition of 'objective' measures to the model accounts for substantially more variance (19 to 47 per cent). Subjective well-being also adds significantly, if less substantially, to the explanation of variance (18 to 35 per cent). The total amount of variance ultimately accounted for by the questionnaire is between 63 and 69 per cent for the phases IV and V and 61 per cent in the 'all survey' analysis. The findings derived from the UK studies were slightly stronger in this respect than those reported by Lehman, which explained 58 per cent of the variance of the delighted–terrible scale and 51 and 48 per cent of two other global well-being measures. The general observation is that criterion validity (via concurrent analysis) is strongly supported and that the results are stable to a considerable degree across settings and cultures, which indicates reliability.

DISCUSSION

The interview technique gives information regarding the state of health and welfare of any one individual, and informs professionals about the nature and extent to which a client is objectively most advantaged or most disadvantaged and subjectively most or least satisfied. Due to the close correspondence between the defined areas of social care and quality of life, this assessment could, in turn, be regarded as contributing to the basis of judgements about need for various aspects of community care.

Quality of life observations on individuals can be aggregated to provide interesting information on specific groups which could serve as the basis for future comparisons. Also, the interview should be able to provide information as to how any individual's profile currently compares with established norms.

As a survey tool, it is to be expected that the profile will give a good baseline measure against which to judge the direction which future community mental health services will have taken and the amount of progress which they have made. As an outcome measure, it should provide evidence which will allow joint community care plans to be partially evaluated. However, this point requires further confirmation, since other authors have reported concern over the insensitivity of some quality of life measures (Baker and Intagliata 1982). Further research which has been undertaken and which is reported in the following chapters, should help to clarify this.

Arguments about reliability and validity are incomplete at the levels of both basic and applied research into quality of life. In this chapter, data analysis has been restricted to the presentation of preliminary results focused largely on subjective well-being measures which were drawn from two development phases. Additional work, which looks at the entire range of questionnaire features, is being undertaken, along with the production of norms relating to a UK population. Nevertheless, even this limited degree of analysis lends limited support to the questionnaire's usage under operational conditions.

The profile includes a variety of well-known indicators of quality of life which conform to contemporary thinking. When used together for assessing chronically mentally ill people, they appear to stand up well under a variety of conditions. Not surprisingly, the best measures of reliability are obtained when the profile is employed under optimum circumstances, such as in a clinical setting (e.g. community mental health centres), with a restricted number of interviewers, or where specially trained interviewers have been used. These levels decline as the number of interviewers increases, as their level of training decreases and as the knowledge and commitment of their line managers diminishes. Also, the variability of samples, as seen through the amalgamated analysis of all study data, does show some of these effects. Nevertheless, internal reliability coefficients for multi-item scales was consistently above .5, which has been said to be acceptable for group comparisons (Aaronson 1990). This produces a pattern of associations comparable to quality of life instruments produced for use with patients suffering from other medical conditions.

In some samples, infrequently occurring phenomena such as subject reactivity or interviewer influence become apparent, though the magnitude of these influences is not great. Any degree of reactivity of mentally ill respondents may be an issue in more general quality of life evaluations and, although they may be small in number in any one survey, the issue should be considered, since the effects may or may not become evident during data analysis. It is of particular importance in studies of services for mentally ill people, since the association with symptomatology appears to limit the findings reported previously by Lehman (1983b). Other sources of unreliability have not been accounted for in this research and these still require addressing. For example, high levels of socially desirable responses have been reported among the chronically ill in quality of life studies of patients with other medical conditions (Hurny et al. 1987).

Thankfully, negative subject reactivity appears to have been the exception rather than the rule. Overall, the combined data did show a small but significant shift towards improved satisfaction. While this is undesirable from a scientific viewpoint, from a clinical perspective it may reflect a degree of improvement. Further research will need to be undertaken to identify exactly the nature of changes during interview. It is interesting to speculate that service characteristics may interact with client characteristics to produce slight improvement. Also, not surprisingly, not all of the individual measures are equally reliable. For example, perceived quality of life measures appear more internally reliable than affect measures. Ultimately, these differences are most probably a function of the affect balance scale's larger number of items, though other competing explanations cannot be excluded. It is generally accepted that measures of psychological well-being such as self-esteem and mental health present special problems in establishing cross-cultural validity (Poortinga 1989) or in respect of application to this client group (Lehman 1983b). We have shown how the presence of specific mental symptomatology such as loneliness or boredom can be associated with inaccuracy. Practically, accuracy is dependent upon things such as perception, interpretation and expression – all factors likely to be difficult to control for in such situations. The same will apply equally to such 'objective' measures as the quality of life uniscale, where intra-cultural variation among professionals may be sufficient to produce significant score disparities.

The validity of the questionnaire also appears satisfactory. Attempts to examine content, construct and criterion validity produced uniformly favourable, if qualified, results. Considering the general level of psychological impairment present in such a population, the questionnaire has held up well under a range of conditions, from relatively benign circumstances (i.e. one specially trained academic colleague interviewing clients in a community mental health centre) to extreme conditions which approximated testing it to destruction (ninety-one interviewers, without uniform training from twenty-two different social work teams). Initial comparison with published work from the USA (Lehman *et al.* 1982) is also encouraging, with the abbreviated profile accounting for more than 60 per cent of total variance for global well-being. This is supported also by the findings of others, who have reported that brief quality of life interviews utilising closed questions yield 'results generally consistent with' more extensive, open-ended interviews (Baker and Intagliata 1982). Nevertheless, the value of this comparison is limited by the considerable differences existing between the sample characteristics of the different studies, and further, more exacting, study is required.

The results of the regression analysis are also important in that they support the theoretical points made in Chapter 1. The amount of variance contributed to explaining global well-being by objective indicators, including social and economic indicators, is very considerable. While the r-squared change for objective indicators was much less than that produced by subjective indicators in the Lehman study, the opposite was reflected in our studies. The minimum amount of influence shown by objective well-being was 33 per cent, a very substantial and significant amount and more than the subjective measures. To develop a quality of life interview which excluded these measures in order to concentrate exclusively on subjective measures would overlook this and, hence, be less valid. This is evidence that quality of life interviews are likely to be best constructed to include a wide range of both objective and subjective measures. To maximise success, work oriented to improving a chronically mentally disordered individual's quality of life must concentrate on both subjective and external, environmental influences.

Practically, the interview itself has always met with favour from mentally disordered clients. During piloting, very few clients have complained about the interview and most (75 to 90 per cent) have indicated that they would be happy to be interviewed again at a later date, with 99 per cent agreeing under the most favourable conditions. One client comment frequently reported by quality of life interviewers is that such professional contact represents the first time that clients have had the opportunity to discuss at length their own welfare. Also, individual clients have frequently complied with profile administration out of an expressed desire to support research which could be of use in helping others with similar mental health problems.

Such approval by the clients is one 'acid test' for a monitoring tool, though it may have been achieved at a cost to the scientific basis of the instrument. For instance, earlier piloting revealed that clients experienced considerable difficulty in following the questions of the affect balance scale. The positive and negative affect questions were intermixed, and the continued change of train of thought from one focus to another was distressing to people, some of whom had thought disorders. Questions were left unanswered or were answered recklessly. Subsequently, in order to overcome the confusion, the questions were re-ordered, i.e. grouped distinctly into positive and negative affect scales rather than the two being staggered. This re-ordering probably created response sets which help to account for lowered validity coefficients. In reality there are 'trade offs' in such applied research. To accommodate the requirements of clients with mental characteristics such as severe thought disorder into a brief subjective appraisal, a slight decrease in validity is tolerated for a general increase in client compliance and response accuracy.

Quite another problem with the interview has been the unwillingness of some health and social care workers to employ it. To date, no data has been gathered systematically on worker response but it is an area worthy of further investigation. Worker willingness to employ the questionnaire during the piloting must be characterised as 'mixed'.

On the positive side, the profile has been successfully employed in various settings for the purposes of surveying agency caseloads and monitoring client change within specific services. Workers have reported that they found the profile a useful means of gathering initial information about new clients, uncovering additional information about the lives of clients already known to the service and, when appropriate, engaging clients in the process of change. These uses correspond to the traditional purposes of any social anamnesis. The profile's structure also has helped workers conducting interviews to manage client anxiety and focus attention. Workers have also welcomed the addition of the uniscale, which gives professionals the opportunity to make a global assessment of well-being based on the experience of the interview. Periodic application of the profile clearly aids in the task of monitoring client movement. Feedback of results of aggregating client data has informed, to varying degrees, in-house training and planning. Client quality of life profiles have been included in the requirements for evaluation of new community mental health services, and quality of life interviewing is included in job descriptions of staff now being employed to deliver these services.

However, overcoming resistance, where it has existed, has proved challenging. The sources of such disquiet are many and cannot be explored in detail here but they influence interview utility (further discussion on this point can be found in Chapter 12 of the present volume). The evidence shown above is that a lowering of satisfaction and, probably, mood can occur during interviews. Thus, infrequently, interviews need to be discontinued due to the client's deteriorating mental or emotional state. Where this is severe it may involve the worker in dealing with a crisis which he or she feels would not have occurred if the interview had not taken place. This itself leads to heightened worker reluctance to participate in future evaluation exercises. Careful selection of cases, the structured nature of the interview and application by qualified workers should reduce, but will not eliminate, such difficulties.

A second point is that, as shown, a small number of interviews can take longer than expected. There is no 'ideal' length for such an interview. As discussed, many workers and clients choose to use the interview positively as a starting point for discussion, picking up and expanding on important details as they arise. Obviously, in other instances, people may choose to see quality of life interviewing as 'just another burdensome task to be got through'. It is easy to understand that where pressures on professional time exist workers feel that they cannot afford the luxury of such lengthy discussion and, as a consequence, become resistant to future interviewing. Also, the difficulty of eliciting information from an individual with pronounced thought disorder can be considerable and is a tiring exercise, even with a brief, structured questionnaire requiring concrete answers. This was exaggerated in the experience of a few workers who took part in piloting early versions (which were lengthy and included substantial numbers of 'open-ended' questions), leading them to be unenthusiastic about future interviewing. It must be said, however, that in these authors' experiences, workers tend to be more troubled than clients by occasional lengthy interviews when, after all, the purpose of the interview is to concentrate on the client's satisfactions and concerns as he or she perceives them.

CONCLUSION

The current version of the Lancashire Quality of Life Profile has both strengths and weaknesses. To its credit, it briefly covers a large number of areas linked to the social care directive, thus adding very little to the costs of an organisation employing it. It is also structured and corresponds to many other questionnaires used elsewhere for similar purposes.

The tight structure of the questionnaire is also very important from a clinical perspective.

In the instances of both reliability and validity, much more work with client surveys such as these is required. This is being encouraged currently by the WHO, which is now recommending intensive research into quality of life indicators with this client group among others (WHO 1991). However, the construction of the 'perfect instrument' may be illusory. Certainly it will take a long time.

In practical terms, it has been our view that it is better to produce something, perhaps less than perfect, but feasible, useful and with an ethical basis, capable of being employed now. Ultimately, we concur with Malm *et al.*, who developed a quality of life checklist and who observed that reliability and validity are important and it is 'right and proper that investigators be concerned with instrument reliability' (Malm *et al.* 1981). However, there is far more to the employment of quality of life in rehabilitation practice than that. As we proceed to consider the *application* of quality of life in practice, we leave the reader with the following thought:

> An instrument must measure a variable which has meaning and reality for the patient and society. A crude or somewhat unreliable measure of an important variable is preferable to a highly precise but irrelevant measure – or to put it more poetically, a candle in the dark may add more to our knowledge than a floodlight at noon.
>
> (Malm *et al.* 1981:484)

Chapter 4

Quality of life in the mental health service context

Any patient, however seemingly intractable the condition, retains the capacity to surprise the persistent therapist.

(Wing and Brown 1970)

INTRODUCTION

Having examined the theoretical and conceptual background to quality of life and described our attempts to develop an operational measure, we now turn our attention to the context in which most of the applications of the LQOLP have taken place. In thinking about the application of quality of life assessment in mental health we have developed an instrument which specifically addresses the needs of people with long-term, persistent and recurrent episodes of disorder, much of which can be described as neurobiological in origin (Francell 1994).

In general terms, people with psychiatric illnesses fall into three main groups in terms of the prevalence of the illness. The first group are people with common illnesses, which are usually mood related and which consist of a mixture of anxiety-related and depression-related symptoms (Goldberg and Huxley 1992). These illnesses occur in about a third of all patients consulting their family doctor (Bridges and Goldberg 1992; Ormel and Giel 1990), and many approaches which attempt to retain the locus of care in primary care have been established in recent years (Strathdee and Williams 1985; Mitchell 1985; Pullen and Yellowlees 1988; Creed and Marks 1989; Darling and Tyrer 1990).

The second group are people with less common illnesses, such as obsessional disorders, eating disorders and episodic forms of psychotic illnesses, who need more specialist attention from social services and secondary health care services in either outpatient, day hospital or inpatient settings. Since psychiatric services have become more community orientated, many of these people have benefited from more innovative generic services in a variety of settings (Falloon et al. 1990; Creed et al. 1991; Muijen 1992; Dean et al. 1993; Jackson et al. 1993). In many of these people with mood-related or episodic psychotic illnesses social factors often have etiological importance (Goldberg and Huxley 1992). In addition, many of these people may experience some social dysfunction. However, restitution of normal functioning is usually contingent upon short-term models of care and time-limited interventions aimed at improving the psychological state and social circumstances.

The third group consists of people with long-term psychiatric illnesses which are either continuous or fluctuating in severity and which are usually associated with persistent forms of social disability. The most common of these illnesses are chronic schizophrenia, chronic somatisation, and chronic organic brain syndromes. People with these long-term disabilities have complex needs and require a network of coordinated services based on a long-term model of care and a titration of various forms of intervention throughout an illness career (Bridges *et al.* 1994b). An essential element of this model is the need to provide continuity of care, i.e. the process which enables a person to have an orderly and uninterrupted involvement with a network of services for as long as he or she needs them (Bachrach 1981, 1993; Borus 1978; Bridges *et al.* 1994b; Shepherd 1990b, 1991)

This chapter is concerned with this third group and describes a broad framework by which to conceptualise the complex interactions which are thought to effect the course and illnesses. We will draw upon some of the literature on schizophrenia in order to illustrate this framework, but readers may find it applicable to other disorders as well. The factors which we describe are as follows: biological, social disabilities, environmental, psychological and premorbid factors. Having described our framework we will present a definition of rehabilitation and draw attention to some points relevant to people will specific disorders who should be targeted by dedicated services.

BIOLOGICAL FACTORS

The biological aspects of an illness such as chronic schizophrenia include psychopathology, an intrinsic vulnerability to destabilisation, and co-existing physical disorders. In addition, some people with schizophrenia take illegal drugs, which can have adverse effects on the mental state, but this is not discussed here.

Psychopathology

Psychopathology can include anxiety- and depression-related symptoms, positive and negative psychotic phenomena and cognitive deficits. These psychotic phenomena have been given different labels by different authors. Positive phenomena have been referred to as 'florid', 'productive' or a Type I syndrome (Crow 1985; Wing 1986), whilst negative phenomena have been described as 'deficits', 'defects', 'primary impairments', 'primary handicaps', 'primary disabilities', 'primary dysfunction' or Type II syndrome (Wing and Brown 1970; Shepherd 1984; Wing 1986; Crow 1986; Falloon 1986; Liberman 1988).

Treatment of a depressive syndrome associated with schizophrenia will depend on its cause but could include use of antidepressants, antiparkinsonians and a reduction in neuroleptic medication. Positive phenomena tend to respond to neuroleptics (Stahl and Wets 1988) and some more intractable forms may respond to specific psychological intervention such as cognitive behavioural techniques (Tarrier *et al.* 1993; Kingdom *et al.* 1994). Catatonic features may only remit following electroplexy, and severe behavioural disturbances may respond to specific behavioural approaches (Barker 1982; Butler and Rosenthal 1985). In general, negative phenomena respond poorly to neuroleptics but tend to improve as a consequence of psychosocial interventions (Wing and Freudenberg 1961; Wing and Brown 1970; Hyde *et al.* 1987).

Intrinsic vulnerability to destabilisation

The intrinsic vulnerability to destabilisation or relapse has been described as an 'invisible impairment' (Wing 1986) and refers to the extent the mental state is reactive either to understimulation and inactivity, which can increase the intensity of negative phenomena, or to overstimulation and social intrusiveness, which can reactivate positive phenomena (Wing and Freudenberg 1961; Brown *et al.* 1966; Wing and Brown 1970) Between these destabilising factors lies the optimal social environment (Wing 1986) which has important therapeutic properties (Drake and Sederer 1986). The size of this 'therapeutic window' will vary between people and over time (Carpenter and Heinrichs 1984).

Although a minority of patients (for example, 20 per cent) may remain relapse-free without maintenance medication (Johnson *et al.* 1986; Carpenter *et al.* 1987), in the majority of cases of chronic schizophrenia the long-term use of neuroleptics reduces the risk of destabilisation of the mental state and its social consequences, such as burden on the family and effects on the patient's employment (Hogarty 1984; Johnson *et al.* 1986). In addition, some patients may benefit from symptom-monitoring techniques which aim to identify features (for example, mild dysphoric symptoms) that may herald an impending relapse of florid phenomena (Birchwood *et al.* 1989). Following this identification, the use of specific 'early interventions' may help to mitigate subsequent pathogenic developments. These interventions could include the temporary use, or increase in the amount, of neuroleptics, stress management, diversionary activities, and counselling directed towards resolving aetiologically significant events (Brier and Strauss 1983; Carpenter and Heinrichs 1983; McCandless-Glincher *et al.* 1986).

Coexisting physical disorders

Physical disorders and dental problems are common in people with chronic schizophrenia (Wing 1986; Taube *et al.* 1988; Brugha *et al.* 1989; O'Driscoll *et al.* 1990). Serious coexisting physical morbidity in people with long-term schizophrenia may result from excessive tobacco smoking, being overweight, poor physical fitness, and squalid living conditions with dampness and no heat (Wing 1986). In addition to the personal burden of a physical disorder, its coexistence can play a part in destabilising the mental state and have a significant impact on social functioning and adjustment of patients in the community (Tessler and Manderscheid 1982; Bellack 1989).

Many people may lack the skills to maintain an adequate level of hygiene and nutrition or to seek medical and dental attention. Some people may neglect their physical problems, lack insight into their significance or the value of medication, or report no discomfort even when they have a severe illness (Wing 1986; Wing and Furlong 1986). Others may avoid seeking help because of the anxiety this process may evoke and it may prove to be very difficult to engage appropriate primary health care services (Johnstone *et al.* 1984).

Attention to the need for appropriate prosthetic devices, such as spectacles, hearing aids and dentures, can be just as crucial as the control of symptoms (Shepherd 1983). In addition, many patients may need interventions concerned specifically with problems associated with their sexuality and fertility. These problems may include exploitation by others, risking contraceptively unprotected coitus, and other consequences of their judgement about their sexual behaviour (see, for example, Clough *et al.* 1976; Lyketsos *et al.* 1983; Kuipers and Bebbington 1990). Consideration of the respondents' physical health and disabilities is specifically included in the Lancashire Profile but, as we have already seen, questions about sexual behaviours have been excluded.

SOCIAL DISABILITIES

The Profile includes a number of items which address the issue of social disability. Social disability is concerned with the performance of social roles and tasks normally expected of the person (Jablensky *et al.* 1980; Wiersma *et al.* 1989; Bennett and Morris 1983; Liberman 1988; Wing 1990; Shepherd 1991). It is also referred to in terms of 'disablement' (Wing 1981, 1990) and 'functional limitation' (Goldman and Manderscheid 1987). It is a relative concept and there are no universally accepted norms for social functioning. Its assessment, therefore, is based on: the extent to which the person fails to perform roles and tasks to a standard that he/she would normally have achieved premorbidly; the opportunities available to the person to perform; and a normative notion and expectations of the socio-demographic and cultural group of people to which the person belongs (Wiersma *et al.* 1981).

Social roles can be regarded as instrumental or expressive and involve many areas of social functioning. These include roles concerned with self-care and self-management, family and domestic roles, sexual and marital roles, parental roles, social roles, occupational and professional roles, leisure and recreational roles, and community and citizen roles (Jablensky *et al.* 1980; Wiersma *et al.* 1981; Bebbington *et al.* 1981; Schubert *et al.* 1986). The ability to fulfil social roles enables the person to contribute to and be valued by his or her social network (Bennett and Morris 1983).

The causes of social disabilities include direct results of the mental disorder, such as negative phenomena or cognitive deficits, and the consequences of contemporaneous social circumstances, such as having to live in socially impoverished places, the lack of opportunities to use latent skills and abilities, and the negative expectations of other people in the person's life. The nature, severity, mix and significance of disabilities will vary from one person to another. These will be contingent upon the biological characteristics of and fluctuations in the person's illness, socio-demographic factors (age, sex, ethnicity and culture), the impact of environmental factors, and the person's own attitude towards his or her illness and the use of health and social services. They will also be affected by premorbid factors, which will be discussed later.

The consequences of social disabilities will be dependent on their characteristics and the person's circumstances. They can aggravate the negative psychopathology (Wing and Freudenberg 1961; Wing and Brown 1970) and are associated with an increased risk of hospitalisation as a consequence of a destabilised mental state (Linn *et al.* 1980). In some people severe deficits can result in extremely poor self-management (for example, personal hygiene, sexual activity, budgeting, toiletry behaviour), gross self-neglect and squalid living conditions – similar to the appalling living conditions of the Diogenes syndrome found in old age (Berlyne 1975; Clark *et al.* 1975). These consequences may persist to a significant extent despite input from care staff (Bridges *et al.* 1991a; Bridges *et al.* 1991b). Some people may drift into destitution (Wing and Furlong 1986). Many people may become open to various forms of exploitation, including financial and sexual, and to attack or robbery, especially in socially deprived inner-city areas (Kuipers and Bebbington 1990). Some people may become very dependent on others.

The non-specific term 'dependency' indicates a high all-round level of need for care (Wing and Furlong 1986). Some degree of dependence on support and material resources is inevitable when serious impairments and disabilities are present, persistent and irremediable (Bennett and Morris 1983; Wing 1983; Kuipers and Bebbington 1990). In other people, maintaining some degree of dependency on staff or relatives may be important in order to facilitate interventions which aim to improve functional abilities in other areas (Farkas *et al.* 1989). However, over-provision of services can de-skill and thwart individual growth and development, and the performance of social roles can reduce the risk of passive and inappropriate levels of dependence. It therefore seems important to maintain a balance between enabling a person to achieve his or her optimal level of functioning and accepting appropriate levels of dependency (Bennett and Morris 1983). Determinants of the extent to which a person remains dependent and the nature of the support he or she may need include: the person's ability to perform basic self-management skills, such as care of clothes, budgeting and cooking ability (Presly *et al.* 1982; Brown and Munford 1983); and competence and flexibility in use of social and problem-solving skills to cope with various stressors and challenging vicissitudes of life (Libermann *et al.* 1986; Shepherd 1990a).

Factors which may affect the efficacy of interventions concerned with the development of skills include: lack of environmental opportunities (Wing 1986); irremediable and intractable negative phenomena (Bennett and Morris 1982); the extent to which interventions are congruent with the specific needs of a patient; and cognitive deficits concerned with attention and information processing, maintaining new skills, and diffi-culties in generalising from a training situation to real-life settings (Wing and Freudenberg 1961; Paul and Lentz 1977; Libermann *et al.* 1986; Shepherd 1988, 1990a).

Interventions aimed at improving social skills may be more successful for some people if they are based on a 'criterion-oriented' approach. This is based on the identification of problem areas and goal-setting tasks relevant to the person's real-life circumstances, i.e. 'in vivo' rather than in settings which are different from those where the new skills are meant to be used. By working with the patient in a flexible way contingent upon his or her needs in real-life situations, a criterion-oriented approach aims to broaden the person's range of behaviours by strengthening coping skills already in use as well as by teaching new skills relevant to the environment where they are needed (Shepherd 1990a). Prior assessments will usually be necessary in order to make initial decisions, for example, with regards to deciding on the nature of support required before someone moves from one setting to another. Many people may have limited potential for acquiring and generalising functional skills and are likely to remain dependent on supportive and prosthetic services indefi-nitely (Libermann *et al.* 1986).

ENVIRONMENTAL FACTORS

Major areas of the Lancashire Profile are concerned with the assessment of the objective or material aspects of the lives of these patients. Environmental factors are thought to increase the risk of a destabilisation of their mental state and social functioning (Wing 1981, 1983, 1986, 1990). Unfavourable social factors giving rise to social disadvantages have been referred to as 'tertiary' or 'extrinsic' handicaps (Shepherd 1984), of which there appear to be at least two different forms: material disadvantages and adverse aspects of the social environment. In addition, the illness and its consequences can have a negative impact on people directly involved in the person's life. This 'burden' is often experienced by relatives and friends (the person's 'primary support system') but can also be experienced by people who are directly involved for professional or voluntary reasons (the person's 'secondary support system').

Material disadvantages

Material disadvantages tend to accumulate over time and can include poverty, poor housing, homelessness, unemployment or poor opportunities for meaningful, work-related and recreational activities, and lack of a supportive social network and appropriate services (Wing 1986). Social disadvantages with no prospects of improvement in opportunities can cause a sense of despair and apathy (Wing 1983), while social assets may enable the person to cope with and adapt to his or her illness and reduce that person's risk of destabilisation in the face of various stressors.

Poverty

Poverty prevents people from having access to many ordinary activities and good-quality material possessions, especially those which are desired but not indispensable (Ramon 1990). The extent to which people remain trapped by poverty is determined mainly by: the size of state benefits; reduction in these benefits when a person is an inpatient for more than six weeks; the person's disabilities relevant to budgeting skills; excessive smoking addiction; restrictive rules concerned with the acquisition of further income from employment of some kind; and the lack of gratuitous opportunities provided by relatives. As a consequence, the social aspects of intervention programmes involving use of local facilities, being appropriately dressed, developing leisure and recreational pursuits are invariably limited by the costs involved.

Accommodation

People who suffer from schizophrenia over a long period have a range of accommodation needs, and these arise in various ways. There are those who are actually homeless; those who have unstable places of residence and an itinerant existence associated with unstable illnesses; those who are inappropriately hospitalised; those lodging in inappropriate residential settings; and some who are at risk of eviction because of the consequences of intolerable and persistent forms of psychopathology and disabilities (Priest 1976; Weller and Jauhar 1987; Weller *et al.* 1987; Lelliot *et al.* 1993).

The majority of homeless mentally ill may not perceive a need for psychiatric services but want assistance with basic needs such as housing, food, clothing, work-related services, and with welfare benefits. Many studies conclude, in fact, that services should be flexible, address the basic physical needs and that they should be introduced in places where these people normally are (Leach and Wing 1978). Once engaged in a rehabilitative process, success of their long-term support is likely to be contingent upon a multi-agency and multi-disciplinary service, case management arrangements (as in Chapter 9 of the present volume), provision of permanent accommodation (as in Chapter 5 of the present volume) and long-term support (as in Chapter 7 of the present volume). Effective services available to the homeless with chronic schizophrenia in the UK, however, are often inadequate.

Many authors have advocated that a given geographical area should have a spectrum of supported residential provision (Gibbons 1988; Garety 1990; House of Commons 1994). However, the extent to which this is achieved varies from district to district depending upon local political issues, resources available (particularly for supportive personnel) and the extent to which a particular type of service is emphasised in the light of locally held views about service principles and models of care (Gibbons 1988; Garety 1991).

It is now accepted that in order to cater for the most severely disabled or behaviourally disturbed as well as those people who are less disabled, the range of accommodation should cover all degrees of clinical need. This range should include hospital-based as well as community-based provisions. Hospital-based provisions include the acute admission wards for periods of severe disturbance of the mental state which cannot be managed in the community. In addition, separate specialist inpatient services are needed for a relatively small number of people who need to return to remain in hospital for long periods (O'Driscol *et al.* 1990; Wing 1990; Clifford *et al.* 1991; Bridges *et al.* 1991a; Dayson *et al.* 1992; Liddle 1992; O'Grady *et al.* 1992; Bridges *et al.* 1994a).

Community-based accommodation should include special forms of residential care such as the 'hostel ward' for people who need twenty-four-hour nursing care in addition to a multi-disciplinary input into their rehabilitation (Wykes 1982; Hyde *et al.* 1987; Gibbons 1988; Garety *et al.* 1988; Hyde *et al.* 1987; Bridges *et al.* 1991a). Also required is

group-living or single-living accommodation supported by staff in situ, a
resident caretaker, and/or a peripatetic support team (Pritlove 1983;
Anstee 1985; Colgan and Bridges 1990; Oliver and Mohamad 1992).
Family placement or fostering schemes are also useful (Howat *et al.* 1988;
Bridges *et al.* 1993).

The community-based accommodation available to many severely
disabled people is usually sited in inner-city areas. The advantages of this
policy may include cheaper rents and lower costs for travelling to various
amenities and services. However, the disadvantages may include having
to live in poorly maintained and sub-standard buildings, coping with
neighbourhood problems, and difficulties in getting household insurance.
Even when residential units are available, their design, size, operational
policies and forms of care may not be appropriate for the needs of their
residents. In addition, support staff may not have had any specific
psychiatric training.

Work-related activities and leisure pursuits

Many people with schizophrenia have a reduced capacity to cope with
the demands of employment and associated interpersonal relationships
with supervisors and co-workers. Work-related activities challenge cognitive abilities and emotional resilience and carry with them the risk of
yet another failure. The benefits of work-related activity include increase
in self-esteem, reduction in symptomatology (Wing and Brown 1970),
decreased need for other health care services, such as admission to
hospital (Anthony *et al.* 1984; Colgan *et al.* 1991), improvement in
work-related skills, willingness to work and social interactions, having a
purpose or role and a routine or structure to the day (Bennett 1970; Warr
1987; Rowlands and Perkins 1988) and improvement in quality of life
(Huxley and Warner 1992).

Factors associated with engagement in work-related activities have
included social stimulation (Wing and Freudenberg 1961), appropriate
levels of supervision (Wadsworth *et al.* 1962) and some reward contingent upon performance (Walker 1979). Factors associated with a successful return to employment include social relationship skills, good
performance in realistic work settings and ego-strength (Anthony and
Jansen 1984), and an employment situation which is not too stressful and
over-stimulating and which offers clear feedback on performance and
social support (Floyd 1984).

At present, employment prospects in the UK are poor. Few opportunities exist for disabled people who could cope with open employment
and a number of sheltered schemes may offer only low-grade forms of
work and are unable to cater for the range of intellectual abilities these
people have (Gloag 1987; Wing 1986). Realistically, many severely

disabled people would not be able to cope with open employment. Even when colleagues in the Employment Services make energetic attempts to help these people they are usually unsuccessful, in part because of the prevailing climate of unemployment but also because of the stigma attached to mental illness. Further, if disabled people can work, the current rules linked to the state benefit systems limit the amount of earnings which can be paid as part of their rehabilitation.

In a climate of high unemployment the development of leisure and recreational pursuits is likely to become increasingly more important and could lead to benefits similar to those that work could provide. For many chronically disabled people, however, recreational opportunities are often limited to the pub and watching TV and, even if they are involved in sheltered schemes or being supported by a regular input from a peripatetic team, they are likely to have long periods of free time on their hands, especially when statutory services are closed in the evenings and at weekends (Liberman 1988; Colgan and Bridges 1990). In addition to potential benefits similar to those provided by work, recreational pursuits facilitate the development of social networks, self-esteem, social competence and social integration (Rosenfield and Neese-Todd 1993; Chapter 11, this volume). These pursuits also provide an important source of pleasure and may even provide a means of engaging people with prominent negative symptoms into services which can help them.

Given the known benefits mentioned earlier, it is important that sheltered services are developed which can offer choice and cater for the range of interests, intellectual abilities and the latent skills which many people with schizophrenia actually have. Many schemes exist in many parts of the country which have been developed by various organisations (Lloyd 1986; Gloag 1987; Pilling 1988; Bridges and Brown 1989; Colgan et al. 1991; Nehring et al. 1993). Some are more structured than others and they usually provide opportunities for people to become involved in a range of activities which may even include outdoor adventure (Stich and Senior 1984; Holloway 1988). Recreational and work-related schemes may be integrated in a way similar to the 'clubhouse' model developed in the USA (see, for example, Beard et al. 1982; Bridges and Brown 1989; Nehring et al. 1993; Chapter 11, this volume). However, the range and number of schemes in any particular area of the UK are usually inadequate (Pilling 1991; Shepherd 1991).

Supportive social networks

Supportive social networks have been divided into: primary – friends, relatives and acquaintances – and secondary – relationships with statutory and non-statutory services (Bennett and Morris 1983). Social relationships may have several potential functions (Weiss 1974; Brier and

Strauss 1984). For example, they may provide a sense of security, companionship, shared experiences, a sense of responsibility for others, reassurance of worth and social competence, a reliable source of practical help, and may give emotional support and assistance when sorting out stressful situations (Weiss 1974). For practical purposes, these functions have been reduced to two main categories (Alloway and Bebbington 1987): the provision of practical support (instrumental or behavioural); and emotional support (expressive or affective). The qualitative nature of a relationship, i.e. feeling supported, may in fact be more important for some people than the objective aspects of a network (Henderson *et al.* 1981).

The social networks of people with schizophrenia are reported to be small, especially in relation to non-kin members, and these relationships tend to be asymmetric in that they are directed more by the other person than by the person with schizophrenia (Pattinson *et al.* 1975; Tolsdorf 1976; Sokolovsky *et al.* 1978). Different people have different social support needs and these needs are likely to vary over time. Some people appear to want only a non-intrusive, low-key relationship –'company without intimacy' (Mitchell and Birley 1983). Social withdrawal may occur as an adaptive response to perceived difficulties in cognitive function, and the reduction in the number of contacts may be a protective measure which enables the person to cope better with the illness (Brown *et al.* 1972). Increasing the levels of social integration for some people with schizophrenia can lead to relapse rather than improvement in their mental state (Wing 1978a).

It is uncertain whether the association between social support and illness is causal, effect, or a mixture of both. However, deficiencies in a primary social network may result in an increased risk of destabilisation of the mental state and hospitalisation (Anthony *et al.* 1983). A decreased ability to cope with the stresses and demands of everyday life has been observed (Bachrach 1978), as has an increased risk of social disabilities and a lack of opportunities to feel and give affection and to experience normal social interactions with a close friend.

Possible causes of a deficient primary network in people with non-psychotic disorders (Henderson *et al.* 1981) may also apply to those with a chronic psychotic illness. These include: the 'repelling' effects of psychopathology and their consequences on friends and relatives – the person would become less attractive in social encounters and less sought after; disinterest in social activity, such as negative phenomena, social anxieties or a depressed mood, resulting from psychopathology; loss of social skills needed in order to perform social transactions; and premorbid difficulties in establishing and maintaining mutually rewarding personal relationships. In addition, as a consequence of their social circumstances – such as instability of residence and having to live in socially deprived, inner-city areas – people with schizophrenia may have difficulties in maintaining contact with old friends and establishing new relationships. And their social circumstances offer few links into other networks for them meet new people.

It is thought that the long-term, day-to-day support of the most vulnerable patients with chronic disabilities should be provided by a specialist, rather than a generic, team (Reed 1984; Ekdawi *et al.* 1987). Such teams have been given various names, such as 'community support team' (see Chapter 7 in this volume) 'continuing community care team', 'continuing support service team', 'network team' (Reed 1984; Holloway 1988; Bridges *et al.* 1993). Their approach is based on four important factors (Bridges and Cresswell 1994). First, an 'in vivo' or 'criterion-orientated', approach to improving social functioning (Shepherd 1990a, 1991; Stein and Test 1980) is thought to be more effective in helping many disabled people deal with the challenges of living in the community than the 'in vitro', educational approaches, which may have problems of generalisation (Liberman 1988). Second, the 'in vivo' locus of care enables practitioners to have a more meaningful assessment of the problems faced by disabled people living in the community, as well as their latent abilities and strengths (Thompson *et al.* 1990). Third, even when people have specific skills for daily living they often depend on on-going support in order to maintain these and to cope with the vicissitudes of life. Fourth, this approach can enable people with certain irreducible disabilities to live in less dependent forms of accommodation, which may allow them to have a better quality of life than they would have in more institutional settings. In addition, the therapeutic alliance which can develop when working with people in this way gives many the opportunity to discuss their thoughts and feelings about how their illness has affected their life and ambitions – an important process which may help some people adapt to their current circumstances and potential losses.

The working of community mental health support teams is thought to be most effective if they are multi-professional and also involve para-professional staff (Ekdawi *et al.* 1987; Stein 1990; Bridges *et al* 1993; Lamb 1993) and if they are specific about which patients they are targeting and about their service objectives (Huxley 1990). Other requirements for effective working include: including direct client contact through the provider role (Rapp and Chamberlain 1985; Chapter 9, this volume); a flexible use of the time of individual members in order to respond to the changing clinical needs of patients (Reed 1984); the use of a supervised keyworker system; the overall responsibility of patient care being shared by the team rather than being taken by the keyworker alone; stand-ardised procedures for assessing needs and for formulating and reviewing care plans; sensitive but assertive approaches; and good forms of liaison with other services and agencies for the purpose of continuity of care.

In view of the nature of a team's daily work and its long-term commitment to individual patients, the caseload size of these teams has to be limited, and the accretion and turnover rates of patients are likely to be small. The implications of this include the need to decide on who should be targeted by specialist and dedicated teams rather than by generic teams (Creed *et al.* 1993).

Adverse aspects of the social environment

The adverse features of the social environment, other than those concerned with under- and overstimulation discussed earlier, include the stigma of mental illness, the inappropriate expectations of patients and of the roles of relatives, and the expressed emotion of carers. These topics are beyond the scope of this brief review and do not, in any event, feature prominently in the assessment of quality of life as we have construed it.

The burden of chronic mental illness

We have been asked on a number of occasions to produce a quality of life assessment which focuses on the carer, on whom, arguably, where one of the greatest burdens of mental illness falls. We have attempted to do this, by using the Lancashire Profile, but the results of this study are not yet available. Preliminary evidence suggests that the profile performs just as well as it does in patient populations.

Burden on the primary support system

Many patients remain in contact with relatives and depend on their support and care (Sturt *et al.* 1982). This dependence is likely to increase as services become more community orientated. Factors which can cause much distress to relatives include worries over whether the patient would be a danger to themselves or others, disturbed nights, aggression and embarrassing behaviour, florid psychotic phenomena, extreme seclusiveness or social withdrawal, and incapacity for self-care.

For many relatives, caring for the patient may result in objective and subjective forms of burden which may increase the longer the person remains ill (Gibbons *et al.* 1984; Hoenig and Hamilton 1966). Objective burden includes significant effects on health, social and leisure activities, and financial difficulties. Subjective burden refers to the extent to which a relative feels that they carry a burden. Relatives show remarkable levels of tolerance in trying to support patients with very problematic behaviours; they rarely complain about their difficulties and tend to expect help from statutory services but get little, except at times of crisis (Fadden *et al.* 1987). In marriages where one partner has schizophrenia, rates of divorce and separation can be significantly higher than national averages (Brown *et al.* 1966).

Coping with long-term mental illness is a difficult and unending task. Interventions based on working in partnership with families can help to enhance the relative's ability to cope and reduce relapse rates for patients, as discussed earlier (Kuipers and Bebbington 1990; Barrowclough and Tarrier 1992). Interventions aim to address a variety of the family's needs by helping the family to understand the problems that beset patients, to formulate their own problems in coping with the demands and needs of the patient and to deal with these by using the resources they have available (Kuipers and Bebbington 1990; Barrowclough and Tarrier 1992a, 1992b). Interventions which are thought to be most effective are those which focus on both family members and patients; are based on a positive attitude towards relatives and their value as a resource in the management of schizophrenia; have a sensitivity towards the family's specific needs; have a relationship which is frank and open; show a willingness to share information, knowledge and ignorance; and which have realistic goals. Care needs to be provided in the context of a long-term model of care, maintained over an extended period, integrated with other aspects of the patient's care plan and provided by staff with specialist training (Kuipers and Bebbington 1990; Barrowclough and Tarrier 1992a, 1992b; Smith 1992).

A range of interventions may be needed to suit the needs of different families. These may include: education about the illness in order to increase understanding, tolerance and empathy; a cognitive behavioural approach to solving or coping with specific problems and sources of stress experienced by the relatives; a goal-setting approach aimed at improving the social functioning of the patient within the family setting; and facilitated relatives' support groups (Falloon *et al.* 1984; Leff *et al.* 1985; Smith and Birchwood 1987; Barrowclough *et al.* 1987; Kuipers *et al.* 1989; Leff *et al.* 1989; Tarrier *et al.* 1993a, 1993b). Interventions specifically concerned with engaging relatives who are reluctant to be involved may also be necessary (Smith 1992).

Burden on the secondary support system

The main resource of a mental health service is the people who provide it and the frequency and quality of their interactions with themselves, the patients and carers (Watts and Bennett 1983; Shepherd 1984; Lavender and Sperlinger 1988; Pilling 1991). There are at least five causes of stress on these staff which, if they are not seriously addressed, may lead to a reduction in the quality of care, such as the development of negative institutional practices and, eventually, low staff morale and 'burn out'.

This is characterised by apathy about work tasks, resentment towards patients, high rates of absenteeism and high rates of staff turnover (Pilling 1991).

The first cause of stress is when staff experience a low level of intrinsic satisfaction from their work which, in turn, causes demotivation. This may occur when care is based on unrealistic expectations, such as staff aspiring to goals such as 'cure' or 'independence', and dull routine work with little reward (Brown 1973; Shepherd 1984, 1988; Huxley 1993c). The second cause of stress is when staff do not receive appropriate and adequate levels of supervision and support when dealing with emotionally demanding situations and behaviours of patients. These can include management of difficult behaviours such as hostility, inappropriate sexual activity, self-injury and offensive toiletry habits, such as a patient repeatedly defaecating in bed or a bedroom (Bridges *et al.* 1991a). They can also include dealing with suicide or other causes of death, particularly of someone who had established a close therapeutic relationship with a member of staff. Difficulties experienced in dealing with these types of problems may be compounded by staff having a sense of isolation if they do not perceive themselves as being integrated with other components of the services.

The third cause of stress is when staff feel overloaded and are having to struggle to meet the needs and demands of several patients at the same time. Examples of this occur when caseloads are inappropriate and too large to enable staff to spend sufficient time on one person or be sufficiently flexible in the use of their time in order to respond to adverse changes in a person's mental state or social circumstances. This can also occur when services are established on a shoestring and are unable easily to accommodate staff being on leave (holidays, sick, maternity, study) without it having a significant effect on the demands on the rest of the team members – a situation which can be made worse by the temporary transfer of staff from specialist services to other services (for example, acute services) when there are staff shortages.

The fourth cause of stress is when a service infrastructure is substantially inadequate, with no immediate prospects for improvement, and funding of current services is unstable or subject to future cuts. As a consequence, staff have to make compromises in their clinical decisions and care planning. These carry with them risks of adverse consequences for the patient and personal dissatisfaction and frustration for staff.

The fifth cause of stress is the personal cost to staff – men and women – of having to work in inner-city areas characterised by a combination of social deprivation and criminal activity, such as drug addiction, theft, muggings, rape, and use of guns. In the UK, at a time when services have endeavoured to become more community-orientated and available twenty-four hours a day these problems appear to be escalating.

Factors thought to be important in helping to ameliorate the burden on staff include: the development of an integrated and cohesive style of teamwork, which includes senior staff being readily available when significant problems arise; staff participation in the formulation of service philosophies, operational policies and management issues; direct staff involvement in individual care planning and reviews; setting clear, specific and limited goals and monitoring achievements, even if a positive outcome is maintaining the status quo or slowing down deterioration; providing opportunities and encouragement to develop new ways of dealing with old problems; the involvement of senior staff in direct care and regular supervision; providing opportunities and mechanisms for educational endeavours and appraisal of personal development; regular contact with people of other components in the network of services; staff support groups, team-building events and therapeutic 'holidays' for staff and/or patients; managerial teamwork and a proactive approach to maintaining the quality of current services and to the development of new services; and sensible policies for staff protection (Watts and Bennett 1983; Shepherd 1984; Lavender and Sperlinger 1988; Pilling 1991).

PSYCHOLOGICAL FACTORS

Adverse personal reactions associated with the illness include those in response to: the illness experience itself and recurring stress; attitudes towards the utilisation of services; and the characteristics of the supportive environment.

The illness experience

The impact the experience of an illness has on a person's attitudes and feelings will vary, to some extent, depending on the phase of his or her life-cycle. People with long-term mental illness have the same existential concerns as anyone else and have to cope with the normal stresses and concerns of each phase of their life. For example, early adulthood brings with it many new and challenging opportunities and tasks, including those concerned with familial separation, moving to independent life-styles, intimate relationships and marriage, parenthood, vocational choices and career developments, and changes in self-definition and identity. Early middle-age brings with it the process of consolidating progress in these areas and for appraising one's achievements, less impulsivity and a more philosophical attitude in the face of adversity and disappointment (Lamb 1982).

The personal experience of a long-term illness, its negative effects on social functioning, and the discordance between a person's aspirations and actual achievement of personal life goals can lead to the development of a persistent negative self-image, low self-esteem, lack of self-confidence, demotivation, lack of self-determination, and the development of a constricted passive stance in relation to life (Lamb 1982; Dingman and McGlashan 1986; Wing 1981, 1983, 1986, 1990). In some people, this may eventually lead to depressive states, passivity and overdependence (Wing 1983; Harris and Bergman 1984a, 1984b). The absence of a negative attitude may be associated with a better outcome (McGashan 1982, 1983) whereas an overpositive attitude may lead to depression when expectations are not met. Some young adults, however, may become defiant and rebellious, volatile and impulsive, assaultive, difficult to engage in services and poorly compliant with medication. Some may have an itinerant existence, have problems with drugs such as alcohol and illegal substances, utilise psychiatric services in a revolving-door manner and usually through emergency services, and may frequently become involved in the penal system. As a consequence, they are often labelled 'problem patients', 'negativistic' and 'difficult', and can evoke serious countertransference reactions and perfunctory treatment (Bachrach 1982; Lamb 1982).

Some people may develop persistent maladaptive responses (such as substance abuse, parasuicidal or suicidal behaviours, or chronic abnormal illness behaviour) to stress and mood disorders (Markowe *et al.* 1967; Miles 1977; Tsuang 1978; Roy 1982; Dingman and McGlashan 1986). Factors reported to be associated with increased risk of suicide in people with schizophrenia include being male, having relatively high premorbid educational and social achievements, being aware of the damaging effects of one's illness, having multiple admissions to hospital, having high internalised standards of performance, and experiencing a deteriorating course (Dingman and McGlashan 1986; Drake *et al.* 1984).

Attitudes towards the utilisation of services

Many patients, even after they have been in hospital, may not have any meaningful contacts with services (Johnstone *et al.* 1984; Kendrick *et al.* 1991). Factors which will influence a person's involvement with services will include the effect that positive and negative phenomena have on his or her judgement and behaviour, his or her attitude towards and beliefs about his or her service needs, and the extent to which he or she has been satisfied with previous service experiences. An important key to the engagement of people with services is the therapeutic alliance. Therapeutic relationships can be conceptualised in terms of: the quality of the interaction between the service provider and the patient, rather than the individual people involved; the continuation of contacts with the individual provider; a relationship with a team rather than a specific keyworker; and, for those patients who have difficulty tolerating interpersonal closeness, the relationship between the patient and an institution (Lamb 1977; Bachrach 1981).

Elements of establishing and maintaining a therapeutic relationship include: adopting an appropriate attitude about interpersonal transactions – for example, by being nonjudgmental, consistent, straightforward, empathetic and having a willingness to learn from the patient what the illness means to him or her; the flexible use of the time, frequency and location of involvement with the patient; using a communication style which is conversational, friendly in tone and signifying to the patient both respect and commitment; and offering practical advice, based upon empathy with the patient's needs of the moment, on how to solve particular problems (Dingman and McGlashan 1989; Huszonek 1987).

Priebe and Gruyters (1993) assessed patients' views of the helping alliance between themselves and their clinical case managers and found that, on the whole, the alliance was viewed positively. Patients who felt more understood and less criticised by their case managers, who felt better immediately after the session with them and who viewed their treatment as more correct than not, had a better outcome. The positive effect of the quality of life assessment on patients and its utility in establishing a relationship with the patient (see Chapter 2) might make a contribution to the formation of a therapeutic alliance, to a more positive attitude to treatment and care and, indirectly, to a better final outcome.

Characteristics of the supportive care environments

A person may develop adverse attitudes also as a reaction to particular features in his or her care environment. These will include the propensity to succumb to the process of institutionalism. This is defined as the gradual acceptance of and contentment with the values and routine of an institution, so that the person no longer wishes to live any other sort of life (Wing and Brown 1970). This attitude has been reported to occur in various care settings, including hospitals, day centres, hostels and group homes. The development of this attitude in some people may be adaptive and appropriate (see Chapter 5). However, in others, it may prevent the achievement of greater functional abilities and cause them to remain in forms of services that they may not necessarily need.

PREMORBID PERSONAL FACTORS

Premorbid personal characteristics can have either an aggravating or protecting (or ameliorating) effect on the extent to which a person becomes socially disabled following the onset of schizophrenia.

Aggregating factors which can affect social disabilities in terms of their severity or perpetuation include poor education and vocational attainment, low intelligence, unsatisfactory work records, lack of recreational skills and interests, and poor abilities to cope with the vicissitudes of life (Wing 1983; Bellack 1989). These may put the person at a social disadvantage even without schizophrenia, but the experience of schizophrenia and the timing of its development can compound the functional difficulties a person may have (Wing 1978a). These characteristics have been referred to as 'premorbid handicapping factors' (Wing and Brown 1970). In addition, coexisting, personality-related problems could be an important determinant of enduring social difficulties particularly in people who come into conflict with the law (Gunn and Taylor 1983). In general, the higher the person's level of social adjustment or attainment prior to the development of an illness, the better their outcome in terms of social functioning (Strauss and Carpenter 1972, 1977; Hersen and Bellack 1976; Liberman 1988).

Personal assets may have a protective or ameliorating effect on the development or persistence of social disabilities. These personal assets include intelligence, perceptual and problem-solving skills, personality strengths, and social competence, all of which will enable the person to cope with and adapt to various stressors, such as stressful life events and environmental challenges (Falloon 1986; Liberman 1988). Coping refers to the process of striving to deal with these stressors in adaptive ways. This will depend on insight, self-confidence, motivation, repertoire of personal skills, opportunities available to the person for soliciting the help of others or for acquiring material resources required, and gaining personal reward for achievement (Liberman 1988; Wing 1986). Coping skills can help to minimise the negative effects of a stressor by decreasing the severity and duration of its impact and, in some cases, by enabling the person to circumvent it entirely (Bellack 1989). Coping strategies may include stress-management strategies, conflict-resolution skills and social survival skills (Clements and Turpin 1992).

The conceptualisation of the patient as essentially helpless in the face of disease and as a passive recipient of care may cause the person's assets to go unnoticed. Many people will experience difficulties that are outside their competence to deal with (Wing 1986), but interventions which build upon the person's existing resources and repertoire of skills may help the person develop new adaptive behaviours and indirectly reduce some of the disabling effects of psychopathology (Liberman et al. 1988b).

A FRAMEWORK FOR REHABILITATION

This overview of some of the personal costs associated with an illness such as chronic schizophrenia indicates that we are concerned with a system involving complex interactions between the person and his or her environment. The nature of these interactions will vary throughout the person's illness career. This needs to be reflected in the definition of rehabilitation. Conceptually, during the early developments of rehabilitation services in the UK, the 'ladder model' of rehabilitation (Wing 1986) dominated thinking and was particularly important with regard to the discharge of patients from mental hospitals. According to this model, the aim of the rehabilitation process is to enable a person to move through stages, from the most supportive setting to other, less supported facilities and, eventually, to independent living. However, its current utility for the majority of people with chronic illnesses – in a variety of dispersed locations within the community – is questionable for several reasons. These include: its potentially disruptive nature, especially with regard to accommodation and the phenomena of 'specificity' and 'generalisation'; its potential lack of flexibility regarding the adjustment and provision of service input contingent upon the changing needs of patients and their wishes over time; and its link with the notion of 'throughput', an inappropriate organisational concept to apply to many people, who need services throughout their illness careers (see, for example, Shepherd 1984, 1991; Garety 1988).

Published definitions of rehabilitation vary in terms of emphasis. Some definitions differentiate rehabilitation from treatment insofar as the latter is concerned only with the removal of symptomatology, while the former deals mainly with the acquisition of functional skills which will enable a person to live as independently as possible, with minimum support (Freudenberg 1967; Farkas et al. 1989). Other definitions are broader and include other goals in addition to improvement in social functioning. These have evolved in recognition of the dynamic interactions between the person and his or her environment, of the fact that all biological and social characteristics are not remediable and of the fact that improvements may be limited. The natural history (course) of the illness is often not linear but variable, and a relatively small number of patients have extremely severe illnesses characterised by progressive deterioration. Published aims of rehabilitation, therefore, have included helping the person and his or her social environment to adapt to the characteristics of the illness and to his or her difficulties in coping with the vicissitudes of life (Bennett and Morris 1983; Shepherd 1991). For some people this may mean remaining in a highly dependent role and living in very supportive settings with specialist staff available *in situ* or on a peripatetic basis.

In general, the main therapeutic aims of psychiatric rehabilitation are interrelated and need to be flexible and contingent upon the changing needs of the patient over time. According to the literature, these aims can be summarised as follows:

1 To prevent or reduce impairments, social disabilities and environmental handicaps.
2 To restore potential abilities to perform social and instrumental roles.
3 To strengthen latent abilities, assets, skills and residual capacities.
4 To facilitate psychological and social adaptation to the effects of irreducible impairments and social disabilities.
5 To slow down the rate of further deterioration.
6 To enable optimal levels of self-determination, execution of personal responsibilities and independence.
7 To improve the person's overall sense of well-being.
8 To minimise the burden on the primary support system.
9 To minimise the burden on staff of services.

(For more details see, for example, Freudenberg 1967; Anthony *et al.* 1983; Shepherd 1984; Tanaka 1985; Liberman *et al.* 1986; Liberman 1988; Wing 1988, 1990; Pilling 1991.)

Overall, rehabilitation is concerned with minimising the negative effects of the dynamic relationships involving the biological, psychological and environmental factors described in the previous section, and maximising the person's latent abilities and strengths. Its long-term goal is to help a person travel through his illness career at minimal personal cost and maximal personal benefit, particularly in terms of achieving an optimal level of functioning and well-being – even if the illness has a deteriorating course. Hypothetically, the maximum personal cost which a person could accumulate over time would occur if he or she never received any help from primary and secondary support systems (Bridges *et al.* 1994b).

This gestalt perspective of rehabilitation will involve a titration of conjugated biological, psychological and social interventions throughout the person's illness career. These multi-modal interventions can be categorised in terms of their purposes:

1 To prevent destabilisation of the mental state and social functioning.
2 To effect restitution of a destabilised mental state and/or social functioning.
3 To maintain stability of an optimal mental state and social function, i.e. homeostasis.
4 To minimise the burden on carers.

The word 'rehabilitation' may seem inappropriate when applied to services based on this gestalt perspective of helping a person through his or her career of illness. However, at present there is no other word or phrase used in the UK which is as well established and which readily brings to mind the long-term service needs of severely disabled people. Potential candidates could include 'continuing support services' or, as in

North America, 'community support system', although this does not normally include hospital-based services and refers to rehabilitation mainly in terms of helping people to develop social and vocational skills (Anthony and Blanch 1989; Stroul 1989). In the UK, where there is an acceptance that the hospital should be part of the range of services needed (DHSS 1975; Reed 1983), other potential candidates include 'long-term community management' (Reed 1984) and 'continuing care services' (Holloway 1988).

TARGETING SERVICES FOR PEOPLE WITH CHRONIC DISABILITIES

In a climate of limited resources it is important to clarify which patients are to be prioritised and thus targeted by dedicated and specialist services. Although this chapter has been concerned largely with schizophrenia, in general targeted patients would not consist of a homogenous group. There will be variation in diagnosis, severity and characteristics of the illness, social disabilities and environmental factors. Several authors provide operational criteria for defining these patients. They usually list three main criteria which have to be satisfied: diagnosis, disability and duration (Goldman *et al.* 1981; Giel 1986; Goldman and Manderschied 1987; Bachrach 1988). Social disability needs to be sufficiently severe to have a significant impact on role performance (although there appears to be no clear agreement on which aspects of social functioning should be regarded as more important than others), and chronicity is defined as a duration of at least twelve months. As a network of services is likely to be required for these people, an additional criterion could be 'the need for multi-professional involvement in the formulation, review and provision of care plans' (Bridges *et al.* 1994c:5).

In addition to these criteria are factors which could be taken into account if services need to be more specific when selecting patients within this group. These have been chosen because they are likely to occur in patients who are particularly vulnerable – a significant and persisting burden on their primary support system, such as relatives, often associated with young adults – or who are a cause of significant difficulties for generic psychiatric services. These factors include:

1 Unremitting psychopathology, anti-social behaviour and significant social disabilities.
2 Significant propensity to experience a relapse of illness, or destabilisation of an already disturbed mental state or of social functioning.
3 Unsuccessful attempts to be supported in the community and experience of recurrent hospital admissions.

4 Changeable attitudes towards collaborating with care planning process and agreed plans.
5 Persistent problematic factors in the patient's social environment (for
example, high EE, exploitation, personal abuse).
6 Instability of place of residence.
7 Persistent relapse associated with severe mental illness.

There are groups of patients, other than schizophrenia sufferers, with
illnesses associated with severe forms of social disability, who need
specialist and dedicated services. These include people with chronic
somatisation and people who have organic brain syndromes, such as
those caused by head injuries.

Chronic somatisation

This occurs in a broad range of medical and surgical settings as well as
in primary care (Deighton and Nicol 1985; Bass and Benjamin 1993). In
the general population its prevalence may be greater than schizophrenia.
Some chronic forms have been reified as a distinct nosological group
known as 'somatoform disorders' (American Psychiatic Association
1987; WHO 1988), although it is probably best regarded as a process
rather than a syndrome or diagnosis (Bass and Benjamin 1993).
   Common characteristics include an excessive use of medical services
for physical complaints, failure to be reassured by negative results of
investigations, 'doctor shopping', reluctance to recognise the relevance
of psychological factors in the development and long-term maintenance
of somatic symptoms, and mutual hostility between patients and their
doctors (Escobar et al. 1987; Bass 1990). Chronic somatisation usually
occurs when physical complaints result from established and chronic
psychiatric disorders – usually mood-related – and the person becomes
frozen into a long-term sick role. Complaining about bodily symptoms
and a preoccupation with illness form a central part of the person's
behaviour as a means of dealing with various stressors – a form of illness
behaviour which may continue to exist even after a psychiatric illness has
been treated.
   Many of these people become chronically disabled and highly dependent (Follick et al. 1984; Barnes and Benjamin 1987) and impose a
considerable burden on their family and other carers (see, for example,
Norfleet and Burnell 1981; Flor et al. 1987; Turk et al. 1987). Their high
use of medical resources has significant financial implications (Bass and
Murphy 1990; Shaw and Creed 1991; Benjamin and Bridges 1993).
Specific interventions include close liaison between practitioners involved
in their care, with an emphasis on recognition of the nature of the
disorder, limiting unnecessary consultations, investigations and treat-

ment, followed by containment rather than cure, through the use of regular, scheduled appointments (Kellner *et al.* 1987; Sayce *et al.* 1990; Bass and Benjamin 1993). Some people, particularly those for whom there is a coexisting affective disorder, may benefit from antidepressants and anxiolytics (Fienmann *et al.* 1985) and from techniques which help to re-attribute their somatic symptoms to underlying psychological dynamics (Gask *et al.* 1989; Goldberg *et al.* 1989). Psychological approaches to treatment based on psychodynamic, behavioural and cognitive models, have been described (Fordyce 1973; Kellner *et al.* 1987; Benjamin 1989; Wesseley *et al.* 1989; Guthrie 1991.

Organic brain syndromes

Head injuries are very common. Accident and Emergency departments in the UK are reported to receive one million head injury patients each year, of which 150,000 are admitted and, of these, only 4 per cent are subsequently transferred to neurosurgical units (Mendelow 1990). The rate for people with associated severe disabilities has been estimated as 150/100,000 (Jennett and Braakman 1990), and between 66–114/100,000 are thought to have moderate or severe brain injury which requires rehabilitation services (Brookes *et al.* 1989). This estimate would be much greater if other forms of organic brain syndromes are included. However, rehabilitation services in the UK for these people are poorly developed (Royal College of Psychiatrists 1991). Local epidemiological surveys are required in order to have a clearer understanding of the mental, social and material consequences experienced by patients and relatives.

Brain injury results in a wide variety of long-term needs, affecting physical, psychological and social functioning. There is a wide range of interventions which address these needs (Lishman 1987; Rosenthal *et al.* 1990). The range of interventions for social disabilities and for affected families and other carers, including respite care, is similar to that described earlier for chronic schizophrenia. This range of services will be important to consider for people with brain disease from other causes.

CONCLUSION

The main aim of this chapter has been to describe a broad framework for conceptualising the complex relationships existing among a variety of factors which can determine the outcome of people with long-term illness careers. Taken together, they represent a 'system of care'. At least three important operational principles arise from this gestalt perspective: the need for planners and practitioners to have longitudinal and cross-sectional concepts of care; the need for multi-professional and multi-agency teamwork; and the need for effective information systems. In our view, quality of life is an important and major outcome variable when considering the benefits of each of the components in this system of care. The following chapters illustrate its utility when it has been used to assess a number of these components.

Part II

Service applications

Chapter 5

The quality of care and the quality of life in independent-sector residential homes

INTRODUCTION

Independent-sector provision of residential care in the UK has grown considerably over the past ten years, from a very low (DHSS 1975) and, some would argue, inadequate baseline (House of Commons 1994a). Much of the growth in provision has been in private homes for elderly people (OPCS 1987), but there has also been a growth in community residential facilities for mentally ill people in the UK (Huxley 1993a) and in the USA (Randolph *et al.* 1991). Large institutions have been reduced in size and smaller units developed in community settings, along with independent living for less dependent people. There has been considerable controversy about the place of residential units in community care (Huxley 1992) and great concern, particularly in the USA, about the inappropriate placement of mentally ill people in nursing homes (these are not the same as nursing homes in the UK because relatively little nursing care is provided in them, and many residents are not in need of physical care) (Warner 1985). Geller and Fisher's (1993) argument that mentally ill people move, over time, through a series of residential settings, from the more restrictive to the less restrictive, is not supported by the evidence. Segal and Liese (1991) also found that though service providers assumed a continuum of care was provided, residents were, in fact, obtaining residential care at critical periods in their lives (perhaps for long periods) rather than progressing through a continuum. Lelliot and others (1993) suggest that the provision of residential services in the UK still remains below recommended levels, and that more, not less, residential accommodation is required. The House of Commons Health Committee (House of Commons 1994a) recommended that the Department of Health issue instructions on minimum acceptable levels of provision for 'staffed community houses' and that services should be inspected every three years and rated against these national minimum standards.

In the UK, evaluation of the quality of residential care for mentally ill people has been limited and has tended to be conducted in local authority homes. Fewer studies have been concerned with independent-sector or private homes (Oliver and Mohamad 1992) and fewer still have tried to relate the quality of care provided to the quality of life as it is experienced by the residents. One study, in the USA, which did attempt such a comparison (Lehman *et al.* 1986), examined the objective and subjective quality of life of four groups of chronic patients, who were categorised according to whether they were inpatients of a state hospital or residents of a supervised community residence and whether their current length of stay had been less than or greater than six months. Regardless of length of stay, the community residents perceived their living conditions more favourably, had more financial resources and were less likely to have been assaulted in the past year than the inpatients.

The present chapter reports a study of residential services for mentally ill people. This study is potentially important in several ways, in that:

1 It is a study which is provided by the independent sector and not by local authorities or health authorities.
2 It uses standardised measures of the quality of care, previously reported in the UK only in residential homes for dependent elderly people.
3 It uses standardised assessments of the quality of care reported in similar client groups in the USA.
4 It uses the Lancashire Quality of Life Profile to assess resident life satisfaction and well-being.
5 It permits, for the first time to our knowledge, the opportunity to compare quality of care and quality of life on these scales (Oliver and Mohamad [1992] used an earlier version of the quality of life and sheltered care environment scales). This will enable us to explore, to a limited extent, the relationship between characteristics of the homes and the views of the residents concerning their quality of life.

Improving and maintaining the quality of life of mentally ill people in the community is a central objective of government policy and is one of the aims of locally developed services. While there is a considerable amount of rhetoric about what is the best form of provision, there is a dearth of empirical evidence. This survey of one independent-sector agency contributes something to the empirical basis of our understanding.

THE INDEPENDENT-SECTOR HOMES (ISH)

The homes in the present study were established by independent-sector (non-statutory) organisations, which began life as a regional breakaway group from a national organisation. The twelve residential homes in the study are, for administrative purposes, run by three separate organisations, partly reflecting the chronology of the development of the homes in different towns in North-West England. The organisation's philosophy is based on the assumption that some form of residential care will always be needed for mentally ill people, either because their behavioural problems can only be managed in a sheltered setting, or because of the need for twenty-four-hour supervision, or because carers are no longer able to cope at home and need temporary or permanent respite. All the managing organisations are companies limited by guarantee, and they also provide day services, workshops and family support workers, none of which is considered in the present chapter. At the time this research was conducted there were over ninety successful projects operating in the region. The organisation continues to meet a demand for care and support, especially from schizophrenia sufferers and their relatives, and continues to grow. The organisation has its critics, especially among some social workers, who see the provision of residential solutions in homes and hostels of this sort as being inappropriate and inconsistent with the principles of normalisation. It has also been pointed out that the organisation may be atypical in that the standard of care it provides could be higher than that in most parts of the independent sector. It may not be representative, therefore, of the whole of the independent sector but only of the best parts.

The size of the homes ranges from ten to thirty places, and all are staffed. The organisation also runs sheltered housing in apartments but these are not included in the present study. Eight of the homes are occupied predominantly by male residents, and the average age in the homes varies from a low of 40 to a high of 65. It is, therefore, a relatively elderly population, and many residents were discharged from long-stay wards of mental hospitals. This group is older and much more impaired than the younger residents, who tend to have more behavioural problems and florid symptoms. All of the residents of the homes have major mental illnesses, of some considerable duration, and require continuing medication.

THE PRESENT STUDY SAMPLE

All of the homes participated in the project. The staff members completed the sheltered care environment scale (SCES) and the residents completed the Lancashire Quality of Life Profile. The SCES forms one part of the multiphasic environmental assessment procedure (MEAP) developed by Moos and Lemke (1984). MEAP is a set of five instruments, which can be used separately or in conjunction with one another. It is designed to evaluate the social and physical environments of residential settings for older adults. Normative data exist for different types of settings in the USA.

The SCES consists of sixty-three yes/no questions and is completed by the staff of the home. The questions evaluate seven areas of interest, or sub-scales: cohesion, conflict, independence, self-disclosure, organisation, resident influence and physical comfort. The sub-scales and dimensions are defined as follows:

1 *Cohesion*: how helpful and supportive staff members are toward residents and how involved and supportive residents are with each other.
2 *Conflict*: the extent to which residents express anger and are critical of each other and the facility.
3 *Independence*: how self-sufficient residents are encouraged to be in their personal affairs and how much responsibility and self-direction they exercise.
4 *Self-disclosure*: the extent to which residents express openly their feelings and personal concerns.
5 *Organisation*: how important order and organisation are in the facility, the extent to which residents know what to expect in their daily routine, and the clarity of rules and procedures.
6 *Resident influence*: the extent to which residents can influence the rules and policies of the facility and are free from restrictive regulations.
7 *Physical comfort*: the extent to which comfort, privacy, pleasant décor and sensory satisfaction are provided by the physical environment.

For the SCES to provide an accurate and durable impression of the usual atmosphere at each home, every staff member was approached to complete the questionnaire. A total of 175 staff were approached and 153 replies were received, giving an overall response rate of nearly 90 per cent. Demographic data were available for all the 169 residents in thirteen homes. Only twenty-nine either refused to participate in the quality of life interview or were considered too unwell by the staff (an 83 per cent participation rate in the quality of life study; n=140).

THE QUALITY OF CARE IN THE HOMES

The findings from the SCES can be compared with the results of applications in other places, notably in the USA and in Netten's (1991) study of local authority homes for old people with dementia (which included some people suffering from functional and organic mental illnesses).

Moos provides normative data for three types of settings: nursing homes, residential care facilities and congregate apartments (Moos and Lemke 1984). From these three indicators, an overall measure of environment is derived. In this chapter, only the norms for residential homes

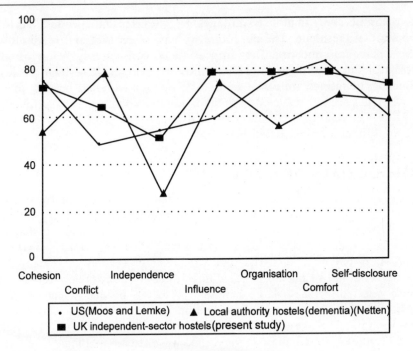

Figure 5.1 SCES scores in residential homes

and nursing homes will be used, where appropriate, for comparative purposes.

Netten examined thirteen homes for elderly people in various locations in England. She describes the residents under examination to be: 'more dependent than residents in care generally' and the staffing levels at the homes to be 'similar to national levels [although] there was a higher proportion of qualified staff, particularly with a nursing background' (Netten 1991:48). Netten collected data from the staff members at each home. She does not indicate the size of the sample drawn from each home.

Figure 5.1 shows, for comparative purposes, the results from Moos and Netten's studies, together with the findings from the present study. One can see immediately that the residents of the homes for the elderly in the UK sample were much less independent, and this reflects their greater degree of impairment and other dependency factors. Although the UK group has a slightly higher degree of influence than its US counterpart, it has a quite substantially greater conflict score. It is worth noting at this point that the conflict rating represents the extent to which residents can express conflict, and so the higher the score the more they are able to express it, rather than a high score indicating that there *is* a lot of conflict in the home.

The scores of the US residential homes for mentally ill people and the independent-sector homes in the present study are, for the most part, comparable. Any major advantages lie with the independent sector homes. The residents are more able to express conflict and to disclose their personal concerns. They appear to be considerably better off in terms of the amount of influence which they can exert in their homes. Since these ratings are based upon staff opinion, it could be that these advantages are not reflected in the individual resident's perceived quality of life. The relationship between quality of care and quality of life will be considered in more detail below.

THE QUALITY OF LIFE IN THE HOMES

There are considerable amounts of data available from community samples on the use of the Lancashire Quality of Life Profile but fewer data available on its use in residential settings. The analysis of quality of life in this chapter uses data from several different sources. First, Oliver and Mohamad (1992) (O&M: n=60) used an earlier and much larger version of the present instrument, and so much of their data is directly comparable. Second, we have selected, from a large community survey in one social services department, all the residents of local authority hostels (LAH: n=36). Third, we occasionally make use of the larger community (social services) sample (CSSS: n=384; see Chapter 7) for comparative purposes. Finally, we have drawn a comparison sample of residents of hostels from the final data-set (n=1,575) accumulated from different settings (mainly in the north-west of England) (database hostel [DBH] sample: n=131).

The comparison with the community sample is a rigorous test of the ability of the homes in the present study to produce community integration, satisfaction with the quality of the home and subjective well-being, since one might expect these things to be better in the community samples where, generally speaking, clients have greater independence and require less supervision. It is helpful to be able to compare hostels and community service in the same authority where, in other respects, service and community characteristics are similar.

The average age at first admission to hospital in the O&M sample was 27, and ranged from 14 to 50. In the present sample, the range is 14 to 63 (although only one client was over 53) and the mean is also 27. The age at first admission in the sample drawn from the full data-set (DBH) is 25. However, the age distribution of the present sample is quite different from the age distribution in the LAH. Only 23 per cent of the present sample are under 40, compared to 62 per cent of residents in the hostels, and 35 per cent of the present sample are over 60, compared to only 9 per cent in the LAH. The mean ages of the samples are significantly different (multiple comparison test [Scheffe method] F=40.67; p<.00001).

On the basis of the existence of these differences, one might argue that further comparison is rather misleading. However, given that we acknowledge these differences, further comparison is important for several reasons. First, there is a widespread, often unstated, assumption that living in the community is always superior in all respects to living in residential care, and we therefore need to examine the extent to which this might be true in the present samples. Second, there are doubts about the capabilities of the independent sector to produce an adequate quality of care and an adequate quality of life for residents. Third, there is a dearth of comparative information which makes use of standardised information. Many previous tests of the comparative adequacy of community living over residential care have not used the same instrumentation in each setting. Finally, this sort of comparison can be expected to become more common as the mixed economy of welfare continues to develop and purchasers and providers seek meaningful ways to assess – and, more importantly, to compare – the outcomes of different modalities of care.

Demographic characteristics: age and gender

The demographic characteristics of the present sample are that the respondents are predominantly male (60 per cent) and the mean age of the sample is 56, somewhat older than the other groups of respondents (for example, the mean age in other hostels [DBH] is 44 years). Only 8 per cent of the residents in other hostels are from minority ethnic groups, compared to 5 per cent in the ISH homes.

Oliver and Mohamad (1992) report that their sample in residential care was: 74 per cent male; had a mean age of 52 (with a range of 22 to 80); and that 66 per cent were single and 81 per cent childless; 71 per cent were previously long-stay patients in hospital; 82 per cent of the people in hostels were male; 84 per cent in boarding-out schemes; and 74 per cent in group homes. The mean age of hostel residents was 35 years (range 21 to 55 years), and in the group homes it was 64 years (range 38 to 80).

Objective indicators

Marital status

Figure 5.2 shows the marital status of the different samples. The vast majority of the respondents are single, but the proportion in the hostels is much higher than in the CSSS.

Work/education

There is a significant difference in school leaving age between the ISH group and the others (for example between ISH and DBH, 14.7 years and

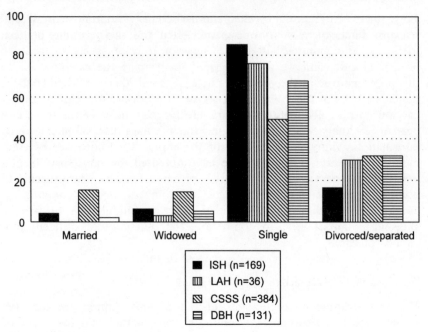

Figure 5.2 Marital status

16 years respectively; F=6.58; p<.01). Almost all (99 per cent) of the ISH sample left school before the age of 16. In spite of their advanced age, 23 per cent (n=40) of residents in the ISH sample were engaged in some form of sheltered work, compared to only 3 per cent of the 'residents of LAH. About half of the forty worked for more than twenty hours a week.

Leisure activities and community participation

Even though residents in the present sample were older, they were less active than people in the local authority homes and community residents only in relation to sport. They had higher rates of going out shopping (83 per cent) and for rides in a car (92 per cent) than the DBH sample (74 and 79 per cent respectively). A slightly greater percentage of the DBH sample (42 per cent) than of the ISH sample (35 per cent) expressed a desire for more leisure activities.

Religious activity

While virtually everyone identified themselves as a member of a religious faith (the largest group being Protestant [62 per cent], similar to the LAH sample [68 per cent]) very few people had been to a religious service in the past month; 79 per cent of this sample and 75 per cent of the LAH residents had not. Twenty-one per cent of the sample were regular attenders (25 per cent in LAH).

Finances

The weekly pay of the ISH residents, even though more of them were in 'work', was lower than that of the residents in the DBH sample (F=6.04 p<.05) (a similar result is reported in Chapter 11). None of the ISH residents compared to 10 per cent of the DBH sample had applied for and been refused any social security benefits during the previous twelve months.

Living situation

Twenty-six people (19 per cent) had lived in their present home for less than six months, and a further six had lived there for between six months and one year. The longest period of residence was eight years (three people), and eighteen people had been in their present home for between five and eight years. The bulk of the sample (n=63) had lived in the present home for between two and five years. Of those who replied to the question, just over one-quarter felt over the past year that they wanted to move or improve their circumstances. This is significantly fewer than in the other hostels (DBH), where 61 per cent expressed a desire for such a change.

Legal and safety issues

In LAH four clients (13 per cent) had been accused of a crime in the past year and eight (25 per cent) had been the victim of violence or robbery. In the present sample, only one resident had had contact with the police in the past year and none had been the victim of crime. Not surprisingly, the ISH residents did not express a desire for more help, whereas one in ten of the DBH sample did.

Family relations

Eighty per cent of the ISH sample do not have children. Only one-third of the sample have weekly contact with a relative, compared to two-thirds of the LAH residents; about one-fifth of each sample have monthly contact. However, over one-third of the present sample have annual or less than annual contact with relatives, compared to only 18 per cent of the DBH residents and 3 per cent of the LAH residents (F=20.56; p<.001).

Social relationships

Two-fifths said that they had a close friend, compared to half of the DBH sample and two-thirds of the LAH sample. Even fewer in the present sample had a friend that they could turn to for help (reliable alliance) – only one-fifth – and in the past week only 18 per cent had visited a friend. These figures were considerably higher in both the LAH sample (56 per cent and 38 per cent respectively) and the DBH sample (54 and 55 per cent respectively).

Health

Fifty-five per cent had consulted a doctor for an episode of physical illness during the past year (not dissimilar to the regional average and identical to the DBH group), and a similar percentage had seen a doctor for their nerves in the last year. Almost all (95 per cent) of the respondents in all the samples were on medication. However, their visits to the doctor in connection with their mental health problems varied from a low of 60 per cent in the ISH group to 75 and 80 per cent respectively in the LAH and DBH groups. There were also differences in rehospitalisation rates, with the ISH again being the lowest. Sixteen per cent of the ISH residents had been readmitted to hospital because of relapse in the last year, compared to 30 per cent of the DBH residents and 44 per cent of those in the LAH sample ($F=6.50$, $p<.05$).

SUBJECTIVE WELL-BEING

Subjective well-being scores are the ratings made by the respondent in each of the nine life domains. The data are compared using one-way analysis of variance (multiple comparison test – Scheffe's method). A few of the residents were unable to understand the procedure required for completing the quality of life scale. A number of them had been institutionalised for many years and their cognitive abilities were significantly impaired. These cases are missing but should not be regarded as refusals (only twenty-nine cases actually refused to complete the quality of life scales, an 83 per cent participation rate). All the remaining residents participated and all those capable of expressing an opinion did so. Some of the items, such as work, religion and family relations, did not apply to the residents. There were missing cases in the community sample too, where clients were not working or had no family. Because of the amount of missing data in the independent-homes sample, we compared those who were able to respond to those who were not and found that the non-respondents tended to be older (a mean age of 58 years compared to 53 years: $F=5.59$; $p<.05$) and had left school at the slightly earlier age of 14 years and 3 months, compared to the respondents whose mean school leaving age was 15 years (F=18.76l; p<.001). It is possible, therefore that the missing group did contain a greater proportion of people with cognitive impairment. They did not differ from the respondents on any of the other major demographic or 'objective' quality of life items.

Table 5.1   Living situation ratings in different residential settings

Setting	Mean
Independent-sector hostel[1]	5.7
Group home[2]	5.3
Hostel ward[2]	4.8
Board and care[3]	4.5
Other hostels[1]	4.4
Local authority hostels[1]	4.3
State hospital[3]	3.9
Psychiatric ward[2]	3.7

Note: 1 This chapter
2 Simpson et al. (1989)
3 Lehman et al. (1982)

Table 5.1 summarises the difference in subjective ratings in respect of 'living situation' in several residential settings. It may be worthwhile mentioning that the rating for living situation given by Andrews and Withey (1976) for their community sample of 1,297 cases, was 5.3.

Table 5.2 Subjective well-being: a comparison between the local authority hostels (LAH) (n=35), the community social services sample (CSSS) (n=387) and the independent-sector hostels (ISH) (n=140).

	Location	Means (SD)	(95% confidence intervals)	F	p
Work/education	LAH	4.4 (1.5)	(3.6-5.1)	7.02	.001
	CSSS	3.8 (1.5)	(3.6-3.9)		
	ISH	4.4 (1.5)	(4.1-4.7)		
Leisure	LAH	4.8 (0.6)	(4.5-5.0)	23.76	.000
	CSSS	4.5 (1.1)	(4.5-4.6)		
	ISH	5.3 (0.9)	(5.1-5.5)		
Religion	LAH	4.1 (1.6)	(3.5-4.8)	2.94	N.S.
	CSSS	4.6 (1.1)	(4.5-4.6)		
	ISH	4.8 (1.0)	(4.6-5.0)		
Finances	LAH	3.4 (1.5)	(2.8-4.0)	9.71	.000
	CSSS	3.4 (1.5)	(3.3-3.6)		
	ISH	4.2 (1.4)	(3.9-4.5)		
Living situation	LAH	4.3 (1.0)	(3.9-4.7)	16.75	.000
	CSSS	4.6 (1.1)	(4.5-4.7)		
	ISH	5.2 (0.9)	(5.1-5.4)		

Table 5.2 (contd)

	Location	Means (SD)	(95% confidence intervals)	F	p
Legal/safety	LAH	4.7 (1.0)	(4.3-5.1)	13.01	.000
	CSSS	4.8 (1.3)	(4.6-4.9)		
	ISH	5.5 (0.9)	(5.3-5.7)		
Family relations	LAH	4.5 (1.5)	(4.0-5.1)	10.94	.000
	CSSS	4.5 (1.4)	(4.4-4.7)		
	ISH	5.3 (1.2)	(5.1-5.6)		
Social relations	LAH	4.5 (1.2)	(4.0-5.0)	4.33	.01
	CSSS	4.6 (1.3)	(4.5-4.7)		
	ISH	5.1 (1.2)	(4.8-5.3)		
Health	LAH	4.5 (1.4)	(3.9-5.0)	26.24	.000
	CSSS	4.3 (1.2)	(4.2-4.4)		
	ISH	5.3 (1.1)	(5.1-5.6)		

Table 5.2 shows major differences between the LAH, ISH and CSSS samples in all domains except finances. In each instance, apart from work, it is the ISH residents whose ratings are highest.

Figure 5.3 provides a direct comparison between the profiles of the ISH and DBH samples. None of these differences is significant at the .05 level, although three – health, family relations and living situation – do come close. ISH residents' subjective well-being is rated above that of DBH residents in all the life domains.

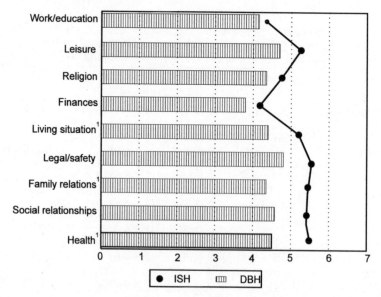

Figure 5.3 Subjective well-being in hostel residents
Note: 1 p<.1

INDEPENDENCE, INFLUENCE AND PRIVACY

These variables have been rated on the same seven-point scale as the subjective well-being scores. The ISH rating is significantly higher than the CSSS and LAH samples in respect of current living arrangements (Table 5.3: F=22.36; p<.001). Although the rating for degree of independence in the home is highest for the ISH, the difference is not a significant one. However, the CSSS is not superior to the residential settings. The amount of influence which the person feels they have and their feelings about their relationship with others who share their home are not significantly different in the four samples. Feelings about privacy are substantially different, and the ISH report greater satisfaction than the DBH, in this respect (F=4.59; p<.01).

Table 5.3 Independence, influence and privacy: a comparison between the local authority hostels (LAH), the community social services sample (CSSS), the data-base sample (DBH) and the independent-sector (ISH) hostels

	Location	Means (SD)	(95% confidence intervals)
Living	LAH	4.3 (1.0)	(5.1–5.9)
arrangements	CSSS	4.7 (1.5)	(4.5–4.8)
	DBH	4.9 (1.5)	(4.6–5.1)
	ISH	5.7 (1.1)	(5.4–5.9)
Independence	LAH	4.6 (1.4)	(4.0–5.1)
	CSSS	5.0 (1.5)	(4.9–5.2)
	DBH	4.9 (1.6)	(4.6–5.1)
	ISH	5.3 (1.5)	(4.9–5.6)
Influence	LAH	4.4 (1.4)	(3.9–4.9)
	CSSS	4.7 (1.5)	(4.6–4.9)
	DBH	4.2 (1.2)	(3.9–4.4)
	ISH	4.7 (1.5)	(4.4–5.1)
Privacy	LAH	4.9 (1.6)	(4.3–5.5)
	CSSS	4.9 (1.5)	(4.8–5.1)
	DBH	4.8 (1.6)	(4.5–5.0)
	ISH	5.5 (1.2)	(5.2–5.7)
Continued			
residence	LAH	3.6 (1.0)	(2.9–4.4)
	CSSS	4.3 (1.9)	(4.2–4.5)
	DBH	3.6 (1.7)	(3.2–3.9)
	ISH	4.9 (1.6)	(4.5–5.3)

When asked how they feel about the prospects of living in this home for the foreseeable future the ISH residents feel (significantly) happier about the prospect than either the hostel residents or the CSSS (F=7.12; p<.001). The strongly positive ratings given in these sections are in marked contrast to the sharply negative response to the idea of returning to a hospital. The mean score in all three samples for this final question was 2 – the idea could hardly be worse! It is perhaps no surprise then that the ISH residents differed significantly from the community residents in their attitude to the current living situation. The ISH group felt significantly better about the level of privacy afforded to them than the other groups, including the CSSS.

On the LQOLP ratings of their living arrangements the residents' general satisfaction with their living arrangements was related to their satisfaction with privacy and with independence. Their rating of their living arrangements was unrelated to the amount of influence they had or to their feelings about their fellow residents. This suggests that the former variables are more important than the latter in producing satisfaction with the homes.

THE RELATIONSHIP BETWEEN QUALITY OF LIFE AND QUALITY OF CARE

Because the quality of care data relate to the homes rather than to the individual residents it is not possible to make a direct comparison for each person in the study between his or her quality of life and his or her quality of care. In order to compare the quality of life and quality of care ratings we ranked the twelve homes according to the proportion of positive staff responses in respect of the sixty-three SCES questions. The highest ranked home had the highest proportion of positive responses and the lowest ranked home the lowest proportion of positive responses on each question. For a large number of the SCES questions there was insufficient variance in the responses to make an analysis meaningful. In the end, only fourteen questions were used and these related to the physical characteristics of the homes, independence, social activity, practical skills and the atmosphere in the homes.

We ranked the twelve homes according to the proportion of residents scoring above the mean on major quality of life items. Once again, the highest ranked home had the highest proportion of residents scoring above the mean, and the lowest ranked home had the lowest proportion of residents scoring above the mean. The quality of life items we used were those which related to the living situation in the home (five questions) and two or three of the life domains (health, leisure, social and financial). We then carried out correlations (Spearman) between the two sets of rankings of quality of life and quality of care items. An indicator of the validity of the rankings was that similar SCES items were highly correlated (for example, the physical comfort rating and the rating of the quality of the décor: $r=.72$; $p=.008$).

The results of the comparison show that the more comfortable and physically homely the home, the more likely the residents were to be satisfied with the amount of privacy afforded them (r=.58; p<.05). The more residents talked about their personal problems (according to the staff ratings) then the less well rated were their feelings about fellow residents (r=−.63; p<.05). This might mean that there were some inter-personal frictions, which were reflected in the staff's ratings, or that some residents, in talking about themselves, alienated their fellow residents in some way. The main set of relationships was between the amount of social activities (according to the staff) and the residents' feelings about privacy, influence, independence and the living arrangements generally. All of these items were negatively correlated at the .05 level, with a greater amount of social activity. This means that the homes where there was a lot of social activity were those where the residents had less satisfaction with influence, privacy, etc.

DISCUSSION

Bearing in mind that the ISH sample residents are older, more often single, and have less contact with their families, where they have them, they are, in many respects, no worse off than the younger residents in hostels or the community residents. The only major disadvantage for the ISH residents lies in the domain of social relationships, where they are much less likely than the other samples to have developed close friendships. Nevertheless, almost one-fifth had visited a friend in the week before the interview and, as a group, they are less active in community participation only with regard to sport, which, given their mean age, is perhaps understandable. In shopping, travelling outside the home, and attending religious services they were somewhat more active. In terms of sheltered work, substantially more of the ISH residents were engaged, and half of those who were (n=40) worked for more than twenty hours each week.

Residents in other hostels were more likely to have seen a doctor for their nerves and also more likely to have been admitted for inpatient care. This may be because they are a group with more florid illnesses and greater behavioural problems. Their legal/safety domain results might also be accounted for by their age, since four (13 per cent) had been accused of a crime in the past year, and one-quarter had been the victim of a crime over the same period. The ISH residents led a much less eventful life, in the sense that only one resident had had any contact with the police over the past year and none was a victim of crime.

It would not have been surprising to find that the ISH group of residents, given their age, had a worse health record than they did. It is possible that their health care needs are picked up early and addressed in the residential context. The residential setting of the ISH homes seems to be a good protection against a hostile and unsafe external world, and while this increase in safety is not at the expense of participating in fewer activities in the local community, there are deficiencies in the residents' friendship networks.

The average satisfaction scores indicated a significantly higher quality of life for ISH residents than for the other groups in most life domains. The ISH ratings for subjective well-being were also higher than both the LAH and CSSS samples for leisure activity, living situation, legal and safety, family relations and health. These subjective well-being differences are in similar domains to the objective differences outlined above.

However, the ISH residents also felt better off in respect of social relationships and finances, where the objective differences between the groups were not marked. In fact, the community sample had a greater frequency of close friendships (two-thirds) and visited friends more often than the ISH residents (39 per cent). Each of the samples received similar benefit payments, suited to their particular circumstances and, of course, those who worked could usually achieve only therapeutic earnings. Even the small amount of weekly cash which this produced for the ISH sample was probably greater than they had experienced in hospital, and this may account for their greater perceived well-being in this domain. Likewise, the opportunity to visit a friend, although exercised by only 18 per cent in the week before the interview, has to be set against the infrequency of visiting in the hospital setting, the inability to choose where and when to meet, and the fact that, in some of the ISH homes at least, they may already be living with their close friends and have no need to 'visit' them, in the sense implied by the question.

The relationship between high levels of social activity and lower satisfaction ratings could be explained by the residents feeling that too many supervised social activities were organised for them and that this impinged upon their freedom to do what they liked. Given the fact that many of them might have preferred to withdraw from social activities, perhaps because the activities were overstimulating, or because the residents were unmotivated, these negative associations may be understandable. The difference in the staff and resident perceptions in this area is consistent with the residents' feelings that they had few friends. Ex-hospital residents do not have large social networks, and staff may be working hard to establish more relationships through social activities in the homes. Some of the residents clearly feel this as some sort of imposition. However, this has to be balanced against the danger for some of them that without this activity they might begin to withdraw and become at risk of relapse.

CONCLUSION

The SCES results show that the ISH homes perform well when compared to SCES results elsewhere. However, the results of the comparison must be treated with some caution, because the SCES ratings are made by the staff of the establishments, and one really needs independent corroboration of the standard of care in the homes before one can accept that they are genuinely better in any respect than other homes or other settings. There is some evidence from the LQOLP that the lives of the residents of the ISH were better than comparable patients living in the community in the same area. The ISH residents were as well integrated into the community as the community sample on a limited number of items, even though one might have expected the older ISH residents to be less active than the younger patients in the community. The community cases were in receipt of standard social services care and might not, therefore, have been receiving optimal care and stimulation. In contrast, the ISH staff spend time and effort ensuring that a lot of social activities are organised for residents. In the comparison with the quality of care ratings, this organised and supervised social activity was not popular with many of the residents, although it may have been essential to their continued well-being. In spite of the organised social activity, the ISH residents have fewer close friendships than the community residents.

These negative aspects of the lives of the ISH residents may be seized upon by proponents of the 'all residential care is bad' school of thought as evidence of failure. Local authority social workers, in particular, hold negative views about residential care, and one has to surmise that their view must be, partly, a result of their experience of residential care as provided by their employers. Social services departments have not given high priority to residential services, and poor conditions of employment for staff and inadequate standards of care have been common. Under these circumstances, any alternative is viewed positively and, given the poor quality of care provided, it is perhaps understandable that social services department workers find this unacceptable; they may not have seen acceptable residential care.

The greater desire for change expressed by the residents of the other hostels (DBH) might be interpreted by opponents of residential care as evidence of their greater capacity for choice, and the lesser desire in the ISH residents as evidence of the consequences of paternalism, institutionalisation, or both. Now, while this might be the case, it rather flies in the face of the evidence. The ISH residents' objective circumstances are not, with the exceptions of the negative results just mentioned, worse than those in LAH and are, in some respects, better. Fewer wish to change their circumstances and more feel adequately provided for. By contrast, the residents in other hostels wish for change and have a greater desire for improvement. The views of the independent interviewers confirm the advantage held by the ISH group in terms of overall quality of life. Additionally, as one might expect, the readmission rate is significantly lower among the ISH residents.

The ISH residents' quality of life and care appears to be good, and they are reluctant to contemplate returning to live in hospital. They are more secure than their community counterparts and the physical standards of the homes are high. They value their independence and the privacy afforded to them in homely surroundings. Whether their quality of life and care would be superior in any alternative setting is beyond the scope of this enquiry, but this seems doubtful. Many of the residents had behavioural problems which made it impossible for them to live in unsupported accommodation, and few had the social skills necessary to transfer to more independent living, although the organisation was able to provide this for those who made sufficient progress and wished to move on.

The results of the present study lend weight to the argument that most residents are using hostel accommodation during a lengthy and critical life-period (Segal and Liese 1991) and that only a minority require care as part of a short-term, transitional arrangement. If Lelliot and others (1993) are correct and more residential care is needed, then, on the present evidence, the independent sector might well be able to provide the quality of care and quality of life demanded by the public, provided that this was done within the context of an adequate range of community services, as recommended by the House of Commons Health Committee (House of Commons 1994a).

Chapter 6

Quality of life of clients of a social services department

INTRODUCTION

There have been few worthwhile surveys of the mental health caseloads of social services departments in England and Wales. As was mentioned in the introduction, this study is particularly relevant for two reasons. First, in the UK, social services departments (SSDs) are designated as the lead agencies in respect of the provision of social care in the community for resettled individuals with serious and disabling mental disorders. Second, service impact has been identified as being the keystone of evaluation.

The few studies which do exist are more about services than the actual impact of services on the lives of clients within those services. For example, Fisher *et al.* (1984) studied, in detail, the mental health social work services of an English county but did not look into the lives of clients, concentrating, rather, on their views of services. This is to say, the study directed its attention to service processes and outputs rather than outcomes.

One important piece of research undertaken to rectify this paucity of client-centred research has been reported by Jones *et al.* (1986). They studied the quality of life of ninety-eight patients discharged from Clifton, Naburn and Bootham Park hospitals in York, UK. Two samples were chosen. The first included all ex-long-stay patients (n=50) who had been continuously in hospital for one year prior to discharge. More than one half of this group were schizophrenic and only five were living with their own family or in their own homes. The second was an elderly, confused group (n=203 aged 65 or older) 58 per cent of whom had died or returned to hospital prior to the survey.

Interviewers completed a battery of in-depth interviews, checklists and detailed case studies on each patient. The interviews varied in length, between one and three hours. Unexpectedly, they found most patients unable to complete the interview using the York scale. Consequently, in the end, most information was taken from 'people such as relatives, officers in charge of homes, landladies, hostel wardens, and hospital staff' (Jones *et al.* 1986:539). According to the definition and methods discussed previously, this would not have constituted a sufficiently adequate assessment of subjective features such as self-esteem, affect and satisfaction to be considered as a true quality of life study.

The findings of this study justified further work in several respects and we understand (personal communication) that Jones asked to extend this research but was unable to obtain the support to do so. A much larger and, if possible, more representative sample was required if a true picture of community care was to emerge. The research needed to be duplicated in a much larger geographical region, one which included within its catchment area the range of rural, suburban and urban settings. In addition, a briefer questionnaire, which patients themselves could complete, needed to be developed. A questionnaire which cannot be completed by most respondents cannot be expected to give reliable and valid information concerning their satisfactions.

A COUNTY-WIDE SURVEY: AIMS AND CONTENT

Full-scale employment of the quality of life interview, surveying the long-term mental health caseload of a county council social services department, was undertaken between 1990 and 1992. The purpose of this work was twofold. The first objective was to gain a cross-sectional picture of the agency's caseload at this time. This was important, as the agency was about to reorganise in order to conform to the changes required of agencies by government under its 'community care' legislation. The survey would provide a useful baseline against which to judge the post-reorganisation agency's progress, or otherwise, in relation to a meaningful outcome – client quality of life. The second objective of the survey was to get some information as to what changes in ethos and procedure might be required to make quality of life evaluation an integrated part of future professional work practices.

At the time, the department was structured into six divisions, each roughly coterminous with a local health district, managed by a central headquarters group. In turn, each division had up to six teams (organised variously on either local area or district boundaries), each one containing a mental health team. Also contained within the county catchment area were two large, long-stay hospitals which were being run down, in accordance with government policies.

Obtaining a sample

Readers familiar with the day-to-day workings of large, public-sector health and social care agencies will recognise that there are considerable difficulties in obtaining a sample truly representative of the operations of such an agency. As the purpose of this book is to examine examples of the implementation of quality of life measures in the evaluation of services, it is important to consider in some detail these difficulties and how they were resolved.

A preliminary survey was made of the caseloads of the agency's social workers. This effort to gain an accurate estimate of the actual workload proved to be, in itself, quite a novel undertaking. All operational groups were contacted and all responded. One hundred and twelve specialist mental health social workers, from all six social services divisions, returned lists which detailed the contents of their caseloads. For each client on his or her caseload, workers were invited to give the individual's name (or an identification number), whether or not the client had been formerly a resident of a long-stay mental hospital, their current type of accommodation and the status of the case (i.e. open/closed).

Workers were given several strict criteria upon which to base their selections. Individuals were to be selected who, at the time of selection, were suffering from severe mental illness. The histories of the selected individuals, as revealed by the case record and/or personal knowledge of the case, should have indicated clearly that their disorder was of long standing (i.e. two years or more) and that the individual's mental condition had been confirmed previously by psychiatric diagnosis. Each selected individual should have had 'illness careers', characterised by frequent contact with the specialist services, including frequent or lengthy periods of inpatient treatment by the specialist psychiatric services and maintenance on psychotropic drugs. At the time of their selection for the survey, the individuals should have been resident (normally) in the community.

In determining case status, workers were invited to classify their cases into the following two categories: *closed cases*, i.e. those clients who, after a period of care or treatment, were no longer in regular contact with the agency or under statutory care; and *open cases*, i.e. those who were still in contact either on a regular basis (*active*) or on a sporadic or infrequent basis (*inactive*). Closed cases were excluded, but all open cases were included. Workers were invited to indicate which clients they thought unsuitable for interview for clinical reasons – usually interpreted as acute illness or temporarily in hospital. Also excluded from the count were clients who suffered from conditions which were complicated by severe learning difficulties, or who were so severely afflicted by dementia as to make them completely unable to respond to the interview, or whose diagnosis and treatment would fall properly within the remit of child and adolescent psychiatry services.

The caseload of every specialist mental health fieldworker (i.e. professionally trained social workers and untrained staff in posts such as those of community support workers) in all fieldwork bases were reviewed. Judgements about inclusion on the case list were made by specialist social workers and their managers, with reference to their own knowledge of the individuals and their case records. Using these criteria, agency social workers reported 1,424 open mental health cases of individuals with severe, long-term mental health problems resident in the community. As the result was to be a survey of the agency caseload, every effort had been made to collect a sample which was restricted to those individuals considered to be clients of the agency. As it transpired, identifying them became a very daunting task as, for the first time, selection procedures were making an attempt to differentiate between classes of cases. Also, at the time of the study, the agency caseload had not yet been computerised and most record keeping was manual.

Divisional responses

This study was intended to produce a profile of the population of the entire county. Considerable effort was expended in accruing a randomised quota sample from each specialist team and individual worker in it. As the usefulness of the findings depend on the success of this sampling, the structure of the sample finally obtained is presented and discussed first.

The researcher (JO) selected a random, stratified sample of 1,034 cases, out of a total agency caseload of 1,424 cases from the caseloads of 112 area team and hospital mental health social workers, as being potentially suitable for interview. This averaged out at nine interviews per worker during the period. No worker was requested to complete more than sixteen such interviews, entailing slightly more than eight hours interviewing during the survey period. Workers and teams were excused from interviewing for various reasons:

1   *A lack of suitable cases on their caseloads.* One area team dealt exclusively with acute cases, work with long-term cases being undertaken by the local hospital team. In other instances, workers dealt exclusively with clients with learning disabilities. In other instances, the emergent community mental health support teams had begun to take over the long-term cases of the area teams.

2   *Inadequate staffing.* In one instance, an entire area team was excluded because it had no members currently in post. In the instance of several area teams and one hospital team, staffing levels were so low that routine operational duties were in danger of being neglected. This included teams with a very high level of work associated with emergency admissions or the activities of Mental Health Act Tribunals.

3   *Changes in described functions of posts.* In other instances, posts had been redesignated away from mental illness since their establishment. Some workers, it transpired, dealt exclusively with clients with learning disabilities, even though their official job designation described them as working with all forms of mental disorder.

4   *Clinical pressures.* Workers from county drug teams were excluded. The nature of their clientele was such that managers feared these clients might cease contact with the agency if approached for details of their personal life.

Also, an individual client could be excluded from the study if he or she was judged to be too ill to benefit from the interview, if the interview was likely to lead to a deterioration in his or her clinical state, or if he or she declined to be interviewed for any other reason.

Prior to the survey, social work teams did not have a standard definition of what was meant by an open and closed case and many found the descriptions supplied by the researchers difficult to apply to their own working practices. Many of the cases described initially as open but inactive were, in effect, closed. This had the unpleasant effect of inflating the size of the agency caseload for this client group. Despite detailed enquiries, it proved subsequently impossible to tell exactly how great this effect was, but it doubtless accounted for a great proportion of those who were selected for interview but who were not interviewed. Later work, which introduced an annual audit of the agency caseload, confirmed a great deal of confusion within the agency on this matter. This was partly procedural – i.e. people were not used to thinking of cases in this way. It also highlighted the lack of a proper information system. The latter is a failing of community care in other parts of the UK (Huxley and Oliver 1993).

Numbered forms were then returned to each team with instructions for completion of interviews. In instances where cases initially selected for interview turned out eventually to be unsuitable, a random selection procedure was implemented for case replacement. This was based on the teams selecting the next available case from their list, in descending alphabetical order of last name. Where there were no more available cases on a worker's list, the next appropriate case to enter the worker's caseload during the course of the study was to be interviewed. An administrative procedure was implemented for tracking cases.

Special local training sessions were arranged upon request to clarify issues arising from the project. During this period, detailed discussions took place between the fieldworkers, their managers and the researcher. The contents of the original lists and the selection procedures were reviewed in great detail and clarified with managers and individual professionals. When adjustments were made every precaution was taken to ensure that cases were being included or excluded according to the study criteria alone. While what emerged was a true picture of the caseload of the agency as the operational staff were able to deliver it, there was a general pattern of reduction in the number of cases deemed to be available and a readjustment of the interview quotas. The time-span of the survey was planned for no more than twelve weeks, i.e. July to September 1990. However, as insufficient numbers of completed interviews were received by this deadline date (i.e. less than fifty), a series of new deadlines ensued. The last interviews to be included in the survey analysis were received in May 1991. A total of 422 questionnaires were finally received and processed. This represented 29.6 per cent of the total caseload and 40.8 per cent of the cases originally suggested for interview.

Within and among the divisions there was a range of successes in contacting users and completing interviews. All teams responded and, eventually, twenty-four teams conducted interviews. These included sixteen area mental health teams, three district general hospital psychiatric social work teams, one long-stay hospital team and four community mental health support teams. Where teams responded, the number of interviews per team ranged from six (1.4 per cent of the total sample) to seventy-two (17.1 per cent of the total sample). It transpired that teams such as hospital teams carried a disproportionately large share of the aftercare work (the client group on which the survey focused), while area teams were focusing on crisis work and first-time hospital admissions. Only three teams actually refused ultimately to take part in the data gathering, these objections being due to other severe work pressures at the time. All refusals were also authorised/confirmed by the Divisional Director (Senior Operational Manager) for that area.

A CLIENT GROUP PROFILE: RESULT

In reporting the results of the County Social Services Department Survey, figures presented are based on the entire sample, unless otherwise stated. In many cases, some information was missing. However, cases were not excluded from analysis where the amount of missing data was modest (i.e. less than ten items per interview) as this was not felt likely to affect the overall results of the survey. Where information was available (i.e. in respect of demographic characteristics and objective quality of life indicators), the sample has been compared to the general population of Lancashire or the United Kingdom.

Demography

Age

The average age of respondents was 45.7 years and they ranged in age from 17 to 91 years. Chronically mentally disordered respondents were frequently in their middle years, the 35-to-49-year group or younger. In fact, 14.3 per cent of the caseload was at or beyond retirement age. This distribution is important, in that it reflects the reality that mental disorder affects people of all ages. The age structure indicates that maintaining such individuals in the community will continue to be a long-term endeavour which requires services relevant to all age-groups from adolescence to old age.

Comparison with the general Lancashire population shows that the structure of this group does not conform to normal demography (Chi-squared = 11, p=.001) with some 'selectivity' of the caseload derived from age bias (Figure 6.1). Due to mismatches in age ranges between the two populations (i.e. county statistics refer to 15–19 years age-group while the survey refers to 18–19 years only), those individuals below the age of 20 years have been excluded from this comparison. However, this group is likely to be far below the proportion of the general population for its age group. Chronic severe mental disorder is rare in people under 20 because of the lengthy period (i.e. two years) for which individuals must have severe disorders before many clinicians will consider their conditions as chronic or long term.

It is important to view the age structure of such a group in the context of respondents' disorder (Figure 6.1). It is probable that the average age of onset of illness approximates age at first admission. In this instance, average age of first admission was 29.6 years, with some users having been admitted for the first time as early as age 2 or as late in life as 87 years. This seems unusual and doubtless reflects some inaccuracy. However, it may well reflect a degree of truth. Severe childhood disorders, such as early infantile autism or disintegrative psychosis, might begin to manifest themselves even during the pre-school period of development, while disorders of the elderly, such as dementia or late-life depression, can show no signs until well after retirement age. The tragedy of mental disorder, however, is that frequently occurring severe mental disorders, such as schizophrenia, do manifest themselves so frequently in late adolescence and young adulthood. This is reflected in our survey, where nearly two-thirds of the sample had onset of illness prior to the age of 30 years. Many people in this group do not recover completely and require monitoring and support by community services. Hence, they are overrepresented in the caseloads and produce this distortion in the statistics. The distribution of the survey group can be seen to be

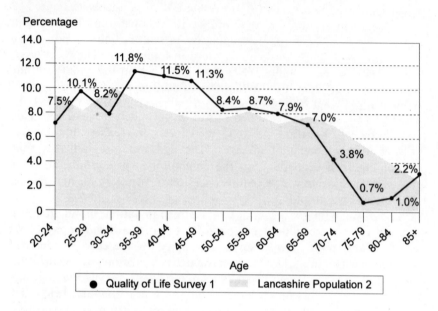

Percentage

Figure 6.1 Phase V quality of life survey sample and Lancashire population, age 20 years or older, compared
Note: 1 Quality of life survey sample: average age = 45.7 years: range = 17–91
2 Friedman two-way Anova: Chi-squared = 11.0; D. F.=1 p=.001

multi-modal (i.e. presenting many points of increased frequency). The ages of onset roughly correspond to periods of adult human growth and development described by some psychoanalytic theorists. This interesting finding is being investigated for its implications for professional case-work practice.

Gender

There was little variation from the normal distribution of Lancashire residents in the distribution of cases according to respondents' gender. The SSD's sample comprised 46.9 per cent males and 53.1 per cent females, corresponding closely to the 48.2 per cent male and 51.8 per cent female distribution of the county for members of the same age-groups.

Ethnic origins

The predominant ethnic group from which each respondent originated was identified. Ethnicity was taken to denote a sense of individual or corporate identity derived from having a religion, language or specific area of individual or family origin. White UK respondents accounted for 96.18 per cent of the entire sample, with 3.8 per cent belonging to different ethnic groups. It would appear that the survey population mirrors the distribution of ethnic groups in Lancashire. The most recent reliable data to be consulted (Eriksson 1987), found the county's ethnic population to account for a virtually identical 3.52 per cent of the general population of Lancashire at the time of the survey.

Objective well-being in nine life domains

As mentioned above, information was gathered in respect of discrete life domains, or areas of activity. The information taken was highly selected, with the intention of producing a picture indicative of key features of the lives of users, rather than a comprehensive picture. We begin by discussing the external, or 'objective', facts of users' lives as they were described to the interviewers. Where possible, these are compared with relevant government statistics for the area. The previous discussions concerning similarities and discrepancies in demographic characteristics of the sample must be borne in mind. Table 6.1 summarises the comparison of selected demographic and social indicators with data drawn from studies of the general population.

Table 6.1:   Social and demographic indicators compared: objective well-being of the survey and general populations compared

Indicator	Survey group	General population
Employed	12.8%	74.2/52.0%
Work (hrs/week)	23.6 hrs	42/37.5 hrs
Leisure	95.3%	99%
Income (£/week)	£67.56	£259.50/182.30
Living alone	35.6%	26%
Victims	15.4%	16%
Criminality	6.7%	3.5%
Single state	43.6%	30%
GP consultation	67–78.1%	13–19%
Chronicity	100%	26–63%

Employment

One of the first observations to be made concerning the way in which continuing mental health problems affect an individual's life is in respect of employment. Early onset of illness, long periods of hospitalisation and a long period of taking powerful medication result in severe disability. Marking such disability are cognitive, affective, volitional, perceptual and behavioural deficits. Biographies frequently emerge which are characterised by long periods of economic inactivity, loss of the initiative to gain employment and maintain work routines and the inability to develop a stable career pattern or pursue either vocational training or academic education.

Not surprisingly, only fifty-four respondents (12.8 per cent) were employed at the time of interview, leaving 368 (87.2 per cent) unemployed. These rates compare very unfavourably with the general economic activity rates of 74.2 per cent for men and 52.0 per cent for women over the age of 16 reported for the North-West region (Central Statistical Office 1991b:151). Even accounting for people beyond retirement age, there remains a substantial difference in rate of unemployment among our respondents compared with the general population (Chi-squared = 62.8; p=800).

Taking all respondents together, the average number of hours worked per week by the sample was 4.3. This was taken to include sheltered as well as open employment. Of those users who were employed, around three-quarters (75.9 per cent) worked less than full time. The average number of hours per week worked by all employed respondents was 23.6. This can be compared with, for example, all full-time men in the North-West region, whose average weekly working hours reported for the year 1990 are 42.3, and women, whose hours are 37.5 (Central Statistical Office 1991b:165-6).

Consequently, the gross weekly pay for the group as a whole was low – only £10.51. Considering only those who were in employment, the incentives for working were few. The average gross pay was £60.52 per week, with 50 per cent of the sample receiving less than £15.00 per week from wages or salaries and only 20 per cent receiving £100.00 per week or more.

Leisure activities

Respondents were interviewed about a selection of their leisure-time and recreational activities. In view of the high level of unemployment just cited above, knowledge of which activities are available and utilised by community residents is especially important. Previous pilots showed that sports, shopping, use of bus or car transport and television or radio were activities which most contributed to global quality of life. Only eighty-five (20.1 per cent) had been engaged recently in watching or playing a sport. Most had, however, been shopping (358, or 84.4 per cent) or utilised bus or cars for leisure (338, or 80.1 per cent). Almost all had either watched or listened to television or radio (402, or 95.3 per cent). This rate was nearly identical to the 99 per cent participation rate reported in the UK for these home-based leisure activities across all age-groups (Central Statistical Office 1991a:60). Unfortunately, the majority (253, or 60 per cent) had experienced recently some form of inhibition in respect of leisure. This is to say that they had been prevented from pursuing leisure activities when they would have preferred to have done so.

Religion

Religious practices and beliefs are difficult to measure in the population, and these difficulties are exaggerated in populations with certain types of severe mental health problems. Nevertheless, when asked, most users considered themselves Protestant (225, or 53.3 per cent). The second largest religious group was Roman Catholic, accounting for 104 (24.6 per cent) of users. Approximately 10 per cent of users were of other minority religions such as Muslim, Hindu or 'other' (8.7 per cent). Only one in ten had no religious affiliation.

However, subscribing to a religion is not the same as practising one. Most (291, or 69 per cent) had not attended church in the previous month. The average church attendance rate was once per month.

Finances

The evidence of the survey suggests that there is little accurate knowledge as to the finances of these users. Weekly income was said to range from nothing to £400.00 per week. The average income reported was £67.56. This was in sharp contrast to the mean national income for all employees of £269.50 for men and £182.30 for women (Central Statistical Office 1991a:40). A large proportion of users were in receipt of state benefits of some sort. However, whether they were in receipt of their proper entitlement is unknown, as 89 (21.1 per cent) reported being turned down upon application for a benefit within the previous year.

Clients were asked to estimate the amount of money which they felt they needed to maintain what in their eyes was an adequate quality of life. On the whole, their wants were meagre, with more than half reporting that an additional £30.00 per week would be sufficient and a quarter requiring an additional £15.00 or less. The average required for the entire group was £47.66. If achieved this would bring the total average income of the group to £115.22 per week, or £5,991.44 per year.

Living conditions

Figure 6.2 displays the housing types in which our respondents were most commonly found to be residents. Most were living in owner-occupied private houses (120, or 28.4 per cent), flats (99, or 23.5 per cent) or rented private houses (82, or 19.4 per cent). Supported housing schemes such as hostels and Part III homes, boarding-out, group homes, sheltered

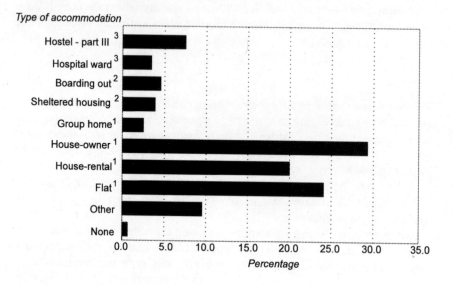

Figure 6.2 Percentage of respondents by accommodation type and level of supervision
Note: 1 No residential supervision
2 Less than twenty-four-hour staffed residential supervision
3 Twenty-four-hour staffed residential supervison

housing and hospital wards, taken together, provided for only 18.4 per cent of users. A crude organisation of these housing types according to levels of supervision provided shows a general trend for those individuals and their families who were on the agency's caseload to tend to be those who were living in housing without any integral form of support.

It was interesting to note that the high levels of homelessness amongst similar groups of users reported elsewhere in the UK did not apply in this sample, with only two users being without accommodation at interview. Of the 2,700 people found recently to be 'sleeping rough' in England and Wales, nearly 50 per cent were in London (Shelter 1992). Many of these have been said to have long-standing mental health problems. If the sampling procedure was correct, few of the respondents who were in regular contact with the county service were homeless.

Clients ranged from one month to sixty years in the length of current residence, averaging 110.9 months or just over nine years. More than one-third (35.6 per cent) of clients lived alone, and just over nine out of ten (90.1 per cent) lived in households of seven or fewer people. Most did not live with a family (261, or 61.8 per cent). A large proportion (64.0 per cent) cited their living situation as inhibiting their quality of life.

While the national trend has been for an increase of one-person households, currently 26 per cent of adults live alone (Central Statistical Office 1992:40), not significantly less than in the present sample.

Legal and safety

Bearing in mind that crime statistics are frequently unreliable, users were questioned as to whether or not they had been accused of a crime, and 6.7 per cent had been within the past year. This rate is 100 per cent greater than the general population. More frequently (15.4 per cent), they had been victims of crimes themselves. This rate is similar to the approximately 16 per cent of the general UK population reported to have been victims of crime in 1988 (Central Statistical Office 1992:207). This contributed to some sense of insecurity, as 17.3 per cent reported that they had required police help within the past year but had not been able to get any. This point might bear further investigation, as these users tend to be vulnerable individuals who are now residing in the general community, which is a less protective environment than the long-stay hospitals which had previously housed many of them.

Family relations

Only 15.4 per cent of the sample were currently married. By far the largest category was 'single,' comprising 184 (43.6 per cent) of the sample. This rate for single people is approximately 50 per cent greater than for the general population. Practically all of the others had been married but were currently widowed (12.2 per cent), divorced (22.7 per cent) or separated (13.8 per cent). The reproduction rate among these users was not high, with 200 (47.4 per cent) childless and an average of 1.2 children per user.

   This high level of individuals who are unmarried in comparison with the general population is typical of this particular user group. It is hardly surprising that people who frequently develop a serious mental disorder during their late adolescence and early adulthood, resulting in prolonged periods of drug treatment with major tranquillisers and of hospital confinement on single-sex wards, neither marry nor reproduce at a 'normal' rate. It is quite possible that one of the underlying rationales of the management regimes to which such individuals have been exposed, particularly in the past, has been to discourage such behaviour. For those who do marry (54 per cent), a severe long-term mental health condition frequently contributes to separation (3.8 per cent) and divorce (22.7 per cent).

   In spite of the above, the users were not without family contact. Only 9.4 per cent had contact with some family member less frequently than annually, and nearly three-quarters (74.1 per cent) of all users were in contact with family at least weekly. The sample was split about evenly over whether or not they had encountered any inhibitors to family contact, with 45.5 per cent reporting that they had.

Social relations

The largest group of users reported that they had no need for friends (60.9 per cent). In spite of this, most did have close friends (269, or 63.7 per cent) and 'reliable alliances' (individuals on whom one can depend) (263, or 62.3 per cent). A substantial number of users (191, or 45.3 per cent) had made contact with their friends during the previous week.

Health

The general state of health for this group was poor. In the previous twelve months, two-thirds (67 per cent) had consulted a doctor for their physical health and more than three-quarters (78.1 per cent) for their mental health or 'nerves'. Regional consultation rates with general practice for the North-West are reported as ranging from 13 to 19 per cent for people of all age-groups beyond the age of 16 years (Central Statistical Office 1991b:116), the differences between the groups being highly significant (Chi-squared = 65.8; p=.001).

All clients were selected carefully for the study as having long-standing conditions. The North-West records between 26 per cent (in the younger age-groups 16–44 years) and 63 per cent (in the over-65s) of the general population as having long-standing illnesses of some description (Central Statistical Office 1991b:116). The subjects' long-term mental disorders were characteristically punctuated by early hospital admissions. Although there may have been some inaccuracy in the data due to respondents' difficulties in recall, it would appear that more than one-quarter of the sample (i.e. 27.4 per cent) was admitted to hospital for the first time for a psychiatric disorder prior to the age of 20, with an average age of first admission of 29.2 years.

Indicators of the serious state of their mental disabilities were the facts that 172 (41.5 per cent) of respondents had been hospitalised for a nervous condition during the previous year and that 313 (76.7 per cent) were currently in receipt of medication for their mental condition. Additionally, 123 (30 per cent) respondents had their mental disorder complicated by a continuing physical disability. These are only indicators, however, and it would have been useful to have had additional information on skills, abilities, signs and symptoms levels to supplement these findings.

A further analysis was undertaken to discriminate between the health conditions of those who were and those who were not currently in receipt of medication. Receipt of medication was not associated with any measures of subjective well-being, including mental health. It was associated with both the use of health services and the duration of the person's illness. In respect of service usage, as one might predict, those who were taking medication were more likely to have been seeing a doctor for treatment (Chi-squared=53.5; D.F=1; p=.000) and to have been recently hospitalised for their nerves (Chi-squared=21.3; D.F.=1; p=.000). Those who were taking medication were, on average, younger (44.5 years) than those who were not (48.7 years) (t=2.34; D.F.=401; p=.02) and had a shorter duration of illness (14.8 years) than those who were not on medication (18.4 years) (t=2.0; D.F.=340; p = .05).

In the whole group, approximately one-quarter of the clients interviewed were living drug-free lives at the time of interview. This does not mean that they had never been mentally disordered, or that they did not have a chronic condition. They were simply functioning without medication at the time. Their quality of life was neither enhanced nor diminished by being off drugs. They tended to be older people with longer histories of illness, though not significantly so. These findings perhaps correspond with those of other studies, which have found that community residents with chronic, recurring psychiatric conditions may experience less symptom severity after a long period of time.

Subjective well-being

Perceived quality of life

A principal measure of subjective well-being incorporated into the interview is that of 'perceived' quality of life, or the degree of satisfaction of respondents in respect of life in each domain. Average scores were computed for life satisfaction measures for each domain respectively. Inspection of these scores reveals that the highest level of expressed satisfaction was in respect of legal and safety (Figure 6.3). Following that, religion was rated second; social relations, third; living situation, fourth; leisure, fifth; family relations, sixth; health, seventh; work, eighth; and finance, ninth and lowest.

In view of the great impact which work has in Western society, it is customary to break down the satisfaction figures for that domain between those who are employed and those who are unemployed. When this happens, great disparities appear. The average work satisfaction level for those unemployed was 3.62, while the level for those in employment was much higher, at 4.59 (thus ranking fourth in average life satisfaction levels among domains). It would appear that some work, even if often poorly paid and part time, is associated with higher levels of satisfaction.

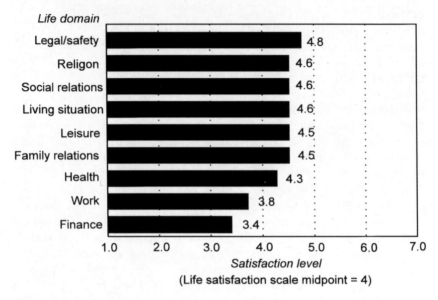

Figure 6.3 Perceived quality of life: profile of average life satisfaction levels across all life domains

In fact, despite the objective indicators cited above, most respondents tended to be satisfied, even if marginally so, in most life domains. Some of the average satisfaction scores cited above were very close indeed, and it is not easy to see the differences among domains. To illuminate the differences, scores can be broken down into three categories – i.e. 'clearly satisfied', 'clearly dissatisfied' and 'uncertain' – with every attempt being made to minimise the size of the last group. This presents a slightly different picture of the rank order among life domains, with living situation (71.3 per cent satisfied) and leisure (67.4 per cent satisfied) moving into second and third position. Only in work (39.7 per cent) and finance (32.1 per cent) are levels of satisfaction outweighed by levels of dissatisfaction.

Self-esteem

Psychology provides many conflicting definitions of the 'self' and proposes many potential features of the 'self system', including, for example, 'self-control', the 'social self', the 'ideal self', the 'real self' and 'self-respect'. Nevertheless, psychological constructs such as the 'self' are important foci for direct interventions in social casework. For research purposes we have focused on one central aspect of self system, i.e. self-esteem. Self-esteem may be thought of as a psychological quality which results from reflective evaluations or appraisals an individual makes of him or herself and the degree of approval or disapproval which results. The level of self-esteem is presumed to play an important role in determining a person's attitudes (levels of aspirations, satisfactions and self-acceptance) and individual and group behaviour (including competence) (Rosenberg 1965; Wells and Marwell 1976). Not surprisingly, although the research evidence is ambiguous, self-esteem which tends towards the 'high' or 'positive' is usually held to be indicative of healthy mental adjustment and social effectiveness, while 'low' or 'negative' suggests the converse.

More than half the respondents (58.8 per cent) had self-esteem which was 'positive', while 31.8 per cent were, on balance, 'negative'. The remaining 9.5 per cent were evenly balanced between the two. Considering the long-term effects on the individuals' 'selves' of multiple social and economic deprivations as well as hospitalisation and symptomatology, it could be interpreted as a strength that fewer were not located in the 'negative' category.

Mental health

In view of the fact that social services departments provide 'mental health' services to the public it seems particularly appropriate to have some direct measure of this state in users. We have taken mental health to be a complex state, more than simply the absence of mental illness. It can be represented as a balance between a person's present acute symptomatology (i.e. 'negative affect') and their strengths. This latter feature is taken to be indicated by adaptability or ability to cope with novelty ('positive affect'). While it is a subjective measure it is not a direct measure of life satisfaction. One might view mental health as a constituent part of overall well-being or, clinically, at least a partial reflection of 'ego strength'; though the point is made (Bowling 1991:156) that the scales employed (Bradburn 1969) are said to be more a reflection of happiness than mental disorder.

In spite of the continuing nature of their psychiatric conditions, many respondents (39 per cent) had a positive mental health rating at present, a point which must not be overlooked when dealing with this group. Often, recurring bouts of illnesses, and even the residue of chronic symptoms accompanying such serious illnesses, are themselves accompanied by intermittent periods of relative 'health'.

Cantril's ladder: a disparity between expectations and achievements

The LQOLP incorporates various measures of overall or 'global' well-being. Some, while intending to take into account both objective and subjective factors of life, are actually subjective appraisals by the user. One such measure is Cantril's ladder (Cantril 1965), a widely used, 100-point scale which adjudges current life from 'the best' which the user could have expected to 'the worst'. Despite the objective facts of life, there is a general tendency towards overall satisfaction. However, approximately two-fifths (39.4 per cent) rated life overall below the scale midpoint of 50.

It is observed quite often that there is a wide discrepancy between the 'objective' facts of one's life and what one makes of these facts, i.e. our subjective appraisals. It is difficult to make direct comparisons between the two types of information principally because they are different types of information. How does one compare level of income with a subjective state? In the development of theory, perceived quality of life was one advance, as it allows for a domain-by-domain assessment of self-appraisal against material, external circumstances. The same comparisons are not easily made for global well-being, however. While it is possible to give, subjectively, an overall appraisal of one's life it is not easy to summarise the objective features of that life into a single, cardinal score for comparison. One alternative is to compare a user's subjective appraisal of global well-being with that of an independent source. We have adopted this approach, employing a contiguous global appraisal by the interviewer, the user's social worker.

Figure 6.4 shows a comparison of global well-being measured by users (Cantril's ladder) and workers (quality of life uniscale, also a 100-point analogue scale). The mean scores of the two appraisals were both

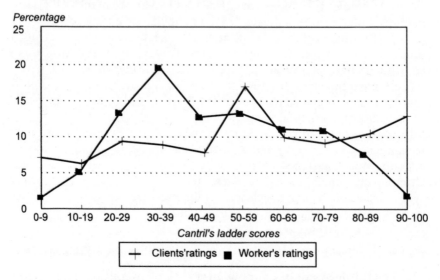

Figure 6.4 Two global well-being scales: clients'[1], and workers'[2] global quality of life ratings compared[3]
Note: 1 Cantril's ladder
2 Quality of life uniscale
3 t=4.66; D.F.=402; p=.001

substantially and significantly different, with users giving a higher (54.9) average rating to their well-being than workers (47.8). While the two measures were significantly correlated, the correlation was not a strong one (r=.31). The fact that some differences between the two were detected is not surprising in that the general well-being measures are taken from different perspectives, which will include different values and experiences and the fact that both are possibly addressing somewhat different parameters of well-being. It is rather as if the two groups (i.e. clients and workers) were talking about the same thing (i.e. well-being) but had divergent opinions as to its nature and degree.

Happiness

Another separate, but related, measure of global well-being is the subjective appraisal of 'happiness'. Happiness is a generalised state of well-being which probably incorporates moods – e.g. 'gaiety and elation' – attitudes and many other felt factors (Campbell *et al.* 1976). Clients most frequently described themselves as either 'pretty happy' (53 per cent) or 'very happy' (9.9 per cent). Nevertheless, a substantial proportion of more than one-quarter (27.2 per cent) described themselves as 'not happy'.

THE LONG-TERM MENTAL HEALTH CASELOAD: A SUMMARY

It is always difficult to aggregate human experiences. In doing so, some of the individual differences which people display are invariably lost. This is possibly magnified when the manner of investigation stresses a quantitative data and a structured approach to information gathering such as the one employed here. In reality, each person's quality of life profile is presumed to be essentially unique. It is arrived at as a sort of balance which each user was in the process of negotiating out of his or her current total life situation. Accepting this makes us cautious about over-generalising from what has been found. This generalisability is also restricted by a lack of 'normative' information from studies of the general population, particularly in respect of mental health and life satisfactions. Nevertheless, other studies of the mentally ill in the community in the UK and elsewhere tend to substantiate some of our findings (Lehman *et al.* 1982; Jones *et al.* 1986; Pryce and Preston 1988; MacGilip 1991).

The first aim of the study was to gain a cross-sectional picture of the agency's caseload prior to reorganisation. It transpires that lives of Lancashire Social Services Department caseload clients who have continuing and serious mental health problems and who are resident in the community can now be described in considerable detail. As we are moving into an era of community care, it is critical for a service agency to have such a revealing profile. Both in terms of health and welfare, the lives of such users are strongly characterised by 'multiple disadvantages'.

Demographically, the users interviewed approximate the general population distribution for Lancashire in terms of gender and ethnicity. However, their age distribution differs noticeably from the general population in two areas. First, people whose ages fall within the 35-60 age bands were overrepresented. This is important because this is a period in the life-cycle associated with economic and social/family activity. Among other things, these vital functions appear profoundly influenced and require a degree of external support. Second, the very elderly were underrepresented. Certainly, at the time of the survey, many elderly mentally disordered were being cared for in residential or nursing homes or being supported at home by social workers from elderly services and were not on the caseloads of mental health specialists. Estimates of the national proportions of elderly residents nationally with mental disorders vary widely but one estimate (probably an underestimate), generally employed for local government planning purposes, has placed the number at 30 per cent of all elderly residents (see Welsh Office 1989).

Economically, users tend to be disproportionately unemployed, have lowered levels of disposable income, and are frequently dependent on state benefits. The disadvantage is not simply a matter of objective comparison to community standards. Clients also felt less satisfied. In these respects, material deprivation was found to be translated into lowered subjective well-being. Yet their economic aspirations were found to be modest – i.e. to increase their standard of living to the lower rungs of the average income range. As discussed in Chapter 2, one important means of rectifying these disadvantages – education – was so poorly utilised among this group that the relevant questions were discarded from the interview after earlier pilots and were not then investigated in this survey.

Not surprisingly, there were some 'knock-on' effects of economic deprivation in the social sphere, though the actual mechanics of this process have not been investigated in the present study. For example, we do not know if it is a simple a lack of money which causes directly the experience, so frequently reported, of inhibitions in leisure pursuits. It is more than likely that the truth would prove to be complex, as the demonstrable health factors are inescapably intertwined with social and economic factors in the lives of such users.

Socially, and in respect of its living circumstances, the group produced a slightly atypical profile, though not a necessarily unpleasant or unsatisfactory one. Users are more frequently unmarried and childless than the local population, and this is an area also ranked lower in satisfaction, though not to the extent that most were dissatisfied with this aspect of their lives. Many encountered inhibiting factors to establishing or maintaining family contacts. Nevertheless, within the confines of their own expectations, many users seemed to be 'getting on with life', organising what they considered to be, both objectively and subjectively, acceptable social lives. This frequently, though not necessarily, was found to include making friends and maintaining social contacts. Also, proportionally more users lived alone than in the general population. However, the percentage difference was not great and, in comparison with other areas of life, living situation was a domain of at least moderate satisfaction. Very few users interviewed were homeless. While most users considered themselves as belonging to some discernible religious group, most did not attend services regularly and, as a group, they were comparatively satisfied with incorporating religion in their lives in this way. Respondents were more often the victims of crimes than the perpetrators.

Given the scale of overall deprivation, considerable scope was indicated for ongoing social work to ameliorate poor environmental conditions among this group. Certainly, users' general state of health, both physical and mental, was poor. They had psychiatric histories of longstanding and were currently involved in, and dependent upon, receiving health care. Their health was an area of identified low satisfaction. As a group they tended to display poor mental health at the time of interview and many were excluded from the study for that reason. However, many displayed a positive 'balance' psychologically. Likewise, though a noticeable proportion displayed poor self-esteem, the majority had a positive self-concept. Mental health and self-esteem are essential ingredients of a psychosocial assessment. The research produced evidence of personality strengths, existing in the face of serious, long-term mental health problems, and professional social work activities, such as direct casework or long-term case management, might be considered on the evidence of these strengths.

Considering all of the above, the general opinion of users concerning the quality of their lives was positive. Most expressed degrees of overall satisfaction with life in general and happiness, and most rated the quality of their lives more positively than the professionals who interviewed them.

The second aim of the study was to investigate the organisational ethos and its preparedness for the task of employing quality of life evaluations in routine service operations. This proved more problematic. On the positive side, the survey did begin to address the central challenge of the White Paper, i.e. how to move the user back to the centre of planning through individualised, consumer-based interviews. It is unclear as to whether it is a point of self-congratulation or an indictment of public services that many local authorities have not yet begun this task.

The 422 interviews recorded represents one of the largest surveys ever to be undertaken with this user group. Results could provide very useful information for planning for each of the districts who took part. This series of pilots and county-wide surveys reflects a considerable commitment by many social services staff and the entire project, from its beginning phases, has been encouraged and supported by many individual social workers and teams throughout the county. The interview itself, when applied, has been generally well received, as more than 90 per cent of users appear to be willing to be interviewed again in future. This continued cooperation is essential to any monitoring exercise. Where it has not worked well, further information could be sought to establish the circumstances under which it should or should not be applied as a means of informing any further use.

On the 'down side', the survey greatly exceeded the stated time-frame. This was coupled with a great difficulty in obtaining the cooperation of some teams, despite the fact that the survey was planned agency business. Deficits (endemic in health and social care agencies, in our experience) in an organisation's ability to define case status severely restrict the possibility of it conducting useful monitoring exercises. There was, in places, a worrying attitude among a few workers and managers that users and professional staff should not be 'bothered' by such interviews. This attitude is certainly not characteristic of the services solely in the county under study. Doubtless this attitude was sometimes justified as, for example, in the cases where users were currently acutely distressed and relapsing or where teams were genuinely understaffed. However, this reluctance to engage users was associated sometimes with the notion that if opinions were required as to the users' well-being, these should be given by professionals.

In other instances, reluctance to engage the users appeared to be related to a more general reluctance to work directly with the client group. This hesitation is not totally justified by the findings of the study, which indicated that many of the clients had many positive psychological and social characteristics which could serve as a basis for direct work should it be undertaken. This corresponds with the findings of Fisher et al. (1984), who found the same reluctance, on the part of staff in another large agency, to get down to work alleviating mental health problems, in spite of such work being the expressed preference of the mental health clients interviewed. As educators, we find it a matter of deep concern that agency staff, for whatever reasons, are no longer inclined towards undertaking such essential work as suggested by the survey's findings.

This negative disposition did not always manifest itself directly. In some instances it took the form of continued resistance to the survey for seemingly endless minor reasons (e.g. questioning the need for any information; portraying the exercise as an invasion of user privacy, instead of seeing it as an opportunity for their well-being to be made paramount, etc.). This runs directly against the current of consumer involvement prevalent in community care thinking, and such reluctance should be looked into in further detail in future research (see also Chapter 13).

Two very important points emerge concerning agency information and information strategies, of which such outcome research is part. The difficulty in identification of mental health 'caseness' produced problems in conducting a survey such as this. The ability to identify cases according to desired criteria is not a capacity which people planning service research should ever take for granted, as we have done in this instance. Rather, the agency's capacity to define cases must be understood and, if necessary, developed as a first step. With the best will in the world, busy practitioners cannot hope to assist fully unless they, in turn, are fully supported. Of considerable importance here is the installation of modern management information systems, which should be of help. (At the time of writing, the local authority has gone far to rectify this deficit by introducing 'new technology' into team management.) However, it would be wrong to let the opportunity pass to comment on the complacency existing at the time in permitting (or being ignorant of) the lamentable situation which we discovered with respect to local authority mentally ill clientele. What makes matters worse is that we know that the situation is (or, at least, was at the time) just as bad in neighbouring authorities and, perhaps, in most other parts of the UK. It can hardly come as a surprise that departments which do not have a clear record of which cases are open and which are closed (and which fail to address the obvious material and psychosocial needs of clients) and which, partly as a consequence, cannot convey meaningful information to other agencies, find themselves the subject of investigation, criticism and public indictment. The Christopher Clunis Report (House of Commons 1994b) is full of justifiable complaint about this state of affairs and its tragic consequences.

CONCLUSIONS

This survey represents the first of such efforts on broad-scale monitoring and evaluation undertaken by a large English county in connection with community care legislation. To the date of the survey, quality of life research in social care operational contexts had shown promise, but the survey cannot be called an unqualified success. Several positive and negative points concerning the employment of quality of life evaluation in routine service operations have arisen from this study. The survey has accomplished both of its intended objectives to a degree, but neither completely. Many issues have been raised – in particular, the need for the organisation to change its ethos towards a greater sympathy for monitoring and evaluation, both for the benefit of the organisation and its accountability to the public, and, more importantly, for the benefit of its service users, their families and friends.

Chapter 7

Community-based support and community mental health support teams

INTRODUCTION

This chapter describes the development and implementation of community mental health support services and focuses on teams specifically designed for the purpose. It examines one crucial dimension in the overall performance of community mental health support teams (CMHSTs), and that is the outcome or impact of the service on the quality of lives of clients receiving the service. The results and their implications have a bearing on service planning and the evaluation of the service in the future.

BACKGROUND

The policy guidance contained in the White Paper, *Better Services for the Mentally Ill* (DHSS 1975) encouraged the development of locally based health and social services in the UK. However, new community services, the responsibility of the local authority, were slow to develop and, unfortunately, many of those which appeared were institutionally based, rather than providing flexible services geared to meeting individual needs in normal surroundings. More recently, *Caring for People* (DHSS 1989) and the subsequent *NHS and Community Care Act* (DHSS 1990) have shifted the focus of the provision of community care from institutional models towards services which meet individual needs by providing 'domiciliary, day and respite services to enable people to live in their own homes wherever feasible and sensible' (DHSS 1990:5).

The rundown of the long-stay mental hospitals in recent decades and scandals of homeless mentally ill people have put the needs of people with long-term mental health problems on the political agenda. The review of community care procedures for the mentally ill commissioned by the Secretary of State and currently under way is a further reflection of these concerns. Both the Care Programme Approach (CPA) and the

Mental Illness Specific Grant (MISG) are attempts to ensure coordinated and improved community services.

People with long-term mental illness require intensive, flexible support in the community over long periods of time. By definition, such conditions require complex packages of help, including acute treatment, continuing rehabilitation and supportive health and social care (Lamb et al. 1993). Critically, a lack of social support for such people is recognised as a risk factor for rehospitalisation (Dayson et al. 1992) or criminal justice system contacts (Caton et al. 1993). Support services are often essential in compensating for the lack of a family network or alleviating burden on caregivers. Consequently, and thus not surprisingly, social support is becoming an integral part of community services in countries around the world, including Singapore (Tan 1993), Thailand (Ransibrahamanakul 1991), the USA and Canada (Torrey et al. 1993) and the UK (Dean et al. 1993; Anderson et al. 1993).

A general look at the literature, drawing on foreign as well as UK sources, reveals that a range of different types of community services actually provides support to individuals with long-term mental illnesses, including ex-psychiatric patients, though these vary widely in type. Recent published examples of services which include substantial support dimensions for the mentally ill exist in respect of: housing support schemes (Hogan and Carling 1992; Carling 1993); nursing home care support schemes (Blazek 1993); advocacy and support schemes for the homeless (Freddolino and Moxley 1992; Nordentoft et al. 1992); family psychoeducational programmes (Posner et al. 1992); hospital reprovisioning schemes (Anderson et al. 1993); and transitional resettlement schemes (Murray and Baier 1993). Frequently cited sources of community support are case management services (Curtis et al. 1992; Solomon 1992; Wasylenki et al. 1993; and see also Chapter 9, this volume) and there is evidence that the assessments made by case managers of clients' needs for support are valid (Widlak et al. 1992). One survey of case managers identified support needs of more than 1,400 clients (Ford et al. 1992). These needs included medication, monitoring, therapy, psychosocial treatment, day and employment activities and supported residential options.

However, quality of life is still to find its way into the routine evaluation of such services, though aspects of quality of life are ever present in service descriptions and evaluation criteria. For example, Boydell and Trainor (1988) described an imaginative income maintenance programme which successfully improved the financial situation of its clients by 30–40 per cent in the first thirty months of operation. An exploratory evaluation was conducted on one American community mental health support service (CSS) by Baker and Intagliata (1982) as outlined in previous chapters. They studied the quality of life of 118 clients selected from two CSS programmes in the western region of New York state: one a voluntary programme serving both rural and urban areas, and the second operating out of a state mental hospital and serving chiefly a rural one. Their findings were essentially positive. Due to the lack of established norms, however, they suggested that future evaluations focus on changes in the quality of lives of clients. Also, Baker in another study (Baker et al. 1992; Baker et al. 1993) followed up 729 patients. This work has shown that adequacy of social support successfully predicts change in global well-being assessments. Both adequacy and availability of social support were strongly related to both mental health and perceived quality of life, including changes in the latter.

Wright et al. (1989) evaluated the first four years of a community programme which offered intensive support to ex-patients who were selected because of their demonstrated inability to manage their own lives in such a fashion as to avoid frequent episodes of rehospitalisation. The study showed that, for the 196 patients in the programme, there were significant reductions in objective indicators such as hospitalisation (number of inpatient days) and criminality (number of criminal charges and subsequent custodial sentences), as well as improvements in subjective well-being and service satisfaction levels. Of course, this group was highly selected, affecting the study's external validity.

While many models exist for delivering support, a recent review by Carling (1993) explores the emergence of 'supported housing'. Reviewing many studies, the author concludes that despite their diversity such schemes generally emphasise the use of integrated community housing, flexibility in the provision of services and the provision of consumer choice. While the contents of a model community support service are still unclear, help in maintaining and improving life quality in areas such as finances, housing, leisure, assistance with medication and peer support all appear as desirable programme objectives, which probably apply to home-based care schemes (Muijen et al. 1992) in general. Importantly, 'empowering' social support services which positively affect patients' perceptions of their own mastery has been shown to improve quality of life (Rosenfield 1992; Rosenfield and Neese-Todd 1993).

Few studies exist into the development of community mental health teams in the UK. Sayce et al. (1991) reported on a survey conducted on behalf of the Sainsbury Centre during the late 1980s. More recently, in 1993, the Sainsbury Centre usefully surveyed the organisational and operational aspects of UK community mental health support teams (CMHSTs) (Onyett et al. 1994). The researchers investigated both general team characteristics and team processes in 302 teams. As will be seen below, several of their findings were very relevant, providing a useful backdrop against which to gauge the service we proceed to describe in more detail.

THE DEVELOPMENT OF COMMUNITY MENTAL HEALTH SUPPORT TEAMS (CMHSTs) IN LANCASHIRE

Against this background, in 1988, Lancashire County Council adopted a policy, 'New Futures', which aimed to provide community care services that would enable clients to live at home enjoying, while maintaining or enhancing, their quality of life. A network of community mental health support teams (CMHSTs) was established to do this.

These teams were introduced following the successful piloting of a scheme in Skelmersdale, West Lancashire, which began in 1985. Subsequently, three more teams were established in Preston (East), Blackburn and nearby Accrington. The number has expanded gradually to thirteen. In addition to those cited above, other teams operate in Fylde, Blackpool, Wyre, Darwen, Lancaster, Preston (South), Clitheroe/Ribble Valley, Chorley and Ormskirk. The first team was financed initially by central government through round two of the 'Care in the Community' initiative. Subsequently, funding was found, through the mainstream social services budget, to expand this team and establish the subsequent three. The newer teams, which commenced in 1991 or 1992, were funded through the Mental Illness Specific Grant, which was also used to fund expansions of the existing teams.

Each team consists of a social worker and varying numbers of community support workers (who are paid on the residential care officers scale, which permits work to take place out of the usual office hours). Teams are based in small-scale, ordinary premises, often private dwellings on estates, though a few still operate from social services office premises. At the time of writing, the smallest team has five full-time equivalent (FTE) members and the largest eleven and a half. All teams have on-site administrative support. A variety of management arrangements are being tried and tested and, apart from the first team established, until now all have been managed by specialist senior mental health social workers already based in area teams. Although the CMHSTs are funded through the County Council, they have been planned jointly with others (for example, health authorities and voluntary services) and, in some instances, provide a community base for workers from other disciplines, such as community psychiatric nurses (CPNs) (in the Lancaster, Blackpool and Blackburn teams).

The CMHSTs have three primary aims. First, they help to enable people with severe mental illnesses to remain living in their own homes by offering clients practical, social and emotional support, with an emphasis on improving their quality of life. Second, they offer help to carers and relatives. Third, teams link with other professionals to develop integrated community mental health services. In addition, teams have other, secondary, aims such as developing community resources, providing a link between hospital-based rehabilitation services and resettled individuals, and serving as a crucial resource in the key-worker structure demanded by the Care Programme Approach (CPA).

Support workers tailor their roles according to the needs and wishes of the service users. Overall, the support workers seek to promote integration into ordinary community life – for example, leisure centres, pubs, social outings. They act as advocates for the service users with psychiatric services, the Department of Social Security (responsible in the UK for income maintenance), legal services, employment services, housing services, etc. They provide a level of psychological security for people who are vulnerable and many of whom would have required previously long-term residential care – often in hospital.

The teams are able to monitor the mental state of individuals and, where necessary, to work with key professionals from health and social services. This may include managing the anxiety of relatives, neighbours and other professionals so that inappropriate hospital admissions do not occur. The teams attempt to promote the service users' independence and personal growth. The development of self-help support groups and various groups facilitated by team members has been an important element of the work of the teams. Men's, women's, social skills, anxiety management, and problem-solving groups have all developed as needs arise. An invaluable aspect of the teams is to provide a drop-in facility, especially at weekends when other specialist and ordinary facilities are closed. Sunday lunch groups, where service users purchase and prepare the meal, have been developed by some teams. The operational policies of all teams accept that many of the most vulnerable service users will require a long-term commitment, and in some instances life-long commitment, although the intensity of support can vary over this time.

As a matter of county policy, all the teams have attempted to translate principles of 'normalisation' into their daily practice. They provide intensive support to a small number of clients on an individual, needs-led basis. This means being available evenings and weekends and, if required, sleeping in the client's own home. Employing the community support workers on residential conditions of service has helped to achieve these objectives.

In accordance with the government's mandate to ensure the quality of services and to focus on the outcome of services, all of the teams are being evaluated in order to determine their utility and potential benefit to service users. Hence, teams regularly gather information in the form of a common referral monitoring procedure, a common periodic service audit and a quality of life interview with the client (using the LQOLP). The LQOLP was developed for operational use and, at the time of writing, had been employed in various settings within the local authority for the evaluation of mental health services. The analysis of this information and the feedback to teams form the basis for periodic reviews of their effectiveness.

The experience of planning and starting these teams has resulted in a strong initial impression about the key factors which have contributed to their success. These include: establishing local joint implementation groups, together with a county steering group, which developed clear and explicit operational policies within a clear values framework; staff selection procedures to identify effective team workers; a robust in-house training and staff development programme designed by team leaders, and an external programme of training at Manchester University School of Psychiatry for new team members; a management learning set for team leaders; a cross-team support group for the team social workers; a team approach to service users; regular individual and group supervision, including a forum for resolving staffing problems associated with interpersonal dynamics; a commitment to data collection and evaluation from all staff; and the active involvement of team managers, staff and service users in the review process. On the operational side, it appears that a major contributing factor to the success of the teams has been a strict workload management, which has allowed staff to work intensively with small numbers of clients.

A formal review of each team was completed in 1992 in conjunction with the Mental Health Social Work Research Unit (MHSWRU) at Manchester University for each of the four original teams. This process included: detailed management reports being prepared in conjunction with team members and service users; a review of the management of the teams by senior staff of social services headquarters using a semi-structured interview and meetings with key managers and teams; and data analysis, drawing on the LQOLP and referral data. The results of that initial review indicated that, with commendable effort, the CMHSTs had been successfully targeting their service on clients with serious long-term disabilities. The selection process identified a group of disabled clients with psychiatric diagnoses of chronic psychosis and histories of multiple admissions to psychiatric hospital. Targeting procedures had excluded people with learning difficulties, people whose problems are primarily alcohol and drug related, people with gross organic brain dysfunctions and people identified as likely to present a serious risk to staff working alone in their homes. The findings of this internal review were partially corroborated following a visit from the Health Advisory Service, which commended one CMHST as a service of national significance.

While the majority of referrals to CMHSTs have come from social workers, a significant number of service users have been referred by CPNs. Initially, few direct referrals were received from psychiatrists. However, the experience of the periodic review procedures since that initial report has shown an increase in referrals from both psychiatrists and general practitioners, though the patterns have been uneven across the county. Also, given the difficulties of working with this client group, a noteworthy initial finding was that staff sickness and turnover were low, while staff morale and commitment remained high.

Several characteristics of this service can be compared with or contrasted to what has been reported nationally (Onyett *et al.* 1994). Nationally, community mental health teams more frequently operate from health bases, such as community mental health centres (44.4 per cent) and hospital or inpatient units (14.2 per cent). Few operate, as do these teams, from other, more 'normalised' settings, such as houses or locality-based offices (8.6 per cent). Nationally, community mental health teams are multi-disciplinary, including, principally, social workers and nurses but also the other disciplines, such as psychiatrists and clinical psychologists. While these teams do include trained social workers and some have one or more community psychiatric nurses attached, most staff are generic social services mental health employees. The latter are usually young, somewhat inexperienced and, typically, without basic professional qualifications. Nationally, most teams have access to hospital beds. This is not generally the case with the support teams, whose relationship (i.e. level and type of contacts and links) to specialist psychiatric services varies greatly. Interestingly, user involvement is central to this support service whereas, nationally, less than half of surveyed teams sampled users views (42.7 per cent). The policy of controlled access to the team was also at variance to national practices, which tend to favour open referral systems.

It must be said that, given our primitive state of knowledge it is not always certain whether approximating a national norm with respect to organisational or working practices is always desirable. For example, community mental health team services which are more typical seem to have several disadvantages by comparison. According to Onyett *et al.* (1994), social workers and other staff employed within them are more likely to be experiencing staff burn-out than departmental reviews have found to be the case with the Lancashire service (possibly a consequence of features such as tightly managed access, caseload size and regular training). Also, the report concludes that support services located away from more conventional clinical settings and working with people in their own homes may be better able to keep their focus upon severely disabled individuals than those located in more conventional settings.

In conclusion, the experience of developing community support services for persons with serious long-term mental health problems has been positive, so far. Initial experiences were drawn on in planning the new community support teams funded by the Mental Illness Specific Grant. As mentioned above, this involved bringing together staff and managers of the established teams with planners and managers of the new teams in order to share experiences. The establishment of a group learning set, which set in motion continued development through a 'trickle down' effect, has been one of the innovative hallmarks of the service's evolution to date. There remain questions about the nature of the client group served by the 'targeted' service, given that the most dangerous patients were excluded. The target group is likely to be different from those of assertive outreach case management teams (such as the one described in Chapter 9), which specifically set out to include the most difficult patients. Whether the teams are dealing with many of the patients described in Chapter 12, those with such difficult behaviours that even 'hostel wards' (Gibbons and Butler 1987, Simpson *et al.* 1989; Bridges *et al.* 1991a, 1991b) find it impossible to cope, must remain speculative, though some quality of life research suggests that 'normal' community services rountinely do this (Oliver 1991b).

METHOD OF EVALUATION

The overall performance of teams is being assessed by various means, which cover their inputs, outputs, outcomes and relevant processes. Of the many potential targets, evaluation has tended to focus on producing descriptions of each team and its work as an agency resource; analyses of the 'economic dimension'; and a study of the quality of life of service recipients. A fourth dimension – client satisfaction – has been evaluated by means of an in-house survey. \

In addition to completing quality of life interviews with clients (as described below), each team:

- holds regular review meetings, which are attended not only by team members and management but also by headquarters policy and research staff, as well as by colleagues from health services;
- produces periodic reports which have been compiled by headquarters staff and summarised;
- produces audit information annually for the Department. This information is then reported back to the Social Services Inspectorate who, in turn, oversees MISG spending within local authorities for central government.

To facilitate this flow of information, each team keeps management information on financial, administrative and staffing matters, as well as client information, currently recorded on the client referral monitoring form developed previously for the purpose by the Department of Health. As teams develop, it is expected that they will also gather and use additional information relevant to their specific needs (for example, measures of behavioural competence to capture the impact of social skills training; measures of psychiatric morbidity as a means of establishing service need and ensuring accurate service targeting, etc.). The management learning set, mentioned above, is geared to help in the production of a uniform standard of evaluation.

A longitudinal evaluation design has been employed, with measurements being taken at set intervals to show changes in the quality of life of CMHST clients. Each client has been interviewed first at, or immediately after, the time when the CMHST has accepted the referral ('before'). Hence, clients who have been referred to the service but who have not been taken on as cases receiving ongoing support work have been excluded from the study. Clients have been interviewed again following a period of support ('after'). Though the interval was to have been one year, in fact the interval has averaged 21.5 months (range 11–27). Interviews have been undertaken by the appropriate key workers.

The evaluation procedures employed routinely should be sufficient to answer questions of service utility and benefits. The latter are highlighted by the pattern of changes shown in specific areas. Readers are reminded, though, that evidence of change, of itself, is not evidence of effectiveness. The establishment of service effectiveness is a more complex matter, requiring information on the performance of a control or comparison group. Controlled studies are possible only if there is an opportunity to restrict access in some way to a particular service, and the service users in index and control conditions must be the same. If CMHSTs are narrowly targeted and eventually provide services to all clients with particular characteristics in an area, then this is a 'fully saturated programme' (see Chapter 13), and randomised case-controlled studies become impossible within the service. The gradual introduction of CMHSTs permits comparison of similar clients in adjacent districts with and without teams and is known as a 'non-uniform full coverage programme' (see Rossi and Freeman 1993). In fact, a comparative study of individuals who have not received the service over the same period and whose life quality has been measured in before–after fashion, over a similar interval and at similar points in time to clients within the CMHST service, is underway currently. Until the results of this study become available any suggestions that the CMHSTs are effective must remain somewhat provisional.

SAMPLE

All clients were taken from the CMHST caseloads. To date, 233 people have become ongoing clients of the CMHSTs and have been interviewed using the LQOLP. Of these, seventy-eight (33.4 per cent) were clients of the original four CMHSTs at the time of the county-wide quality of life survey, in 1990–1 (which is reported in Chapter 6), when the profile became available for routine operational use. A further 155 cases have been opened and interviewed by six new teams. No results are yet available from the three most recently formed teams.

On maintaining clients within the CMHST service

To date, of 233 cases opened, fifty-two (22.3 per cent) have been re-interviewed at one year and thirteen (5.6 per cent) re-interviewed at two years. Importantly, of the seventy-eight cases opened originally, thirty-eight (48.7 per cent), or approximately half, were open for the necessary period of one year and agreed to be re-interviewed. Before proceeding to an analysis of all data available, however, the issue of case closure requires further elaboration. In a service which has, as its principal function, the maintenance of contact with and support of clients resident in the community, the proportion of clients whose cases remain open across a given period must be regarded as a valid, direct measure of service outcome.

As reported in Chapter 6, prior to the county-wide survey of quality of life undertaken in 1990, preliminary inspection of caseloads revealed that large numbers of mentally ill clients had their cases effectively closed (i.e. they were considered as either closed or inactive). This was one reason given, at the time, for the failure of some teams to respond fully to the survey. Unfortunately, it has not been possible to establish in retrospect whether or not these individuals were also those who required the ongoing support of the agency in order to remain in the community. When developing a new form of community care, the purpose of which was to supplement existing services, these points were carefully considered by managers. The community support teams were designed and brought into action precisely to give ongoing support to individuals deemed in need. Maintaining continuing contact with these individuals was seen to be an essential prerequisite to the department meeting its responsibility to provide and coordinate community-based social care, particularly as an alternative to long-term hospital care (i.e. supervision and control) and treatment.

The first seventy-eight cases opened represented those clients who were assessed as being appropriate cases for the new service in its developmental stages. Yet by the end of a relatively brief period, approximately half of the clients selected were no longer actively in contact with the service set up to support them or, which is less likely, judging by our experiences elsewhere, refused or were unable to be re-interviewed. As cases kept in treatment must be regarded as a serious indicator of the degree to which the service is targeting correctly those most relevant and/or the degree to which they are managing the difficult task of providing continuing, long-term support, this represents a clinically noteworthy finding.

Fortunately, this finding for drop-out rates established by completed quality of life interviews has been supported by statistical returns based on information from other sources (i.e. referral monitoring forms) included by many teams in their evaluation reports. It is true that a small number of clients were absent from the follow-up because they were unwell or declined re-interview. However, in order to compensate for this, the evaluation procedure left a degree of flexibility in the timescale of interview, allowing workers to re-interview when it is most likely that they will be successful. Examination of returns suggests that teams have made considerable efforts to interview again after an initial failed attempt and have been largely successful.

ANALYSIS OF RESULTS

Differences between the quality of life of CMHST and other mental health clients

As planned, one of the benefits of having expended the considerable effort required to conduct the survey described in Chapter 6 was that it would give the department valuable information against which to evaluate new services in future. This evaluation of CMHSTs, a major frontline service development, is a case in point. As they were all interviewed as part of the county-wide survey, we are able to begin our evaluation by considering the special nature of the seventy-eight clients originally selected for CMHST service, not from their clinical characteristics alone but from an appraisal of their life characteristics. These initial CMHST cases are compared with 344 other agency caseload clients, who also had long-standing and severe mental health conditions, but who had not been referred for such support at the time. In this way, based on the relative characteristics of the cases accepted for support, we are able to increase our knowledge of the selection procedures of the teams. We begin a discussion of our results with an examination of areas of substantial and significant difference between the 'run of the mill' long-term mental health caseload and that of the CMHSTs.

Personal characteristics and objective features of life

To begin with, looking at objective indicators and personal characteristics, differences occurred between the two groups in several areas. For the sake of convenience, several of these are grouped together and presented in Table 7.1. Average values, t-test results and levels of probability are also included. Clients who eventually became CMHST cases have identifiable demographic characteristics which differentiate them, as a group, from those who have not. In respect of age, they are significantly younger on average, though like most such clients they are middle aged (with a mean of 42.6 years). CMHST clients are also significantly more likely to be male (61.5 per cent) than other mental health cases (43.6 per cent) within the agency (Chi-squared=7.5; p=.006). No differences in ethnicity were apparent.

Table 7.1   Objective well-being comparison: analysis of differences[1] between mean values of CMHST and other clients

Objective indicator/characteristic	CMHST clients	Other clients	t value	Probability
Global QOL				
QOL uniscale	43.7	48.7	1.8	.08
Demography				
Current age	42.6	46.4	2.3	.02
Health				
Age at first Psych. admission	26.4	29.9	2.3	.03
Employment				
Total weekly Income	£60.13	£69.21	2.17	.03
Hours worked per week	1.4	5.1	3.4	.001
Living conditions				
Number of other residents	1.0	3.2	5.73	.000

[1] Established by t-test

The age of onset of their illness, as indicated by the age at which they were first admitted to hospital, was significantly younger. The younger onset for severe illness prevents the establishment of families and carers. Clients lived more frequently alone or with a small group of others. Their type of accommodation was most frequently a flat (37.2 per cent), while other clients were to be found residing most frequently in their own homes (30.6 per cent) (Chi-squared=22.3; p=.01). CMHST clients total average income was significantly less (£60.13) and, on average, they worked significantly fewer hours per week (1.4) than other clients. These features are also a reflection of their higher levels of disability.

In respect of overall well-being, as measured by professional appraisal on the quality of life uniscale, the CMHST group was rated as having a lower quality of life (43.7) than other mental health clients (48.7). This finding is noteworthy, though it failed narrowly to attain statistical significance (p=.08).

Thus, the set of personal characteristics of this group of clients is one likely to render members particularly vulnerable and suggests that they are individuals who are likely to be in need of community mental health support services.

Subjective well-being

To a limited degree, the information about the personal characteristics of clients and the objective indicators of their lives helps us to understand the differences occurring among the subjective measures. There was a general trend for the CMHST clients to have a relatively diminished perceived well-being. With the exception of the satisfaction with employment by employed clients, all levels of satisfaction were lower for the community support service clients. In particular, differences in dissatisfaction with legal/safety (t=2.3; p=.02) and health (t=2.1; p=.03) were especially pronounced, reaching statistical significance, while religion narrowly missed being significant (p=.06).

Differences existed at selection between CMHST clients and others in respect of mental health. CMHST clients showed a general trend towards worse mental health than others. Positive affect was generally lower and negative affect higher (Chi-squared=11.5; p=.04) for those selected for the support service. In particular, two symptoms – boredom (Chi-squared=3.7; p=.05) and depression (Chi-squared=4.8; p=.03) – stood out as very predictive of referral. Likewise, differences existed in respect of self-esteem. Here, the general trend was for CMHST clients to entertain less strong positive self-attitudes and stronger negative or self-critical ones (Chi-squared=21.7; p=.001). In particular, feelings of failure (Chi-squared=14.3; p=.001), depleted self-respect (Chi-squared=4.5; p=.03) and feelings of uselessness (Chi-squared=6.6; p=.01) were very pronounced.

Changes in the life quality of CMHST clients

Sample

During the period of evaluation, data from a total of 298 client interviews were coded, entered and processed from the thirteen teams. Of these, 233 (78.2 per cent) are for first-time interviews, fifty-two (17.4 per cent) second-time interviews and thirteen (4.4 per cent) third-time interviews. Because of the small number who were interviewed a third time, the analysis of changes concentrates on identifying differences between the first two occasions.

Personal characteristics

The quality of life interview gathers basic demographic information on the clients. The sample characteristics were drawn from the entire population of CMHST cases interviewed at least once (n=233). As the number of teams grew, so did the variety of geographical areas covered by the teams, as well as the number of clients serviced. This raises the possibility, for example, of the demographic characteristics of the clientele changing. Demographic information is a particularly useful means of establishing the parameters of your group and enabling comparisons among similar or dissimilar teams – factors which must be monitored by managers and planners (see also Chapter 12).

CMHST clients have an average age of 43.6 years (range from 18 to 77 years) with only 3 per cent above the age of 65. The proportion of male clients (56.8 per cent) exceeds that of females (43.2 per cent). The sample has an average school-leaving age of 15.5 years, with 13.4 per cent having remained at school beyond the age of 16. However, as it has transpired, of the 233 clients of the expanded service, fifty-four clients (23.6 per cent) come from minority ethnic groups. This represents a dramatic increase over the original intake of the 'old CMHSTs' (Chi-squared=39.81; p=.001) which, as reported earlier, closely mirrored the survey sample which, in turn, approximated the general population for the region. This change is particularly apparent in the reported caseloads of three of the expanded teams, in each of which the minority ethnic groups were larger than the white group.

Also, as demographic information is recorded at each interview, it is possible to check it for changes over time. This allows potential sources of variation to be identified and, by identifying sources of error, provides a simple means of increasing the reliability of the data-gathering exercise. For subjective and objective measures, changes have been calculated on those clients (n=52) who remained in the service.

Quality of life indicators for specific life domains

There were few notable changes in the objective well-being of clients. We report only some of the more noteworthy aspects. Most clients were unemployed when they came to the CMHST (92.1 per cent) and they remained this way (89.5 per cent). Most clients led lives of limited leisure activity. Everyone watched television or listened to the radio and almost all shopped (88.4 per cent) or took bus or car rides (86.6 per cent), while a minority engaged in any sport (26 per cent). This all remained unchanged during the period of study. Interestingly enough, the number reporting that their use of leisure time had been inhibited during the period declined noticeably from nearly two-thirds (65 per cent) to half (51 per cent), narrowly missing statistical significance (p = .06).

While 7.3 per cent of clients had been accused of a crime in the year prior to coming to the CMHST, only 1.9 per cent were accused during the period of the survey. While the percentage was quite small to begin with, this does represent a substantial, and clinically rather than statistically significant, improvement. The proportion of clients reporting themselves to have been victims of crimes before coming to CMHSTs diminished from 13.4 per cent to 9.6 per cent during the course of the study, and slightly fewer had required the assistance of police during the study (from 20.1 to 16.7 per cent). Socially, there were also noticeable but insignificant gains. Those reporting themselves requiring close friend-ships increased from approximately two-thirds (65.9 per cent) of the sample to approximately three-quarters (74.5 per cent). Those reporting a 'reliable alliance' increased from 68.3 per cent to 79.6 per cent.

Some of the few areas of significant change were in respect of some aspects of health. While there was no substantial change in the rates at which clients saw doctors for physical illness nor in their development of physical handicaps, there was a change in respect of their 'nerves'. Figure 7.1 shows that in the year prior to the CMHSTs, 82.2 per cent had seen a doctor for nerves. After CMHSTs this number had decreased to 71.2 per cent. This difference was a substantial change, bordering on significance (Chi-squared = 3.2, p = .07). Interestingly enough, the decrease in use of medical/psychiatric services was accompanied by a reduction of more than half in rehospitalisation rates (from 42.6 per cent to 17.6 per cent) (Chi-squared = 11.03; p = .001). Practically all clients continued to be maintained on psychotropic medication (86.7 per cent, as compared to 88.5 per cent). As will be seen below, this fits into a general, though weak, pattern of improvement in subjective well-being. This increase in community survival rate is a very important indicator of a positive outcome in a most crucial area of service performance.

Subjective well-being measures: perceived quality of life

Above we have defined 'perceived' quality of life as being the sum total of an individual's appraisals of his or her levels of satisfaction in various specific life domains. While changes did not generally reach levels of statistical significance, there is a reasonably consistent pattern of move-ment towards increased satisfaction. A slight downward trend was noticed in respect of life satisfaction with work among the employed. However, except for this, all other satisfaction measures either remained stable (e.g. religion) or increased slightly (finance, legal/safety, family relations, social relations, health). The single exception was the sub-scale score for leisure. This increased significantly (from 4.4 to 4.8) (t = 2.45; p = .01).

The specific life satisfaction items within the subjective well-being scales were each investigated separately for evidence of change. Linked to the sub-scale findings, clients who remained in contact with the service were found to be more satisfied with the amount of money which they had for enjoyment of their leisure (from 3.2 to 3.7) (t = 2.06; p = .045). They were also more satisfied with the notion of remaining in their current residence (from 4.2 to 4.8) (t = 2.2; p = .029).

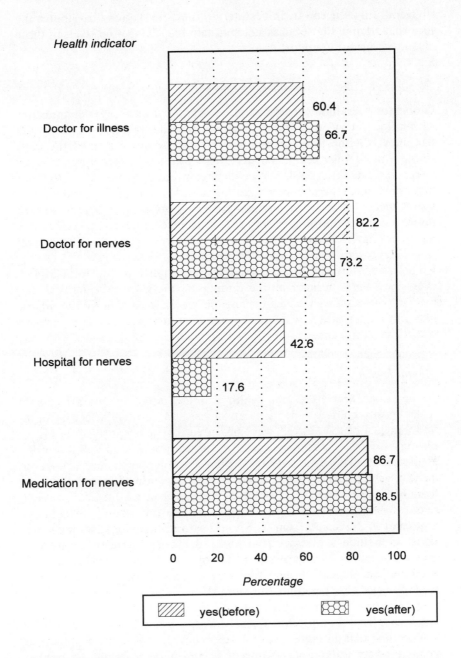

Health indicator

Figure 7.1 Changes in health indicators: percentage of affirmative responses to objective health questions before and after exposure to CMHSTs
Note: Chi-squared=11.0; D.F.=1; p=.000

Overall (like the results in Chapter 9), these results tend to support the idea that community services can maintain life satisfaction levels of those clients whom they support.

Global well-being: three subjective and one objective measure

Global, or overall, well-being was measured by several separate measures within the interview: Cantril's ladder, the life satisfaction scale and happiness. Of the three measures, happiness scores remained the most stable with 14.5 per cent of clients at first assessment reporting that they were 'very happy', 53.4 per cent 'pretty happy' and 32.1 per cent 'unhappy' and these percentages remained unchanged. Ladder scale scores displayed a clear, though statistically insignificant, trend toward improvement (from 56.9 to 68.1). Average life satisfaction scale scores improved significantly (from 4.1 to 4.6) (t = 2.36; p = .02). The general trend was towards improved self-assessment.

This trend towards an improved overall quality of life for CMHST clients was substantiated by the findings of the workers' quality of life ratings. These showed a mean change in scores from 45.8 to 51.8 which, like the ladder scale, was substantial but narrowly failed to achieve statistical significance (t = 1.82; p = .07).

Mental health

As described above, mental health was measured by two affect sub-scales: positive affect (adaptive capacities) and negative affect (symptomatology). Positive affect was measured by self-report of levels of feelings of accomplishment, success, pride, interest and high spirits. While not statistically significant, with a few exceptions, most changes in positive affect were favourable (i.e. increased): sense of accomplishment, from 65.9 to 61.7 per cent; feelings of success, from 65.0 to 65.3 per cent; sense of pride, from 59.1 to 51 per cent; interest, from 57.8 to 62 per cent; and high spirits, from 33.5 to 37.5 per cent. Negative affect was taken to include restlessness, boredom, depression, loneliness and feelings of upset. In all instances, levels of these negative characteristics remained unchanged or improved (i.e. decreased) slightly: restlessness, from 51.6 to 46.2 per cent; boredom, from 70 to 66.7 per cent; upset, from 37.3 to 32.7 per cent; depression, from 66.5 to 61.5 per cent; and loneliness, from 51.6 to 46 per cent.

Assuming that an increase in the frequency of affirmative responses to positive affect (adaptability) questions and a decrease in the level of affirmative responses to negative affect (symptomatology) both represent improvement, mental health showed general benefit. General mental health scores are sometimes computed by summing the two scales into a single 'affect balance scale', showing the degree and direction of mental balance between symptomatology and adaptability. This degree of psychological balance is thought to be a good indicator of overall ego strength. On a scale from − 5 to +5 the group displayed a marginal, if insignificant, tendency towards improvement (from − .5 to +.2).

Self-concept

An important factor in psychological well-being lies with the construct which we call 'the self'. This is seen as a socially derived set of mental constructs including both cognitions and affects. While the entire sense of self is too broad to measure under such conditions, self-esteem, a certain antecedent of a strong sense of self, has been chosen as an indicator of well-being. Two dimensions of self-esteem − positive and negative self-concept − have been measured.

Positive self-concept is composed of self-enhancers such as high self-worth, recognition of one's good qualities, possession of abilities, a positive attitude towards one's self and a sense of self-satisfaction. Changes in scores tended (with one exception − possession of abilities) to reflect either generally stable patterns or improvements (i.e. increases) which were, in a few instances, substantial, though none reached statistical significance: self-worth, from 74.3 to 86 per cent; recognition of one's good qualities, from 85 to 85.4 per cent; possession of abilities, from 64.6 to 62.5 per cent; positive attitude towards one's self, from 65.2 to 75 per cent; and sense of self-satisfaction, from 57.6 to 66 per cent.

Negative self-concept is composed of self-detractors such as feelings of failure and uselessness, lack of pride, low self-respect and self-worth. Here, a decrease in percentages represents an improvement in mental state. Universally, changes in scores reflected general improvement (i.e. they decreased): feelings of failure, from 45.5 to 37 per cent; lack of pride, from 45.9 to 34.7 per cent; low self-respect, from 62.3 to 44 per cent; and feelings of uselessness, from 72.1 to 69.2 per cent. One element − self-respect − improved significantly, from 62.3 to 44 per cent (Chi-squared = 5.57; p = .02).

Assuming that improvement is represented by an increase in the frequency of clients expressing self-enhancing attitudes and deterioration by a decrease in the frequency of self-detracting attitudes, then the group improved in nine aspects of self and deteriorated in one. This finding displays a weak but general trend towards improvement similar to that shown by the mental health measure.

As with mental health, an average score can be computed between the two dimensions, producing a score range from − 5 to + 5. In this instance, self-concept increased slightly but insignificantly across the period of the study (from .7 to 1.2).

Looking at subjective well-being, we see a general picture of benefit during the period of the service. While the level of changes was usually small, the general picture was quite consistent. Clients' general vision of life, the degree to which they were happy, satisfied and achieving what they were capable of, tended to improve. Looking at specific domains or areas of life, there was a general trend for people to feel that life was marginally more satisfactory. Mental health dimensions and self-esteem are measures of psychological well-being. While not changing dramatically, these, too, showed a general trend towards improvement. In total, the group profile showed that there was a trend to benefit from the service, though the degree of these changes was small.

Diagnosis, affect and subjective well-being

In the CMHST study we were able to obtain a clinical diagnosis for nearly 200 cases. The vast majority of the cases being supported by the CMHST are suffering from schizophrenia (n=133). Twenty-six individuals were diagnosed as manic-depressive and a further ten were chronically depressed. The remainder (n=30) were suffering from organic, personality or affective disorders such as chronic anxiety state. The subjective well-being scores were computed for the three main diagnostic groups and the results are shown in Figure 7.2. While the manic-depressive clients felt better about their leisure and safety (t = 6.6; p=.002), for the most part they and the schizophrenia group had similar

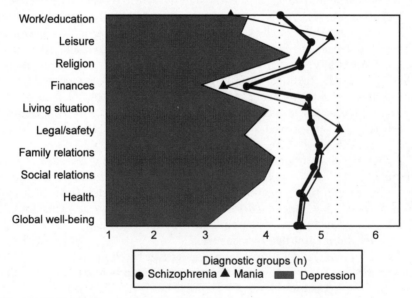

Figure 7.2 Subjective quality of life by diagnosis

scores. The small number of chronic depressed patients had markedly lower scores, although one can see that they were, nevertheless, still able to discriminate between life domains in very much the same way as the other two groups.

The significant differences (Scheffe) between the diagnostic groups are the depressed group's health (F=7.0; p=.001) and social relationships (F=3.1; p=.05) compared to the schizophrenia group, and the depressed group's leisure ratings (F=7.0; p=.001) compared to those of the manic patients. None of the other differences shown in Figure 7.2 reaches any level of significance.

Because these findings showing the impact of clinical depression on subjective well-being reports have been identified by others (Lehman, personal communication), we re-analysed the CMHST data using the respondents' scores on the affect balance scale. Respondents scoring four or five on the five negative affect items are regarded as possibly depressed, and the remainder not. In terms of the ability of the affect balance scale to assess psychopathology accurately, we found that while the single question about depression on the affect balance scale does discriminate between the diagnostic groups, the total negative affect score (of 4 or 5) is a significantly better measure (F= 25.6713; p<.001). In the chronic depression group, 90 per cent scored 4 or 5, compared to 42 per cent of the manic group and only 22 per cent of those people with a diagnosis of schizophrenia.

Figure 7.3 shows the subjective well-being scores for the two groups. The pattern is similar to the diagnostic group analysis, in that the

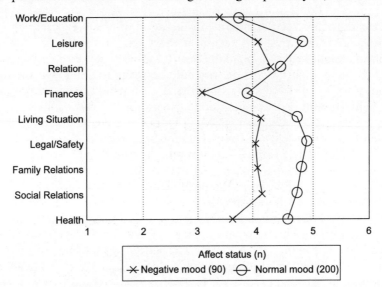

Figure 7.3 Subjective well-being and negative affect

negative affect (depressed) group score consistently lower than the others. It is worthwhile noting that only about one-third of the cases are affected and that, even so, they are still able to discriminate between domains. In addition, some of the domain differences fail to reach significance (work and religion). In fact, for the small number of people in work the subjective well-being score of the depressed respondents is higher than that of the non-depressed group. When repeated on another sample from another culture (seventy-six cases from Boulder, Colorado), similar but not identical results were found. In the Boulder sample, work, religion, legal/safety and family domains were not significantly different.

Taken together, these findings suggest that the result of a high negative affect score is not to produce a blanket effect on the individual's capacity to respond, but rather to produce a 'portside' effect (moving the whole profile to the left). Clients remain able to provide answers which produce a profile discriminating between the domains, but most of the scores fail to reach the levels attained by other respondents. Treatment which improves their clinical state may improve their quality of life ratings by bringing them up to the level of their peers. On the other hand, simply to be relieved of the symptoms of negative affect may not be a guarantee that subjective well-being will improve. It may be that both symptoms and subjective well-being are determined by other factors, material or biological. Drug treatment may remediate the latter but do nothing about the former. Stress is produced by both environmental and emotional factors, as recent studies using sophisticated multivariate statistics have shown (Lobel and Dunkel-Schetter 1990).

Extending this discussion to a consideration of positive affect may help us to understand what the nature of these relationships is. A mood of euphoria might lead to a blanket effect on subjective well-being scores so that the individual fails to discriminate between domains. On the other hand, it might produce a 'starboard' effect (moving the whole profile to the right), retaining discrimination in the profile but raising all the scores above the level of the peer group. Figure 7.2 suggests that for manic patients, in whom elevated mood might be expected, there is no 'starboard' effect. The profile is very similar to the other patients, and is higher in two domains and lower in two. We decided to calculate an 'elevated mood' factor from the positive affect scale to see whether, for those with elevated mood, there was a 'starboard' effect. No effect would suggest that positive mood affects subjective well-being in a different way from negative mood and would reduce the case for subjective well-being being mood dominated. A 'starboard' effect would suggest that the relationship between mood and subjective well-being is a linear one. However, as the reader can see in Figure 7.4, the 'starboard' effect is limited and only reaches significance in three domains: health, leisure

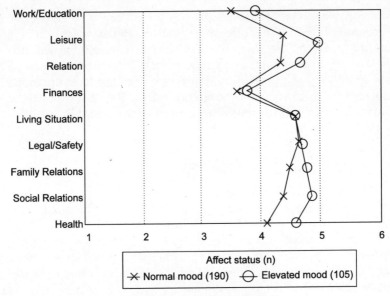

Figure 7.4 Subjective well-being and positive affect

and social relationships. We repeated the analysis on a completely different data set from another culture (the seventy-six cases from Boulder, Colorado) and found the same results. An elevated affect score was significantly related to the same three life domains only.

It is possible that greater positive affect is the result of high subjective well-being in these life domains. On the other hand, it is possible that reporting subjective well-being in these areas is more sensitive to positive affect. We know, for instance, that Henderson *et al.* (1981) have argued, for non-psychotic patients, that it is the perception of social relationships which is important to the individual rather than the absolute size of their social networks. In their study, inadequate social relationships predicted future morbidity, but only in the face of social adversity. Goldberg *et al.* (1990) found different social factors to be associated with different mood states; depression was related to a lack of support from close family, and dissatisfaction with interaction with relatives.

It might be the case that those people who subscribe to the argument that affect dominates self-reported states are paying selective attention to the relationships between affect and reported subjective well-being which exist in certain domains. If one is preoccupied with treating people with affective problems, particularly in the context of a medical model and within a health service, then one attends to those areas affected by mood, such as health, leisure, social and family relationships, to the exclusion of other areas, such as religion, finances or living situation. In fact, it may be the case that clinicians have learned to use the data about these aspects of social relationships as (surrogate) indicators of recovery from the depressed mood, because these are the areas where there is a relationship. Over time, therefore, one may be clinically misled into the view that affect dominates everything, which is far from the case. That is not to say that serious clinical depression does not have the 'portside' effect referred to above; we believe that it does. But that is not the same as saying that subjective well-being is simply the same thing as affect or is always dominated by it.

DISCUSSION AND CONCLUSIONS

The analysis of quality of life data from the CMHSTs gives a reasonably complete, if not particularly detailed, portrait of their caseloads. A great number of points are raised by this research, but this discussion will concentrate on those relating most closely to the potential benefits of CMHST services to clients. In this respect, we hope that these comments will be of use both to service providers, interested in seeing their clinical practice described in a more systematic way, and to service purchasers, interested in the impact which a community care service has on the general public.

First, a question must arise as to the number of cases which, having been accepted for team support, were closed within periods which must be described as relatively brief, in the context of the careers of long-term mentally disordered clients. The reasons are doubtless complex and cannot be answered by the presence or absence of completed quality of life forms alone. Nevertheless, these figures correspond with those gained from other sources, such as team reviews and evaluation reports, which indicated a return to hospital and case closure as the outcome the clients preferred. A primary aim of the teams is to engage clients in need of long-term support by providing vital contact with the social care agency charged with taking the lead in organising their community care. All community services report a need for some clients to return to hospital periodically. These findings confirm that reality.

When compared with other clients who were not brought into contact with the service, those who have appear to be people with greater degrees of social disadvantage and psychological debility. They represent some of the more vulnerable of an already vulnerable group, though they may not be the most difficult cases to manage.

Most objective well-being indicators remained unchanged, but where change did occur it was for the better. For example, the area of client health was particularly prominent, with sharp decreases in the rate of rehospitalisation (reflecting other findings – for example, Wright *et al.* 1989) and levels of reliance on medical services. Survival in the community, when combined with other positive indicators, should be construed as a benefit to the client which is probably also producing cost savings across both the health services (for example, bed usage) and social services (for example, 'approved social worker' and hospital social work services).

Among the objective indicators of life quality, the issue of rehospitalisation rate deserves special mention. A halving of the rate for hospital admissions during the previous year is certainly substantial, whether or not the differences achieved statistical significance. Nevertheless, such a result cannot be judged a 'good thing' in isolation of other factors. For example, fewer hospital admissions might be associated with lower satisfaction with health, more criminal convictions and/or victimisation, more homelessness and general decreased access to health care. In such instances, fewer admissions would be a reflection of a deteriorating quality of life. Hospital admissions are, sometimes, a necessity, and one to which clients have every right, and they should certainly not be denied access (see Chapter 12). Here, this decline in rate is associated with other improvements judged favourable by both the clients and the professionals, and it is within such a context that such facts must be understood. This is the purpose of having a quality of life *profile*: many facts concerning many dimensions, ultimately allowing us to deal with the complexities of an individual's situation.

However, it must also be noted that many case closures during the course of the evaluation were due to the re-admission of CMHST clients. These individuals dropping out of the evaluation must have skewed the readmission figures favourably.

CMHSTs have the avowed aim not only of keeping individuals out of hospital but also of helping vulnerable clients to gain access to health care provisions when these are required (Baker *et al.* 1992). Very importantly, there was no demonstrable change in the criminal status of these clients. Clients who remain within the service are not entering the criminal justice system as the alternative to long-stay hospitalisation, a most disturbing trend reported elsewhere by studies of community support provisions (Caton *et al.* 1993).

Though global well-being, as rated by professionals, showed improvement, the results must be viewed with caution, as professional opinion is thought not truly to reflect quality of life (Slevin *et al.* 1988). The increase in similarity between client and worker ratings probably reflects the professionals revising their opinions upwards. Just possibly, this represents an increased awareness on the part of the staff of the strengths which clients actually possess in their lives towards adaptation, despite their outward levels of disability and disadvantage (Waltz 1986). This interpretation is the one most supported by research feedback and training sessions with CMHST staff across the county. A common feature is that workers are surprised to discover new aspects of the client through the interviewing process, and these are not always client weaknesses. Often reported are discoveries of client strengths and abilities which have led to alterations of the workers' opinions about clients towards more favourable appraisals.

To say that the objective, external, material conditions of anyone's life have improved is one thing. Life, however, is also to be measured by what the individual him or herself makes of it. Here, two complex but highly relevant indicators – i.e. mental health and self-esteem – showed reasonably uniform, though weak, trends towards increased strength and lessened symptomatology. These changes are essential, as all mental health services should, by definition, maintain or improve the service recipients' mental health if nothing else. These services did that. Also, community services which provide community-based care, aimed at 'normalising' individual's lives by destigmatising them and treating clients as valued people, should show improvements in client self-esteem. The services apparently do that as well. In both of these crucial areas the clients showed clinically important, if not always statistically significant, gains in subjective well-being, similar to those reported elsewhere of successful support services (Rosenfield 1992; Baker et al. 1992).

Also, satisfaction with everyday life in the range of life domains increased generally. While these changes were often slight, there was a demonstrable trend towards a brighter view of the various areas of life. This may be related to improvements in mental health (poor mental health, especially negative affect, can depress life satisfaction scores), but this pattern is unlikely to be completely explained by this. It is not only psychotherapy and drug treatment which can benefit such clients, since it is not solely the health domain of an individual's life which becomes disrupted by a continuing severe mental health condition. All of the social and economic areas of life become involved. This is the reason for having both health and social care services available to these clients and of measuring both the health and social dimensions of impact. The systematic enhancement of people's lives in so many aspects (other than health) would strongly suggest that the range of supportive, social care activities being directed at various life circumstances are beginning to show some positive effects.

Some would argue that the only true basis of comparison for a person, especially one with the complexities of mental illness, is him or herself. A point to be borne in mind when evaluating any such service is that both aggregated data and individual case studies are useful in obtaining a more complete picture of how the services are operating. Examples of both drawn from this study are given below in Chapter 13 and both, within limits, tend to support the outcomes of the service.

This study confirms again the usefulness of quality of life information in the evaluation of community mental health services. Doubtless, the same would prove true should quality of life techniques be put into play in evaluating similar services for other client groups, such as the elderly, those with physical disabilities and those with learning difficulties, involved in community care. Studies such as this also form the basis for future studies of a similar type, allowing us to monitor service development through continuing client progress over many years (Brekke and Test 1992). Accumulating such a database will allow us to have complementary styles of service assessment, an essential ingredient to multidisciplinary clinical work and inter-agency planning, for employment by both health and social care agencies.

In conclusion, there are clearly benefits to the service, corresponding with findings reported elsewhere. Changes have occurred in many clients and these have largely been in the desired direction, though the magnitude of improvement has been generally weak. This is predictable, as quality of life measures are very stable, though not so stable as to be unable to detect changes in individuals as they occur. People lacking good education but with a long history of intractable, severe mental problems tend to remain disproportionately unemployed and on low incomes. A year with a support team such as this should not have been expected to have produced more. Here, maintenance of quality of life levels in itself is a fair outcome and substantial change, if it happens, will appear gradually over many years. Certainly, modest, gradual increases in standards are indicators of progress and would be acceptable standards against which to judge future activities.

But these advances neither obviate the need for nor diminish the efforts of other existing patterns of community care. The changes which are occurring through support team efforts may well – indeed should – also be occurring in clients cared for by other workers using other methods in other settings. As there are many more clients on the caseloads of hospital and area team social workers than are cared for by CMHSTs, so their total benefit to the public may be expected to be greater. Also, CMHSTs do not take all of the 'difficult' cases. As mentioned above, evidence as to disability levels of clients has not been gathered, perhaps a severe limitation of the evaluation, given that the intent of much work in many instances must be rehabilitative. CMHSTs cater for an atypical group and might not be capable of providing for all those with severe, continuing need. Many clients dropped out of the evaluation. They may have been those for whom CMHST contact did not have a positive effect.

This is one study with change measures available on less than half of the existing teams, and the established teams may prove different in some crucial way from the newer teams. The service will require longer-term evaluation for a clear picture of its benefits to emerge. Trends towards improvement in the first year or so may not be maintained over the longer term. This is a crucial point, as a long-term service will require continued monitoring and we know from research elsewhere that the effects of introducing community-based services may not show a significant positive effect for two years or more (see Creed *et al.* 1993; and Holloway 1991).

Chapter 8

Activity-based services

INTRODUCTION

In Chapter 4 we suggested that the majority of people with long-term social disabilities are able to use normal community facilities. However, despite this, many people also need various forms of 'prosthetic' or sheltered services. In that chapter we pointed out that in a 'system of care' these services should include various forms of accommodation, specialist peripatetic support teams, work-related activities and recreational pursuits. This chapter is concerned with activity-based services. It will describe some benefits with reference to two popular projects known as 'START and SNAPS STUDIOS' and 'the ROVERS', which are located in an inner-city area of Manchester. The case study of John presented in Chapter 10 illustrates how these services work in collaboration with other components of a rehabilitation service – an operational principle which we believe is very important.

THE BENEFITS OF ACTIVITY

There are two main forms of activity-based pursuits: those which are work-related and those which are more concerned with recreational activity. We use the term 'work-related' to refer to any purposeful activity, even if it does not attract any financial remuneration as in employment. In a climate of high unemployment and because many people have long periods of free time on their hands, particularly in the evenings and at weekends, the development of recreational pursuits is particularly important. Work and recreational activities are similar: both provide 'an opportunity to do something'. Leisure also provides 'a chance to do nothing' but may not be valued unless we have been occupied by some endeavour. The benefits of these endeavours are very important to the majority of disabled people. In addition, some benefits, such as the structuring of time, may help some people overcome the considerable difficulties they may have in initiating and maintaining various recreational pursuits (Collis and Ekdawi 1984).

As mentioned in Chapter 4, research and clinical experience have shown that the benefits of work-related activity can include an increase in self-esteem, a sense of purpose, a routine and structure to the day, an opportunity to improve interpersonal interactions and work-related skills and to develop friendships, and an improvement in a person's quality of life. In addition, meaningful activity can play a part in reducing symptomatology and may reduce a person's need for other services, such as admission to hospital. Its loss may cause significant degrees of psychological distress in some people (Platt 1984; Warr 1987), and prolonged periods of unemployment may lead to a reduction in motivation and apathy (Nehring *et al.* 1993). Work, even in the most sheltered settings, provides a means by which people with a mental illness can have a social role which is valued (Collis and Ekdawi 1984; Warner 1985). The potential benefits of leisure and recreational pursuits are probably similar: they may facilitate the development of social networks and integration and they provide an important source of pleasure. In addition, they can be a means of engaging some people into services which can help them – this, in fact, has been one of the aims of the ROVERS.

Overall, sheltered services need to offer people choice and cater for their range of interests, intellectual abilities and their latent skills. They should also facilitate the development of personal autonomy (Nehring *et al.* 1993). START and SNAPS STUDIOS and the ROVERS in Manchester are described here for the purpose of illustration. These three services are part of a rehabilitation network which has been developed in a multi-cultural inner-city area ranked as one of the worst areas in the country in terms of social deprivation (Jarman 1984).

START AND SNAPS STUDIOS

START was established in 1986. It is a community-based project which encourages people with chronic disabilities to work as artists, alongside practising artists and craftspeople. It is directed by a very experienced artist, and his team includes two other experienced artists. It also involves a number of associated artists, volunteers, students on placement from local colleges and, occasionally, school pupils on work experience schemes. In 1989 it won joint first prize in the visual arts category of a BBC television national competition for community initiatives linked by a television programme series called 'It's My City' (Bridges and Brown 1989).

START STUDIOS is based in a building about ten minutes' walk from the main hospital campus in a leafy area of Manchester known as Victoria Park, which has an interesting social history (Spiers 1976). It occupies many rooms as studios and uses a large garden for displays and other outdoor activities. SNAPS STUDIOS is based in a nearby building where there is a darkroom for photography.

The working environment is relaxed and informal, and artists and members often continue their work into the evenings and at weekends. Much of the artwork occurs in other locations and in places where specific projects have been commissioned, such as in schools, hospitals, health centres and various other places in the community. These projects are often permanent additions to the visual environment – for example, the large ceramic mural in the foyer of the Rawnsley Building, Department of Psychiatry, Manchester Royal Infirmary, called 'Head for the Hills' (Bridges and Brown 1989).

The activities offered are wide ranging and include painting, ceramics, screen printing, textiles, pottery, wood carving, stained glass work and photography. Patients are called 'members', and in addition to arts activities they participate in the administrative and executive activities of the project as well as in the organisation of exhibitions and the marketing and commissioning of their work. In these respects, it is similar to the 'clubhouse' model seen in the US (Beard *et al.* 1982). Several members have now moved on either to start a college course in the arts, or to set up their own business, or to develop a similar project elsewhere, known as 'STARTOUT'.

The main principle on which this project is based is that members should benefit from being actively involved in some creative endeavour, from being the artist and from being part of a shared experience which can give pleasure to others. In addition, we have found this project successful in many ways similar to the 'latent' functions of employment. START helps many people to focus their thoughts on activities which have not been concerned with illness and offers the opportunity for people to occupy their time in more structured, meaningful and enjoyable ways. This has been particularly important for those who are bored and who have much time on their hands. It gives people the opportunity to express themselves and their creativity, particularly when they have not been able to do so through words. Allied to this, we have found that a number of people have drawn upon the experience of their mental illness in terms of it making a positive contribution to their creative work. START helps to restore a person's self-esteem and self-confidence by allowing him or her to be a member of a social group with common interests. People can feel valued by their peers; they have the opportunity to feel a sense of responsibility for others; and they can experience camaraderie and friendships. In addition, their work is valued by the community generally through exhibitions, commissioned work and retail success. It helps people to use and develop their entrepreneurial and organisational skills.

In an audit of this project we found that members had a significant reduction in the number of referrals to other services and re-admissions to inpatient wards and an acute day hospital, indicating an advantage to health services as well as to its members (Colgan *et al.* 1991).

THE ROVERS

The ROVERS – a roving day care service – was formed in 1989. Its aim is to help people with long-term psychiatric disabilities, who are unable to work in an unsheltered workplace, who lack leisure or recreational pursuits, who spend a substantial proportion of their day doing very little, and who have proved difficult to engage in other rehabilitation services already established by the health service, social services and voluntary organisations. It is a team consisting of an occupational therapist, a mental health worker with psychiatric nurse training, an artist, a gardener and a woodworker.

It is based in the same building as START. However, each member of the team works in a variety of locations in the community, including the patient's home. For example, the gardener has rented some allotment sites where he meets certain people on a regular basis. Contingent upon the resources available and member's individual personal skills, the team has developed a wide choice of activities based on a flexible approach and the interests of their members. Its main operational principles are similar to START. Each member of the team provides a choice of activities, a skilled input, a relaxed and informal approach, and each operates in different locations in the community. In addition, each member has a flexible attitude towards the commitment they expect from individual people, and attempts are made to overcome the barriers to involvement, such as, for example, transport difficulties or lack of motivation, by working in the client's home.

An example of the work of the ROVERS in supporting a person (John) is described in Chapter 10. It will be seen that he was a very dependent person experiencing a significant degree of social disability. Yet, eventually, he was able to arrange an exhibition of his own art work in a local library with support from the ROVERS team. He had been able to build up a good relationship with the artist over the time he had been attending and was able to talk to her easily. With her he enjoyed his art and he was able to distract his attention from his dissatisfaction with life elsewhere. He was able to relax and his achievements in this field appeared to boost his self-esteem.

In the first year of this service we carried out an audit to assess whether it would lead to an improvement in its clients' general well-being associated with occupational, leisure and social life domains. Before they became involved, the first consecutive series of people who were taken on by the team were assessed by an independent researcher using the LQOLP (Oliver 1991a). This assessment was then repeated after one year, though not all the original subjects were included at this time, mainly because some had only engaged in the project for a brief period or only needed to be involved for a short time before moving on to some other service. Overall, no significant changes in subjective scores were reported.

There may have been at least two important reasons for these results. First, any personal benefits gained during times of direct contact with the service were not generalised to other occasions because of on-going problems experienced by their clients, such as those concerned with motivation, volition or lack of other opportunities. This would be in keeping with other studies, which showed that several factors – for example, social stimulation (Wing and Freudenberg 1961), supervision (Wadsworth *et al.* 1962) and reward contingencies (Walker 1979) – may be important if people are to remain engaged in activities.

A second reason may have been the fact that the team was unable to provide sufficient input, because of its limited resources, to have an overall and sustained effect on the person's well-being generally. It had to limit the amount of time it could offer to each individual because of its size and the number of people wanting its service. In practice, this amounted to only one morning or afternoon each week for each person, which was recognised by the team as very inadequate for the majority of its clients – most would have benefited from being involved every day of the week. Had it been able to provide a greater level of input then it might have been able to have had a significant effect on the subjective ratings. This is supported by the following unsolicited report from the independent assessor who carried out the follow-up assessments. He had worked as a social worker and probation officer.

> When I started the interviewing I was fairly confident that I knew what to expect. Unfortunately, I didn't. Many of the people interviewed appeared to lead lives that could only be described as impoverished. Whilst I had expected limited access to resources and poor accommodation I was appalled at the poverty of people's relationships both in terms of family ties and friends. The desolation which I encountered saddened me very much.
>
> If there was a bright spot in my interviewing it was the impact that the Roving Day Care Team have made in terms of people's quality of life. Many of the people I spoke to clearly relied very heavily on the ROVERS who they see as being hard working, friendly and committed. Whilst it might be expected that the work of the ROVERS would have little impact in such impoverished circumstances, I was surprised at the examples of innovation, personal commitment and determination that people talked about.

Whilst I have no idea what results the Quality of Life questionnaires will produce, I feel that if no clear evidence of 'improvement' is seen, this will merely reflect the degree of difficulty faced. I would suggest that any future hopes of many of those interviewed lie with the continuation and hopefully extension of the Roving Day Care service.

Of course, a study with a comparison or case-control group could tell us whether the programme was helping to maintain the quality of life of participants over time compared with similar patients who were not in receipt of the service. We know that maintenance of people with long-term severe mental illness is a legitimate service objective (see also Chapter 9).

THE NEED TO DEVELOP FURTHER ACTIVITY-BASED SERVICES

For many disabled people, the goal of gaining open employment is unrealistic even when employment is plentiful, but we need to expose many more people to the opportunity of the benefits of being involved in sheltered schemes. Various forms of successful activity-based services exist in many parts of the UK (Nehring *et al.* 1993; Ekdawi and Conning 1994; Pilling 1988). However, the extent to which these services have been developed in most areas is inadequate and there is a real worry that this situation may worsen.

For example, with regard to START and SNAPS STUDIOS and the ROVERS, only about forty-five people can be involved with each of these because of their size (and usually only for one session per week), whereas at least another 500 people with serious social disabilities are known in the district who would probably benefit from the forms of activity they provide – an estimated figure which does not take account of other people who would benefit, such as those with chronic somatisation or organic brain disorders. Both projects have waiting lists and a very low throughput, because the majority of the people using them need to be involved on a long-term basis and, when possible, offered more time in each service. Clearly, these types of services need to be replicated several times over – if only the funding was available.

With regards to paid work, we believe that many socially disabled people are able to cope with open employment, as exemplified by the successful development of social firms. Further, even when this is a realistic goal and colleagues in the employment services (disablement employment advisors) make energetic attempts to help people find work, they are usually unsuccessful – particularly with people who have schizophrenia. There are two obvious reasons for this. The first is a high rate of unemployment, which makes it difficult to compete with well people who have satisfactory work records. Of interest, the outcome of schizophrenia is thought to be better in countries with nearly full employment than other industrial nations (Warner 1985). The second is the stigma attached to mental illness. Strong negative attitudes continue to exist in society, and these stigmatise the person with mental illness (Goffman 1963; Maclean 1968; Rabkin 1972; Davies and Morris 1989; Huxley 1993d). This is particularly the case when the characteristics of the illness are publicly visible or when the person comes into conflict with the law (Gunn and Taylor 1983). Apart from being unsuccessful in getting work, these negative attitudes reflect back to the person a low social status and an expectation of failure which can only worsen an established negative self-image and low self-esteem (Wing 1983). Stigma associated with mental illness is perpetuated by ignorance and continues to have an important effect on the allocation of opportunities and resources.

An example will, in part, illustrate these points. Bernard was a 33-year-old man who applied for a job as a kitchen porter in a large institution. He was born in a mental hospital, where his mother had been a long-stay patient and had become pregnant. He was fostered and brought up by various families. He first became ill in his late teens and has had three admissions with schizophrenia. After his last admission his care was transferred to his local rehabilitation services. He lived in a hostel ward (an example is described in Chapter 12) for about eighteen months and was then able to move to a council flat, where he has been living for the last five years with some support from a peripatetic team. About three years ago he applied for the job and was short-listed. In his interview, when he had to compete against three other applicants, he was successful. However, this was subject to a medical assessment by the works doctor, as he had told his prospective employer that he was on a regular depot injection to prevent him from becoming ill. Following this medical assessment he was informed that he could not be employed, and this was in spite of his references from the support staff and from his psychiatrist.

THE NEED FOR INTEGRATION WITH OTHER SERVICES

Activity-based services need to be integrated with other rehabilitation services (Ekdawi and Connings 1994). There are two main forms of integration. First is the 'cross-sectional' integration of a person's involvement in activity-based services with other service provision relevant to different aspects of his or her overall care plan. The involvement of some people in activity-based services may not, in fact, be coordinated with other services. At present, some people continue to hold the spurious belief that 'clinical' and 'social' care are separate entities and, as a consequence, do not seem to appreciate the important relationships that exist between social, biological and psychological interventions. In addition, the integration of services – within the 'system of care' described in Chapter 4 – is likely to lead to far greater effectiveness and efficiency in the use of limited resources and appropriate levels of support to patients and their relatives (Ekdawi and Conning 1994).

The second form is 'longitudinal' integration. The emphasis on a 'ladder' model of rehabilitation, with success being measured in terms of movement 'up the ladder' to more skilled work or valued work, risks exposing people and staff to the negative consequence of failure (Pilling 1988). However, there will be some people who will gain skills and want to progress in taking on more challenging opportunities. This will often be possible only if there is a coordinated chain of provisions and key personnel acting as coordinators (Gloag 1985).

CONCLUDING COMMENTS

The experience of these two projects in Manchester, in keeping with the literature, indicates that activity-based services have an important part to play in the 'system of care' that disabled people need. They also highlight the fact that people with special skills but without specific training in psychiatry, can make a valuable and significant contribution to rehabilitation programmes which improve the client's quality of life.

START STUDIOS and the ROVERS have been working to capacity for a long while and, as a consequence, are only able to take other people by reducing time available for their current clients and members. With further investment in these and similar services we should be able to transcribe the recommendations arising out of research which demonstrates the importance of patients spending their time on meaningful activities.

Chapter 9

Client subjective well-being in a case management service

INTRODUCTION

This chapter reports on an assessment of case management clients in a service in North America, and compares the quality of life and psychiatric symptoms of clients of the case management service with comparable patients in the UK. Comparisons are also made between the quality of life of the sample in 1989 and two years later, in 1991.

CASE MANAGEMENT

Case management services for mentally ill people in the USA, by comparison with the UK, have a relatively long and substantial history, and studies have suggested that there are indeed many benefits which might accrue to patients in the UK. There are, however, many different models of case management, and it is not always clear whether the different models have different 'active ingredients'. Moreover it is not entirely clear which clients benefit most from case management (Clark and Fox 1993), although it seems likely that there is a minimum intensity of provision which is required in order to achieve lower hospitalisation rates in frequently hospitalised patient groups (Dietzen and Bond 1993). Case management services for people with a history of frequent and lengthy admissions also need to be offered assertively (Dincin et al. 1993). There is also evidence that a continuing relationship with a case manager over a long period of time is necessary in order to produce improvements in the mental health and quality of life of community residents who have had a long-term mental illness (Huxley 1991). While it is not clear whether this relationship needs to be with the same person, or a team of case managers, in order to be most effective, there are some indications from empirical work (see Chapter 7) that, for successful community outcome, the keyworker should be trained in community support work. Finally, case management may not be more effective than standard services if the latter are offered in areas which are already well-resourced and integrated (Franklin *et al.* 1987; Hornstra *et al.* 1993) or it may work better when a comprehensive range of other services is already in place.

In adopting a case management approach in the UK, the terminological change to 'care management' has rather obscured the lessons learned about it in North America in particular (see Huxley 1993b). At the time this book goes to press there are growing indications that the UK government recognises that there are different models of case management and that the particular form of care management adopted in the UK to provide services for elderly people is not necessarily the correct model for mentally ill people. Whether this is a genuine insight and whether the NHS and Community Care Act reforms really are going to facilitate the development of more sophisticated and appropriate models of care management for mentally ill people will, in time, become clear. However, a number of Department-of-Health-funded investigations are enabling us to examine the benefits and limitations of different models in the UK (RDP 1991; Muijen *et al.* 1992) and the most recently funded tri-centre study should shed further light on questions of the active ingredients, optimal caseloads and suitable client groups for case management, and the costs (Creed *et al.* 1993).

The case management services in Boulder

The mental health services in Boulder County, Colorado, have a number of different case management modes of operation. Therapists in the mental health centre act as case managers for clients with long-term needs, while continuing to carry a typical outpatient caseload. The most difficult-to-help clients, with the longest histories and most frequent hospitalisations, have case managers who are specifically dedicated to this client group. They carry small caseloads and work intensively in small teams (community support systems [CSS] teams). The CSS services were set up in Boulder in the 1980s with advice and guidance from Len Stein (the originator of the innovative community services in Madison, Wisconsin). They use an assertive outreach model and a mixed model of individual and team responsibility. There is a psychiatrist member of each team and medication compliance is one of the central service goals. Several different disciplines are represented in each team, including a former service user trained in a special programme. One team is located in county health premises and the other in a small, relatively anonymous house in the university part of the town. One of the case managers is the director of the sheltered workshop, which is located in a business park.

Patients assigned to the more intensive treatment on the CSS team were selected after assessment indicated a need for one or more of the services provided by the team – for example, a need for medication monitoring due to treatment noncompliance, or a need for management of the client's funds, supervised housing, frequent and flexible therapeutic contacts, and so on. These were generally the clients at greatest risk of relapse and hospital admission.

SAMPLE AND ENQUIRY METHOD

The data reported here are based on an analysis of the sample of sixty-eight cases interviewed in 1989 and reassessment of forty-one of the same group in 1991.

Eighty patients with a diagnosis of psychosis were randomly selected from all patients with psychosis treated by the Community Mental Health Centre of Boulder County Inc., Boulder, Colorado. The patients were in receipt of outpatient services from therapists in the centre and from CSS teams in the community. For a number of patients, case management services were provided from an acute inpatients facility and a sheltered workshop.

A computerised list of all the patients with a psychotic diagnosis was provided from the Center's record system. This list of names was checked with each team to remove patients who were deceased or no longer in contact with the service. A one-in-three sample was drawn from the list using random numbers. The case managers were asked to obtain the agreement of the selected patients until a quota of approximately fifteen patients in each setting was obtained. The patients were then interviewed, mostly at the sheltered workshop or in their own homes. The interview consisted of the LQOLP and the General Satisfaction Questionnaire (Huxley 1990). The interviewed patients were subsequently rated on the KGV (Krawiecka *et al.* 1977; see below) by the psychiatrist responsible for their medical care.

Measures

The General Satisfaction Questionnaire (GSQ) is based on the work of Larsen *et al.* (1979) in California. It has been piloted in the UK and has been the subject of a field trial (Huxley 1988, 1990). It consists of twenty items (eight on a four-point scale and twelve on a seven-point scale), two sections for the patients to give a free response, and a section for demographic data. Four sub-scores can be produced representing 'general satisfaction', satisfaction with access to services, satisfaction with the help given, and satisfaction with the 'acceptability' of the service provided.

The treating psychiatrists also made ratings of each patient who agreed to be interviewed, using the Manchester scale (the KGV). The KGV is a brief measure of psychopathology – including negative, positive and affective symptoms – developed by Krawiecka *et al.* (1977) for the assessment of long-standing psychiatric illness. It is suitable for use with patients in community settings. Five treating psychiatrists were responsible for completing these assessments, and to improve inter-rater reliability the rating criteria or 'anchors' were described in detail, item by item, on each copy of the ratings scale completed. No inter-rater reliability tests were conducted.

Further information was obtained from the computerised record, including the number of days during the past year the patients had spent in hospitals of all sorts, the number of outpatient and case management contacts, the date of first service contact, and the amount of time spent in sheltered work and day care during the year.

Because there were no LQOLP or GSQ data available on non-psychiatric populations in the USA, we also arranged to interview a sample of patients from a local health clinic for people on low income. These patients were paid for their participation in the study and were self-selected volunteers.

Results

Of the eighty selected patients, seven refused to be interviewed and five were unavailable to be interviewed because they were in hospital or jail. Of the sample, 46 per cent were female and 95 per cent were white; 55 per cent were single and only 8 per cent were married, the remainder being widowed, divorced or separated. Of the sample, 51 per cent (n=38) had a diagnosis of schizophrenia and a further 16 per cent (n=12) of schizoaffective disorder, while 20 per cent (n=15) suffered bipolar disorder and the rest had some other form of psychosis. Some patients had a case manager who was their outpatient therapist, others were in the CSS schemes, some had case management services provided by staff while they were in the acute unit and, for a number of others, their case manager was the senior worker at the sheltered employment setting. The mean age of the sample was 40 years.

Comparison between case management clients and the low-income group in the USA

The mean age of the low-income group was 34 years; 60 per cent were female, 93 per cent were white and 33 per cent were single. The quality of life interview obtains a global quality of life rating by the client on Cantril's ladder. Figure 9.1 shows the results for all the patients in this sample, the case management patients, the CSS patients, and the low-income comparison group. The CSS group has the largest proportion of all the samples of people who appear to be ambivalent (12 per cent).

Percentage

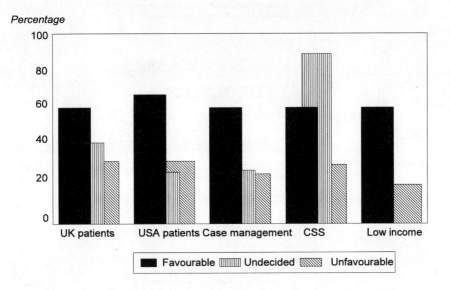

Figure 9.1 Global quality of life
Source: All Boulder data except UK patients

The quality of life interview is divided into different domains, and the mean scores for each of these is given in Figure 9.2. Four of the nine domains show a higher quality of life for the low-income group (health, social relations, legal and safety, and family relations). Two domains – religion and leisure – are approximately the same, and three – living situation, work and education, and finances – are superior in the psychiatric patients. The differences are significant only with regard to social relations, family relations, and work and education.

Quality of life comparisons between US case management and UK services

The case management clients in Boulder were compared with similar patients in South Manchester, using results obtained by Simpson *et al.* (1989). The Simpson study included patients who were long-term sufferers and for whose needs existing acute hospital provision was unsuited. A number of their sample remained long-stay (more than six months) on an acute hospital ward, while others, who had previously been long-stay on the acute hospital ward, were placed in a small, well-staffed hostel ward in the community. The remainder were a relatively stable group of long-term patients residing in group homes in the community. Their sample is therefore comparable to the present sample, in that it contained some long-term psychotic patients who were

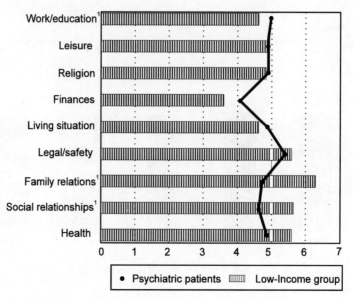

Figure 9.2 Quality of life of the low-income comparison group
Note:1 t=2.10; D.F.=29; p<.05
2 t=3.12; D.F.=35; p=<.01

receiving routine outpatient psychiatric care while others proved too difficult to provide for in traditional inpatient and outpatient services. The solution for this latter group was, in the USA, case management and, in the UK, long-term institutional care.

In an earlier publication (Warner and Huxley 1993), we compared the quality of life ratings in the US and UK settings. The significant differences (at the .05 level) were that the Manchester hospital patients were significantly less happy about their safety than the patients in the acute treatment unit in Boulder. The Manchester hospital patients were also less happy about their living situation than the outpatient case management patients in the Boulder service. Finally, the Manchester hospital patients were less happy about their living situation than the group home residents.

Psychiatric symptoms in US case management clients and comparable UK samples

The psychiatrists in the Boulder service rated the patients in this sample using the KVG (the same instrument as was used in the UK study) and found that the US patients tended, if anything, to be more disturbed than their UK equivalents. The psychopathology scores differed in this respect: positive symptoms were greater in the case management clients in

Boulder than those of the patients in the Manchester group homes. Affective symptoms were greater in the outpatient case management service clients than in the district general hospital patients. Negative symptoms did not differ across the groups.

The relationship between case manager activities and quality of life

When the case management cases were examined, monitoring was the only variable which was associated (positively at the .05 level) with quality of life. When the CSS cases were removed and the analysis repeated, monitoring remained positively associated with quality of life. In both analyses, brokerage activity was unrelated to quality of life. In all case management cases, total treatment contacts were inversely related to global quality of life ($r=-.470$; $p<.001$), and the same finding held for the CSS patients only ($r=.-488$; $p<.01$).

The relationship between case manager activities and service satisfaction

In an earlier paper (Huxley and Warner 1992), we reported that brokerage was the only case manager activity which was negatively associated with the GSQ acceptability score. Assertive outreach variables, including out of office visits, were positively correlated with the service accessibility satisfaction score. Monitoring activity was significantly associated (at the .01 level) with a higher score on the acceptability of services (in the analysis without CSS cases).

In the total sample, the total number of case management contacts in the last year was associated with less satisfaction (the correlation with the GSQ total was $-.268$, $p<.05$), as was the total number of all treatment contacts ($r=-.297$, $p<.05$).

Two-year follow-up

Two years after the original data collection, forty-one of the same patients were followed up to reassess their quality of life. Data collection took place over six weeks and the reduction from sixty-eight cases is entirely due to the limited time available. In order to see whether the 1991 sample of forty-one was a skewed sample of the sixty-eight original cases, we compared all major demographic and clinical variables. No significant differences were found. The mean global quality of life score (on Cantril's ladder) in 1991 (64 per cent) was higher than in 1989 (58.6 per cent), but the difference was not significant. However, the mean quality of life rating made by the interviewer (on the quality of life uniscale) is significantly higher in 1991 (58.2 per cent) than in 1989 (49.1 per cent) ($F=5.32$, $p<.05$). The mean satisfaction score (15.3

per cent) is also higher in 1991 than in 1989 (14.6 per cent), but is not significantly so.

The distribution of individual percentage change scores is approximately normal for the thirty-six clients for whom data are available. Twenty-six clients remained within 25 per cent of their original score. Over the two-year period, out of thirty-six patients, five deteriorated by more than 25 per cent of their initial score and five patients improved by more than 25 per cent. The mean scores of the two groups of patients in 1989 and 1991 are remarkably similar, as Figure 9.3 shows.

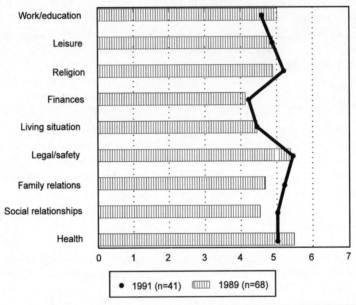

Figure 9.3 Quality of life comparison 1989 and 1991

DISCUSSION

Low-income clinic comparison

The face validity of the LQOLP is supported by the fact that the low-income group had the highest global quality of life. It is also clear that family relations and social relations are important components in the superiority, since they are significantly different from the psychiatric patients' scores. Even though the low-income group was attending a clinic for physical health problems, patients' perceived health is better than that of the psychiatric patients, albeit that this is not a statistically significant difference. Had they been a low-income non-consulting group, then this difference might have been significant.

The work and education result favoured the patients, because the low-income group were mostly not in work and a substantial proportion of the patients attended the sheltered work setting. This improved their income compared to other patients and to the low-income group.

UK–US quality of life comparison

The study reported here was conducted before the increase in the popularity of case management in the UK and before the legislative changes which introduced the care programme approach and care management in local authorities. In spite of these changes, most of the hospital patients in the Simpson study are almost certainly still being cared for in twenty-four-hour staffed accommodation of some sort (Goldberg, personal communication). It comes as no surprise that the patients in the hospital ward in Manchester felt least happy about their personal safety. Overcrowded, understaffed wards with a high proportion of detained patients can be a hazardous environment. In contrast, safety was better in the small, more domestic acute unit in a house in the community in Boulder. However, both the Boulder and Manchester inpatients would rather not have been in hospital and this is reflected in their lower living situation scores. The more stable community residents (in group homes in Manchester and outpatient care in Boulder) felt significantly happier about their living situation.

Psychiatric symptoms

Keeping the Boulder patients in the community is perhaps achieved at some clinical cost, since their KGV ratings were higher than those of the patients in the hospitals and community settings in the UK. We have discussed elsewhere the possible reasons for this finding (Warner and Huxley 1993). It is possible that this result is due to selection bias, because the group home patients are chosen because of their low level of clinical disturbance. However, most of the group home residents do experience repeated episodes of disorder and were certainly not selected because they had a good prognosis, either clinically or socially. It is true, though, that the patients who were long-stay in the hospital were unsuitable for group home residence because of their clinical and behavioural problems, which required twenty-four-hour supervision.

Assuming that the clinical ratings were not biased and that there were not substantial differences in medication doses or compliance, the Boulder patients were possibly more unwell, because of greater levels of stress in their living situations. Hospital wards and hostel wards are, whatever their problems, structured settings in which symptoms and behaviour can be treated and controlled. Intensive community case management, even with daily contact, cannot provide the same degree of control of the external environment. Finally, it could be argued that the lack of availability of psychiatric beds in the Boulder service means that patients who, in the UK, would be long-stay in hospital or in a hostel ward, have to be treated in community settings (for a more detailed consideration of this point see Warner and Huxley 1993).

Case manager activity, quality of life and satisfaction with services

In the sample as a whole, there was a tendency for satisfaction to be lower the greater the number of case management contacts and total treatment contacts (as reported by the service data base). This suggests that the patients perceived the services as too intrusive. Case managers are (presumably) giving most of their attention to clients who have the lowest quality of life and satisfaction ratings and who are seen by the case managers as most in need or most at risk. This is consistent with other reports from similar services elsewhere (Brekke and Test 1987; Dietzen and Bond 1993). Dietzen and Bond found that the quantity of services was unrelated to their outcome measures (change in hospital use and client satisfaction). However, their high-contact groups had clients with significantly higher rates of prior psychiatric admissions. They argue that some clients benefit more from office-based interventions than from assertive outreach, and that low-contact groups have a significant proportion of schizophrenia sufferers in them. These patients may be resisting the intensity of the service contact (Dozier *et al.* forthcoming). It becomes critical to predict which service packages are of most benefit to which clients. However, there may have to be a trade-off between the degree of assertiveness and the level of satisfaction and quality of life. Without the assertive approach, many of these patients would have to be re-admitted to hospital, and most were clearly expressing a preference for community living and reporting better quality of life than hospitalised patients. To reduce the assertiveness of the case management service would simply put them at greater risk of receiving care and treatment in less 'popular' institutional settings. One patient complained of having to go each day to receive her medication from the case management team; however, prior to this arrangement, she had spent several years having regular and long admissions to the state hospital. She remained quite deluded but she had acquired her own home and had not been admitted for more than a year at the time of this study.

This research lends further weight to the argument that it is a long-term relationship between worker and client which is the key to successful community treatment and that continual monitoring is a crucial part of the process. The brokerage component of assertive case management does not appear to have any influence over quality of life for mentally ill people, and in the present investigation, was actually unpopular. This could be because the case managers required more initiative to come from the client than they did when they were monitoring progress and that clients found the activity associated with contact with other agencies overstimulating or, alternatively, they lacked the motivation required to undertake the associated tasks.

Two-year follow-up

An important part of the process of service evaluation is to provide feedback to the clients and to the workers. Only one person who was approached for the follow-up study refused to be re-interviewed. He did so because he had had no feedback from the previous interview. As a direct result, we computed individual profiles and offered a graphic copy to each participant (Figure 9.4 is an illustration of one of the actual profiles). This exercise of providing feedback was popular with nearly all of the clients and some asked for the information to be shared with their helpers or carers. It seems possible that graphic quality of life feedback might be used as a form of goal-attainment scaling. In this case, a middle-aged man who lived alone and who had no family (hence the absence of ratings in these domains in Figure 9.4) had returned to work as a postman in 1990. The improvement in his financial situation is reflected in his improved subjective well-being in the financial, work and leisure domains. He remained a devout worshipper and so rated his

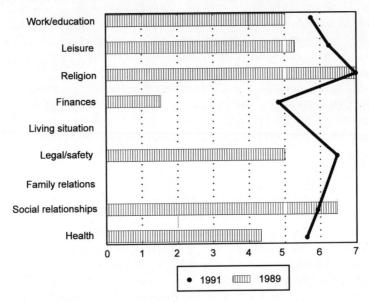

Figure 9.4 Individual client comparison

satisfaction with his religious faith and its teachings very highly on both occasions.

Feedback to the providers and the purchasers of services is sometimes as important as feedback to clients, and we have used versions of Figure 9.3 in this way in presentations to health and social services executives. It shows the aggregated data for the sample at times one and two. Given that the objective of the case management service is to coordinate care so that the clients are maintained in the community with an acceptable quality of life, then Figure 9.3 could be regarded as showing the successful accomplishment of this objective, in terms of subjective well-being, for the case managers' clients as a group.

CONCLUSIONS

The availability of a computerised information system, in existence because of the need to track output for billing purposes, is, nevertheless, an invaluable tool in evaluation research. It can act as a sampling frame and can distinguish between patient sub-groups in terms of demographic details and treatment history.

Comparability between the different patient groups is of fundamental importance. The comparison here was international and required even greater efforts than usual to ensure comparability. As Shepherd (1993) has argued, patient comparability cannot be ensured by using service-use characteristics or definitions of sub-groups of patients with long-term needs. Comparability of groups of patients has to be developed from individual assessments (of their health and welfare characteristics). Aggregated information, which can be used in service planning and provision, can be drawn from this individual assessment (Ryan *et al.* 1991; Huxley 1994a; 1994b).

So far as information about provision of services is concerned, there is evidence that the size of the provision – i.e. the volume of activity or the number of contacts – is far too crude a measure of impact. This study and a number of others show that the relationship between activity and outcome is a complex one. In some cases, more activity appears to be associated with a worse outcome and lower levels of satisfaction on the part of the recipients. Two factors which should be taken into account are: more contact may be required for the patients with the greatest levels of need, who may have the most intractable problems; and patients who either are served against their will or who are reluctant to be helped may have different satisfaction profiles from those who are helped willingly.

Finally, the importance of providing feedback to participants cannot be more powerfully illustrated than by the case of the man who refused to participate a second time because he had had no feedback two years previously. The excuse that it had taken two years to finalise the report on the project was irrelevant (and we did not use it!). Not only is feedback a legitimate part of the contract of involvement in the evaluation, it might also prove to be clinically useful. Showing the patients their own graphic picture of their progress over the two years produced many positive responses. It seemed likely that the procedure could be adopted in clinical practice, in the same way that goal-attainment scaling uses feedback to the patient on the achievement of goals.

Chapter 10

Individual case studies using quality of life assessment in routine practice

INTRODUCTION

The studies described in this book have been based on the nomothetic method of investigation, i.e. data based on groups of subjects. This methodological approach is very important in research such as epidemiological surveys and in the assessment of aetiological factors and the effectiveness of different interventions (Goldberg and Huxley 1992). However, some practitioners have found it helpful, as part of routine practice, to assess changes in the quality of life of an individual. This has been a useful means of identifying areas of unmet need and of auditing the outcome of individual care plans. This approach, based on an individual person, is known as the idiographic method of investigation (Barlow and Hersen 1984; Bech 1990). This chapter gives two examples of this approach by describing the changes in subjective quality of life over time as assessed by the repeated use of the LQOLP.

The first example is of a 42-year-old man with a twenty-three-year history of a persistent psychotic illness which has varied in severity. We have called him John, and his quality of life was assessed over four years. The second example is of a 30-year-old man with at least a fifteen-year history of a psychiatric illness. We called him Ralph, and his quality of life was assessed over a two-year period.

CASE STUDY: JOHN

Details of this case are described elsewhere (Bridges *et al.* 1993). Briefly, he is a man with a twenty-three-year history of a persistent schizophreniform psychosis associated with temporal lobe epilepsy which have both varied in severity. The positive psychotic phenomena have included third person auditory hallucinations, thought insertion and withdrawal, and persecutory beliefs. Associated with these have been serious behavioural disturbances, especially when he has been exposed to various social stressors. These have included antisocial acts such as destructive, combative, disruptive, restless, intrusive, pestering and abusive behaviour; fleeting thoughts, threats and actual episodes of parasuicidal behaviour (for example, superficial self-cutting and self-poisoning); and importunate illness behaviour associated with the desire for money, cigarettes and failure to accept responsibility for his own actions. Other features of his illness have included episodes of marked sleep disturbance, periods of dysphoria and a persistent negative self-image. To date he has required at least nine inpatient admissions to psychiatric hospitals and lengthy day-hospital admissions on four occasions.

Following the onset of his illness he became very dependent on his elderly mother, but by the age of 34 years he had imposed an excessive burden on her. He was drinking and smoking heavily, his daily living skills were extremely limited, he made no significant contribution to household activities and often went to bed early complaining he could not sleep. Eventually he was persuaded by social services to live in a local authority staffed hostel for mentally ill people. During the following five years he benefited from intensive support, provided by a network of services. This included staff at the hostel, a day centre, a day hospital, two rehabilitation projects run by artists which offered arts-related activities (Bridges and Brown 1989), a mental health social worker, a support worker, a psychiatrist and his family doctor.

Initially he required a lot of supervision and personal attention; otherwise he would drift off to pester people, including his mother, for cigarettes and money. However, with time and with this range of support, his mental state became more stable and his involvement with his structured programme became more sustained. His involvement with the arts-based rehabilitation services (known as START and the RO-VERS: see Chapter 8) was particularly successful and, eventually, he was able to arrange an exhibition of his own work in a local library with support from the team. At the end of this period the hostel was closed by social services and replaced by a dispersed network of supported accommodation. Before he had to move, his quality of life was assessed using the LQOLP. The results of his subjective responses at this time are summarised in Figure 10.1 ('hostel').

He moved to a group home, along with three other people who were thought to need twenty-four-hour supervision and support. After four months this support was changed by social services, mainly because of shortages in resources, to a peripatetic service. This eventually resulted in a marked deterioration in John's mental state, social functioning and relationships with other people living at the group home and in the local community. Another resident of the group home developed a hostile attitude towards him and often accused him of stealing money, food and clothes. On at least one occasion such accusations led to fighting between them. His support worker helped and encouraged him to keep his

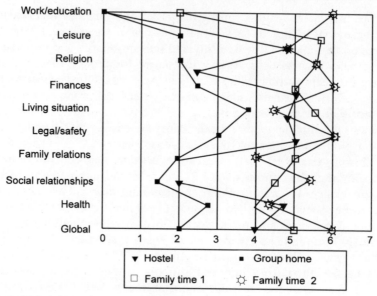

Figure 10.1 John's changes of accommodation

bedroom in a reasonable state, to attend to his personal hygiene, laundry, budgeting his money, shopping and cooking. This became more and more difficult. He often ate food before it was properly cooked, frequently he was awake at night demanding cigarettes from other residents, and he was banned from the local pub for pestering customers. In addition, he frequently requested a move elsewhere, including into hospital. On the positive side, he maintained a good relationship with the artist at the ROVERS and was able to talk to her easily. He often expressed feelings of loneliness, especially at night, a sense of insecurity, a lack of friendships and his difficulties in living in a group home. However, he enjoyed his art and he was able to concentrate on it and apply himself when supervised by the teacher. It enabled him to distract his attention from his dissatisfaction with life elsewhere and he enjoyed the trips to various places arranged by the ROVERS, during which his friendly and generous nature was often seen. The LQOLP was completed again one year after he moved to the group home as shown in Figure 10.1 ('group home').

The deterioration identified by application of the LQOLP led to the involvement of the adult fostering service of the local social services department (the Family Placement Scheme), which successfully placed him with someone who was willing to foster him. The Family Placement Scheme recruits and supports a 'host family' – a single person, couple or a family – who have the physical space and personal ability to offer a warm and supportive home environment to another adult. The move resulted in a gradual and significant improvement in John's mental state and behaviour. His involvement with day-time support services also improved and eventually included work in a voluntary sheltered work-shop where he helped to make plastic bags. His week remained very structured, though with more of an emphasis on domestic and social activities. After about a month, his neuroleptic medication was reduced, because he often felt sleepy during the day and because his psychotic phenomena had remained quiescent since he had settled into his more relaxed home environment. Reviews of his progress involved repre-sentatives from the network of services and were held at his new home. On these occasions he would usually and spontaneously make the tea for everyone. After six months he had established a trusting relationship with his 'host' carer and had become integrated into her own social network and activities in the evenings and at weekends. It is interesting to note that his placement was in an area ranked as one of the worst in the country in terms of measures of social deprivation (Jarman 1984). The assessment of his quality of life was repeated twelve months after he moved to his current home, and is shown in Figure 10.1 as 'family time 1'.

John has been in his current home for over three years. Overall, his mental health and social functioning have improved considerably and he has been able to establish a meaningful friendship with another person living in the same place. To a large extent these improvements have been due to the excellent quality of the support provided by his 'host' carer. John continues to be pleased with his living arrangements, although after two years he developed a desire, eventually to move to more independent accommodation. He now has a job as a cleaner for about thirteen hours a week in a public institution, where he is popular and valued. After being in this home for two years his LQOLP was repeated and shown as 'family time 2' in Figure 10.1.

CASE STUDY: RALPH

All of the information for this case study was drawn from the LQOLP forms completed by a community support team. Ralph was chosen because he was assessed at three points in time: at the time of acceptance of case by the teams; at the end of one year of team support; and at the end of two years of team support. Ralph is a 30-year-old man who was referred to the support team because of serious, long-term mental disorder. He left school at age 15, when he was first admitted to hospital because of his mental illness. At the first assessment he was seeing doctors for a physical illness as well but this did not appear to be serious, and he was in receipt of medication for his 'nerves'. Ralph was single and had been living in a flat with a girlfriend for over two years. He had daily contact with his family. During this period he thought of moving but had

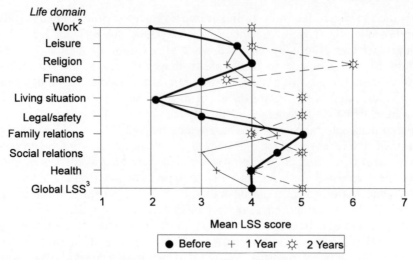

Figure 10.2 Perceived quality of life for Ralph: three assessments of life
satisfaction levels[1]
Note: 1 Life satisfaction scale (LSS) = 1–7
2 Ralph became employed year 1–2
3 Global well-being by LSS scale

not done so. He saw himself as a person who did not need friends but,
nevertheless, had regular contact with some. At least one friend was a
person on whom he felt he could rely if needed. He did not attend church
regularly. At the time, he had neither been a victim of a crime nor
accused of one but he had required help from the police within the
previous year. He was unemployed, with an income of £56 per week from
state benefits.

Figure 10.2 shows his subjective quality of life ratings. When he was
referred to the team his living situation and work were particularly
unsatisfactory life domains. His assessment was essentially positive but
markedly higher than the assessment of the key worker (Figure 10.3).

After one year he was reassessed. By that time, some things in his life
had changed. In particular, he had moved from his flat and was now
living in a larger rented house. He was still unemployed but his weekly
income had risen to £80. His social and family life, health and the
legal/safety aspects of life remained as before and he had again needed
the help of the police. His perceived quality of life ratings remained
similar, though his satisfaction with both social relations and health were
diminished noticeably. Interestingly enough, a degree of concordance
began to emerge between the client and worker concerning his overall
quality of life (Figure 10.3).

At the end of a second year, his life showed further signs of change.
For example, by now he had not been hospitalised for mental disorder

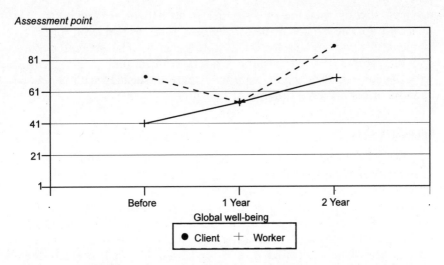

Figure 10.3 Global quality of life for Ralph: three assessments by worker and Ralph of global well-being
Note: Both rated on 100-point scale

during the previous three years and was no longer seeing a doctor for physical health problems. He was still seeing a doctor for his psychiatric illness and was continuing to receive medication for this. He had changed his place of residence; he was no longer living in a private home but had moved to a group home with five other residents, none of whom was his family. Interestingly, he had begun to see much less of his family and he had finished his relationship with his previous co-habitee. In addition, he had begun to attend church more frequently during the period. He was employed, working thirty hours per week, but his overall income had dropped marginally to £76.

   In addition to this idiographic approach, these data can be compared with group data of others who have similar circumstances. A comparison of Ralph's perceived quality of life with that of other men living in the same district who are also on the social services department's caseload and who suffer from long-term, severe mental health problems similar to his shows that, on initial assessment, Ralph's life satisfaction levels were appreciably lower than the average. In fact, only in the area of family relations did his satisfaction appear above average, and that difference was only marginal. In some areas, such as his living situation, they were very much worse. At two years, however, the situation had changed. By then, most areas of life satisfaction either approximated or exceeded the local norms. As shown above, his living situation was not only an area of objective change but one of subjective change as well. Inexplicably, family relations had declined to below average. Likewise, income had declined slightly, making one wonder if he had been caught up in a poverty trap where gains made through employment had led to impoverishment through greater losses in state benefits. The general picture, including global life satisfaction indicators, confirm that his involvement with the community support team was clearly associated with beneficial changes in his perceived quality of life.

DISCUSSION

The personal costs of a chronic and disabling illness are high, and we need to judge the effectiveness of different forms of intervention in terms of how they reduce these non-monetary costs and how they facilitate the development and maintenance of personal strengths, abilities and adaptation to the persistent impairments and social dysfunction related to the illness. In addition, when evaluating the benefits of services, we need to take notice of how satisfied people are in relation to the effects these services have on different aspects of their lives. These two case examples of the idiographic approach illustrate the utility of assessing quality of life in routine practice. We have found the LQOLP to be a useful tool for indicating areas of unmet need and for auditing the outcome of the individual's care plans. A general point to be borne in mind when evaluating services is that both aggregated data and individual case studies are useful in obtaining a more complete picture of how the services are operating.

As well as illustrating the use of the LQOLP in routine practice, these case studies draw attention to several important operational principles. First, when formulating care plans, a variety of biological, social and personal factors need to be assessed, collated and reviewed. The care process must be underpinned by a 'long-term' model rather than one which is episode orientated and focused upon acute presentations of illness. Plans need to be realistic and flexible and should not be based on the expectation that the majority of people will emerge from the intervention able to lead independent lives (Bennett and Morris 1983; Shepherd 1991).

Second, people with long-term and/or recurrent episodes of disorder depend on a 'system of care' (described in Chapter 4), which involves a multiplicity of organisations. Patients need a variety of services and each of these has its own longitudinal dimension. In general terms, the 'system of care' for people with long-term disabilities must be flexible and well coordinated so that people, depending upon their needs at the time, can move easily within it (Bachrach 1981; Bennett and Morris 1983). In order to develop and maintain such a system, organisations need to work in partnership and encompass both longitudinal and cross-sectional concepts of care. If the cross-sectional aspect of care is not acknowledged and planned for, uncoordinated changes in some services can have an adverse effect on patients; for example, John experienced a major change in his mental state after he moved to the group home and when the mode of staff support was changed.

Third, the 'system of care' depends upon a multi-disciplinary approach and dedicated staff with specialist knowledge and skills. John's case illustrates that some workers without specialist training in psychiatry can make an important contribution to the overall care of an individual because of their personal skills, experiences and personalities. As Shepherd (1991) concludes, the process of rehabilitation is about people and how we behave towards each other. Although John benefited from the care and support of many people, he gained most from his involvement with the artist and his 'host' carer (who continues to be very important in his life).

Finally, these two cases remind us of the principle that we are working with people who, despite their illness, have freedom of choice regarding the way in which they conduct their lives and the extent to which they accept the services which are on offer. Economists refer to this in terms of the principle of 'consumer sovereignty' (Mooney 1986). This raises the issue (considered in Chapter 1) of the extent to which an individual is the best judge of, or is actually able to judge, his or her own welfare and service needs. Of course, services cannot be compulsorily imposed on someone unless his or her needs fulfil the requirements of the Mental Health Act. Fortunately, in the main, we are working with people who are not helpless in the face of disease and who are able to have an impact on the illness process. There are many factors which remain under the direct control of the person and which can have either a positive or negative effect on the overall outcome or course of the illness (Wing 1986).

CONCLUSION

Within the lifetime of John and Ralph, many changes have occurred in the provision of mental health services in the UK. If John and Ralph had been adults three decades ago they may have become two long-stay patients of a mental hospital. In the past thirty years we have learned that, when appropriate resources are available, coordinated and used flexibly, it is possible to enable people with disabling illnesses to have a reasonable quality of life in the community. The 'Care Programme Approach' (in the UK) may become meaningful only when a comprehensive infrastructure of services – especially personnel with relevant skills – is in place. Unfortunately, we know that this infrastructure is inadequate in many parts of the UK and there is a real danger that the situation may deteriorate. If more resources are invested in education, research and the development of rehabilitation services we might stand a chance of maximising the quality of life of many people like John and Ralph. One could be forgiven, however, for observing that their needs have a longer shelf-life than the average professional and the below-average politician.

Chapter 11

The quality of life of clubhouse members

BACKGROUND

There is no doubt that, irrespective of one's mental health status, work plays an important role in the creation of individual well-being. The difficulties of placing mentally ill people directly into the work environment have grown during the years of recession, and efforts to enhance this process, usually subsumed under the title 'vocational rehabilitation', have been expanded and developed accordingly. A review of research on vocational programmes, reported by Anthony and Blanch (1989), found mixed results, with twice as many programmes failing to show an effect than reporting positive outcomes. In terms of sheltered workschemes, seven of the eight studies reported better results for the programme subjects than for the control subjects.

A number of different approaches have been taken to address the problem of organising vocational programmes. In traditional schemes, the participants are trained or prepared in advance of the placement in competitive employment. The relative failure of this approach led to the development of the concept of supported employment, in which participants are placed and trained in the workplace (Sciarappa *et al.* 1994) and provided with whatever support is required. This may include on the job 'coaching' or job-sharing (Wehman *et al.* 1989). Kaufmann *et al.* (1989) report on a project which combines peer support groups combined with vocational counselling and job-placement services. One component of the programme involves a consumer-oriented self-help employment centre. Another approach is to combine vocational and case management services through the assignment of vocational rehabilitation specialists to case management teams in an integrated approach (Mowbray *et al.* 1992). The costs and benefits of the various approaches have not been compared, although benefit–cost analysis of supported employment has shown some promise. Sciarappa *et al.* (1994) found participants experienced significant monetary and non-monetary benefits and reduced service utilisation. However, service costs were increased due to the increased advocacy efforts of staff.

An increasingly common approach to vocational rehabilitation is the clubhouse model. The first clubhouse, Fountain House in New York, was established in 1948 by a group of ex-patients as a social club for former patients and was turned into a vocational programme, emphasising transitional employment, by John Beard. Mastboom (1992) estimates that the number of clubhouses in operation has more than doubled over the past ten years, and they now operate all over the world. Standards for clubhouse programmes have been developed through collaboration with clubhouses worldwide, and in 1991, 90 per cent of clubhouses were said to be trying to follow the thirty-five standards (Propst 1992).

The programme components at the original Fountain House are prevocational day programme, transitional employment programme, apartment, reach-out, evening and weekend programmes, therapeutic interventions and clubhouse evaluation. Four hundred members attend the clubhouse to participate in the day programmes. Beard *et al.* (1982) describe the four fundamental principles of the programme as: the clubhouse belongs to its members; daily attendance is expected and makes a difference to other members; members feel wanted as contributors; and, consequently, members feel needed. Staff are treated in the same way and are usually indistinguishable from members. The model encourages withdrawal at times of stress, peer networks of high-intimacy friendships, and positive approaches to stressful requirements of the work.

According to Mastboom (1992) the target population for the clubhouse consists of people suffering usually long-term and serious psychiatric problems, who, 'in addition to the disorder and intense treatment. . .have sustained social and psychiatric impairments' (Mastboom 1992:10). Intervention overtly recognises and accepts the psychiatric disorder and offers purposeful support and reinforcement of the patient's remaining strengths. One of the central features of the approach is the Transitional Employment Program (TEP), which is 'based on agreements made with business enterprises that promise to provide employment opportunities for clubhouse members, enabling them to gain job experience in a normal working environment. . .The clubhouse guarantees the employer actual daily staffing for the employment position' (Mastboom 1992:12). One clubhouse director graphically expresses the effects of this process on new members:

> It never ceases to amaze me as I witness the literal transformation that takes place as members discover their roles in the clubhouse and begin to use their own ideas, talents, and abilities to enhance part of the clubhouse for the benefit of the membership. It is as if you can watch the layers of armour

shielding them from ignorance, contempt, and indifference gradually drop off to expose feelings of power, mastery, confidence and self-esteem.

(Waters 1992:41)

The approach is a 'form of psychosocial rehabilitation and intends above all to improve the quality of the daily lives of its members' (Mastboom 1992:10). Given this central objective, it makes sense to assess the impact of clubhouses on their members' quality of life. The present chapter reports preliminary results from the assessment of the quality of life of members of the Chinook Clubhouse in Boulder, Colorado.

Previous empirical investigations

There have been a number of empirical investigations of clubhouses, including a survey of fifty by Mastboom (1992). Much of the work is descriptive, and only two studies have undertaken methodologically sophisticated investigations (Wilkinson 1992; Rosenfield and Neese-Todd 1993). In one of the few studies of staff members, Finch and Kranz (1991) found that staff at Fountain House had longer tenure and fewer symptoms of burn-out than staff in traditional mental health settings.

Mastboom's survey (1992) had an 80 per cent response rate. The average membership of a clubhouse was 107, with an enormous range from forty to 2,000 registered members (this depended on the age of the clubhouse). Irrespective of the age of the clubhouse, the number of active members tended to be about half of those registered. There were, on average, ten members to each staff member. Of the active members, 63 per cent were schizophrenia sufferers and the next largest group, at 12 per cent, was bipolar disorder. Forty-one per cent had spent more than two years in hospital, and only 4 per cent had never been admitted. Fifty-four per cent of members are male, and the modal age is between 31 and 40 years of age. Nineteen per cent live alone, and 35 per cent live in some form of housing programme connected to the mental health services. The proportion living alone in the Amsterdam Clubhouse is much higher at 65 per cent.

Exclusion criteria operating in the USA were alcoholism and drug addiction (twenty-nine entries); mental retardation (twenty-nine); organic brain disorder (eighteen); former aggressive behaviour (eighteen); travel time greater than one hour (fifteen); lack of psychiatric problems (eleven); the inability to travel independently (eight); and an insufficiently chronic case history (eight). Although the members of most clubhouses have long-term problems and most have had psychotic illnesses, these exclusion criteria mean that the most difficult patients, who have a combination of drug abuse and assaultive behaviours and who lack motivation or refuse help, may be excluded in some instances.

Wilkinson (1992) studied thirty-two clubhouse members, aged between 22 and 50, from the New Day Clubhouse in Spartanburg, South Carolina. Members attended for a minimum of one day a month for twelve consecutive months and their frequency of hospitalisation during the period before regular membership was compared with their period of regular membership. The number of hospital days and admissions was reduced from 2,064 days and twenty-seven admissions in the pre-clubhouse period, to 420 days and fourteen admissions in the period afterwards. The average length of stay in the hospital was reduced from seventy-six days to thirty days. The analysis of costs shows that the thirty-day stay in an acute psychiatric facility in the general hospital is $14,868, $8,585 in an acute psychiatric hospital bed and $5,555 in a mental hospital bed. Thirty days' provision at the clubhouse costs $550. Depending upon the facility to which the patient is admitted, the cost savings of a reduction in the length of stay from seventy-six to thirty days is approximately in the range $5,000 to $14,000. However, Wilkinson does not assess whether there has been any increase in the use of other services in the post-clubhouse period.

Rosenfield and Neese-Todd (1993) interviewed 157 clubhouse members (93 per cent of those attending for one consecutive month) and compared their quality of life with various programme components and members' views of the extent to which the service empowered them. Empowerment (rated on a specially devised scale, RNES) was related to satisfaction with living arrangements, social relations, family relations, prevocational activities, safety, health and leisure activity. Members' level of functioning and mood were not responsible for the associations. Those with more social contacts were more satisfied with their social relations and their leisure activities. Transitional employment was related to greater satisfaction with finances, but satisfaction with finances and employment status were unrelated to empowerment.

Graves (1991), the Director of the National Institute on Disability and Rehabilitation Research, has called for applied research that engages consumers in the quest for information about their own rehabilitation programme.

THE PRESENT STUDY

The present study is in two parts. Part I examines the impact of the introduction of a clubhouse into the community services in Boulder, Colorado, and examines the members' satisfaction with services and their quality of life compared to non-members. This study was undertaken, in part, to assess improvements in the clubhouse group, and to investigate changes in service use following its membership. While advocates of the clubhouse have argued that it does produce improvements, it is possible that clubhouse membership affects the way in which members access services, so that, following membership, they actually consume more resources than before. It is also possible that people who become regular clubhouse users are not those people who have the highest levels of psychiatric morbidity. This part of the study was, therefore, a before-and-after two-year follow-up of a group of psychotic patients in touch with services before the clubhouse was instituted as part of the service provision. Patients thought suitable by the service providers were offered the opportunity to use the clubhouse when it opened and this part of the study was uncontrolled.

Part II involves the comparison of two matched groups, one of regular users and the other of non-users, matched for diagnosis, age, gender, length of history and previous service use. This part was conducted on a larger case-comparison group to establish whether the clubhouse produced quality of life and satisfaction with service improvements, in comparison with a matched group who were not in receipt of the clubhouse service. The opportunity was taken, as suggested by Graves (1991), to involve members in the evaluation. Indeed, the evaluation was their idea and they selected the LQOLP as the instrument they wished to use. Six members of the Chinook Clubhouse in Boulder, Colorado, were trained to use it (by PH) and conducted most of the interviews themselves. The Chinook Clubhouse was established in 1990, following the principles established by Fountain House, and has a transitional employment programme. Clubhouse activities include prevocational activities from 9 a.m. to 3 p.m. daily and social activities, usually between 5 p.m. and 8 p.m. In July 1991, the opening hours were extended to include Saturdays from 11 a.m. to 3 p.m.

Part I: Sample

From an original survey of sixty-eight psychotic patients conducted in 1989, forty-four were followed up in 1991. Cases which were not available for follow-up were not significantly different on any variables of major importance from those who were followed up; the limitations of time available to collect the sample was the cause of the reduced number of cases successfully followed up. Of the forty-four successfully followed up, twenty-four patients had become clubhouse members. This group of forty-four was using the clubhouse with the same frequency as all other users (in 1991).

The group which went on to become members of the clubhouse (twenty-four of the original sixty-eight) and the group which did not (forty-four of the original sixty-eight) were compared to see whether any variable obtained in 1989 discriminated between the groups. They were similar in terms of age, school-leaving age, and age at first admission. The group which did not become clubhouse members tended to work longer hours and earn slightly more. The group which went on to become clubhouse members had a significantly greater desire for more leisure activities (Chi-squared =4.37, D.F.=1, p=.03). This suggests that it might be a more highly motivated group, certainly where social activities are concerned.

Clinical status

The clinical status of patients in 1989 was related to their subsequent clubhouse membership in 1991. A high positive symptom score in 1989 is related to being an infrequent user in 1991. A similar relationship holds for negative and total symptom scores in 1989, but the former is an insignificant relationship. This suggests that the most disturbed patients (in 1989) were not recruited to clubhouse membership by 1991.

Service use

Table 11.1 is based on data from the Mental Health Center information system. They show that 'group (long)' and 'inpatient days' have decreased for clubhouse users (but not significantly). All other service use has increased; 'group (regular)' and 'group (short)' have increased significantly. There is little evidence that the clubhouse members are using fewer other services. An effect of this sort (reduction in the use of other services) may take longer to appear and probably requires an examination of a larger sample.

Table 11.1 Service use before and after clubhouse membership

Service item	Mean before	Mean after	p
Inpatient status	3.1	0.8	.15
Individual (regular)	6.2	8.3	N.S.
Individual (brief)	16.05	17.55	N.S.
Group (regular)	18.65	26.35	.05
Group (short)	5.11	9.75	.02
Group (long)	17.3	13.8	N.S.
Brief Medication	11.1	15.45	N.S.
Residential support	13.45	15.65	N.S.
Vocational rehab.	32.25	36.2	N.S.
Case management	7.35	8.35	N.S.
Total service use	148	183	.12

Note: Based upon service use data for the months of clubhouse use compared with the same number of months before clubhouse use (for each of twenty-four patients)

Comparison of the members and non-members in the 1991 follow-up sample (n=44)

There are no major social or demographic differences between the two groups of clients. There are a number of significant differences between the groups and these are shown in Table 11.2. Frequent users have better social relationships and higher satisfaction levels. The infrequent and regular members have lower scores.

Table 11.2 A comparison between the clubhouse members and the non-members re-interviewed in 1991

Item	Non-member	Member	p
No.	20	24	
Age	50	43	
Income	201	123	
Positive symptoms[1]	2.2	5.3	.002
Negative symptoms[1]	3.5	4.8	
Affective symptoms[1]	3.3	3.5	
Total symptoms[1]	9.0	13.4	.02

	Non-users	Infrequent members	Regular members	Frequent members
QOL social relations domain, (F=4.86; p=.006)	5.5	4.1	4.5	5.3
Satisfaction with services (out of 20) (F=3.27; p=.03)	17	12	14	18

Note: 1 These data are from 1989 and were collected using the Manchester Scale (KGV)

Subjective responses to clubhouse

As Table 11.2 shows, the infrequent and regular users have lower satisfaction levels. This could be because people with low satisfaction scores are selected or self-selected for membership, or because there are aspects of the service which produce greater dissatisfaction. Interviews with the members suggest that both processes are probably in operation.

Some members have found existing services do not meet their needs, and the clubhouse is popular with these clients. They may be looking for work or to increase their social contacts (frequent members do have better social relationships, although the number of frequent members is small). Some said that they found the activities at the clubhouse suited them and that they were able to learn new skills (for example, computer work) or do things they found undemanding and enjoyable (for example, helping with meals). Others, particularly infrequent users, have found that the clubhouse does not meet their needs. One or two said that they felt unwelcome and used this as an excuse to leave after one or two visits.

Others found that they did not like the activities available, although this may have been a function of the early development of the programme. Some said that the programme times overlap with the availability of other services and that they would rather use these other services than start to use the clubhouse.

Part I: summary

One should treat these findings with some caution because the numbers involved are small. The 1991 sample does, nevertheless, seem to be representative of both the 1989 sample and clubhouse members. The clubhouse is not being used by those people who were more unwell in 1989. However, in comparison with the twenty non-members interviewed in 1991, they have more positive symptoms and a higher total symptom score. It is perhaps being used by those whose existing needs were not well met by services available in 1989 and who were, at that time, motivated to do more. Those who use the clubhouse frequently have better social relationships and are more satisfied with services than members who use the clubhouse less often.

Part II

A comparison group was obtained from a neighbouring area without a clubhouse. We expected that, compared with the comparison group, the clubhouse members might have better outcomes in terms of their current: quality of life scores; costs; hospitalisation rates; social contacts, especially trusting and reliable ones; leisure activities; involvement in work; and symptom scores.

The service utilisation data and the cost information were not available at the time this book went to press, but we will be interested to see whether the clubhouse members have changed the pattern of service use since becoming members and whether they have been hospitalised less, compared with their own rate before membership. The comparison group of non-members will be assessed over the same time periods in terms of their service utilisation to see if their pattern of use or hospitalisation rate differ in the same way or to the same extent as that of the clubhouse members. On the basis of part I of this study one might expect to find an increase in service use and, hence, costs in the clubhouse group.

Matching the samples

Matching was undertaken on the basis of sex, age and diagnosis (295, 296 or 298), with an attempt to match for past service use and length of contact with the Mental Health Center services. Sixty-eight clubhouse members met the diagnostic and age criteria. It was possible to match fifty-four clubhouse members with comparable clients elsewhere (79 per cent of available clubhouse members; 77 per cent of the males available and 88 per cent of the females). When we excluded the less successful matches in terms of service utilisation and length of contact, bringing us down to a total of forty, there were 75 per cent of available females and 54 per cent of available males. Table 11.3 shows the matching characteristics of the close (n=40) and less closely matched groups (n=54).

Table 11.3   Matching characteristics at selection

	Mean age	
	Clubhouse members	Matched group
n=54	37.92	38.83
n=40	39.64	39.12
	Mean number of years since first contact	
	Clubhouse members	Matched group
n=54	11.0	9.0
n=40	7.8	8.2
	Diagnosis	
	n=54	n=40
Females		
Schizophrenia	6	5
Affective psychosis	8	7
Males		
Schizophrenia	26	16
Affective psychosis	12	11
Other non-organic psychosis	2	1

Even after matching, the mean number of recent service contacts was higher in the clubhouse sample by an average of forty contacts per person (1,600 more contacts by forty people). The average number of clubhouse contacts per person is, however, greater than forty, at 102.8 for the fifty-four matched cases and 108.6 for the forty matched cases.

Results

A number of the selected cases were unavailable, mainly because they had moved. A number of substitutions were made (from the fifty-four matched cases) and the final number of matched cases was seventy-six in total (thirty-eight pairs). The results of the matching process produced quite comparable groups, as Table 11.4 shows. They differed in three respects from the clubhouse group. They were less mobile (F=4.26; p<.05), tended to live to a greater extent with members of their family

(F=8.14; p<.01) and to have left school earlier (F=5.97; p<.05). In other important respects (age, sex, diagnosis, ethnicity, marital status, number of children, type of accommodation, family contacts and age at first admission) the two groups were very similar.

Table 11.4 Matching characteristics of the final sample

Matching item	Index	Matched cases	p
Mean age	40.2	38.3	N.S.
Males	76%	76%	
Females	24%	24%	N.S.
White	84%	89%	N.S.
Marital status			N.S.
% single	66%	67%	
%married	14%	17%	
Other	20%	24%	
Number of children			
None	65%	63%	N.S.
1	14%	16%	
2–4	21%	21%	
Accommodation type			
Rented apartment or house	23 (72%)	24 (69%)	N.S.
Mobile home	2 (6%)	3 (9%)	
Own house	2 (6%)	5 (14%)	
Other	5 (15%)	2 (6%)	
Missing data	6	3	
Other family in residence	29%	63%	.004
Number of other residents	1.08	1.4	N.S.
Length of residence	29 mths	56 mths	.04
Family contacts			
Daily family contact	43%	50%	N.S.
Weekly family contact	23%	28%	
Less than weekly	34%	22%	
School leaving age	25	19	.02
Age first admission	23.77	24.18	N.S.

Note: Statistical tests used were cross-tabs or t-tests

In terms of outcome (Table 11.5), more of the clubhouse group was in work but its mean total income is less than that of the comparison group. This is, in part, because the comparison group works longer hours and earns more per hour. Both groups obtain approximately half of their income from work. Being in work makes a weekly difference in income of $11.50 per week to the clubhouse members compared with those not currently in work ($146.55 compared with $135.05) but a difference of $33.17 to those in work in the comparison group compared with those not in work ($203.00 compared with $169.83). Being in work therefore represents an 8.5 per cent improvement in income in the clubhouse but a 19.5 per cent improvement in the comparison group.

Table 11.5 Outcomes

	Clubhouse cases	Matched cases	p
In employment	18 (47.4%)	13 (34.2%)	N.S.
Rate of pay per week	$97.47	$172.77	N.S.
Under $100	22%	20%	
$100–$200	65%	46%	
Over $200	13%	34%	N.S.
Hours per week worked	14	19.5	N.S.
Hourly pay from work	$4.98	$5.23	N.S.
Mean total income (from all sources)	$146.65	$203.00	N.S.

Areas in which there were differences in outcome for the two groups are in social relationships and self-esteem. The clubhouse group members more often said that they had close friends (92 per cent compared to 62 per cent of the comparison group: Chi-squared = 7.95; p< .01) and someone whom they could rely on and turn to for help when they needed it (100 per cent compared to 63 per cent in the comparison group: Chi-squared = 14.79, p< .001). Only one of the self-esteem items is significantly different: the clubhouse members have higher self-worth than the comparison group (Chi-squared = 4.49; p< .05). There were no significant differences in use of health services (according to the LQOLP results). More of the clubhouse members had seen a doctor for a physical illness (58 per cent compared with 50 per cent), but fewer had seen a doctor for psychiatric reasons (92 per cent compared with 100 per cent). The same percentage in both groups (32 per cent) had been hospitalised during the year, and somewhat fewer of the clubhouse group were on medication (82 per cent compared with 95 per cent). There were no differences of significance in the ratings of positive and negative affect between the groups. In terms of subjective well-being (Figure 11.1) there were three differences between the groups: the clubhouse members were more satisfied with their financial circumstances (F=5.96; p< .05) and with their safety (z=2.79, p<.01) and there was a significant difference in global well-being in favour of the clubhouse group (z=2.37, p< .05).

DISCUSSION

So far as we are aware, this is the first empirical investigation of the effects of the clubhouse on members' quality of life to be suggested and carried out by members themselves. This is an interesting feature

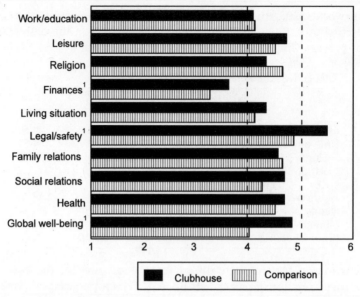

Figure 11.1 Subjective quality of life in clubhouse and comparison group
Note: 1 Clubhouse superior (.02)

of the present work which will be considered in detail elsewhere. The LQOLP was designed to be used in service evaluations and to require very little training for professionals. The members in this study had brief training sessions with one of us (PH) and feedback sessions on their use of the profile. They managed the collection of the clubhouse data with little difficulty.

The age and sex distribution of the present sample is fairly similar but not identical to that found by Mastboom (1992), in that the mean age is about 40, but the proportion of males in the present sample is 76 per cent. This difference may be due partly to the restricted diagnostic groups in the present study. Twenty-nine per cent of the present sample live with family members; Mastboom found 29 per cent lived with partner or family.

In the present study, according to the LQOLP results, there were no significant differences between the members and the matched group in the use of health services, but further information will become available from the Mental Health Center records in due course. It will then be possible to see what the costs of providing the clubhouse services are and to relate these cost data to the outcomes described here.

Rosenfield and Neese-Todd (1993) found that members with more social contacts were more satisfied with their social relations and their leisure activities. In the present study, the regular clubhouse members felt subjectively better about their social relationships than infrequent users.

Non-members in 1991 felt equally good about their social relationships. This perhaps suggests that the regular members of the clubhouse are deriving benefit from their attendance, rather than that the clubhouse selected all those already feeling better about their social relationships. If that had been the case then the non-members' scores would be lower. The finding that the social relationship results may be due to the programme effect rather than a selection effect is supported by the findings from the matched comparison group study. The mean subjective well-being scores in the social relationship domain are higher for the members, but fail to reach significance. Members said, significantly more often than the comparison group, that they had close friends and someone on whom they could rely and turn to for help when they needed it. Ely (1992) from Fountain House says: 'That's all I really have to say, that he's always been there for me. . . .I really have a real friend now' (Ely 1992:62).

Those patients surveyed in 1989 who went on to become clubhouse members had a significantly greater desire for more leisure activities (in 1989). This suggests that they might be a more highly motivated group, certainly where social and leisure activities, rather than social contacts per se, are concerned.

Rosenfield and Neese-Todd (1993) also found that transitional employment was related to greater satisfaction with finances. In the present study, while the overall earnings in the comparison group are higher, and the economic advantages non-members gain from work are twice those of the clubhouse members, the members still experience greater satisfaction. This may be due to their previous lack of work experience and their difficulty in obtaining gainful work of any sort. The improvement of $11.50 a week over those in the clubhouse not currently working may be of greater significance in the clubhouse context, where personal productivity is highly valued, than the $33.17 increase in the comparison group. The clubhouse members are all able to see and help one another make gains in work hours and pay, and this positive feedback to one another may enhance their financial well-being. The comparison 'group' are not a group in the same sense, being simply an aggregation of individuals for the purpose of this study. They cannot directly compare themselves so easily with other similar patients as they can with their peers in the workplace. Mowbray (1993) in her study of combined vocational rehabilitation and case management teams found that participants rated money or material goods as the most likely area in which they noticed the impact of a job. An impact on their relationships came fifth, with only 13 per cent of respondents rating this area as important. The global well-being of the members in the present study is better than that of the participants in Mowbray's scheme, but the results in terms of satisfaction with work and social support are very similar.

The members feel better about their personal safety, positive self-esteem and their overall well-being. There is no space here to investigate the causal directions within these relationships and, in any event, as we have argued elsewhere in the book, this is really only possible with much larger data-sets than a single clubhouse study can provide. A more substantial follow-up investigation, using the LQOLP in a much larger number of clubhouses with similar member characteristics, would be one way to explore the causal relationships at work and to assess the impact of clubhouse membership on the determinants of quality of life.

Chapter 12

Long-stay patients and quality of life

INTRODUCTION

So far, we have examined the quality of life of people who are receiving mental health services in the community rather than in hospital. We regard the hospital services as one form of care which is an essential part of the spectrum of resources available and which should be made available to those who need it, for as long as they need it. In Chapter 5 we described a residential provision which, in many respects, was superior to the standard care provided by local authority residential and community services. Our conclusion from findings such as these is that the population in need is heterogenous and that within it there will be people for whom a brief or extended period in residential care or in hospital makes an essential contribution to their care in the community. Everyone is agreed that such periods should be no longer than necessary.

Earlier, we made the point that a 'system of care' in a community should be able to cater for the most severely disabled or behaviourally disturbed as well as those who are less disabled. A small number of severely disabled people have illnesses which may include intractable positive phenomena, a lack of internal motivation to persist at any task unless closely supervised and behaviours which either put themselves at risk or are a major imposition on others. They need a service with a high staff complement, highly skilled multi-disciplinary teams, dedicated services for as long as they need them and services which are integrated with a range of others concerned with rehabilitation.

'LONG-STAY' PATIENTS

Previous writers have described the characteristics of the most disabled patients, many of whom are the 'long-stay' residents of mental hospitals and many psychiatric units of district general hospitals (O'Driscoll *et al.* 1990; Lawrence *et al.* 1991; Bridgés *et al.* 1991a; Clifford *et al.* 1991; Dayson *et al.* 1992; Liddle 1992). This was a label originally given to people after they had been in hospital for a long period (Wykes 1982; Wykes and Wing 1991). However, other people with long-term disabilities will also need these services at some stage in their illness career, even if they have not been in hospital or have been admitted for only a brief period. Other labels have also been coined to refer to them: members of the 'high-dependency group' (Wing and Furlong 1986); 'hard core' (Stone and Nelson 1979); those with 'special needs for continuing care' or 'particular challenging behaviours' (Tannahill *et al.* 1990) and the 'difficult to place' (Coid 1991). Some have to be managed in regional secure units where the emphasis is on shorter-term and medium security care (Lodge 1991; Smith 1991). However, although some may have a history of recidivism, many may not have any forensic history (O'Grady *et al.* 1992).

The following vignettes are examples of people with chronic psychotic illnesses who have required specialised, hospital-based care for prolonged periods (Bridges *et al.* 1994a). The first is a person who was a patient on an acute psychiatric ward of a district general hospital and who proved impossible to care for in a community-based hostel ward. The second is a person who needed care in a secure unit for extended periods but who is now living in the community and has a life with much variety.

A twenty-six year old man with an illness characterised by prominent catatonic features and a marked deterioration of his personality. His behavioural problems included smearing faeces on walls when stressed, alcohol abuse, stealing clothes from other patients, stealing from shops and immediately gorging food snatched from shop display counters, defecating in the neighbourhood, and inappropriate sexual activity in public places. He failed to become involved in his care plans despite agreeing these with staff. Before his admission he had been excluded from a variety of sheltered residential facilities. When he was in the community-based hostel ward he required three readmissions to the acute ward of hospital because of unmanageable behaviour and eventually a permanent transfer after he made several attempts to set fire to the building.

A twenty-seven year old man with a nine year history of a very unstable episodic psychotic illness and who had several admissions to hospital. The total cumulative time spent in hospital exceeded six years, of which three and a half years were in secure settings. When floridly disturbed the characteristics of his illness included marked lability of mood (including periods of euphoria, anger, hostility and depression), flight of ideas, incoherent screaming, preoccupation with self-injurious thoughts and delusions (persecutory, grandiose, and passivity), auditory hallucinations and markedly disturbed insight. When floridly disturbed persistent behavioural disturbances included following people in an intimidating manner, smearing faeces over his body, physical and verbal hostility towards others, smashing reinforced windows, pulling wash basins off walls, burning own clothes, throwing himself through doors, punching himself, and laceration of penis, groins and legs.

(Bridges and Cresswell 1994)

The most appropriate form of service for patients with these characteristics, and the type of hospital service required, will be considered later in this chapter.

QUALITY OF LIFE ISSUES

Whether in hospital or not, there are problems in the assessment of quality of life, particularly with regards to the reliability of patients' subjective ratings. Very severe forms of psychopathology affect the cognitive processes involved in the perception and evaluation of personal experiences. When working with severely ill people this needs to be taken into account, and greater importance may have to be given to objective assessments made by staff and independent assessors. Simpson *et al.* (1989) make the fundamentally important point that levels of severe psychopathology should be controlled when comparing different facilities, otherwise apparent benefits 'may be illusory, reflecting only differing population characteristics' (Simpson *et al.* 1989).

There is some evidence that even the most severely disabled person, known to be incapable of living outside hospital, can make worthwhile gains in levels of social functioning and in quality of life when provided for in a specialised rehabilitation unit (Atkins *et al.* 1991). Atkins *et al.* assessed quality of life using the Social Behaviour Schedule (Wykes and Sturt 1986), direct observation, using a time sampling schedule drawn from Alevizos *et al.* (1978) and another measure of progress in rehabilitation. To our knowledge, only one study has reported an assessment of the quality of life of long-stay patients using the LQOLP (Simpson *et al.* 1989). Another study has been completed and is at the stage of data analysis (Mechenzie, personal communication). In both these studies, the LQOLP was used to assess patients in district general hospital units and residents of 'hostel wards'.

The first study used an earlier version of the LQOLP, and the analysis took account of the level of psychopathology experienced by the patients. There was an overall tendency for the quality of life to be better in groups homes, with higher levels of global well-being, subjective satisfaction with the living situation, total social contacts, better finances and comfort. For the long-stay patients on the acute wards the situation was less impressive, although there were higher levels of cohesion, objective leisure and subjective satisfaction with the living situation. However, the district general hospital wards had the highest levels of victimisation, a finding also reported elsewhere (Lehman *et al.* 1986). The 'hostel ward' residents appeared to occupy an intermediate position. Their environment was socially cohesive, comfortable, had a higher level of total social contacts and appeared to be the safest. However, they were disadvantaged financially, as they were officially inpatients and therefore entitled to lower state benefit payments (Simpson *et al.* 1989). The authors concluded from this work that the placement of patients within the spectrum of services studied corresponded to the severity of psychopathology. Both the group homes and 'hostel ward' fulfilled important functions, but the care received on acute wards of a district general hospital left much to be desired.

In the study by Mechenzie an association was found between the degree of negative phenomena experienced by patients and whether the assessor rated their responses to the subjective assessments of different life domains as reliable. The details of this study are to be reported elsewhere but, in essence, it found that patients with high scores for negative phenomena, as assessed by the Psychological Impairment Rating Scale (Jablensky *et al.* 1980), were more likely to have been rated as unreliable (Bridges *et al.* 1994c). This gives further support to the suggestion put forward in Chapter 2, that people with the most severe cognitive impairments may not be suitable subjects to provide self-reported assessments.

DISADVANTAGES OF LONG-TERM CARE ON ACUTE ADMISSION WARDS

The policy changes which reduced the role of the mental hospital and fostered the development of the admissions unit within the general hospital failed to appreciate the disadvantages of this location for the treatment of people with long-term problems, many of which are social in origin. There are disadvantages, too, for the acute services in terms of the consumption of resources needed for acute admissions (Hirsch 1992). In addition, there are at least three clinical reasons why this location is an inappropriate setting for long-stay patients (Bridges *et al.* 1994a).

First, the ward can become too arousing and disruptive because of acutely disturbed patients. Long-stay patients may have to be moved to different beds and wards in order to accommodate new admissions – a situation that is likely to occur more often with the further loss of acute beds faced by many districts. As a consequence of these moves, long-stay patients lose their personal space. In addition, care on acute wards exposes them to a busy, crowded, noisy and volatile environment with hardly any privacy for long periods and with the risk of victimisation (Simpson *et al.* 1989).

Patients with continuing needs do not respond well to stress: often there is a relatively narrow line between the risk of developing negative symptoms when understimulated and equally of developing florid disturbances of their mental state as a consequence of overstimulation.

Second, staff on acute wards are likely to spend more time on recent admissions or disturbed behaviour at the expense of time needed for long-stay patients and there is some evidence that the latter are more likely to have unqualified rather than qualified staff spending time with them (Bridges *et al.* 1994a). Furthermore, nurses allocated to work with long-stay patients may not be able to dedicate their time to them because of the demands of having to spend the whole of a shift nursing other patients or 'specialing' a disturbed patient for long periods. Junior doctors may also prioritise their work in a similar way, particularly when their work is demand-led, in terms of dealing with new admissions and acutely ill patients. Involvement with long-stay patients may be limited only to those occasions when their clinical state is deteriorating.

Third, it is very difficult, in an acute ward, to establish a consistent therapeutic regime which is suitable for long-stay patients. In such an environment the implementation of an agreed programme can be very difficult because of poor resources, low staffing levels and the diversion of staff elsewhere. It is very difficult to carry out meaningful assessments of behaviour and skills, and such places are not good environments in which to develop and maintain new skills. In fact, places such as acute wards where basic needs are met through the provision of the so-called hotel services, may actually de-skill some patients.

THE NEED FOR DEDICATED SERVICES

It is our view that people with long-term service needs can only achieve the best quality of life through the provision of dedicated services. Those people who need twenty-four-hour nursing care and a multi-disciplinary input to their care plans can, based on the location and type of specialist care they require, be divided into three main groups: those who could receive their care in special residential facilities in the community away from the hospital campus, those who need to be in hospital and those who need to be in a locked hospital-based facility (secure or medium-secure units). We suggest that people with a severe organic brain syndrome (for example, head injuries; dementia) should receive care in separate facilities dedicated to their special needs rather than be shared with services for people with functional illnesses. Staff in specialist facilities should be able to assess, plan and implement care plans which would enable individual patients to have a more meaningful time while they remain in specialist residential facilities or in hospital.

Estimating the number of people in a district who would benefit from such services is problematic (Wing and Furlong 1986; Clifford *et al.* 1991; Hirsch 1992). In the UK at present, these estimates tend to be based on an extrapolation of acute hospital bed occupancy; this is rather limited since it is based on demand rather than need and does not take account of people in other inappropriate locations, such as those who are destitute. Furthermore, data for one district may not be applicable to another, as figures are likely to be influenced by a number of factors specific to a locality, such as the availability of effective local community rehabilitation services and differences in socio-demographic indices and geographical factors. For example, a higher number of places are likely to be needed in areas characterised by high social deprivation (Jennings and Callahan 1983). Units with rehabilitation programmes based on high staffing ratios are likely to be expensive (Goldberg 1991).

The hostel ward

The 'hostel ward', with a multi-disciplinary team providing input to individualised rehabilitation programmes, has been conceived as a possible solution to providing care for people who need prolonged periods of twenty-four-hour nursing support but who do not need this in hospital (DHSS 1975). The first three were opened in Camberwell, London (111 Denmark Hill), in South Manchester (Douglas House) and in Southampton (Cranbury Terrace). Some of their clinical, social and economic benefits have since been reported (Wykes 1982; Wykes and Wing 1982; Garety and Morris 1984; Gibbons and Butler 1987; Hyde *et al.* 1987; Simpson *et al.* 1989). Since these earlier reports, several units have opened in other areas of the country and further reports have appeared supporting their utility as well as drawing attention to some of their limitations (Bridges *et al.* 1991; Creighton and Hyde 1991).

In general, the 'hostel ward' is thought of as a cost-effective solution to providing care in a more domestic, community-based setting, particularly when it is part of a range of integrated rehabilitation services, and there now seems to be increasing agreement about its potential value as part of the range of services needed by a health district (Young 1991). Hostel wards can be located away from the hospital site. Some may be financed by organisations other than health, which gives some financial advantages to their residents as their state benefits are based on their status as an outpatient rather than as an inpatient of a hospital.

The overall aim of these units is to provide a quality of care appropriate to the needs of the residents and to help each achieve his or her optimal level of social functioning. Care is provided for as long as it is needed and those who are ready are relocated into homes in the community. When a resident leaves a hostel ward there is a need for close liaison with other services, such as peripatetic support staff, which will be involved in his or her future care (Bridges and Cresswell 1994).

The form of care will vary from one place to another but, in general, the care of an individual is eclectic and dependent on the characteristics of his or her illness, his or her behaviours and the nature of his or her social disabilities. For example, at the Anson Road project (Bridges *et al.* 1991b), the form of care includes medication, personal counselling, educative procedures, practical support and advice. Medication is usually administered by the nursing staff but, when possible, residents are encouraged to manage their own medication and go to a local health centre for their depot injections when these are prescribed. Each person is allocated a specific keyworker and a co-worker, though the day to day aspects of a rehabilitation programme are shared by all the staff.

At the Anson Road project, the needs of each person are assessed periodically throughout the admission using a semi-standardised format. These assessments are based on regular discussions with the resident and on observations made by the staff and they attempt to identify potential abilities and assets as well as disabilities. Several areas are covered, including self-care, domestic skills, social and community skills and specific problem areas such as budgeting skills or medication problems. Individual rehabilitation programmes are then formulated in collaboration with the resident and are based on a step-wise goal-planning approach, aiming to encourage the resident to work at a small number of specific problems which are realistic and within his or her abilities. In addition to these programmes, the residents are encouraged to pursue their own social and leisure activities; many go out to the theatre, cinema, pubs and restaurants and most have been away for a seaside holiday together with staff.

People receiving care in a 'hostel ward' tend to fall into three main groups (Bridges *et al.* 1991a; Hyde *et al.* 1991; Garety 1991). The first group includes those who are able, eventually, to move on to other settings in the community such as nursing homes, sheltered housing schemes, individual flats, group-living arrangements, and family fostering schemes (see Chapter 10). Following this move, the majority of people have continued to need care and support from peripatetic staff. The second group are those who need the hostel ward for a long time – and some may not ever move on. The third group consists of a small number of people who need to be transferred to hospital-based services. The main reason for this is the occurrence of very severe behavioural disturbances which prove too difficult to manage in this setting. The decision to move someone into hospital would involve consideration of the nature, severity, frequency and mix of behaviours and the effects of the patient's behaviour on the therapeutic milieu of the unit and upon the neighbourhood. Behavioural problems which have led to patients being returned to hospital have included aggressive and threatening behaviour, repeated suicidal or parasuicidal behaviour, frequent absconding, unsafe wandering, intolerable sexual behaviour, frequent substance abuse, and significant fire hazard or arson attempts (Bridges *et al.* 1991b; Hyde *et al.* 1987).

Life quality for 'hostel wards' residents has also been compared with that experienced by people residing in other forms of accommodation, such as group homes, hostels and board and lodging schemes (Oliver 1991b). The research suggested that while the 'hostel wards' were clearly coping with some individuals with very difficult behavioural characteristics, so were the more ordinary residential settings. This research also confirmed the trend for some aspects of life quality to improve as people moved from hospital settings, with most people surveyed being satisfied with their conditions. The general conclusion was that hostel wards, like other forms of residential support, needed to be viewed as one element in a spectrum of provisions and that quality of life could provide very useful data for evaluating this range of services.

Hospital provision

For a relatively small number of very severely disabled people, the location of specialised rehabilitation services needs to be in a hospital setting, where there are advantages of quick access to extra nursing and medical staff when necessary, geographical separation from the local community, and the facility to detain people when it is in their best interests because of very disturbed behaviour and problematic ideation (for example, violence towards themselves or others). These patients may include some long-stay patients who are in mental hospitals scheduled to close or who are on acute psychiatric wards of the district general hospitals, as well as those who turn out to be impossible to care for in community-based hostel wards. In addition, there will be some people who would benefit from elective admissions to hospital for a short period either before, or instead of, transfer to a hostel ward. Several authors, in fact, have recommended that specialised hospital-based services should be available to people who cannot be managed in community settings (Wing 1990; Coid 1991; Clifford *et al.* 1991; Bridges *et al.* 1994a).

When providing care for patients with such persistent and difficult behaviours as in the two earlier illustrations, the known disadvantages of mental hospital-based services of the past need to be avoided and considerable attention needs to be given to design, patient mix and numbers, therapeutic functions, and staff needs (Wing and Brown 1970; Wing 1990; Wilkinson *et al.* 1990). Environments should be designed as domestically as possible but with consideration given to the specific needs of some patients, for example those who are very restless. The hospital services need to be functionally integrated with other services in order to facilitate the person's eventual transfer of care to a community-based network of rehabilitation services or, when required, to other hospital services providing more secure care (Courtney *et al.* 1992). They should be staffed by a specialist multi-disciplinary team to provide individually tailored, flexible and achievable care programmes based on collaboration with the patients, a step-wise goal-planning approach and a combination of biological, psychological and social interventions throughout the person's stay (Hogg and Hall 1992). Finally, whenever possible, they need to provide opportunities for personal strengths and latent abilities to thrive.

There are at least two possible ways of arranging these specialist services. First, some health districts have been able to arrange their district general hospital services so that these patients receive care in dedicated units which are separate from acute wards; examples in the UK include Withington Hospital in South Manchester, Littlemore Hospital in Oxford and The Royal South Hants Hospital, Southhampton (Gibbons and Butler 1987; Pullen 1987). This arrangement should not only cater for patients requiring long-term care but also provide a service for those who require short-term admissions to hospital either before, or instead of, transfer to a hostel ward. However, as far as we are aware, most districts lack this form of inpatient service.

Second, some health services have been able to develop specialist services located on the site of a mental hospital. These have developed either for patients unable to be discharged from the hospital as part of a closure plan (Wing and Furlong 1986), or as a supra-district service – such as the Bowness Unit at Prestwich Hospital in Salford. Supra-district services are particularly attractive if they can help other, perhaps smaller, districts which find it impossible to re-arrange their acute inpatient facilities and have an insufficient number of patients requiring this form of care to justify resources being deployed in this way. This particular approach, however, may result in some operational difficulties concerned with the continuity of care when patients are in the process of returning to their home district services. In both cases, it will be important that these specialist units maintain a close relationship with others so as to minimise the risk of isolation which can occur with remote services (Wilkinson *et al.* 1991).

CONCLUSION

People with very severe forms of psychopathology need expensive services because of their need for twenty-four-hour nursing care, a multi-disciplinary input into their rehabilitation, and specialised facilities. The services described in this chapter have been concerned with patients with either chronic psychotic illnesses or organic brain syndromes. A similar argument for specialist inpatient facilities could also be made for other patient groups, such as those with severe, disabling forms of chronic somatisation (Benjamin and Bridges 1993). People with psychopathology which interferes with the cognitive processes involved in the appraisal of subjective well-being present a particular challenge to the assessment of quality of life. Some people will be more reliable in their responses than others and, it is likely to be more useful, therefore, if the assessor adopts an idiographic approach when making judgements on subjective responses rather than aggregating data as in a nomothetic approach (see case studies in Chapter 10). In any case, a greater reliance on objective assessments, augmented by other information available, will need to be made by practitioners and researchers, preferably by those who know the patient well. One of the major challenges for future quality of life research is to find and test the best means of assessing quality of life in this particular group of patients. One could argue that this is one of the lessons learned from the application of quality of life assessment in mental health services. In the final chapter we look at the other major lessons which have emerged.

Part III

Issues arising from application in service

Lessons learned from the experiences of applying quality of life to mental health services

INTRODUCTION

The programme of work described in the previous chapters really began as a modest contribution towards bringing the concerns and realities of the lives of a group of otherwise rather neglected and voiceless people back to the centre of practice and planning. While, ultimately, it may have come to embrace science and policy, it began as an attempt to serve, more effectively, mentally ill people receiving psychiatric services. Thus, our starting point for this enterprise was clinical practice: the hurly-burly of everyday work, in that far from perfect setting which we all know as the clinic. We are reminded continually of these imperfections by football commentators who have now colonised (grotesquely) the term 'clinical' to describe perfect, clean flawless play: 'The goal was clinical, Jimmy!' Could they really mean a horrible combination of basic skills, politicised negotiation, fly-by-the-seat-of-the-trousers guess-work and dumb luck?

During the course of this work our attentions have been drawn to any number of new insights concerning not only the lives of patients/clients but also a better understanding of the forces which influence them. The assessment of quality of life through interview, like any element of clinical work, brings the interviewers very close to the realities of the lives of the clients whom they serve. These insights precede the analysis of data. They are the result of an exercise designed to satisfy our intellectual and emotional curiosities. This satisfaction is to be found in the act of structured human observation of a phenomenon which is too often overlooked or deliberately ignored: the sifting through of the bric-a-brac of someone else's life – the examination of someone else's life domains. These include: many stories from those whom we have interviewed of their gratitude for the work done by professionals with them and on their behalf; the amazing optimism of some people who have had to endure long years of a chronic mental disorder; the disappointments in not having established careers, of never having married nor having had children; distress at having been continually rehospitalised, loss of contact with their families and poverty; the fact that the treatments which they have sometimes received have been more hindrance than help; and, in some cases, their lost lives as residents of antiquated asylums.

PRINCIPLES

It is convenient to think of at least three principles which have provided guidance for us in this work (Girling and Boswell 1993): ethics, utility and feasibility. Is this exercise right and proper? Is it likely to be of some use and to whom? Is it possible, given the current clinical and organisational situation? We discuss each principle separately.

Ethics

It might seem a straightforward matter that putting the clients' opinions at the centre of planning is a 'good thing', a just and right-thinking thing to do of and by itself. In the real world of seeing this actualised in an agency's operations, things are seldom quite so straightforward. From the beginning, much concern has been expressed that the interviewing process would not be ethical. Many professionals feared that the entire enterprise would be cosmetic, geared simply to justifying government hospital closure policies and community neglect of ex-patients. At worst, some colleagues were convinced that quality of life interviews would lead only to unnecessary upset and prove a danger to health. Consequently, the concerns of professionals have always held strong sway. As the research proceeded, all research projects were first submitted to the ethical sub-committees of local district health authorities and social services committees for consideration. Professionals have always been given the authority to select from their caseloads individuals who, in their opinion, would not suffer negative side-effects from the interviews.

Of course, the concerns for the rights of patients were central. User groups or their spokespeople were contacted and each was given an opportunity to comment on questionnaire design and content. The entire procedure was exposed to professional and consumer criticism through continual presentation of results in public fora such as conferences and workshops. Before interview, clients have always been informed of the nature of the exercise, as best we understood it. Clients have always been free to participate or not and to discontinue an interview when they wished. The conditions regarding confidentiality as outlined in professional codes of conduct have been observed. Likewise, data storage and the processing and analysis of questionnaires have complied with the conditions of the Data Protection Act (1984). Such steps may seem rather fundamental but their observation is a *sine qua non* of any such research activity.

Also within this category one must consider the people's sensitivities, which must be respected in design and use. One classic example appeared in respect of enquiries concerning sexual conduct. Early versions of the questionnaire received from the USA contained questions around these matters. However, when piloting these in the UK, social workers refused to conduct the interviews as a consequence of their presence. Possibly such questions ran across traits held deeply within the national character. Whatever, in their opinion such enquiries represented unwarranted prying into clients' lives, though few maintained that sexual behaviour was independent of life satisfaction. The questions were deleted. Other national groups, however, with whom we have since discussed the LQOLP have not felt so constrained and have tackled the problem in various ways. For example, Priebe (personal communication, 1994) and his colleagues at the Freie Universität Berlin have re-introduced the questions, though they have thought it more useful to portray enquiries into sexuality as matters of need for help rather than as problems with living. Such questions on sexuality are incorporated there into a separate 'needs analysis' which accompanies the quality of life interview.

Utility

Another precondition of the exercise is that it be useful. Aside from the considerable work undertaken to improve the validity of the question-naire format itself, there is the question of usefulness of the entire exercise. At the core is a basic scepticism among professionals and administrators concerning evaluation. For many years and mostly amongst ourselves at the University of Manchester, we have maintained wryly that the rule of thumb for this matter is 'Nobody evaluates anything unless they are made to'. This gross generalisation and un-proven maxim accounts for both the paucity of evaluative research undertaken in the past and the resistance to beginning any now, as experienced in so many quarters. It implies that, in reality, quality of life interviewing must be introduced into the ordinary working procedures of service delivery organisations, where what one should expect to en-counter is a deeply ingrained apathy towards such initiatives.

At a general level, we believe that agencies must move towards becoming 'research minded'. We define 'research mindedness' as having an appreciation for the potential usefulness of the research activity and possession of the capability to be at least good consumers of other people's research. Also, in most cases, it is impractical for service organisations to carry on as they have in the past – i.e. simply coopera-ting with central-government-funded initiatives to investigate this matter or the other; funding independent research into some aspect of provision from time to time. They must develop their own capacities to do this. In the north-west of England the academics have been involved for many years in a partnership with local authorities called the 'consortium'. Local authorities who have lacked the resources independently to undertake all of the evaluative work which they would like group together and have been undertaking projects across authorities, utilising the resources of the university, which has considerable infrastructure which can be turned to such projects. As can be seen from the book, this 'consortium' has resulted in a wide range of evaluative quality of life research, the scale of which would have been far beyond any single authority to finance. Yet the benefits are felt by all, with feedback occurring through local symposia and organisational papers. The work has informed management learning sets and, hopefully, it has had considerable academic spin-off. This plan will continue in the future, with different research and evaluation problems being identified and resolved through joint effort.

Feasibility

Development has always proceeded at a pace which could be supported by the field; this has been differential between social and health care agencies. The former were, on the whole, ready to proceed at an earlier date, because the sensitive issue of hospital closure and potential job loss prevented health authorities from becoming involved until all of these matters had been resolved. All this took some time – in many cases, a matter of years.

As has been described above, desire for a measure of quality of life has been driven by the need for such an instrument in the field. After Culyer (1978) and, subsequently, McEwen (1983), we sought to produce an instrument which was cheap and easy to produce, short and simple to apply, was reliable and valid, was sophisticated enough to encompass a number of models of quality of life and was sensitive enough to be of use in the routine evaluation of clinical work in social and health care settings for this client group. In addition, the questionnaire had to be acceptable to a wide range of people holding quite different perspectives. These are the sort of characteristics which encourage feasibility.

PRACTICAL PROBLEMS AND DILEMMAS IN APPLICATION

Client reactions

The first source of concern is subject reactivity. As mentioned above, a very small proportion of clients reacted badly to the questionnaire. In only one instance was this reported to be serious. In that case the client was required to be re-admitted to hospital following the interview. Considering the approximately 2,000 interviews which we have personally overseen or been associated with, that seems a small figure. Nevertheless, it does highlight the need for caution. In operational contexts, we recommend that interviews be carried out by the professionals who know the patient. This introduces the problems of interviewer bias but reduces the possibility of a person in an unsuitable clinical state being interviewed. Quality of life interviews could be preceded by some other form of screening process and it is part of our research plan to look into how this might be done. Also, being available to answer particular questions following interview or deal with any emotional upset which might occur is also likely to reduce such negative side-effects. It is wise to consider the old maxim that anything which is strong enough to have an effect is strong enough to have a side-effect, and interviews fall into this category.

The second source of concern is social desirability. No firm evidence has been drawn from our data about this phenomenon. Some of the most sophisticated research to date has addressed the question of acquiesence and 'yea-saying', together with 'mood-of-the-day effects'. This has not really thrown any light on the extent to which mentally ill people proffer socially desirable responses (Moum 1988).

Researchers, concerned to establish this aspect of reliability, may wish to cross-validate interviews with an instrument for detecting social desirability. Both the Crowne and Marloe (1964) Social Desirability Scale or Edward's (1957) S.D. Scale (an off-shoot of the Minnesota Multiphasic Personality Inventory – MMPI) exist, are well validated and could, possibly, be considered. The possibility of introducing some screening questions to identify this propensity in individuals or, perhaps, in situations is another part of the planned programme of future research.

The third source of concern is poor compliance from clients. Poor client compliance has not really been a problem which we have encountered, because most of those interviewed, in so far as they have expressed an opinion, have felt that little attention had been given to their lives in the past and have been keen to talk about their circumstances. One author (PH) in his American interviewing has made a special point of giving feedback to individuals. This feedback is given in the form of graphic profiles of clients' perceived quality of life. This is apparently reinforcing and, according to unstructured feedback to us from others who have tried it, decreases resistance, probably for well-established, learning-theory-based reasons.

Also, our experience has taught us that the interview is probably not appropriate for certain people. These include young children, those suffering from some forms of dementia and those with severe learning disabilities (amentia) and, in addition, those with specific symptoms which militate against quality of life interviewing. In some cases the patients are simply unwell at a particular time but will improve sufficiently to be interviewed at a later date. We have not interviewed at admission to hospital or inpatients, unless patients are well enough to be discharged. In the instance of people with impaired memory or poor orientation one encounters those who are well enough for some form of interview but not the entire profile and those who may be able to answer only a single question. Again, experience suggests that a single, global measure of well-being might be a solution for these people. The less satisfactory but partial answer is to enlist the assistance of carers in helping with interviews. Employing carer ratings of client well-being is not really satisfactory. It might inhibit the informant in his or her life satisfaction or other responses. To develop alternative measures, perhaps based on observation of behaviours or even physiological responses, might be alternatives worthy of consideration (see, for example, Alevizos et al. 1978).

As could be seen, many of the people interviewed had very weakened ego structures, and their psychotic symptoms may have become florid under what may seem to others to be a small amount of stress. In these instances it is as well to employ closed questions in structured interviews as opposed to open-ended questions. For those with very concrete thinking and a poverty of affect, rating scales such as the 'delighted–terrible' scale apparently work well, helping clients by providing them with a framework for understanding questions.

As well as the problems of symptoms and response characteristics, failures are strongly related to changes of address. In one set of surveys (phases I and II) we found that over 17 per cent of clients had changed address within a single year and many were, unfortunately, lost to the system. The UK government has since become aware of this and instituted care management and the care programme approach to help and keep people who need help within the system. Linking quality of life interviews to ongoing monitoring and review processes, including computerised record systems, can help to reduce this problem.

Worker reactions

In the case of worker problems we have encountered many but three are particularly noteworthy: shortage of time, misunderstanding about instructions for interviewing and lack of ownership of the product.

First, the interview now takes only about thirty minutes on average to complete. It would have been possible to make it even briefer but not without reducing the number of dimensions measured. In the end, its present length has had the feel of a good compromise between something academically respectable and operationally workable. There is a genuine and quite understandable concern felt by managers and professionals alike that such evaluative activities should not seriously skew the operational activities of the agencies by their scale and we have worked to this as a target. Full-time professional social care workers regularly work slightly in excess of 160 hours per month, for a ten-month year (excluding annual leave, statutory holidays and sick or other emergency leave). As was shown in the survey of the social care agency, while the actual preponderance of such clients on caseloads is difficult to establish unequivocally, social care workers frequently had an average of approximately ten such clients on their caseload. This has meant interviewing approximately one person per month across the year. This rate of interviewing demands that roughly between .5 and 1 per cent of a clinical worker's time be devoted to this task of data collection. The amount is almost negligible and does not require additional financial resources of any substance. Also, interviewing time is time spent in face-to-face contact and not in administration, which is an attractive feature of quality of life assessment.

A second problem with worker implementation has been technical. Although the interview is simple and straightforward, many workers have been unused to the multiple question/answer format, being more accustomed to open-ended recording. Brief periods of training can usually resolve such queries and make staff more confident in their ability to accomplish the task effectively.

A third problem encountered has been in the 'lack of ownership of the product'. Many professionals are resistant to administering a questionnaire because they themselves have not personally designed it. This is a complex issue. Various professionals have involved other professionals in the task and this has sometimes paid dividends. Line managers and clinical staff have been involved in trials and they have had their fears and complaints dispelled. People who resisted the quality of life interviews in the beginning subsequently became their greatest supporters. However, one trial went wrong (i.e. phase III). The questionnaire was not really suitable but it was tried anyway. Word soon spread about what an awful nuisance it was to use. This attitude took a lot of time and energy to undo. Based upon this own experience, one must recommend caution when enlisting the aid of operational staff to pilot a new instrument.

In some agencies, practitioners are the major obstacle to the development of service evaluations while, in the same agency, other practitioners are leading the way in creative use of quality of life and other methodologies of service evaluation. What is this paradox to be called? How is it that some practitioners can develop monitoring tools, outcome measures and evaluation strategies while working in the same organisation as others who say there is no time to do so and who have no inclination to do so? Is this a function of training, professionalisation, staff selection and recruitment, incentives, personality, management, resources, a combination of all of these, or something else?

OPERATIONAL USES FOR QUALITY OF LIFE

Beginning as we have with clinical work and with practice, we have identified some operational uses to which quality of life assessment is well suited.

1   Quality of life assessments can foster putting actual needs, derived from individual assessment, at the centre of service planning.
2   The outcomes of human services are to do with their clients' life conditions. Quality of life assessments offer a useful means of monitoring and reviewing these.
3   Health and social service authorities typically employ different information in planning their services. These differences stem from differing ideologies about the nature of mental disorder which hardly need to be rehashed here. Suffice it to say that there are, in operation, any number of alternative models to those which explain psychiatric disorder in a strictly organic way. Quality of life brings together information of many different types and offers a mutually acceptable common base of information which focuses on the total life circumstances of the individual.
4   Quality of life interviews are generally well received by clients. They provide a possible avenue for opening discussion, engaging clients in the process of helping and maintaining their interest and cooperation over long periods of time.
5   The feedback from the quality of life profile can be used in clinical practice. Already mentioned above is the observations that graphic feedback to clients in the first Boulder study (phase IV) was well received by them. This type of feedback might be useful in helping people to achieve personal goals and reflect upon them. Another clinical use is in the routine gathering of quality of life data from the clients and its use in supervision of the worker or junior doctor, by the team manager or consultant psychiatrist.

Quality of life as an outcome measure

Rossi and Freeman have described evaluation research as 'the systematic application of social research procedures for assessing the conceptualisation, design, implementation and utility of social intervention programmes' (Rossi and Freeman 1993:5). We began our evaluation research very much in this spirit, even though the applications described in the earlier chapters fall within the broad area of social or community psychiatry, which some people would not consider 'social intervention programmes' except in the broadest sense. We think that evaluation research in social and community psychiatry is an essentially social undertaking, and we are pleased, as social scientists, to contribute to it. Moreover, we think that intervention is frequently multifaceted, and the successful achievement of impact measurement demands that social methods and social measures should be integral to the approach. We originally constructed the LQOLP with social care agencies in mind, because we were keen to see systematic social assessments located in these agencies as a matter of course, both for initial and outcome assessments. Our efforts can be seen as a modest attempt to add measures concerned with social care needs to those already developed for the assessment of health needs. It was not our intention to develop another needs assessment schedule but, rather, a measure which reflected the client's social circumstances. In this sense, the research was pursuing a closer and more integrated approach to the assessment of health and welfare. We were responding to our own experience of the provision of social care in the UK since the early 1970s, which we have found, in professional terms, to be increasingly inadequate. Apparently, social workers, in particular, are not only taught less and less about mental illness but are also not taught the skills involved in taking a social history. In practice, they tend to focus too much upon practical matters and, as a consequence, fail to gain an understanding of the client's view of the world and its complexities. As a result, they make passive rather than active contributions to multi-disciplinary teamwork, and the social dimension of the patient, his family and past circumstances are inadequately presented in clinical settings. The ultimate and dramatic consequences of this are painstakingly documented in the powerful report on the care and treatment of Christopher Clunis (a psychiatric patient who tragically murdered the musician Jonathan Zito in London in 1992), in which a core failure was the fact that health and social services agencies had 'lost touch with some of the basic realities of his personal history' (House of Commons 1994b:3.1.6:8).

Since this work began, legislation, service organisation and practice in many Western countries have changed, so that assessment and outcome measurement have a much higher profile and are in considerably greater demand. We are reminded constantly that commercial organisations collect and use much better quality information than health and social care agencies; products are thoroughly tested before being applied; and feedback is critical to the further development of the product. Although there are those people who object to health and, more particularly, to 'welfare' being construed as a product, commercial enterprises are often more sympathetic than their statutory counterparts to the investment in research and development (and, some people would add, more sympathetic to their workforce, investment in which is essential for progress to be made). The argument that a lack of resources prevents investment in research and development in the health and welfare services simply ignores the vast amount of resources wasted by a failure to test *any* service innovation before putting it into operation. Rossi and Freeman, writing about this lack of rigour from the 1960s to the 1980s in the USA, could be speaking of recent developments in the United Kingdom when they say that programme developments and organisational changes were 'hurriedly put into place...poorly conceived, improperly implemented, and ineffectively administered' and lacked any systematic attempt to assess their impact (Rossi and Freeman 1993:22).

In spite of good reasons for putting the client at the centre of evaluation effort and improving accountability through focus on outcomes, providers, professionals and purchasers are not at one in this regard. This is due to the simple fact that everyone has different objectives for the services and ranks different outcome measures differently. A study in California (Styc, personal communication) found that, given an opportunity to state their preferences, clients, carers, professionals, managers and advocates all ranked a different outcome measure top of their list. Patients wanted to be relieved of their symptoms, while carers wanted hospital admission for the patient to be readily available when needed. Advocates differed from all the other groups, including the patients, in their ordering of the importance of particular outcomes. The area which achieved the highest mean agreement level among all those consulted was social functioning. We suspect that quality of life as an outcome would, nowadays, reach a similar level of agreement. We know, however, that individuals will value different outcome measures and that the best approach is to keep a range of outcomes available.

A second reason why outcomes do not produce instant agreement in those trying to use them is that they can become political items. As stated earlier, one of the resistances to using outcome indicators is undoubtedly the fear that they will be misused in politico-economic circles. The demonstration that the case management team can maintain client's quality of life over time can equally be taken to show a failure to achieve significant improvement over time. One positive aspect of the fact that outcome evaluation takes place in a political context is that, in order to defend services against budget reductions, the goals and outcomes of the service become issues to be identified, assessed and debated. On the whole, this can only be a good thing. One cannot, after all, legislate for politicians, but one can perhaps educate them.

A major difficulty in the operational evaluation of outcomes relates to instances where the whole population is subject to the same programme, which makes comparison a non-starter. These are called full-coverage programmes, and the Care Programme Approach in the UK is a good example. This is mandated by the government and applies to all patients in the care of the specialist psychiatric services. Even in the full-coverage case there are one or two ways in which evaluation can still be conducted. First, there is the opportunity, with sufficient warning, to use a system of reflexive controls – i.e. the same patients are compared with one another before and after the introduction of the full-coverage programme. Although not included in this volume, we have such a study under way, in which a panel of 100 patients was assessed before the introduction of the NHS and community care changes in the UK. This panel of patients will be interviewed over a three-year period in order to assess the impact of the changes on the services they receive. A time-series analysis will be used. Rossi and Freeman have observed that 'time series analyses are quite powerful designs for estimating the effects of either instituting or making changes in constant-treatment, full coverage programmes' (Rossi and Freeman 1993:349).

Second, even though a service is supposed to be mandated for full coverage, we know that implementation times vary, and it becomes possible to instigate evaluations which take place in parts of the service which make changes ahead of others. This was the approach used by some researchers in a study of the implementation of the care programme approach in London. This has been called a 'non-uniform full-coverage program'. There are similar opportunities afforded when different sectors of the same authority use pilot schemes in one sector only. Providing the sectors are demographically similar (often not the case, it has to be said) then evaluation can take place. If sectors differ, then a degree of control can be gained from comparing well-matched patients.

FUTURE DEVELOPMENTS

Study limitation

Quality of life assessment will become more prominent as one of a number of outcome measures in service monitoring and evaluation. A substantial amount of work remains to be done, and the authors and their colleagues at the University of Manchester and the field social services and health agencies with which they are associated have several projects in progress which may contribute to this overall objective. In addition to those already mentioned, some specific projects are currently under way.

However, before moving on to discuss them, it is essential to acknowledge that no report such as this would be complete without some energy being devoted to the task of self-criticism. As with any series of projects of this scale, this research has not emerged without its flaws. Because of these, the reader, in turn, must maintain certain reservations when considering applying the results reported here.

1   The particular sub-set of questions arrived at here is a product of a particular time, place and world view. The LQOLP is a 'basket of measures' which is very appropriate for a narrowly defined group of individuals. Nevertheless, though it may well be of use to others, it should not be extended beyond that for which it was specifically designed without consideration. Such limitations are characteristic of social scientific endeavours such as these, where the researcher is making choices as to which route to pursue and which to avoid. The limitations must be more pronounced when these choices are also influenced by the availability or otherwise of resources or, when action research is linked to operational activities, when they themselves are determined by organisational priorities.

In some instances, these limitations are a result of the methodology employed. Questions were chosen ultimately for inclusion only after having been tested empirically. Consequently, some types of questions (for example, on education) were excluded because there was no variation among this particular client group (chronic, adult mentally ill) not because they were irrelevant. Others, such as open-ended questions, were excluded because they may have had some undesired cultural effects and because of difficulties in scoring, not because they are *sui generis* undesirable. Under different conditions, other investigators trying to develop life quality measures might like to reconsider these limitations.

2   Certainly, the idea of research tracking operations has its drawbacks. The services considered here are local services. The larger, county-wide survey had missing data, the ultimate effect of which could only be estimated. The CMHST research was uncontrolled. While the numbers of subjects studied can be seen to compare very favourably with other research undertaken, there are still doubts as to its external validity. Not everyone runs their services as they are run here in the north-west of England. There may be no CMHSTs exactly like these in the world. Likewise, administrators change and it may not be possible to continue to employ the LQOLP in the service within the foreseeable future. How, then, could one truly replicate the study?

3   Undoubtedly, there are culturally specific characteristics to the research. Current values have influenced the method which has, in turn, tended to reinforce certain content being selected in or out. The issue of sex was but one prime example. Being a product of the late twentieth century North-West England context, this research has made many assumptions which would not hold true elsewhere. For example, questions about watching television have been included

while questions about very basic human requirements, like food and clothing, have not. Where television does not exist or where the emphasis is on different forms of recreation or where people are more engaged in social groups (for example, in Norway), they seem marginal, at best. Semantic issues are very pronounced in respect of the translation of various aspects of this work into other cultural settings. Elsewhere, where these basic needs for food and clothing are being satisfied, they might well take precedence over areas which have been included here. The presence of such conditions, for example, would arguably better justify alternative approaches such as Jones *et al.* (1986), who emphasised Abraham Maslow's 'hierarchy of needs' as a foundation for their quality of life research.

4   While the results of validating this instrument are promising, a very great deal remains undone. Outstanding are matters of unproven predictive validity, possible insensitivity, apparently mediocre inter-observer reliability, uncertainty about social desirability and some evidence of subject reactivity. The inability easily to combine objective well-being results is annoying and prevents that information from being better employed once it has been gathered. These matters all require further research. Certainly, some valuable knowledge is to be gained through a more detailed analysis of extant data (for example, power calculations to determine optimum sample sizes for detecting change). Screening questions to identify those individuals who may experience reactivity should be considered when this questionnaire is applied.

5   Finally, one must return to the theory. It is our opinion that the problem with quality of life theory or theories lies not in the fact that there are none but, conversely, in the fact that there are simply too many. The works of important writers such as Alan Maynard have not been included due only to the pressures of space. What has been done is that theories have been selected. As discussed below, the works of Lehman, Baker and Ingaliata and Franklin have been included not only because they have employed life quality measures with this client group but also because they have presented models of life quality which could be tested. This data has already been employed to test these models and the results will be published elsewhere shortly.

Service-oriented research

As mentioned above, other work is in progress. In one study, 100 clients of a community-based team are being assessed regularly over a three-year period. Their quality of life is being assessed using the LQOLP every nine months, and the local services are being assessed using the Robert Wood Johnson Questionnaire in a key-informant study. The three-year period has been chosen to coincide with local and national changes in service organisation and funding, in order to assess the extent to which these changes have an impact upon the quality of life of clients in continuous contact with the services and the direction of changes, if any, in key informants' judgements about the quality of services provided.

In another, the quality of life of a number of the clients of a community-based social work team in Manchester is being assessed, together with an analysis of their needs on a needs-assessment instrument. The purpose of this study is to investigate the extent to which the quality of life and needs assessment variables represent measures of different or related constructs.

The LQOLP is being used as one of two main outcome measures in a study of the effectiveness of different modes of delivery of care to opiate addicts in three Manchester districts. A pilot study showed that the LQOLP was acceptable to drug users as an assessment instrument.

A further study has used the LQOLP to assess the quality of life of carers who are responsible for a family member with a serious and long-standing mental illness. The preliminary results from this study suggest that the LQOLP can be used successfully in this way, and it is planned to do so in an evaluation of family support workers.

A major four-centre study (one in Manchester and three in London) of case management, funded by the Department of Health as one of the national research priorities in the mental illness field, is using the LQOLP as one of the main outcome measures. Experience in using the LQOLP as part of a large battery of tests taking several hours to complete shows that the LQOLP is a popular part of the process, confirming our impression that it is user-friendly for most clients.

Finally, the LQOLP has been incorporated as the first of a library of outcome measures in the Care Programme Approach Support System (CPASS). CPASS is designed to meet some of the requirements placed on health and social services agencies by the NHS and Community Care Act, the Care Programme Approach and the All Wales Strategy Mental Illness. The NHS and Community Care Act, the Care Programme Approach circular and guidance concerning supervised discharge have made the assessment of individual need and the construction of a care plan central to the development of adequate community care for mentally ill people. The care plan requires regular review and an attempt to show what the impact of the plan has been on the users of the services. The purpose of CPASS is: to encourage the systematic assessment of mental health service users and the provision of care based on individual need; to enable operational assessment at first and subsequent contacts, which will provide an indication of individual case outcome; and to encourage the assessment of quality of life and satisfaction, so that individual and aggregated information is available to users, front line workers and managers. The LQOLP has, therefore, been incorporated into the assessment processes to be used in CPASS. The main purpose of its incorporation is to facilitate systematic assessment procedures and systematic measurement of outcomes.

Theoretical research

While applied research has been emphasised in the programme, it has not been exclusively so. Several projects are under way to look into the many unresolved theoretical aspects of life quality.

One observation cited in the social services department survey (Chapter 4) was that the distribution of age of first admission (following or corresponding to age of onset) was multi-modal. This modality appears to correspond closely to various life crises and developmental stages identified by psychologists (Erikson 1965). Research is proceeding to study how the particular developmental period during which an individual becomes seriously mentally ill actually influences subsequent life quality and how this is associated with the type of illness which the individual has developed and its prognosis.

During the course of the research, many theoretical models have been considered. Rather than being based upon its own theoretical model, the LQOLP was designed to encompass essential elements of at least three existing models (Lehman 1983a; Baker and Intagliata 1982; Franklin *et al.* 1986). Each of these models has been outlined in published research but none has been thoroughly tested at the time that the research began. While the models vary in their manner of expression and formulation, they have some points of convergence in their contents, making them ideal for comparative research. In a paper currently in preparation, a series of structural equations has been developed and applied to the database in an attempt to test the models through path analysis.

International collaboration and cross-cultural issues

To date, the profile has been given, along with instructions and computer program to 200 potential users in seventeen different countries. One of the possible uses of the large database which is accumulating in Manchester is to extract matching samples for other researchers.

We are collaborating with researchers in: Oslo (Norway) over use in evaluation of novel community support and leisure services in remote areas; Verona (Italy) in routine monitoring and evaluation of community services; Amsterdam and Utrecht (Netherlands) for the evaluation of community psychiatric services; and in Boulder, Colorado (USA) where the LQOLP will be used as a pre- and post-measure in the introduction of a capitation payment scheme.

Additionally, we are assisting in the translation of the LQOLP into various languages including Chinese, Dutch, German, Italian, Norwegian and Polish. The international collaboration is at an early stage in its development but we already have gained insights into methodological and operational issues which have not arisen from our work in England. We look forward to continuing and extending our international collaboration and have no doubt that, in due course, this will result in a second volume on cross-cultural issues in quality of life assessment and research in psychiatric services.

CONCLUSION

We hope that the reader has found something useful between the covers of this book. What are the main lessons which the authors have learned? In spite of all of the problems of conceptualisation, definition, operationalisation and measurement, we remain convinced that quality of life is a useful concept and one which is understandable and attractive to service users and to some professionals. We hope that others will be encouraged to proffer conceptual improvements and operational refinements and that, as a result, our knowledge about effective care and treatment for people with a serious mental illness will be increased and further developed.

Appendix I

LANCASHIRE QUALITY OF LIFE PROFILE

NAME OR IDENTIFICATION NUMBER _____

ADDRESS (optional): _____

_____

DATE OF INTERVIEW: _____ | ____ 6–11

INTERVIEWER'S NAME: _____ | ____ 12–14

If the client DECLINES to be interviewed, please state the
reason(s) and STOP HERE:

_____ | ____ 15

_____

STARTING TIME: _____

Section 1:   Client's personal details

1.1   The client's age is: _____ years | ____ 16–18
1.2   The client is _____ male _____ female | ____ 19
1.3   The client's ethnic group is: _____ | ____ 20
(a) White (b) Black-Caribbean (c) Black-African (d) Black-other
(e) Indian (f) Pakistani (g) Bangladeshi (h) Chinese (i) Other
1.4   At what age did the client leave full-time | ____ 21–22
education? ——— years

Section 2: General well-being

2.1   Can you tell me how you feel about your life as a whole | ____ 23
today? (LSS) ____

Section 3:   Work/education

3.1   Do you have a job? YES / NO / DK | ____ 24
3.2   (If YES) What is your occupation? _____

	____ 25–26

3.3   How many hours per week do you work? _____ hrs   ____ 27–29

3.4   How much money are you paid weekly (gross)? _____   ____ 30–32

How satisfied are you with: (LSS)

3.5   your job (or sheltered employment;
occupational or industrial therapy; studies)? _____   ____ 33

3.6   the amount of money that you make? _____   ____ 34

3.7   being unemployed or retired? (If appropriate.) _____   ____ 35

Section 4:   Leisure/participation

In the past fortnight, have you: Y N DK

4.1   been out to play or watch a sport?   1 2 3   ____ 36

4.2   been out shopping?   1 2 3   ____ 37

4.3   been for a ride in a bus, car or train, other than
for transport to and from work?   1 2 3   ____ 38

4.4   watched television or listened to radio?   1 2 3   ____ 39

4.5   In the past year, have there been times when
you would have liked to have had more leisure
activity but were unable?   1 2 3   ____ 40

How satisfied are you with: (LSS)

4.6   the amount of pleasure you get from
things you do at home?   _____   ____ 41

4.7   the amount of pleasure you get from
things you do outside your home?   _____   ____ 42

4.8   the pleasure you get from radio or T.V.? _____   ____ 43

Section 5: Religion

5.1   What is your religion now? _____   ____ 44

(a) Protestant   (d) Muslim

(b) Roman Catholic   (e) Hindi   (g) None

(c) Jewish   (f) Other

5.2   How often have you attended religious   ____ 45–46
services in the past month? _____

How satisfied are you with: (LSS)

5.3   your religious faith and its teachings?   _____   ____ 47

5.4   the frequency with which you attend services? _____   ____ 48

Section 6: Finances

6.1   What is your total weekly income? _____   ____ 49–51

6.2   Which, if any, state benefits do you receive?

_____   ____ 52–53

6.3   In the past year, have you been turned down for any
state benefits for which you have applied?   YES / NO / DK   ____ 54

	FOR OFFICE USE ONLY

6.4   About how much more money per week do
you need to be able to live as you would wish? _____ | _____ 55–57

6.5   During the past year, have you ever lacked the
money to enjoy everyday life?   YES / NO / DK | _____ 58

How satisfied are you with: (LSS)

6.6   how well-off you are financially?   _____ | _____ 59

6.7   the amount of money you have to spend
on enjoyment?   _____ | _____ 61

Section 7: Living situation

7.1   The client's current residence is: _____ | CARD 2

(a) Hostel	(f) Private house (owner-occupied)
(b) Boarding-out	(g) Private house (rental)
(c) Group home	(h) Flat
(d) Hospital ward	(i) Other
(e) Sheltered housing	(j) None

_____ 1–2

7.2   How long have you lived here? _____ yrs _____ mths | _____ 3–5

7.3   How many other people live here? _____ | _____ 6–7

7.4   Do your family live here too?   YES / NO / DK | _____ 8

7.5   In the past year have there been times when you
wanted to move or improve your living conditions but
were unable to do so?   YES / NO / DK | _____ 9

How satisfied are you with: (LSS)

7.6   the living arrangements here?   _____ | _____ 10
7.7   the amount of independence you have here?   _____ | _____ 11
7.8   the amount of influence you have here?   _____ | _____ 12
7.9   living with the people who you do?   _____ | _____ 13
7.10   the amount of privacy that you have here?   _____ | _____ 14
7.11   the prospect of living here for a long time?   _____ | _____ 15
7.12   the prospect of returning to live in hospital?
(If applicable.)   _____ | _____ 16

Section 8:   Legal and safety

8.1   In the past year have you been: Y N DK
(a) accused of a crime?   1 2 3 | _____ 17
(b) assaulted, beaten, molested or otherwise
a victim of violence?   1 2 3 | _____ 18

8.2   In the past year have there been any times
when you would have liked police or legal help
but were unable to get it?   1 2 3 | _____ 19

How satisfied are you with: (LSS)

	FOR OFFICE USE ONLY

8.3   your general personal safety? _____   ____ 20
8.4   the safety of this neighbourhood? _____   ____ 21

Section 9: Family relations

9.1   What is your current marital status? _____

(a) Married   (d) Divorced
(b) Single   (e) Separated
(c) Widowed   (f) Other   ____ 22

9.2   How many children do you have? _____   ____ 23–24
9.3   How often do you have contact with a relative? _____

(a) Daily   (d) Annually
(b) Weekly   (e) Less than annually
(c) Monthly   (f) Not appropriate/DK   ____ 25

9.4   In the past year have there been any times when you would have liked to have participated in family activities but were unable?   YES / NO / DK   ____ 26

How satisfied are you with: (LSS)

9.5   your family in general? _____   ____ 27
9.6   the amount of contact you have with
your relatives? _____   ____ 28
9.7   your marriage? (If applicable.) _____   ____ 29

Section 10:   Social relations

People differ in how much friendship they need.

	Y N DK	
10.1 Would you say that you are the sort of person who can manage without friends?	1 2 3	____ 30
10.2 Do you have anyone who you would call a 'close friend' (i.e. who knows you very well)?	1 2 3	____ 31
10.3 Do you have a friend to whom you could turn for help if you needed it?	1 2 3	____ 32
10.4 In the past week have you visited a friend	1 2 3	____ 33

How satisfied are you with: (LSS)

10.5   the way that you get on with other people? _____   ____ 34
10.6   the number of friends you have? _____   ____ 35

Section 11:   Health

	Y N DK	
During the past year have you:		
11.1 seen a doctor for a physical illness?	1 2 3	____ 36
11.2 seen a doctor for your nerves?	1 2 3	____ 37

11.3 been in hospital for your nerves?	1 2 3	_____ 38
11.4 Do you take medication for your nerves?	1 2 3	_____ 39
11.5 Do you have any physical handicap which effects your mobility?	1 2 3	_____ 40
11.6 How old were you when you were first admitted to a psychiatric hospital/ward? (If appropriate.)	_____ yrs	_____ 41–42
11.7 In the past year have there been times when you wanted help from a doctor or other professional for your health but were unable to get it? YES / NO / DK		_____ 43

How satisfied are you with: (LSS)

11.8 your general state of health?	_____	_____ 44
11.9 how often you see a doctor?	_____	_____ 45
11.10 your nervous well-being?	_____	_____ 46

During the past month, did you ever feel:

	Y N DK	
11.11 pleased about having accomplished something?	1 2 3	_____ 47
11.12 that things were going your way?	1 2 3	_____ 48
11.13 proud because someone complimented you on something you had done?	1 2 3	_____ 49
11.14 particularly excited or interested in something?	1 2 3	_____ 50
11.15 'on top of the world'?	1 2 3	_____ 51
11.16 too restless to sit in a chair?	1 2 3	_____ 52
11.17 bored?	1 2 3	_____ 53
11.18 depressed or very unhappy?	1 2 3	_____ 54
11.19 very lonely or remote from other people?	1 2 3	_____ 55
11.20 upset because someone criticised you?	1 2 3	_____ 56

Section 12:   Self-concept

How satisfied we are with ourselves is also a very important part of our lives. Do you agree that the following statements apply to you:

	Y N DK	
12.1 You feel that you're a person of worth, at least on an equal plane with others.	1 2 3	_____ 57
12.2 You feel that you have a number of good qualities.	1 2 3	_____ 58
12.3 All in all, you are inclined to feel that you are a failure.	1 2 3	_____ 59
12.4 You are able to do things as well as most others.	1 2 3	_____ 60
12.5 You feel you do not have much to be proud of.	1 2 3	_____ 61
12.6 You take a positive attitude toward yourself.	1 2 3	_____ 62

<table>
</table>

		FOR OFFICE USE ONLY
12.7 On the whole, you are satisfied with yourself.	1 2 3	_____ 63
12.8 You wish you could have more respect for yourself.	1 2 3	_____ 64
12.9 You certainly feel useless at times.	1 2 3	_____ 65
12.10 At times you think you are no good at all.	1 2 3	_____ 66

Section 13: General well-being

During the course of this interview, you and I have discussed many of the conditions of your life and how you feel about them. Might we try and sum them up now?   CARD 3

13.1   Can you tell me how you feel about your life as a whole? (LSS)   _____   _____ 1

13.2   This is a picture of a ladder. I would like you to imagine that the bottom of the ladder represents the very worst outcome which you could expect to have had in life. The top represents the very best possible outcome you could have expected. Can you please mark (X) where on this ladder you would put your life at present? (Ask client to MARK ladder!)   _____ 2–4

_____

BEST POSSIBLE OUTCOME

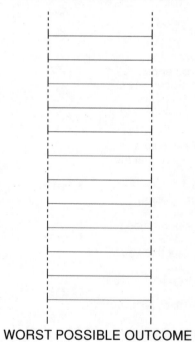

WORST POSSIBLE OUTCOME

13.3   How happy has your life been overall?   _____

(a) Very happy
(b) Pretty happy   ____ 5
(c) Not happy
(d) Don't know

13.4   Can you name anything(s) which would
improve the quality of your life?

1 _____   ____ 6–7

2 _____   ____ 8–9

3 _____   ____ 10–11

Section 14: Final remarks

Thank you for having spoken to me in such an honest
and open way about your life.

14.1   It is possible that we may wish to contact you
again in future, perhaps next year. Would you be willing
to be interviewed again?   YES / NO / DK   ____ 12

Thank you very much for your co-operation.

FINISHING TIME: _____

Section 15: Interviewer comments

Before filing this questionnaire or proceeding on to the next
interview, would you please complete the following section
while your impressions of both the client and the setting for the
interview are still fresh in your memory.
15.1   How long did the interview take?   _____mins   ____ 13–15
15.2   How reliable or unreliable do you think
the client's responses were?   _____   ____ 16
(a) Very reliable
(b) Generally reliable
(c) Generally unreliable
(d) Very unreliable

For the interviewer

15.3   Please complete the Quality of Life Uniscale now.
PLEASE MARK WITH AN X THE APPROPRIATE PLACE
WITHIN THE BOX TO INDICATE YOUR RATING OF THIS
PERSON'S PRESENT QUALITY OF LIFE.

LOWEST quality applies to someone completely dependent
physically on others, seriously mentally disabled, unaware of
surroundings and in a hopeless position.
HIGHEST quality applies to someone physically and mentally
independent, communicating well with others, able to do most
things enjoyed, pulling own weight, with a hopeful yet realistic
attitude.

LOWEST
QUALITY

HIGHEST
QUALITY

———17–19

THANK YOU FOR YOUR HELP.
Please return completed questionnaires to:

© J. Oliver
March 1990

LANCASHIRE QUALITY OF LIFE PROFILE (LQOLP): INTRODUCTION AND INSTRUCTIONS

Introduction

The Lancashire Quality of Life Profile is a structured interview for measuring the health and welfare of mental health clients.

Since its development began three years ago, influences such as the recent United Kingdom White Paper on community care and the Lancashire Mental Health Strategy 'New Futures' have made it important that suitable means of monitoring the progress of mental health cases resident in the community be devised and that these become part of our departmental operational procedures. The Lancashire Quality of Life Profile is our attempt to begin this process.

Our profile builds upon recent American and British questionnaires developed for research on clients with similar life predicaments. In addition, we have both developed our own material and incorporated questions from sources so far not used in this sort of research. We have piloted the questionnaire here in Lancashire on several occasions and it is now ready for employment within the agency.

The Lancashire Quality of Life Profile gives a fairly comprehensive, if brief, profile or outline of an individual client's current level of psychosocial functioning. It combines 'objective', factual material related to several of a client's life areas or domains with 'subjective' material drawn from the client's self-assessments. Also included is a professional quality of life assessment based on observation and prior knowledge of the case.

The interview seeks to strike a balance between the structure required to produce reliable results and the flexibility necessary to produce an interview atmosphere where additional material of a clarifying nature can be safely sought and received. Continuous pruning of the questions has reduced the interview to the minimum length necessary to produce a useful client profile.

General instructions

1 Each questionnaire should, wherever possible, be completed in a single interviewing session. Previous experience leads us to believe that about one hour is generally sufficient time. Only one questionnaire is to be completed for each client. If, for some reason, an interview requires more than one session to complete, the same form should be used, continuing on from where the previous session stopped.

2 Interviews are best conducted in a quite place, with sufficient privacy to allow the client to feel that he/she can speak freely without being overheard. As the interview requires the attention of both the worker and the client, an environment free of unnecessary or frequent interruptions is also highly desirable.

3 In each interview, information is gathered in the following order:
Initial information
Section 1: Client's personal details
Section 2: Client's general well-being
Section 3: Work/education
Section 4: Leisure/participation
Section 5: Religion
Section 6: Finances
Section 7: Living situation
Section 8: Legal and safety
Section 9: Family relations
Section 10: Social relations
Section 11: Health
Section 12: Self-concept
Section 13: Client's general well-being
Final remarks
Interviewer comments

4 All answers for the interview must be made in the spaces available. **Along the right-hand side of each page is a vertical margin containing data column codes. THIS AREA IS FOR DATA PROCESSING ONLY AND SHOULD NOT BE WRITTEN IN**.

5 Please complete all questions.

Specific instructions

1 Name or identifier. Affix the client's name or other personal identifier, such as an identification number. This is necessary to ensure that the same client has not been interviewed twice and that should the client be contacted again, at a later date, that information can be accurately updated.

2 Address. Complete in cases where the client has recently changed address or is planning to do so in the near future. If client is 'homeless', indicate with NFA (No Fixed Abode).

3 Date of interview. In the unlikely event that the interview should take place on two different dates, include only the first date.

4 Interviewer's name. Please state your name on EACH interview.

5 Starting time. Be sure to note the time at which the interview actually begins. This is compared with the FINISHING TIME at the end of the interview, to give a measure of the length of the interview.

6 Before beginning the interview it is necessary to introduce yourself, tell the client exactly what the purpose of the interview is and to gain his/her consent. Following is a model introduction which we have tried previously and which works well.

Thank you for allowing me to speak with you. My name is Mr/Mrs/Miss/ Ms and I work for the Lancashire Social Services Department.

[You can display Lancashire Social Services identification at this point, if required.)

I am visiting you because we are interested in finding out all about the things which go to make up your everyday life and how you feel about them. We want to get a fairly complete picture of the quality of your life at present so that we have a better idea of how to develop our services in the future.

To do this, I will need to ask you questions about many different areas of living. I expect that I shall take about an hour of your time.

Before we begin, I would like to say that anything which you will say to me will be held in confidence. Normally this would mean that only I and my superiors in the Social Services Department would have access to it and no information will be passed on to others without your knowledge and consent. I hope that this will help you to feel that you can speak openly and honestly with me.

Also, you may find some of the questions difficult or too personal to discuss. In either instance, please do not hesitate to say so. You may decline to answer any questions which you like and may also stop the interview at any time. I will certainly understand.

7 Client declines interview. In instances where the client declines to be interviewed please indicate so on the interview form, also stating the reason, if one has been given. Also include here clients who have not been interviewed for other reasons: e.g. they were acutely ill at the time and/or you judged that it would not be in their best interest, etc. In all instances, please give a clear explanation for not proceeding.

Section 1: Client's personal details

1.1 Insert current age to nearest year.
1.2 Indicate sex with a tick or X.
1.3 Insert correct letter for ethnic group.
1.4 Insert age for cessation of formal education to nearest year.

Where a client was unwilling or unable to answer such a question, or where the question was, for some reason, not applicable to the client, please insert only DK, for 'did not know', into the appropriate space.

Section 2: General well-being

Give the client the Life Satisfaction Scale (LSS). He/she should keep it for use throughout the interview. It helps the client to give verbal expression to a range of satisfactions from LOW (i.e. 'couldn't be worse') to HIGH (i.e. 'couldn't be better') and contains a variety of expressions between these extremes (displeased, mostly dissatisfied, mixed feelings, mostly satisfied and pleased). It is numbered correspondingly from 1 (LOW) to 7 (HIGH). Please record *only the number* corresponding to the words chosen by the client.

The use of the Life Satisfaction Scale may be explained to the client as follows:

Please look at this. [Show the client the Life Satisfaction Scale].
This is a chart which will help you to describe how you feel. We will be using it throughout the interview to help you with questions about many areas of your life. All you have to do is to point to the part of the chart which best describes how you feel when you are asked. As you can see, it covers all of the feelings from when you are most satisfied with something or approve of it most strongly to when you are least satisfied or most strongly disapprove.

For example, if I asked you if you liked fish and chips you might say 'couldn't be better' if you really liked them a lot. This would show the strongest possible satisfaction or approval. On the other hand, if you hated fish and chips you might point to 'couldn't be worse'. This would show the strongest dissatisfaction. If you felt about equally satisfied and dissatisfied with fish and chips you would point to the middle of the chart and 'mixed'. This would tell me that you were uncertain or of mixed feelings. As you can see, there is room for many shades of opinion in either direction.

2.1 Enter LSS score.

Section 3: Work/education

3.1 Circle client's answer. Here, as elsewhere, only one answer should be recorded per question. For example:

YES – the client 'agreed' with the statement.
NO – the client 'disagreed' with the statement.
DK – the client 'did not know' or would/could not answer.

3.2   Where employed, please list occupation.
3.3   Indicate number.
3.4   Indicate amount.
3.5–3.7 Enter LSS score.
N.B. Clients who are currently employed will be asked 3.5 and 3.6. Clients NOT currently employed will be asked only 3.7. ALL clients should be asked one or the other.

Section 4: Leisure/participation

4.1–4.5 In some instances where a series of such question are asked, the scoring has been simplified to 1 = YES, 2 = NO and 3 = DK (do not know,

was unwilling to answer, question not applicable). In these instances, however, the same rules apply with *only one* answer being *circled* per question.
4.6–4.8 Enter LSS score.

Section 5: Religion

5.1   Enter appropriate letter.
5.2   Enter appropriate number.
5.3–5.4 Enter LSS score.

Section 6: Finances

6.1   Enter total income before deductions or payment of expenses.
6.2   List benefits.
6.3   Circle client's response.
6.4   Enter amount required.
6.5   Circle client's response.
6.6–6.7 Enter LSS score.

Section 7: Living circumstances

7.1   Enter appropriate letter.
7.2   Enter number of years and months.
7.3   Enter number.
7.4–7.5 Circle client's response.
7.6–7.12 Enter LSS score.

Section 8: Legal and safety

8.1–8.2 Circle client's response.
8.3–8.4 Enter LSS score.

Section 9: Family relations

9.1   Enter appropriate letter.
9.2   Enter number.
9.3   Enter appropriate letter.
9.4   Circle client's response.
9.5–9.7 Enter LSS score.

Section 10: Social relations

10.1–10.4 Circle client's response.
10.5–10.6 Enter LSS score.

Section 11: Health

11.1–11.5   Circle client's response.
11.6   Enter number of years.
11.7   Circle client's response.
11.8–11.10   Enter LSS score.
11.11–11.20 Circle client's response.

Section 12: Self-concept

12.1–12.10   Circle client's response.

Section 13: General well-being

13.1 Enter LSS score.
13.2 Cantril's ladder is a measure of global well-being *scored by the client him/herself directly on the questionnaire.* Have the client look at the ladder and make one mark, preferably an 'X', at the point on the ladder which best expresses his/her current level of life satisfaction. The mark need not rest on any rung but may lie anywhere on the ladder. The mark must lie *within* the ladder, however, and not next to it.
13.3   Enter appropriate letter.
13.4.1–13.4.3 List only one item per line.

Section 14: Final remarks

14.1 Circle client's response.

Section 15: Interviewer comments

15.1 Enter number of minutes.
15.2 Enter appropriate letter.
15.3 Mark with a X for Quality of Life Uniscale.

LIFE SATISFACTION SCALE (LSS)

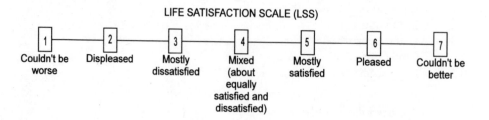

Appendix 2

Table 1 Subjective well-being: mean scores for social and economic indicators

	Mean	STD	Median	95% C.I. for mean
General work satisfaction	5.08	1.32	5	(4.9387, 5.2274)
Earnings	4.14	1.62	5	(3.9440, 4.3342)
Employment status	3.76	1.54	4	(3.6560, 3.8560)
Pleasure from home activities	4.52	1.44	5	(4.4473, 4.5949)
Pleasure from outside activities	4.60	1.47	5	(4.5212, 4.6725)
Pleasure from radio and television	4.97	1.32	5	(4.9010, 5.0356)
Religion overall	4.80	1.39	5	(4.7222, 4.8759)
Frequency of religious practice	4.45	1.43	5	(4.3727, 4.5313)
Financial comfort	3.75	1.59	4	(3.6652, 3.8289)
Money for enjoyment	3.64	1.54	4	(3.5557, 3.7158)
Res. living arrangements	4.82	1.43	5	(4.7451, 4.8916)
Res. independence	5.11	1.38	5	(5.0380, 5.1798)
Res. influence	4.75	1.46	5	(4.6740, 4.8300)
Res. other residents	4.94	1.41	5	(4.6740, 4.8300)
Res. privacy	5.01	1.47	5	(4.9368, 5.0880)
Res. continued residence	4.39	1.78	5	(4.2972, 4.4813)
Res. return to hospital	2.23	1.44	2	(2.1300, 2.3365)
Personal safety	4.85	1.35	5	(4.7783, 4.9171)
Neighbourhood safety	4.84	1.37	5	(4.7741, 4.9154)
General family satisfaction	4.75	1.50	5	(4.6690, 4.8257)
Amount of family contact	4.44	1.55	5	(4.3567, 4.5189)
Family participation	4.84	1.86	5	(4.5974, 5.0735)
Getting on	4.87	1.21	5	(4.8044, 4.9292)
Number of friends	4.40	1.50	5	(4.3249, 4.4798)
General health	4.28	1.51	5	(4.2059, 4.3614)
Frequency for doctor	4.98	1.20	5	(4.9151, 5.0397)
Nervous well-being	4.08	1.58	4	(4.0022, 4.1665)

Table 2 Perceived quality of life: mean life satisfaction scores for nine life domains

	Mean	STD	Median	95% C.I. for mean
Sub-scale for work	4.00	1.52	4	(3.9182, 4.0910)
Sub-scale for employed	4.78	1.22	5	(4.6198, 4.9407)
Sub-scale for unemployed	3.80	1.53	4	(3.7064, 3.9025)
Sub-scale for leisure	4.70	1.02	5	(4.6465, 4.7497)
Sub-scale for religion	4.63	1.08	5	(4.5743, 4.6913)
Sub-scale for finance	3.70	1.47	4	(3.6224, 3.7740)
Sub-scale for living situation	4.64	1.06	5	(4.5891, 4.6973)
Sub-scale for legal and safety	4.85	1.22	5	(4.7844, 4.9091)
Sub-scale for family relations	4.60	1.34	5	(4.5282, 4.6677)
Sub-scale for social relations	4.63	1.18	5	(4.5716, 4.6927)
Sub-scale for health	4.44	1.13	5	(4.3854, 4.5011)

Table 3 Measures of global well-being by age and sex [Cantril's ladder, happiness and LSS total scores]:

	Sex						
	Male			Female			
Age	Cantril's ladder			Cantril's ladder			95% C.I. for mean
	Mean	STD	Count	Mean	STD	Count	
31	53	25.87	173	55	28.82	94	(50.9696, 57.4791)
31–40	56	28.48	162	56	25.70	141	(52.9930, 59.1675)
41–50	56	29.42	189	53	26.82	182	(51.5841, 57.5104)
51–65	60	27.93	211	57	27.37	222	(55.5245, 61.1674)
>65	58	28.23	72	61	29.09	97	(54.7329, 64.3463)
Total	56	27.98	807	56	27.32	736	

	Sex							
	Male				Female			
Age	Happiness				Happiness			
	Very happy	Pretty happy	Not happy	Don't know	Very happy	Pretty happy	Not happy	Don't know
<31	1.3%	5.6%	3.0%	1.9%	.4%	3.3%	2.0%	.5%
31–40	.9%	4.7%	3.5%	1.4%	.6%	4.1%	2.8%	1.4%
41–50	1.5%	7.1%	2.4%	1.3%	1.2%	6.4%	3.3%	1.7%
51–65	1.6%	6.9%	4.0%	.9%	2.0%	7.0%	3.1%	1.7%
>65	.6%	2.7%	.9%	.2%	1.1%	3.8%	.7%	.7%
Total	5.9%	27.0%	13.7%	5.7%	5.4%	24.5%	11.8%	5.9%

Age	Sex						95% C.I. for mean
	Male			Female			
	QOL by average LSS score			QOL by average LSS score			
	Mean	STD	Count	Mean	STD	Count	
<31	4.21	1.36	173	4.22	1.40	94	(4.0453, 4.3742)
31–40	4.26	1.30	162	4.16	1.28	141	(4.0652, 4.3545)
41–50	4.39	1.36	189	4.06	1.43	182	(4.0863, 4.3763)
51–65	4.27	1.41	211	4.30	1.30	222	(4.1554, 4.4210)
>65	4.12	1.38	72	4.47	1.15	97	(4.1226, 4.5222)
Total	4.27	1.36	807	4.22	1.33	736	

Table 4 Perceived quality of life: mean life satisfaction scores for nine life domains

Age	Sex						95% C.I. for mean
	Male			Female			
	Sub-scale for work			Sub-scale for work			
	Mean	STD	Count	Mean	STD	Count	
<31	3.26	1.36	173	3.81	1.51	94	(3.2758, 3.6740)
31–40	3.92	1.55	162	3.79	1.57	141	(3.6659, 4.0616)
41–50	4.04	1.56	189	4.01	1.57	182	(3.8457, 4.2089)
51–65	3.92	1.50	211	4.34	1.41	222	(3.9959, 4.3140)
>65	4.46	1.46	72	4.89	1.11	97	(4.4541, 4.9160)
Total	3.85	1.53	807	4.16	1.50	736	

Age	Sex						95% C.I. for mean
	Male			Female			
	Sub-scale for employed			Sub-scale for employed			
	Mean	STD	Count	Mean	STD	Count	
<31	4.53	1.24	173	4.83	.98	94	(4.2688, 5.0547)
31–40	4.89	1.35	162	4.40	1.19	141	(4.3155, 4.9512)
41–50	5.08	1.17	189	4.94	1.13	182	(4.7269, 5.2883)
51–65	4.62	1.33	211	5.02	1.00	222	(4.5065, 5.1738)
>65	3.71	1.63	72	6.00	.82	97	(3.3583, 5.7326)
Total	4.75	1.32	807	4.82	1.13	736	

Age	Sex						95% C.I. for mean
	Male			Female			
	Sub-scale for unemployed			Sub-scale for unemployed			
	Mean	STD	Count	Mean	STD	Count	
<31	3.03	1.27	173	3.51	1.49	94	(2.9992, 3.4282)
31–40	3.65	1.49	162	3.51	1.65	141	(3.3560, 3.8212)
41–50	3.70	1.55	189	3.71	1.59	182	(3.4965, 3.9179)
51–65	3.75	1.49	211	4.19	1.45	222	(3.8191, 4.1735)
>65	4.61	1.42	72	4.81	1.09	97	(4.5053, 4.9713)
Total	3.62	1.50	807	3.98	1.54	736	

Age	Sex						95% C.I. for mean
	Male			Female			
	Sub-scale for leisure			Sub-scale for leisure			
	Mean	STD	Count	Mean	STD	Count	
<31	4.61	.97	173	4.46	1.10	94	(4.4339, 4.6810)
31–40	4.67	1.03	162	4.58	.98	141	(4.5101, 4.7366)
41–50	4.74	.98	189	4.63	1.03	182	(4.5805, 4.7878)
51–65	4.81	1.02	211	4.78	1.10	222	(4.6882, 4.8960)
>65	4.79	.91	72	4.91	.94	97	(4.7228, 5.0185)
Total	4.72	.99	807	4.67	1.05	736	

Age	Sex						95% C.I. for mean
	Male			Female			
	Sub-scale for religion			Sub-scale for religion			
	Mean	STD	Count	Mean	STD	Count	
<31	4.34	1.33	173	4.52	1.01	94	(4.2351, 4.5612)
31–40	4.50	1.14	162	4.74	1.13	141	(4.4774, 4.7520)
41–50	4.71	.99	189	4.62	1.12	182	(4.5475, 4.7796)
51–65	4.54	1.11	211	4.83	.92	222	(4.5907, 4.8011)
>65	4.56	.88	72	4.91	.84	97	(4.6141, 4.9076)
Total	4.53	1.12	807	4.73	1.02	736	

Age	Sex						95% C.I. for mean
	Male			**Female**			
	Sub-scale for finance			*Sub-scale for finance*			
	Mean	*STD*	*Count*	*Mean*	*STD*	*Count*	
AGE1							
<31	3.37	1.42	173	3.66	1.37	94	(3.3132, 3.6529)
31–40	3.56	1.61	162	3.37	1.41	141	(3.3127, 3.6574)
41–50	3.76	1.48	189	3.41	1.51	182	(3.4318, 3.7467)
51–65	3.97	1.49	211	3.94	1.36	222	(3.8148, 4.0999)
>65	3.74	1.45	72	4.36	1.27	97	(3.8815, 4.3415)
Total	3.68	1.51	807	3.70	1.44	736	

Age	Sex						95% C.I. for mean
	Male			**Female**			
	Sub-scale for living situation			*Sub-scale for living situation*			
	Mean	*STD*	*Count*	*Mean*	*STD*	*Count*	
<31	4.36	1.12	173	4.48	1.06	94	(4.2801, 4.5450)
31–40	4.62	1.15	162	4.52	1.13	141	(4.4395, 4.6964)
41–50	4.66	.99	189	4.58	.99	182	(4.5179, 4.7233)
51–65	4.87	1.04	211	4.88	.92	222	(4.7768, 4.9702)
>65	4.55	1.15	72	4.75	1.06	97	(4.4790, 4.8373)
Total	4.63	1.09	807	4.66	1.03	736	

Age	Sex						95% C.I. for mean
	Male			**Female**			
	Sub-scale for legal and safety			*Sub-scale for legal and safety*			
	Mean	*STD*	*Count*	*Mean*	*STD*	*Count*	
<31	5.02	1.22	173	4.60	1.12	94	(4.7247, 5.0187)
31–40	5.09	1.26	162	4.55	1.34	141	(4.7034, 5.0019)
41–50	4.82	1.34	189	4.64	1.27	182	(4.5955, 4.8679)
51–65	4.99	1.12	211	4.87	1.13	222	(4.8171, 5.0400)
>65	4.54	1.07	72	5.04	.87	97	(4.6692, 4.9998)
Total	4.94	1.23	807	4.73	1.19	736	

Age	Sex						95% C.I. for mean
	Male			Female			
	Sub-scale for family relations			Sub-scale for family relations			
	Mean	STD	Count	Mean	STD	Count	
<31	4.85	1.21	173	4.66	1.40	94	(4.6301, 4.9403)
31–40	4.86	1.38	162	4.39	1.35	141	(4.4943, 4.8090)
41–50	4.63	1.37	189	4.44	1.16	182	(4.3992, 4.6662)
51–65	4.60	1.31	211	4.52	1.44	222	(4.4199, 4.6995)
>65	4.10	1.54	72	4.50	1.29	97	(4.0941, 4.5726)
Total	4.69	1.35	807	4.49	1.33	736	

Age	Sex						95% C.I. for mean
	Male			Female			
	Sub-scale for social relations			Sub-scale for social relations			
	Mean	STD	Count	Mean	STD	Count	
<31	4.48	1.40	173	4.47	1.08	94	(4.3150, 4.6282)
31–40	4.61	1.30	162	4.73	1.20	141	(4.5210, 4.8045)
41–50	4.50	1.28	189	4.54	1.03	182	(4.3987, 4.6408)
51–65	4.78	1.12	211	4.80	1.06	222	(4.6828, 4.8997)
>65	4.76	1.05	72	4.65	1.06	97	(4.5245, 4.8686)
Total	4.61	1.26	807	4.66	1.09	736	

Age	Sex						95% C.I. for mean
	Male			Female			
	Sub-scale for health			Sub-scale for health			
	Mean	STD	Count	Mean	STD	Count	
<31	4.43	1.17	173	4.58	.99	94	(4.3538, 4.6235)
31–40	4.47	1.21	162	4.38	1.04	141	(4.3061, 4.5621)
41–50	4.59	1.16	189	4.05	1.24	182	(4.1878, 4.4440)
51–65	4.48	1.07	211	4.49	1.09	222	(4.3769, 4.5920)
>65	4.64	1.03	72	4.55	.99	97	(4.4046, 4.7356)
Total	4.50	1.14	807	4.38	1.11	736	

Bibliography

Aaronson, N.T. (1990) 'Quality of life research in cancer clinical trials: a need for common rules and language', *Oncology* 4:59–66.

Able-Smith, B. and Townsend, P. (1965) *The Poor and the Poorest*, London: Bell.

Abrams, M. (1973) 'Subjective social indicators', *Social Trends* 4, London: HMSO.

AEP (1994) *Quality of Life and Disabilities in Mental Disorder*, 7th European Symposium of the Association of European Psychiatrists, Vienna, 7–9 April.

Alevizos, P., DeRisi, W., Liberman, R., Eckman, T. and Callahan, E. (1978) 'The behaviour observation instrument: a method of direct observation for programme evaluation', *Journal of Applied Analysis* 11:243–57.

Allebeck, P. (1989) 'Schizophrenia: a life-shortening disease', *Schizophrenia Bulletin* 15:81–9.

Alloway, R. and Bebbington, P. (1987) 'The buffer theory of social support—a review of the literature', *Psychological Medicine* 17:91–108.

American Psychiatric Association (1987) *Diagnostic and Statistical Manual of Mental Disorders* (3rd edition, revised), Washington: APA.

Anderson, J., Dayson, D., Willis, W., Gooch, C., Margolius, O., O'Driscoll, C. and Leff, J. (1993) 'The TAPS project 13: Clinical and social outcomes for long-stay psychiatric patients after one year in the community', *British Journal of Psychiatry Supplement* 19:45–56.

Anderson, M.R. (1977) 'A study of the relationship between life satisfaction and self-concept, locus of control, satisfaction with primary relationships and work satisfaction' (Ph.D. dissertation, Michigan State University), *Dissertation Abstracts International* 38, 2638–9a (University microfilms No. 77–125:214).

Andrews, F. and Withey, S.B. (1976) *Social Indicators of Well-being: Americans' Perceptions of Life Quality*, New York: Plenum Press.

Anstee, B.H. (1985) 'An alternative form of community care for the mentally ill: supported lodging schemes. A personal view', *Health Trends* 17:39–40.

Anthony, W. and Blanch, A. (1989) 'Research on community support services: what have we learned?', *Psychosocial Rehabilitation Journal* 12:55–82.

Anthony W.A. and Jansen, M.A. (1984) 'Predicting the vocational capacity of the chronically mentally ill. Research and policy implications', *American Psychologist* 39(5):537–44.

Anthony, W.A., Cohen, M.R. and Cohen, B.F. (1984) 'Psychiatric rehabilitation' in J. Talbott (ed.) *The Chronic Mental Patient: Five Years Later*, London: Grune and Stratton.

—— (1993) 'Philosophy, treatment process, and principles of the psychiatric rehabilitation approach', *New Directions for Mental Health Services* 17: 67–79.

Arnold, H.D. (1986) 'Heilpadagogik in psychiatrischen Kliniken. Bessere Libens-
qualitat fur die geistib Behinderten' ('Therapeutic education in psychiatric
hospitals: improved quality of life for the mentally handicapped'), *Kran-
kenpflege Soins Infirmiers* 79(4):81–4.

Atkins, T., Meats, P. and Sincock, C. (1991) 'Can we rehabilitate everyone?',
Psychiatric Bulletin 15:10–12.

Bachrach, L.L. (1975) *Deinstitutionalisation: An Analytical Review and Sociological Perspective*, Washington, D.C.: U.S. Department of Health, Education and
Welfare.

—— (1978)'A conceptual approach to deinstitutionalisation', *Hospital and Community Psychiatry* 29:573–8.

—— (1981) 'Continuity of care for chronic patients: a conceptual analysis',
American Journal of Psychiatry 138:1449–56.

—— (1982) 'Program planning for young adult chronic patients', in B. Pepper
and H. Ryglewicz (eds) *The Young Adult Chronic Patient*, San Francisco:
Jossey-Bass.

—— (1984). 'Asylum and chronically ill psychiatric patients', *American Journal
of Psychiatry* 141(8):975–8.

—— (1988) 'Defining chronic mental illness: a concept paper', *Hospital and
Community Psychiatry* 39:383–8.

—— (1993) 'Continuity of care: a context for case management', in M. Harris
and H.C. Bergman (eds) *Case Management for Mentally Ill Patients. Theory
and Practice*, Harwood Academic Publishers.

Baier, K. (1974). 'Towards a definition of "quality of life" ', in R.O. Clarke and
P.C. List (eds) *Environmental Spectrum: Social and Economic Views of the
Quality of Life*, New York: Van Nostrand.

Baker, F. and Intagliata, J. (1982) 'Quality of life in the evaluation of community
support systems', *Evaluation and Programme Planning* 5:69–79.

Baker, F., Jodrey, D. and Intagliata, J. (1992) 'Social support and quality of life of
community support clients', *Community Mental Health Journal* 28(5):397–411.

Baker, F., Jodrey, D., Intagliata, J. and Straus, H. (1993) 'Community services
and functioning of the seriously mentally ill', *Community Mental Health
Journal* 29(4):321–31.

Barker, P.J. (1982) *Behavioural Therapy Nursing*, London: Croom Helm.

Barlow, D.H. and Hersen, M. (1984) *Single Case Experimental Designs*, London:
Pergamon.

Barrowclough, C. and Tarrier, N. (1992a) *Families of Schizophrenic Patients*,
London: Chapman and Hall.

—— (1992b) 'Interventions with families', in M. Birchwood and N. Tarrier (eds)
Innovations in Psychological Management of Schizophrenia, London: John
Wiley & Sons.

Barrowclough, C., Tarrier, N., Watts, S., Vaughn, C., Bamrah, J.S. and Freeman, H.L. (1987) 'Assessing the functional value of relatives' knowledge about
schizophrenia: a preliminary report', *British Journal of Psychiatry* 151:1, 8.

Barry, M., Crosby, C. and Bogg, J. (1993) 'Methodological issues in evaluating
the quality of life of long-stay psychiatric patients', *Journal of Mental Health*
2:43–56.

Barton, R. (1959) *Institutional Neurosis*, Bristol: John Wright.

Bass, C. (1990) *Somatization: Physical Symptoms and Psychological Illness*,
Oxford: Blackwell.

Bass, C. and Benjamin, S. (1993) 'The management of chronic somatisation',
British Journal of Psychiatry 162:472–80.

Bass, C. and Murphy, M. (1990) 'The chronic somatiser and the Government White Paper', *Journal of the Royal Society of Medicine* 83:203–5.

Bauer, R.A. (1966) 'Detection and anticipation of impact: the nature of the task', in R.A. Bauer (ed.), *Social Indicators*, Cambridge, Mass.: M.I.T. Press.

Beard, J.H. (1978) 'The rehabilitation services of Fountain House', in L.I. Stein and M.A. Test (eds) *Alternatives to Mental Hospital Treatment*, New York: Plenum.

Beard, J.H., Probst, R.N. and Malamud, T.J. (1982) 'The Fountain House model of psychiatric rehabilitation', *Psychosocial Rehabilitation Journal* 5(1):47–53.

Bebbington, P., Hurry, J., Tennant, C., Sturt, E. and Wing, J.K. (1981) 'Epidemiology of mental disorders in Camberwell', *Psychological Medicine* 11(3): 561–79.

Bech, P. (1990) 'Measurement of psychological distress and well-being', *Psychotherapeutics Psychosomatics* 54:77–89.

Beiser, M. (1974) 'Components and correlates of mental well-being', *Journal of Health and Social Behaviour* 15:320–7.

Beiser, M., Shore, J.H., Peters, R. and Tatum, E. (1985) 'Does community care for the mentally ill make a difference? A tale of two cities', *American Journal of Psychiatry* 142:1047–52.

Bellack, A.S. (1989) 'A comprehensive model for treatment of schizophrenia', in A.S. Bellak (ed.) *A Clinical Guide for the Treatment of Schizophrenia*, London: Plenum Press.

Benjamin, S. (1989) 'Psychological treatment of chronic pain: a selective review', *Journal of Psychosomatic Research* 33:121–31.

Benjamin, S. and Bridges, K. (1993) 'The need for specialised services for chronic somatizers', in S. Benjamin, A. House and P. Jenkins (eds) *Liaison Psychiatry: Defining Needs and Planning Services*, London: Gaskell.

Benjamin, S., Barnes, D., Berger, S. *et al.* (1988) 'The relationship of chronic pain, mental illness and organic disorders', *Pain* 32:185–95.

Bennett, D. (1970) 'The value of work in psychiatric rehabilitation', *Social Psychiatry* 5:224–30.

Bennett, D. and Morris, I. (1983) 'Support and rehabilitation', in F.N. Watts and D.H. Bennett (eds) *Theory and Practice of Psychiatric Rehabilitation*, London: John Wiley and Sons.

Bennett, D.H. (1978) 'Social forms of psychiatric treatment', in J.K. Wing (ed.) *Schizophrenia: Towards a New Synthesis*, London: Academic Press.

Berkman, P.L. (1971) 'Life stress and psychological well-being: a replication of Langner's analysis in the midtown Manhattan study', *Journal of Health and Social Behaviour* 12:35–45.

Berlyne, N. (1975) 'Diogenes syndrome', *Lancet* 1:515.

Bigelow, D.A., Brodsky, G., Stewart, L. and Olson, M. (1982) 'Chapter 14: The concept and measurement of quality of life as a dependent variable in evaluation of mental health services', in *Innovative Approaches to Mental Health Evaluation*, New York: Academic Press.

Birchwood, M., Smith, J., MacMillan, F., Hogg, B., Prasad, R., Harvey, C. and Bering, S. (1989) 'Predicting relapse in schizophrenia: the development and implementation of an early signs monitoring system using patients and families as observers', *Psychological Medicine* 19:649–56.

Black, D., Morris, J.N., Smith, C. and Townsend, P. (1982, 1988) 'The Black report', in P. Townsend. and N. Davidson (eds) *Inequalities in Health*, London: Penguin Books.

Blazek, L.A. (1993) 'Development of a psychiatric home care program and the role of the CNS in the delivery of care', *Clinical Nurse Specialist*, 7(4):164–8.

Blenker, M. (1954) 'Predictive factors in the initial interview in family casework', *Social Service Review* 28:65–73.

Blinov, N.N., Demin, E.V. and Chulkova, V.A. (1991) 'Cancer research in Russia. Part 1: Some aspects of the rehabilitation of cancer patients in St Petersberg', *Social Work and Social Sciences Review* 3(3):243–50.

Bloom, B.L., Hodges, W.F., Kern, M.B. and McFaddin, S.C. (1985) 'A preventive intervention program for the newly separated: final evaluations', *American Journal of Orthopsychiatry* 55(1): 9–26.

Borus, J.F. (1978) 'Issues critical to the survival of community mental health', *American Journal of Psychiatry* 135:1029–35.

Bowling, A. (1991) *Measuring Health: A Review of Quality of Life Measurement Scales*, Milton Keynes: Open University Press.

Boydell, K.M. and Trainor, J.N. (1988) 'Improving the income support of the chronically mentally ill: a model program to address the needs of ex-psychiatric patients', *Canadian Journal of Psychiatry* 33(1):3–6.

Boyer, C.B. (1985) 'The role of social support and psychological variables on dietary and fluid compliance and the quality of life of hemodialysis patients' (Ph.D. dissertation, State University of New York at Stony Brook), *Dissertation Abstracts International* 47/02–B.

Bradburn, N. (1969) *The Structure of Psychological Well-being*, Chicago: Aldine Publishing Co.

Bradburn, N. and Caplovitz, D. (1965) *Reports on Happiness*, Chicago: Aldine Publishing Co.

Brand, J. (1978) 'The politics of social indicators', in M. Bulmer (ed.) *Social Policy Research*, London: Macmillan.

Brekke, J.S. and Test, M.A. (1987) 'An empirical analysis of services delivered in a model community support programme', *Psychosocial Rehabilitation Journal* 10(4):51–61.

—— (1992) 'A model for measuring the implementation of community support programs: results from three sites', *Community Mental Health Journal*, 28(3):227–47.

Bridges, K. and Brown, L. (1989) 'Psychiatric patients work alongside artists in prizewinning project', *British Medical Journal* 299:532.

Bridges, K. and Cresswell, A. (1994) 'The continuing support service (CSS) for people with enduring disabilities', in J.P.J. Oliver, P. Huxley, and A. Butler (eds) *Mental Health Casework (Vol. 2): Themes from Teams*, Manchester: Manchester University Press.

Bridges, K. and Goldberg, D.P. (1992) 'Somatisation in primary health care: prevalence and determinants', in B. Cooper and R. Eastwood (eds) *Primary Health Care and Psychiatric Epidemiology*, London: Routledge.

Bridges, K., Davenport, S. and Goldberg, D. (1994a) 'The need for hospital-based rehabilitation services', *Journal of Mental Health* 3:205–12.

Bridges, K., Giblin, B. and Sellwood, W. (1991a) 'The Anson Road Project (1989): two wards in central Manchester', in R. Young (ed.) *Residential Needs For Severely Disabled Psychiatric Patients*, London: HMSO.

Bridges, K., Gage, A., Oliver, J., Ewert, C., Kershaw, A. and Wood, L. (1993), 'Changes in social support and quality of life: a case study of a man with an enduring psychotic illness', *International Journal of Social Psychiatry* 39:142–51.

Bridges, K., Huxley, P. and Oliver, J. (1994b) 'Psychiatric rehabilitation: re-defined for the 1990s', *International Journal of Social Psychiatry* 40(1):1–16.

Bridges, K., Mechenzie, M. and Thomas, C. (1994c) 'Negative psychopathology in long stay patients and assessment of quality of life' (submitted to *Social Work and Social Sciences Review*).

Bridges, K., Staufenberg, E. and Moss, G. (1991b) 'High Elms (1985–1989): the first hostel ward in central Manchester', in R. Young (ed.) *Residential Needs For Severely Disabled Psychiatric Patients*, London: HMSO.

Brier, A. and Strauss, J.S. (1983) 'Self control in psychiatric disorders', *Archives of General Psychiatry* 40:1141–5.

Brimblecombe, F.A. (1985) 'The needs of young intellectually retarded adults,' (eighteenth Blake Marsh lecture, February, 1984) *British Journal of Psychiatry* 146:5–10.

Brooks, N., Symington, C., Beattie, A., Campsie, L., Bryden, J. and McKinlay, W. (1989) 'Alcohol and other predictors of cognitive recovery after severe head injury', *Brain Injury* 3 (3) 235–46.

Brown, G. (1973) 'The mental hospital as an institution', *Social Sciences and Medicine* 7:107–24.

Brown, G.W., Birley, J.L.T. and Wing, J.K. (1972) 'Influence of family life on the course of schizophrenic disorders: a replication', *British Journal of Psychiatry* 121:241–58.

Brown, G.W., Bone, M., Dalison, B. and Wing, J.K. (1966) *Schizophrenia and Social Care*, London: Oxford University Press.

Brown, G.W., Carstairs, G.M. and Topping, G. (1958) 'The post hospital adjustment of chronic mental patients', *Lancet* 2:685–9.

Brown, M.A. and Munford, A.M. (1983) 'Life skills training for chronic schizophrenics', *Journal of Nervous and Mental Diseases* 171:466–70.

Brugha, T.S., Wing, J.K. and Smith, B.L. (1989) 'Physical health of the long term mentally ill in the community. Is there unmet need?', *British Journal of Psychiatry* 155:777–81.

Bulpitt, C.J. and Fletcher, A.E. (1985) 'Quality of life in hypertensive patients on different antihypertensive treatments: rationale for methods employed in a multicentre randomised controlled trial', *Journal of Cardiovascular Pharmacology* 7 (Suppl. 1):137–45.

Bunge, M. (1975) 'What is a quality of life indicator?' *Social Indicator Research* 2: 65–79.

Burns, T. (1990) 'Community ward rounds', *Health Trends* 22:62–3.

Butler, R.J. and Rosenthal, G. (1985) *Behaviour and Rehabilitation: Behavioural Treatment for Long-Stay Patients*, London: John Wright & Sons.

Cadman, S.P. (1935) *Adventure for Happiness*, New York: The Macmillan Co.

Cagnoni, G., Guizzardi, G., Giardina, F. and Mennonna, P. (1986) 'Follow up and surgical consideration on a series of patients operated on for non-tumoral aqueductal stenosis', *Journal of Neurosurgical Sciences* 30(1–2):77–9.

Campbell, A. (1976) 'Subjective measures of well-being', *American Psychologist* 31:117–24.

—— (1981) *The Sense of Well-being in America: Recent Patterns and Trends*, New York: McGraw-Hill.

Campbell, A., Converse, P. and Rogers, W.L. (1976) *The Quality of American Life: Perceptions, Evaluations and Satisfactions*, New York: Russel Sage.

Cantril, H. (1965) *The Pattern of Human Concerns*, New Brunswick, N.J.: Rutgers University Press.

Carling, P.J. (1993) 'Housing and supports for persons with mental illness: emerging approaches to research and practice', *Hospital and Community Psychiatry* 44(5):439–49.

Carmines, E.G. and Zeller, R.A. (1978) *Reliability and Validity Assessment*, London: Sage Publications Ltd.

Carpenter, W.T. and Heinrichs, D.W. (1983) 'Early intervention, time-limited, targeted pharmacotherapy of schizophrenia', *Schizophrenia Bulletin* 9 (4):533–42.

Carpenter, W.T., Heinrichs, D.W. and Hanlon, T.E. (1987) 'A comparative trial of pharmacologic strategies in schizophrenia', *American Journal of Psychiatry* 144: 1466–70.

Caton, C.L., Wyatt, R.J., Felix, A., Grunberg, J. and Dominquez, B. (1993) 'Follow-up of chronically homeless mentally ill men', *American Journal of Psychiatry* 150 (11):1639–42.

Central Statistical Office (1991a) *Key Data: 1991/2 Edition*, London: HMSO.

—— (1991b) *Regional Trends* 26, London: HMSO.

—— (1992) *Social Trends*, London: HMSO.

Chang, R.H. and Dodder, R.A. (1983) 'The modified purpose in life scale: a cross-national validity study', *International Journal of Ageing and Human Development* 18(3): 207–17.

Clark, A.N.G., Mankikar, G.D. and Gray, I. (1975) 'Diogenes syndrome: a clinical study of gross neglect in old age', *Lancet* 1:366–8.

Clark, R.E. and Fox, T.S. (1993) 'A framework for evaluating the economic impact of case management', *Hospital and Community Psychiatry* 44: 469–73.

Clements, K. and Turpin, G. (1992) 'Vulnerability models and schizophrenia', in M. Birchwood and N. Tarrier (eds) *Innovations in Psychological Management of Schizophrenia*, London: John Wiley & Sons.

Clifford, P., Charman, A., Webb, Y. and Best, S. (1991) 'Planning community care: long-stay populations of hospitals scheduled for rundown or closure', *British Journal of Psychiatry* 158:190–6.

Clough, L., Abernethy, V. and Grunebaum, H. (1976) 'Contraception for the severely psychiatrically disturbed: confusion, control and contradiction', *Comprehensive Psychiatry* 17:601–6.

Cnaan, R.A., Adler, I. and Ramot, A. (1986) 'Public reaction to establishment of community residential facilities for mentally retarded persons in Israel', *American Journal of Mental Deficiency* 90(6):677–85.

Cochrane, R. (1983) *The Social Creation of Mental Illness*, London: Longman.

Coid, J. W. (1991) ' "Difficult to place" psychiatric patients', *British Medical Journal* 302:603–4.

Colgan, S. and Bridges, K. (1990) 'The development of a community support service for the chronically mentally ill in an inner city health district', *Psychiatric Bulletin* 14:710–12.

Colgan, S., Bridges, K., Brown, L. and Faragher, B. (1991) 'A tentative START to community care', *Psychiatric Bulletin* 15:596–8.

Collis, M. and Ekdawi, M.Y. (1984) 'Social adjustment in rehabilitation', *International Journal of Rehabilitation Research* 7:259–72.

Courtney, P., O'Grady, J. and Cunnane, J. (1992) 'The provision of secure psychiatric services in Leeds, Paper ii: a survey of unmet need' *Health Trends* 24:51–3.

Cooper, J. (1988a) 'The set menu gives way to the mixed grill', *Social Work Today*, 2 June: 14–15.

—— (1988b) 'The mosaic of personal social services: public, voluntary and private', *British Journal of Social Work* 18: 237–50.

Corden, A. (1990) 'Choice and self-determination as aspects of quality of life in private sector homes', in S. Baldwin, C. Godfrey and C. Propper (eds) *Quality of Life: Perspectives and Policies*, London: Routledge.

Cox, D.R., Fitzpatrick, R., Fletcher, A.E., Gore, S.M., Spiegelhalter, D.J. and Jones, D.R. (1992) 'Quality of life assessment; Can we keep it simple?' *Journal of Royal Statistical Society* 155(3):353–93.

Creed, F. and Marks, B. (1989) 'Liaison psychiatry in general practice: a comparison of a liaison attachment scheme and the shifted out-patient model', *Journal of the Royal College of General Practitioners* 39:514–17.

Creed, F.C., Huxley, P.J., Tarrier, N., Murray, R. and Tyrer, P. (1993) 'Comparison of intensive and standard case management programmes for psychotic patients' (research submission to the Department of Health), Manchester University School of Psychiatry and Behavioural Sciences.

Creed, F.H., Black, D., Anthony, P., Osborn, M., Thomas, P. and Tomenson, B. (1991) 'Day hospital for acute psychiatric illness', *British Medical Journal* 300:1033–7.

Creer, C. and Wing, J.K. (1974) *Schizophrenia at Home*, Surbiton: National Schizophrenia Fellowship.

Creighton, F. and Hyde, C. (1991) 'Douglas House: a review of 7 years' experience', *British Journal of Psychiatry* (in press).

Crow, T.J. (1985) 'The two syndrome concept: origins and current status', *Schizophrenia Bulletin* 11:471–86.

Crown, D. and Marlowe, D. (1964) *The Approval Motive*, New York: Wiley.

Culyer, A.J. (1978). 'Need values and health status measurement', in A.J. Culyer and K.G. Wright (eds) *Economic Aspects of Health Services*, London: Martin Robertson.

Cunningham, J.K. (1985) 'Re-examining the apparent lack of covariance between objects and satisfactions', (quality of life, attitudes) (Ph.D. dissertation, Claremont Graduate School), *Dissertation Abstracts International*, 46/08-B.

Curtis, J.L., Millman, E.J., Struening, E. and d'Ercole, A. (1992) 'Effect of case management on rehospitalisation and utilisation of ambulatory care services', *Hospital and Community Psychiatry* 43(9):895–9.

Cutten, G.B. (1926) *The Threat of Leisure*, New Haven: Yale University Press.

Dalkey, N.C. and Rourke, D.L. (1972) 'The Delphi procedure and rating quality of life factors', unpublished, University of California at Los Angeles.

Dann, G. (1984) *The Quality of Life in Barbados*, London: Macmillan.

Darling, C. and Tyrer, P. (1990) 'Brief encounters in general practice: liaison in general practice psychiatry clinics', *Psychiatric Bulletin* 14:592–4.

Davies, T.W. and Morris, A. (1989) 'A comparative quantification of stigma', *Social Work and Social Sciences Review* 1(2):109–22.

Dayson, D., Gooch, C. and Thornicroft, G. (1992) 'The TAPS Project. 16: Difficult to place, long term psychiatric patients: risk factors for failure to resettle long stay patients in community facilities', *British Medical Journal* 305:993–5.

Dean, C. and Gadd, E.M. (1990) 'Home treatment for acute psychiatric illness', *British Medical Journal* 301:1021–3.

Dean, C., Phillips, J., Gadd, E.M., Joseph, M. and England, S. (1993). 'Comparison of community based service with hospital based service for people with acute, severe psychiatric illnesses', *British Medical Journal*, 307, 6902:473–6.

Deighton, C.M. and Nicol, A.R. (1985) 'Abnormal illness behaviour in young women in a primary care setting: is Briquet's syndrome a useful category?' *Psychological Medicine* 15(3):515–20.

Diener, E. (1984) 'Subjective well-being', *Psychological Bulletin* 95(3):542–75.

Dietzen, L.L. and Bond, G.R. (1993) 'Relationship between case manager contact and outcome for frequently hospitalized psychiatric clients', *Hospital and Community Psychiatry* 44(9):839–43

Dincin, J., Wasmer, D., Witheridge, T.F., Cook, J. and Razzano, L. (1993) 'Impact of assertive community treatment on the use of state hospital inpatient bed-days', *Hospital and Community Psychiatry* 44(9):833–8.

Dingman, C.W. and McGlashan, T.H. (1986) 'Discriminating characteristics of suicides. Chestnut Lodge follow-up sample including patients with affective disorder, schizophrenia and schizoaffective disorder', *Acta Psychiatrica Scandinavica* 74:91–7.

—— (1988) 'Characteristics of patients with serious suicidal intentions who ultimately commit suicide'. *Hospital and Community Psychiatry* 39(3):295–9.

—— (1989) 'Psychotherapy', in A.S. Bellack (ed.) *Clinical Guide for the Treatment of Schizophrenia*, London: Plenum Press.

DHSS (1975) *Better Services for the Mentally Ill*, London: HMSO.

—— (1989) *Caring for People*, London: HMSO.

—— (1990) *National Health Service and Community Care Act 1990*, London: HMSO.

DOH (1993) *The Health of the Nation*, London: HMSO.

Dozier, M., Cue, K. and Roach, J.P. (forthcoming) 'When is service intervention coercive for adults with serious psychopathological disorders?', in J. McCord (ed.) *Coercion and Punishment in Long-term Perspectives*, New York: Cambridge University Press.

Drake, R.E. and Sederer, L.I. (1986) 'Inpatient psychosocial treatment of chronic schizophrenia: negative effects and current guidelines', *Hospital and Community Psychiatry* 37:897–901.

Drake, R.E., Gates, C., Cotton, P.G. and Whitaker, A. (1984) 'Suicide among schizophrenics: who is at risk?', *Journal of Nervous and Mental Disease* 172:613–17.

Edgerton, R.B. (1984) 'Anthropology and mental retardation: Research approaches and opportunities', *Culture, Medicine and Psychiatry* 8(1):25–48.

Edgerton, R.B., Bollinger, M. and Herr, B. (1984) 'The cloak of competence: after two decades', *American Journal of Mental Deficiency* 88(4):345–51.

Edwards, A. (1957) *The Social Desirability Variable in Personality Assessment*, New York: Dryden.

Ekdawi, M. and Conning, A. (1993) *Psychiatric Rehabilitation: A Practical Guide*, Chapman & Hall.

Ekdawi, M., Ghadiali, H., Howat, J., Mackay, M., Morris, B., O'Callaghan, M.A.J., Robinson, A. and Rowland, L. (1987) 'National demonstration services: statement on psychiatric rehabilitation and care in the community', *Bulletin of the Royal College of Psychiatrists* 11: 207–9.

Ely, I. (1992) 'Closeness in clubhouse relationships', *Psychosocial Rehabilitation Journal* 16 (2):61–2.

Emerson, E.B. (1985) 'Evaluating the impact of deinstitutionalisation on the lives of mentally retarded people', *American Journal of Mental Deficiency* 90(3): 277–88.

ENMESH (1994) *First International Conference of the European Network for Mental Health Service Evaluation*, Amsterdam, 10–12 June.

Erikson, E. (1965) *Childhood and Society*, Harmonsdworth: Penguin.

Eriksson, R. (1987) 'Survey of ethnic groups in districts with large populations in the county of Lancashire: Blackburn, Burnley, Hyndburn, Pendle, Preston, and Rossendale', Preston: Lancashire County Council.

Fairweather, G. (1978) 'The development, evaluation, and diffusion of rehabilitative programmes: a social change process', in L.I. Stein and M.A. Test (eds) *Alternatives to Mental Hospital Treatment*, New York: Plenum Press.

Falloon, I., Shanahan, W., Laporta, M. and Krekovian, H.A.R. (1990) 'Integrated family, general practice and mental health, care in the management of schizophrenia', *Journal of the Royal Society of Medicine*, 83:225–8.

Falloon, R.H., Boyd, J. and McGill, C. (1984) *Family Care of Schizophrenia*, New York: Guildford Press.

Farkas, M.D., Anthony, W.A. and Cohen, M.R. (1989) 'Psychiatric rehabilitation: the approach and its programs', in M.D. Farkas and W.A. Anthony (eds) *Psychiatric Rehabilitation Programs: Putting Theory into Practice*, Baltimore: The John Hopkins University Press.

Fayers, P.M. and Jones, D.R. (1983) 'Measuring and analysing quality of life in cancer trials: a review', *Statistics in Medicine* 2:429–46.

Feinmann, C., Harris, M. and Cawley, R. (1984) 'Psychogenic facial pain: presentation and treatment', *British Medical Journal* 288:436–8.

Fillenbaum, G.G. (1985) *The Wellbeing of the Elderly: Approaches to Multidimensional Assessment* (WHO Offset Publication 84). Geneva: World Health Organisation.

Finch, E.S. and Krantz, S. (1991) 'Low burnout in a high-stress setting: a study of staff adaptation at Fountain House', *Psychosocial Rehabilitation Journal* 14(3):16–26.

Fisher, M., Newton, C. and Sainsbury, E. (1984) *Mental Health Social Work Observed*, London: National Institute of Social Work.

Flanagan, J.C. (1982) 'Measurement of quality of life: Current state of the art', *Archives of Physical Medicine and Rehabilitation* 63:56–9.

Flor, H., Turk, D.C. and Rudy, T.E. (1987)' Pain and families. II: assessment and treatment', *Pain* 30(1):29–45.

Floyd, M. (1984) 'The employment problems of people disabled by schizophrenia', *Journal of the Society of Occupational Medicine* 34(3):93–5.

Follick, M.J., Smith, T.W. and Turk, D.C. (1984) 'Psychosocial adjustment following ostomy', *Health Psychology* 3(6) 505–17.

Ford, J., Young, D., Perez, B.C., Obermeyer, R.L. and Rohner, D.G. (1992) 'Needs assessment for persons with severe mental illness: What services are needed for successful community living?', *Community Mental Health Journal* 28(6):491–503.

Fordyce, W.E. (1973) 'An operant conditioning method for managing chronic pain', *Postgraduate Medicine* 53(6) 123–8.

Francell, E.G. (1994) 'What mental illness needs: public education and a new name (editorial)', *Hospital Community Psychiatry* 45(5):409.

Franklin, J.L., Simmons, J., Solovitz, B., Clemons, J.R. and Miller, G.E. (1986) 'Assessing quality of life of the mentally ill: a three dimensional model', *Evaluation and the Health Professions* 9(3):376–88.

Franklin, J.L., Solovitz, B., Mason, M., Clemons, J.R. and Miller, G.E. (1987) 'An evaluation of case management', *American Journal of Public Health* 77:674–8.

Freddolino, P.P. and Moxley, D.P. (1992) 'Redefining an advocacy model for homeless people coping with psychiatric disabilities', *Community Mental Health Journal* 28(4):337–52.

Freedman, R.I. and Moran, A. (1984) 'Wanderers in a promised land. The chronically mentally ill and deinstitutionalization', *Medical Care* 22(12):1–60.

Freudenberg, R.K. (1967) 'Theory and practice of rehabilitation of the psychiatrically disabled', *The Psychiatric Quarterly* 41:698–710.

Garety, P. (1988) 'Housing', in A. Lavender and F. Holloway (eds) *Community Care in Practice*, London: John Wiley & Sons Ltd.

—— (1991) 'A hostel ward for "new" long-stay psychiatric patients: the careers of the first ten years' residents', in R. Young (ed.) *Residential Needs for Severely Disabled Psychiatric Patients: The Case for Hospital Hostels*, London: HMSO.

Garety, P.A. and Morris, I. (1984) 'A new unit for long stay psychiatric patients: organization, attitudes and quality of care', *Psychological Medicine* 14:183–92.

Gask, L., Goldberg, D., Porter, R. *et al.* (1989) 'The treatment of somatisation: evaluation of a teaching package with general practice trainees', *Journal of Psychosomatic Research* 33:697–703.

Geller, J.L. and Fisher, W.H. (1993) 'The linear continuum of transitional residences: debunking the myth', *American Journal of Psychiatry* 150(7):1070–6.

Gerson, E. (1976) 'On quality of life', *American Sociological Review*, 41:795–806.

Gibbons, J.S. (1988) 'Residential care for mentally ill adults' in I. Sinclair (ed.) *Residential Care: The Research Reviewed*, London: NISW.

Gibbons, J.S. and Butler, J.P. (1987) 'Quality of life for "new" long-stay patients: the effects of moving to a hostel', *British Journal of Psychiatry* 151:347–54.

Gibbons, J., Horn, S., Powell, J. and Gibbons, J. (1984) 'Schizophrenic patients and their families: a survey in a psychiatric service based on a DGH unit', *British Journal of Psychiatry* 144:70–7.

Giel, R. (1986) 'Care of chronic mental patients in the Netherlands', *Social Psychiatry* 21:25–32.

Gill, W.M. (1984) 'Subjective well-being: properties of an instrument for measuring this (in the chronically ill)', *Social Science and Medicine* 18(8):683–91.

Girling, J. and Boswell, C. (1993) 'The Worth Valley Health Consortium' in V. Peel and R. Sheaf (eds) *Best Practice in Health Care Commissioning*, Harlow: Longman.

Gloag, R. (1987) 'Some approaches to employment problems in chronic psychiatric illness', *Bulletin of the Royal College of Psychiatrists* 11:43–5.

Goffman, E. (1963) *Stigma: Notes on the Management of Spoiled Identity*, Harmondsworth: Penguin Books.

Goldberg, D. (1991) 'Cost-effectiveness studies in the treatment of schizophrenia: review', *Schizophrenia Bulletin* 17:453–9.

Goldberg, D.P. (1972) *The Detection of Psychiatric Illness by Questionnaire* (Maudsley Monograph 21), London: Oxford University Press.

—— (1983) 'Measurement of the benefits in psychiatry', in G. Teeling-Smith (ed.) *Measuring the Social Benefits of Medicine*, London: Office of Health Economics.

Goldberg, D.P. and Huxley, P.J. (1992) *Common Mental Disorders: A Biosocial Model*, London: Routledge.

Goldberg, D.P. and Jones, R. (1980) 'The costs and benefits of psychiatric care', in L. Robins, P. Clayton and J. Wing (eds) *The Social Consequences of Psychiatric Illness*, New York: Bruner Maazel.

Goldberg, D.P., Bridges, K., Cook, D., Evans, B. and Grayson, D. (1990) 'The influence of social factors on common mental disorders: destabilisation and restitution', *British Journal of Psychiatry* 156:704–13.

Goldberg, D.P., Gask, L. and O'Dowd, T. (1989) 'The treatment of somatization: teaching techniques of reattribution', *Journal of Psychosomatic Research* 33:689–95.

Goldman, H.H., Gazzotti, A.A. and Taube, C.A. (1981) 'Defining and counting the chronically mentally ill', *Hospital and Community Psychiatry* 32:21–7.

Goldman, H.H. and Manderschield, R.W. (1987) 'The epidemiology of psychiatric disability', in A.T. Meyerson and T. Fina (eds) *Psychiatric Disability: Clinical, Legal and Administrative Dimensions*, New York: American Psychiatric Press Inc.

Graves, W.H. (1991) 'Participatory action research: a new paradigm for disability and rehabilitation research', unpublished paper presented at the Annual Conference of the National Association of Rehabilitation Research and Training Centers.

Griffiths, R. (1988) *Community Care: Agenda for Action*, London: HMSO.

Gunn, J. and Taylor, P. (1983) 'Rehabilitation of the mentally abnormal offender', in F.N. Watts and D.H. Bennett (eds) *Theory and Practice of Psychiatric Rehabilitation*, London: John Wiley & Sons Ltd.

Gurin, G., Veroff, J. and Feld, S. (1960) *Americans View their Mental Health*, New York: Basic Books.

Guthrie, E.A. (1991) 'Brief psychotherapy with patients with refractory irritable bowel syndrome', *British Journal of Psychotherapy Research* 8:175–88.

Haberman, P.W. (1969) 'Appendix: the reliability and validity of the data', in J. Kosa *et al.*, *Poverty and Health: A Sociological Analysis*, Cambridge, Mass.: Harvard University Press.

Hampson, R., Judge, K. and Renshaw, J. (1984) *Care in the Community Project Material* (Personal Social Services Research Unit Discussion Paper 362/2), Canterbury: PSSRU.

Hankiss, E. (1983) *Socio-Economic Studies 5: Quality of Life: Problems of Assessment and Measurement*', Paris: UNESCO.

Harper, A.C., Harper, D.A., Chambers, L.W., Cino, P.M. and Singer, J. (1986) 'An epidemiological description of physical, social and psychological problems in multiple sclerosis', *Journal of Chronic Diseases* 39(4):305–10.

Harris, M. and Bergman, H.C. (1984a) 'The young adult chronic patient: affective responses to treatment', *New Directions for all Health Services* (21) 29–35.

—— (1984b) 'Reassessing the revolving door: a developmental perspective on the young adult chronic patient', *American Journal of Orthopsychiatry* 54(2):281–9.

Heal, L.W. and Chadsey-Rusch, J. (1985) 'The lifestyle satisfaction scale (LSS): assessing individuals' satisfaction with residence, community setting and associated services', *Applied Research in Mental Retardation* 6(4):475–90.

Heaton, R.K., Grant, I., McSweeny, A.J., Adams, K.M. and Petty, T.L. (1983) 'Psychologic effects of continuous and nocturnal oxygen therapy in hypoxemic chronic obstructive pulmonary disease', *Archives of Internal Medicine* 143(10):1941–7.

Henderson, S., Byrne, D.G. and Duncan-Jones, P. (1981) *Neurosis and the Social Environment*, Sydney: Academic Press.

Hensen, M. and Bellack, A.S. (1976). 'Social skills training for chronic psychiatric patients: rationale, research findings and future directions', *Comprehensive Psychiatry*, 17:559–80.

Hirsch, S.R. (1992) 'Services for the severely mentally ill – a planning blight', *Psychiatric Bulletin* 16:673–5

Hoeffer, B. (1987) 'Predictors of life outlook of older single women', *Research in Nursing and Health* 10(2):111–17 (April).

Hoenig, J. and Hamilton, M. (1966) *Desegregation of the Mentally Ill*, London: RKP.

Hogan, M.F. and Carling, P.J. (1992) 'Normal housing: a key element of a supported housing approach for people with psychiatric disabilities', *Community Mental Health Journal* 28(3):215–26.

Hogarty, G.E. (1984) 'Depot neuroleptics: the relevance of psychosocial factors', *Journal of Clinical Psychiatry* 45:36–42.

Hogg, L. and Hall, J. (1992) 'Management of long-term impairments and challenging behaviour', in M.J. Birchwood and N. Tarrier (eds) *Innovations in* the *Psychological Management of Schizophrenia: Assessment, Treatment and Services*, London: John Wiley & Sons Ltd.

Holloway, F. (1988) 'Day care and community support', in A. Lavender and F. Holloway (eds) *Community Care in Practice*, London: John Wiley & Sons Ltd.

—— (1991) 'Case management for the mentally ill: looking at the evidence', *International Journal of Social Psychiatry* 37:2–13.

Hope, K. (1978) 'Indicators of the state of society', in M. Bulmer (ed.) *Social Policy Research*, London: Macmillan.

Hornstra, R.K., Bruce-Wolfe, V., Sagduyu, K. and Riffle, D.W. (1993) 'The effect of intensive case management on hospitalisation of patients with schizophrenia', *Hospital and Community Psychiatry* 44(9):844–7.

Hoult, J. (1990) 'Dissemination in New South Wales of the Madison model', in I. Marks and R. Scott (eds) *Mental Health Care Delivery: Innovations, Impediments and Implementation*, Cambridge: Cambridge University Press.

House of Commons (1994a) *Report of the Health Committee*, London: HMSO.

—— (1994b) *The Report of the Inquiry into the Care and Treatment of Christopher Clunis*, London: HMSO.

Howat, J., Bates, P., Pidgeon, J. and Shepperson, G. (1988) 'The development of residential accommodation in the community', in A. Lavender and F. Holloway (eds) *Community Care in Practice*, London: John Wiley & Sons Ltd.

Hubanks, L. and Kuyken, W. (1993) *Quality of Life Assessment: An Annotated Bibliography*, Geneva: World Health Organisation (Division of Mental Health).

Hurny, C., Piasetsky, E., Bagin, R. and Holland, J. (1987) 'High social disability in patients being treated for advanced colorectal or bladder cancer: eventual impact on the assessment of quality of life', *Journal of Psychosocial Oncology* 5(1):19–29.

Huszonek, J.J. (1987) 'Establishing therapeutic contact with schizophrenics: a supervisory approach', *American Journal of Psychotherapy* 41(2):185–93.

Hutton, S. (1990) 'Chapter 12: testing Townsend: exploring living standards using secondary data analysis', in S. Baldwin, C. Godfrey and C. Propper (eds) *Quality of Life: Perspectives and Policies*, London: Routledge.

Huxley, P.J. (1986) *Quality Measurement in Mental Health Services: A Discussion Paper on Quality of Life Measurement*, London: GPMH.

—— (1988) *The General Satisfaction Questionnaire Pilot Study: Technical Details*, Mental Health Social Work Research Unit, University of Manchester, UK.

—— (1990) *The General Satisfaction Questionnaire (GSQ). Field Trial Results I: GSQ Subscales*, Mental Health Social Work Research Unit, University of Manchester, UK.

—— (1991) 'Effective case management for mentally ill people: the relevance of recent evidence from the USA for case management services in the United Kingdom', *Social Work and Social Sciences Review* 2(3):192–203.

—— (1992) 'The sociology of size in residential care', in M. Davies (ed.) *The Sociology of Social Work*, London: Routledge.

—— (1993a) 'General psychiatric services in the community as an alternative to hospital admission: a review of recent research evidence', *Health and Social Care in the Community* 1(1):27–33.

—— (1993b) 'Case management, care management and community care', *British Journal of Social Work* 23:365–81.

—— (1993c) 'Resettlement and community care: "the mental hospital as an institution" revisited', *Psychiatric Bulletin*, 17:282–5.

—— (1993d) 'Location and stigma: a survey of community attitudes to mental illness. Part 1: enlightenment and stigma', *Journal of Mental Health* 2:73–80.

—— (1994a) 'The development of the Care Programme Approach Support System (CPASS)', Hull and Holderness Community Health Services, in-service programme for mental health professionals, January 1994.

—— (1994b) 'Quality and outcomes in mental health', University of Manchester, Department of Community Psychiatry (Academic Unit), Day Conference: 'Purchasing mental health services – the way ahead', Royal Preston Hospital, Preston, Lancashire, 24 February.

Huxley, P.J. and Oliver, J.P.J. (1993) 'Mental health policy in practice: lessons from the All Wales Strategy Mental Illness', *International Journal of Social Psychiatry* 39(3):177–89.

Huxley, P.J. and Warner, R. (1992) 'Case management, quality of life, and satisfaction with services of long term psychiatric patients', *Hospital and Community Psychiatry* 43(8):799–802.

Huxley, P.J., Hagan, T., Hunt, J. and Henelly, R. (1990) *Effective Community Mental Health Services*, Aldershot: Gower.

Huxley, P.J., Goldberg, D.P., Maguire, P. and Kincey, V. (1979) 'The prediction of the course of minor psychiatric disorders', *British Journal of Psychiatry* 135:535–43.

Hyde, C., Bridges, K., Goldberg, D., Lowson, K., Sterling, C. and Faragher, B. (1987) 'The evaluation of a hostel ward: a controlled study using modified cost-benefit analysis', *British Journal of Psychiatry* 151:805–12.

Jablensky, A., Schwarz, R. and Tomov, T. (1980) 'WHO, collaborative study on improvements and disabilities associated with schizophrenic disorders', *Acta Psychiatrica Scandinavica* (second supplementum) 285(62):152–63.

Jackson, Y., Gater, R., Goldberg, D., Tantam, D., Loftus, L. and Taylor, H. (1993) 'A new community mental health team based in primary care: a description of the service and its effects on service care in the first year', *British Journal of Psychiatry* 162:375–84.

Jan, M., Bazeze, V., Saudeau, D., Aytret, A., Bertrand, P. and Gouaze, A. (1986) 'Devenir des menigiomes intracraniens chez l'adulte: étude retrospective d'une serie medio-chirugicale de 161 meningiomes' ['outcome of intracranial mening-ioma in adults. Retrospective study of a medicosurgical series of 161 menigio-mas'], *Neurochirurgia* 32(2):129–34.

Jarman, B. (1984) 'Underprivileged areas: validation and distinction scores', *British Medical Journal* 289: 1587–92.

Jenkins, J. (1994) 'The ethical QALY', *Quality of Life Newsletter* 7–8:1–2.

Jenkins, R. (1990) 'Towards a system of outcome indicators for mental health care', *British Journal of Psychiatry* 157:500–14.

Jennett, B. and Braakman, R. (1990) 'Severe traumatic brain injury', *Journal of Neurosurgery* 73(3):479–80.

Jennings, B. and Callahan, D. (1983) 'Social science and the policy-making process', *Hastings Centure Report* 13(1):3–8

Johnson, F.L., Cook, E., Foxall, M.J., Kelleher, E., Kentopp, E. and Mannelin, E.A. (1986) 'Life-satisfaction of the elderly American Indian', *International Journal of Nursing Studies* 23(3): 256–73.

Johnstone, E.C., Owens, D.G.C., Gold, A., Crow, T.J. and MacMillan, J.F. (1984) 'Schizophrenic patients discharged from hospital', *British Journal of Psychiatry* 145:586–90.

Jones, K., Robinson, M. and Golightly, M. (1986) 'Long-term psychiatric patients in the community', *British Journal of Psychiatry* 146:537–40.

Joyce, K., Singer, M. and Isralowitz, R. (1983) 'Impact of respite care on parents' perceptions of quality of life', *Mental Retardation* 21(4):153–6.

Jurmann, J.A. (1986) 'Quality of life improvement after coronary-artery bypass surgery', Ph.D. Dissertation, St. John's University, *Dissertation Abstracts International*: 47/09–B.

Kaufmann, C.L., Freund, P.D. and Wilson, J. (1989) 'Self-help in the mental health system: A model for consumer–provider collaboration', *Psychosocial Rehabilitation Journal* 13 1:5–21.

Kaunitz, A.M., Thompson, R.J. and Kaunitz, K.K. (1986) 'Mental retardation: a controversial indication for hysterectomy', *Obstetrics and Gynecology* 68(3):436–8.

Kedenberg, D. (1980) Quality of life scale: a preliminary analysis, *Professional Psychology* 11(4):599–605.

Kellner, R., Abbott, P., Winslow, W.W. and Pathak, D. (1987) 'Fear, beliefs and attitudes in DSM-III hypochondriasis', *Journal of Nervous and Mental Disease* 175 (1):20–5.

Kendrick, T., Sibbald, B., Burns, T. and Freeling, P. (1991) 'Role of general practitioners in care of long term mentally ill patients', *British Medical Journal* 302:508–10.

Kinard, E.M. (1981) 'Discharged patients who desire to return to the hospital', *Hospital and Community Psychiatry* 32(3):194–7 (March).

Kind, P. (1990) 'Chapter 4: issues in the design and construction of a quality of life measure', in S. Baldwin, C. Godfrey and C. Propper (eds) *Quality of Life: Perspectives and Policies*, London: Routledge.

Kind, P., Gudex, C. and Godfrey, C. (1990) 'Introduction: what are QALYs?', in S. Baldwin, C. Godfrey and C. Propper (eds) *Quality of Life: Perspectives and Policies*, London: Routledge.

Kingdon, D., Turkington, D. and John, C. (1994) 'Cognitive behaviour therapy of schizophrenia', *British Journal of Psychiatry* 164:581–7.

Kleinman, A. and Kleinman, J. (1985) 'Somatization: the interconnections in Chinese society among culture, depressive experiences and the meaning of pain', in A. Kleinman and B. Good, *Culture and Depression*, Berkeley: University of California Press.

Klonoff, P.S. (1984) 'Quality of life in patients with closed head injury: a comparison of patients with and without frontal lobe damage, Ph.D. dissertation, University of Victoria (Canada), *Dissertation Abstracts International*: 46/08-B.

Knapp, M. (1991) 'The direct costs of community care of chronically mentally ill people', in H. Freeman and J. Henderson (eds) *Evaluation of Comprehensive Care of the Mentally Ill*, London: Gaskell Press.

Krauss, J.B. and Slavinsky, A.T. (1982) *The Chronically Ill Psychiatric Patient and the Community*, Boston: Blackwell Scientific Publishers.

Krawiecka, M., Goldberg, D.P. and Vaughn, M. (1977) 'A standardised psychiatric assessment scale for chronic psychotic patients', *Acta Psychiatrica Scandinavica* 55:299–308.

Kuipers, L. and Bebbington, P. (1990) *Working in Partnership: Clinicians and Carers in the Management of Longstanding Mental Illness*, London: Heinemann Medical Books.

Kuipers, L., MacCarthy, B., Hurry, J. and Harper, R. (1989) 'Counselling the relatives of the long term mentally ill. II: a low-cost supportive model', *British Journal of Psychiatry*, 154:775–82.

Lamb, H.R. (1977) 'Rehabilitation in community mental health', *Community Mental Health Review* 2:1–8.

—— (1981) 'What did we really expect from deinstitutionalisation?', *Hospital and Community Psychiatry* 32:105–9.

—— (1982) 'Young adult chronic patients: the new drifters', *Hospital and Community Psychiatry* 33:465–8.

—— (1993) 'Lessons learned from deinstitutionalisation in the US', *British Journal of Psychiatry* 162:587–92.

Lamb, H.R., Goldfinger, S.M., Greenfield, D., Minkoff, K., Nemiah, J.C., Schwab, J.J., Talbott, J.A., Tasman, A. and Bachrach, L.L. (1993) 'Ensuring services for persons with chronic mental illness under national health care reform', *Hospital and Community Psychiatry* 44(6):545–6.

Larsen, D.L., Atkisson, C.C., Hargreaves, W.A. and Nguyen, T.D. (1979) 'Assessment of client/patient satisfaction: development of a general scale', *Evaluation and Program Planning* 2:197–207.

Larson, R. (1978) 'Thirty years of research on the subjective well-being of older Americans', *Journal of Gerontology* 33:109–25.

Lavender, A. and Sperlinger, A. (1988) 'Staff training', in A. Lavender and F. Holloway (eds) *Community Care in Practice*, London: John Wiley & Sons Ltd.

Lawrence, R.E., Copas, J.B. and Cooper, P.W. (1991) 'Community care: does it reduce the need for psychiatric beds? A comparison of two different styles of service in three hospitals', *British Journal of Psychiatry* 159:334–40.

Lawton, M.P. (1984) 'The varieties of wellbeing', in C.Z. Maltatesta and C.E. Izard (eds) *Emotion in Adult Development*, Beverley Hills: Sage.

Leach, J. and Wing, J.K. (1978) 'The effectiveness of a service for helping destitute men', *British Journal of Psychiatry* 133:481–92.

Leff, J., Berkowitz, R., Shavit, N., Strachan, A., Glass, I. and Vaughn, C. (1989) 'A trial of family therapy v. a relatives group of schizophrenia', *British Journal of Psychiatry* 154:58–66.

Leff, J., Kuipers, L., Berkowitz, R. and Sturgeon, D. (1985) 'A controlled trial of social intervention in the families of schizophrenic patients: two year follow-up', *British Journal of Psychiatry* 146:594–600.

Lehman, A.F. (1983a) 'The well-being of chronic mental patients: assessing their quality of life', *Archives of General Psychiatry* 40(4):369–73.

—— (1983b) 'The effects of psychiatric symptoms on quality of life assessments among the chronic mentally ill', *Evaluation and Programme Planning* 6:143–51.

Lehman, A.F., Possidente, S. and Hawker, F. (1986) 'The quality of life of chronic patients in a state hospital and in community residences', *Hospital and Community Psychiatry* 37(9):901–7.

Lehman, A.F., Ward, N.C. and Linn, L.S. (1982) 'Chronic mental patients: the quality of life issue', *American Journal of Psychiatry* 139(10):1271–6.

Lelliot, P., Sims, A. and Wing, J. (1993) 'Who pays for community care? The same old question', *British Medical Journal* 307 (6910):991–4.

Levine, S. (1987) 'The changing terrains of medical sociology: emergent concern with quality of life', *Journal of Health and Social Behaviour* 28:1–6.

Liberman, R.P. (1988) 'Coping with chronic mental disorders: a framework for hope', in R.P. Liberman (ed.) *Psychiatric Rehabilitation of Chronic Mental Patients*, Washington: American Psychiatric Press, Inc.

Liberman, R.P., Jacobs, H.E., Boone, S.E., Foy, D.W., Donahoe, C.P., Falloon, I.R.H., Blackwell, G. and Wallace, C.J. (1986) 'Skills training for the community adaptation of schizophrenics', in J.S. Strauss, W. Boker and H.D. Brenner (eds) *Psychosocial Treatment of Schizophrenia*, New York: Hans Huber Publishers.

Liddle, P.F. (1992) 'Severe persistent mental illness', *Psychiatric Bulletin* 16:743–5.

Linn, M.W., Klett, J. and Caffey, F.M. (1980) 'Foster home characteristics and psychiatric patient outcome', *Archives of General Psychiatry* 37:129–32.

Lishman, W.A. (1987) 'Head injury', in *Organic Psychiatry: The Psychological Consequences of Cerebral Disorder* (2nd edition), London: Blackwell.

Liu, B. (1976) *Quality of Life Indicators in U.S. Metropolitan Areas: A Statistical Analysis*, New York: Praeger.

Ljunggren, B., Sonesson, B., Saveland, H and Brandt, L. (1985) 'Cognitive impairment and adjustment in patients without neurological deficits after aneurysmal SAH and early operation', *Journal of Neurosurgery* 62(5):673–9.

Lloyd, K. (1986) 'The BEC enterprise scheme', *British Journal of Occupational Therapy* 49:257–8.

Lobel, M. and Dunkel-Schetter, C. (1990) 'Conceptualizing stress to study effects on health: environmental, perceptual, and emotional components', *Anxiety Research* 3:213–30.

Lodge, G.J. (1991) 'Whither the disturbed patient: a study of regional secure unit referrals from two health districts', *Psychiatric Bulletin* 15:144–5.

Lusthaus, E.W. (1985) 'Involuntary euthanasia and current attempts to define persons with mental retardation as less than human', *Mental Retardation* 23(3):148–54.

Lyketsos, G.C., Sakka, P. and Mailis, A. (1983) 'The sexual adjustment of chronic schizophrenics: a preliminary study', *British Journal of Psychiatry* 143:376–82.

McCall, S. (1975) 'Quality of life', *Social Indicators Research* 2:229–48.

McCandless-Glincher, L., McKnight, S., Hamera, E., Smith, B.L., Peterson, K. and Plumlee, A. (1986) 'Use of symptoms by schizophrenics to monitor and regulate their illness', *Hospital and Community Psychiatry* 37:929–33.

McClure, R.F. and Loden, M. (1982) 'Religious activity, denomination membership and life satisfaction', *Psychology: A Quarterly Journal of Human Behaviour* 19:12–17.

MacDonald, L., Sibbald, B. and Hoare, C. (1988) 'Measuring patient satisfaction with life in a long-stay psychiatric hospital', *International Journal of Social Psychiatry* 34(4): 292–304.

McDowell, I. and Newell, C. (1987) *Measuring Health: A Guide to Rating Scales and Questionnaires*, New York: Oxford University Press.

MacEachron, A.E., Zober, M.A. and Fein, J. (1985) 'Institutional reform, adaptive functioning of mentally retarded persons and staff quality of work life', *American Journal of Mental Deficiency* 89(4):379–88.

McEwen, J. (1983) 'The Nottingham health profile: A measure of perceived health', in G. Teeling-Smith (ed.) *Measuring the Social Benefits of Medicine*, London: Office of Health Economics.

MacGilip, D. (1991) 'A quality of life study of discharged long-term psychiatric patients', *Journal of Advanced Nursing* 16:1206–15.

McGlashan, T.H. (1982) 'DSM-III schizophrenia and individual psychotherapy', *Journal of Nervous and Mental Disease* 170:752–7.

—— (1983) 'Intensive individual psychotherapy of schizophrenia: a review of techniques', *Archives of General Psychiatry* 40:909–20.

Maclean, U. (1968) 'The 1966 Edinburgh survey of community attitudes to mental illness', *Health Bulletin* 26:23–7.

Malm, U., May, P.R.A. and Dencker, S.J. (1981) 'Evaluation of the quality of life of the schizophrenic outpatient: a checklist', *Schizophrenia Bulletin* 7(3):477–87.

Markowe, M., Steinert, J. and Heyworth-Davies, F. (1967) 'Insulin and chlorpromazine in schizophrenia: a ten year comparative survey', *British Journal of Psychiatry* 113(503):1101–6.

Markson, E.W. (1985) 'After deinstitutionalization, what?' *Journal of Geriatric Psychiatry* 18(1):37–62.

Marnell, M.E. (1987) 'Measuring subjective well-being in daily life in arthritis, heart disease and chronic pain (health, quality of life)', Ph.D. dissertation, Stanford University, *Dissertation Abstracts International* 47–12–A.

Marshall, D. (1986) 'Creative therapy: every picture tells a story', *Nursing Times* 82(18):36–7.

Mastboom, J.C.M. (1992) 'Forty clubhouses: models and practices', *Psychosocial Rehabilitation Journal* 16(2):9–23

Maudsley, H. (1879) *The Pathology of Mind*, London: Macmillan.

Mayo, D.J. (1983) 'Contemporary philosophical literature on suicide: a review', *Suicide Life Threatening Behaviour* 13(4):313–45 (Winter).

Meehl, P. (1954) *Clinical vs Statistical Prediction*, University of Minnesota Press.

Milbrath, L.W. (1978) 'Indicators of environmental quality', in *Indicators of Environmental Quality of Life* (Publication SS/CH/38: *Reports and Papers in the Social Sciences*) Paris: UNESCO.

—— (1979) 'Policy relevant to quality of life research', *Annals of the American Association of Political and Social Scientists* 444:32–45.

Miles, P. (1977) 'Conditions predisposing to suicide: a review', *Journal of Nervous and Mental Disease* 164:231–46.

Mitchell, A.R.K. (1985) 'Psychiatrists in primary health care settings', *British Journal of Psychiatry* 147:371–9.

Mitchell, S.F. and Birley, J.L. (1983) 'The use of ward support by psychiatric patients in the community', *British Journal of Psychiatry* 142:9–15.

Mold, J.W., Steinbaur, J.R., Wunder, S.C. and Small, B. (1987) 'Outpatient multidisciplinary geriatric assessment', *Journal of the Oklahoma State Medical Association* 80(6):367–71.

Mooney, G.H. (1986) *Economics, Medicine and Health Care*, London: Harvester Press.

Moos, R. and Lemke, S. (1984) *Multiphasic Environmental Assessment Procedure (MEAP) Manual*, Palo Alto, California: Social Ecology Laboratory, Stanford University.

Mosher, L.R. and Menn, A.Z. (1978) 'Lowered barriers in the community: The Soteria Model' in L.I. Stein and M.A. Test (eds) *Alternatives to Mental Hospital Treatment*, New York: Plenum Press.

Moum, T. (1988) 'Yea-saying and mood-of-the-day effects in self reported quality of life', *Social Indicators Research* 20:117–39.

—— (1992) 'Self-assessed health among Norwegian adults', *Social Science and Medicine* 35(7):935–47.

Mowbray, C. (1993) 'Integrating vocational services in case management teams: project WINS', paper presented to the Butler County Mental Health Conference, Michigan, 5 June.

Mowbray, C., Rusilowski-Clover, G., Harris, S., McCrohan, N. and Greenfield, A. (1992) 'Project WINS: integrating vocational services on mental health case management teams', paper presented at the International Association of Psychosocial Rehabilitation Services Conference, Anaheim, California, May.

Muijen, M., Marks, I., Connolly, J. and Audini, B. (1992) 'Home based care and standard hospital care for patients with severe mental illness: a randomised control trial', *British Medical Journal* 304 (6829):749–54.

Murray, R.B. and Baier, M. (1993) 'Use of therapeutic milieu in a community setting', *Journal of Psychosocial Nursing and Mental Health Services* 31 (10):11–16.

Musella, G. (1984) 'Reflections sur la condition des personnes agées' ['Reflections on the condition of elderly people'], *Soins-Psychiatrie* 40:43–6.

Nagpal, R. and Sell, H. (1985) *Subjective Well-being*, New Delhi: World Health Organisation Regional Office in South-East Asia.

NATO (1993) 'NATO Advanced Workshop, Il Ciocco, Italy, September 2–5': proceedings to be published as G. Thornicroft and H. Knudsen (eds) *Mental Health Service Evaluation*, London: Churchill Livingstone.

National Association for Mental Health (MIND), World Federation for Mental Health (WFMH) (1985) *Charter 2000*, London: MIND

Nehring, J., Hill, R. and Poole, L. (1993) *Work, Empowerment and Community*, London: Research and Development in Psychiatry.

Netten, A. (1991) 'A positive experience? Assessing the effect of the social environment on demented elderly residents of local authority homes', *Social Work and Social Sciences Review* 3(1):46–62.

New South Wales Department of Health (1983) *Psychiatric Hospital versus Community Treatment: A Controlled Study*, Sydney, Australia: New South Wales Department of Health.

Norfleet, M.A. and Burnell, G.M. (1981) 'Utilization of medical services by psychiatric patients', *Hospital Community Psychiatry* 32(3):198–200.

Nortentoft, M., Knudsen, H.C. and Schulsinger, F. (1992) 'Housing conditions and residential needs of psychiatric patients in Copenhagen', *Acta. Psychiatrica Scandinavica* 85(5):385–9.

North Western Regional Health Authority (NWRHA) (1985) *Plan for the Closure of Four Long-Stay Mental Illness Hospital in the North West*, Manchester: NWRHA.

Norusis, M.J. (1988) *SPSS/PC+Version 2.0 Base Manual*, Chicago: SPSS.

O'Brien, J.E. (1973) 'Components of quality of life among severely impaired urban elderly', *Gerontologist* 13 (3, Part III):85.

O'Callaghan, M.A. (1992) 'Training the trainers (and introducing change): practical aspects of establishing and running a training system in mental health rehabilitation', *Journal of Mental Health* 1:141–7.

O'Donnell, O. (1991) 'Cost-effectiveness of community care for chronic mentally ill', in H. Freeman and J. Henderson (eds) *Evaluation of Comprehensive Care of the Mentally Ill*, London: Gaskell Press.

O'Donnell, O., Maynard, A. and Wright, K. (1992) 'Evaluating mental health care: the role of economics', *Journal of Mental Health*, 1:39–51.

O'Driscoll, C., Marshall, J. and Reed, J. (1990) 'Chronically ill psychiatric patients in a District General Hospital unit: a survey and two-year follow-up in an inner-London health district', *British Journal of Psychiatry*, 157:694–702.

O'Grady, J., Courtney, P. and Cunnane, J. (1992) 'The provision of secure psychiatric services in Leeds. Paper 1: a point prevalence study', *Health Trends* 24:49–50.

Okin, R.L., Dolnick, J.A. and Pearsall, D.T. (1983) 'Patients' perspectives on community alternatives to hospitalisation: a follow-up study', *American Journal of Psychiatry* 140(11):1460–4.

Oliver, J.P.J. (1991a) 'The social care directive: development of a quality of life profile for use in community services for the mentally ill', *Social Work and Social Sciences Review* 3(1):5–45.

—— (1991b) 'The quality of life in community care' in Dr R. Young (ed.) *Residential Needs for Severely Disabled Psychiatric Patients: The Case of Hospital Hostels*, London: HMSO.

Oliver, J.P.J. and Mohamad, H. (1992) 'The quality of life of the chronically mentally ill: a comparison of public, private and voluntary residential provisions', *British Journal of Social Work* 22:391–404.

Onyenwoke, N.O. (1983) 'Urban development and quality of life in the elderly', *Dissertation Abstracts*, Part A, 43:11 3717A, May.

Onyett, S., Heppleston, T. and Bushnell, D. (1994) *The Organisation and Operation of Community Mental Health Teams: A National Survey*, London: Sainsbury Centre for Mental Health.

OPCS (Office of Population Censuses and Surveys) (1987) *The General Household Survey*, London: HMSO.

Ormel, J. and Giel, R. (1990) 'Medical effects of non-recognition of affective disorders in primary care' in H.U. Wittchen (ed.) *Psychological Disorders in General Medical Settings*, Bern: Hogrefe & Huber.

Osborne, S.P. (1992) 'The quality dimensions: evaluating quality of service and quality of life in human services', *British Journal of Social Work* 22:437–53.

Ostrow, D.G., Whitaker, R.E., Fraiser, K., Choen, C., Wan, J., Frank, C. and Fisher, E. (1991) 'Racial differences in social support and mental health in men with HIV infection: a pilot study', *AIDS Care* 3(1):55–62.

Packa, D.R. (1986) 'Quality of life of adults after a heart transplant', dissertation for the University of Alabama in Birmingham, *Dissertation Abstracts International*, 48/01-B.

Patmore, C. and Weaver, T. (1992) 'Improving community services for serious mental disorders', *Journal of Mental Health* 1:107–15.

Pattison, E.M. Defrancisco, D., Wood, P., Frazier, H. and Crowder, J. (1975) 'A psychosocial kinship model for family therapy', *American Journal of Psychiatry* 132(12):1246–51.

Paul, G.L. and Lentz, R.J. (1977) *Psychosocial Treatment of Chronic Mental Patients: Milieu Versus Social Learning Programs*, Boston: Harvard University Press.

Persons, J.B. (1986) 'The advantages of studying psychological phenomena rather than psychiatric diagnoses', *American Psychologist* 41:1252–60.

Pilling, S. (1988) 'Work and the continuing care client', in A. Lavender and F. Holloway (eds) *Community Care in Practice*, London: John Wiley & Sons.

—— (1991) *Rehabilitation and Community Care*, London: Routledge.

Platt, S. (1984) 'Unemployment and suicidal behaviour: a review of the literature', *Social Science and Medicine* 19:93–115.

Poortinga, Y.H. (1989) 'Equivalence of cross-cultural data: an overview of basic issues', *International Journal of Psychology* 24:737–56.

Poortinga, Y.H. and Van de Vijver, F.J.R. (1987) 'Explaining cross-cultural differences: bias analysis and beyond', *Journal of Cross-Cultural Psychology* 18:259–82.

Posner, C.M., Wilson, K.G., Kral, M.J., Lander, S. and McIlwraith, R.D. (1992) 'Family psychoeducational support groups in schizophrenia', *American Journal of Orthopsychiatry* 62(2):206–18.

Powell, T.H. and Hecimovic, A. (1985) 'Baby Doe and the search for a quality life', *Exceptional Children* 51(4):315–23.

President's Commission on National Goals (1960) *Goals for Americans*, New York: Columbia University, The American Assembly.

Presly, A.S., Grubb, A.B. and Semple, D. (1982) 'Predictors of successful rehabilitation in long-stay patients', *Acta Psychiatrica Scandinavica*, 66:83–8.

Priebe, S. and Gutyers, T. (1993) 'The role of the helping alliance in psychiatric community care: a prospective study', *Journal of Nervous and Mental Disease* 181(9):552–7.

Priest, R.G. (1976) 'The homeless person and the psychiatric services: an Edinburgh survey', *British Journal of Psychiatry* 128:128–36.

Priestman, T.J. and Bauum, M. (1976) 'Evaluation of quality of life in patients receiving treatment for advanced cancer', *Lancet* 1:899–901.

Pritlove, J. (1983) 'Accommodation without resident staff for ex-psychiatric patients', *British Journal of Social Work* 13:75–92.

Propst, R.N. (1992) 'Standards for clubhouse programs: why and how they were developed', *Psychosocial Rehabilitation Journal* 16(2):25–30.

Pryce, I.G. and Preston, J. (1988) 'Community care for 20 psychiatrically disabled older men', *Social Psychiatry and Psychiatric Epidemiology* 23:166–74.

Pullen, G.P. (1987) 'The Oxford service for the young adult chronically mentally ill', *Psychiatric Bulletin* 11:377–9.

Pullen, I.M. and Yellowlees, A. (1988) 'Scottish psychiatrists in primary health care settings: a silent majority', *British Journal of Psychiatry* 153:663–6.

Rabkin, J. (1972) 'Opinions about mental illness: a review of the literature', *Psychological Bulletin* 77: 153–71.

Randolph, F.L., Ridgway, P. and Carling, P.J. (1991) 'Residential programs for persons with severe mental illness: a nationwide survey of state-affiliated agencies. Special Section: housing and support programs for persons with severe mental illness', *Hospital and Community Psychiatry* 42(11): 1111–15.

Ransibrahamanakul, S. (1991) 'Community mental health', *Journal of the Medical Association of Thailand* 74(9): 412–20.

Rapp, C.A. and Chamberlain, R. (1985) 'Case management services for the chronically mentally ill', *Social Work* 30: 417–22.

RDP (1991) *The RDP Case Management Project. Information Update*, London: Research and Development in Psychiatry.

Reed, J. (1983) 'The DHSS mental illness policy: a personal view', *The Bulletin of the Royal College of Psychiatrists* 7: 122–4.

—— 'The future of rehabilitation in psychiatry', *Bulletin of the Royal College of Psychiatrists* 8: 47–8.

Rehder, T.L., McCoy, L.K., Blackwell, B., Whitehead, W. and Robinson, A. (1980) 'Improving medication compliance by counselling and special prescription container', *American Journal of Hospital Pharmacology* 37(3): 379–85.

Rescher, R. (1972) *Welfare: The Social Issues in Philosophical Perspective*, Pittsburgh: University of Pittsburgh Press.

Rhodes, A.A. (1980) 'The correlates of life satisfaction in a sample of older Americans from a rural area', Ph.D. Dissertation, University of Arkansas, *Dissertation Abstracts International* 41: 1958–9a (university microfilms No. 80–26, 072).

Roewer, N., Kloss, T. and Puschel, K. (1985) 'Langzeiterfolg und Lebensqualitat nach praklinischer kardiopulmonaler Reanimation' ['Long-term result and quality of life following preclinical cardiopulmonary resuscitation'], *Anasthesie, Intensiotherapie, Notfallmedizin* 20(5): 244–50.

Rosenberg, M. (1965) *Society and the Adolescent Self-image*, Princeton: Princeton University Press.

Rosenfield, S. (1987) 'Services organisation and quality of life among the seriously mentally ill, in improving mental health services: what the social sciences can tell us', in D. Mechanic (ed.) *New Directions for Mental Health Services* 36, San Francisco: Jossey Bass.

—— (1992) 'Factors contributing to the subjective quality of life of the chronic mentally ill', *Journal of Health and Social Behaviour* 33(4): 299–315.

Rosenfield, S. and Neese-Todd, S. (1993) 'Elements of a psychosocial clubhouse program associated with a satisfying quality of life', *Hospital and Community Psychiatry* 44(1): 76–8.

Rosenthal, M., Griffith, E.R., Bond, M.R. and Miller, J.D. (1990) *Rehabilitation of the Adult and Child with Traumatic Brain Injury* (2nd ed.), Philadelphia: F.A. Davis Company.

Ross, W.D. (1947) (trans.) Aristotle's 'Nicomachean Ethics', in R. McKoen (ed.) *Introduction to Aristotle*, New York: Modern Library.

Rosser, R. and Watts, V.C. (1972) 'The measurement of hospital output', *International Journal of Epidemiology* 1(4): 361–8.

Rossi, P.H. and Freeman, H.E. (1993) *Evaluation: A Systematic Approach* (5th ed.) London: Sage.

Rowland, L. and Perkins, R.E. (1988) 'You can't eat, drink or make love eight hours a day: the value of work in psychiatry – a personal view', *Health Trends* 20: 75–9.

Rowntree, B.S. (1901) *Poverty: A Study of Town Life*, London: Macmillan.

Roy, A. (1982) 'Suicide in chronic schizophrenia', *British Journal of Psychiatry* 141: 171–7.

Ryan, P., Ford, R. and Clifford, P. (1991) *Case Management and Community Care*, London: RDP Publications.

Ryff, C.D. (1989) 'Happiness is everything, or is it? Explorations on the meaning of psychological well-being', *Journal of Personality and Social Psychology* 57(6): 1069–81.

Sandberg, S.I., Barnes, B.A., Weinstein, M.C. and Braun, P. (1985) 'Elective hysterectomy: benefits, risks and costs', *Medical Care* 23(9): 1067–85.

Sandhu, H.S. (1986) 'Psychosocial issues in chronic obstructive pulmonary disease', *Clinics in Chest Medicine* 7(4): 629–42 (December).

Sartorius, R. (1983) 'Coercive suicide prevention: A libertarian perspective', *Suicide and Life Threatening Behaviour* 13(4): 293–303.

Sayce, L., Craig, T.K.J. and Boardman, A.P. (1991) 'The development of community mental health centres in the UK', *Social Psychiatry and Psychiatric Epidemiology* 26(1): 18–20.

Schalock, R.L. and Konig, A. (1987) 'Die Entwicklung gemeindenaher Dienste fur geistig Behinderte in den USA – Auf dem Weg zu einem integrieten Leben' ['Development of community-based services for the mentally handicapped in the USA – on the way to an integrated life'], *Rehabilitation (Stuttgart)* 26(1): 28–34.

Schalock, R.L. and Lilley, M.A. (1986) 'Placement from community-based mental retardation programmes: how well do clients do after 8–10 years?', *American Journal of Mental Deficiency* 90(6): 669–76.

Scheibmer, M.S. (1986) '*The quality of life of individuals with insulin-dependent diabetes mellitus*, unpublished M.S., University of Arizona, *Masters Abstracts*: 25/01.

Schmandt, H.J. and Bloomberg, W. Jr (eds) (1969) *The Quality of Urban Life. Vol. 3: Urban Affairs Annual Reviews*, Beverly Hills: Sage Publications Inc.

Schubert, C., Krumm, B., Biehl, H. and Schwarz, R. (1986) 'Measurement of social disability in a schizophrenic patient group', *Social Psychiatry* 21: 1–9.

Sciarappa, K., Rogers, E.S., MacDonald-Wilson, K. and Danley, K. (1994) 'A benefit–cost analysis of a supported employment model for persons with psychiatric disabilities', unpublished, University of Massachusetts.

Segal, S.P. and Liese, L.H. (1991) 'A ten-year perspective on three models of sheltered care. Special section: housing and support programs for persons with severe mental illness', *Hospital and Community Psychiatry* 42(11): 1120–4

Sharpe, M., Peveler, R. and Mayou, R. (1992) 'The psychological treatment of patients with functional somatic symptoms: a practical guide', *Journal of Psychosomatic Research* 36: 515–29.

Shaw, J. and Creed, F. (1991) 'The cost of somatization', *Journal of Psychosomatic Research* 35: 307–12.

Sheldon, E.B. and Moore, W.E. (eds) (1968) *Indicators of Social Change: Concepts and Measurements*, New York: Russell Sage Foundation.

Shelter (1992) *Fact Sheet: Community Care and Housing*, London, Shelter.

Shepherd, G. (1984) *Institutional Care and Rehabilitation*, London: Longman.

—— (1990a) 'A criterion-oriented approach to skills training', *Psychosocial Rehabilitation Journal* 13: 11–13.

—— (1990b) 'Case management', *Health Trends* 22: 59–61.

—— (1991) 'Psychiatric rehabilitation for the 1990s', in F.N. Watts and D.H. Bennett (eds) *Theory and Practice of Psychiatric Rehabilitation*, London: John Wiley & Sons.

—— (1993) 'Differentiation of care for the long-term mentally ill', in J. Wolf and J. van Weeghel (eds) *Changing Community Psychiatry*, Utrecht: The Netherlands Institute of Mental Health.

Shepherd, M. (1983) 'Social criteria of the outcome of mental disease', in G. Teeling-Smith (ed.) *Measuring the Social Benefits of Medicine*, London: Office of Health Economics.

Simms, M. (1985) 'Surgery for retarded infants [letter]', *Lancet* 2(8462): 1014–5.

Simpson, C.J., Hyde, C.E. and Faragher, E.B. (1989) 'The chronically mentally ill in community facilities: a study of quality of life', *British Journal of Psychiatry* 154: 77–82.

Simpson, R.B.S. (1989) 'Expressed emotion and nursing the schizophrenic patient', *Journal of Advanced Nursing* 14: 459–66.

Skantze, K., Malm, U., Dencker, S.J., May, P.R.A. and Corrigan, P. (1992) 'Comparison of quality of life with standard of living is schizophrenic outpatients'. *British Journal of Psychiatry* 161: 797–801.

Slevin, M.L., Plant, H., Lynch, D., Drinkwater, J. and Gregory, W.M. (1988) 'Who should measure quality of life, the doctor or the patient?', *British Journal of Cancer* 57: 109–12.

Smith, J. (1991) 'Beyond mental hospital sites', *Psychiatric Bulletin* (letter) 15: 40–1.

—— (1992) 'Family interventions: service implications', in M. Birchwood and N. Tarrier (eds) *Innovations in Psychological Management of Schizophrenia*, London: John Wiley & Sons.

Smith, J. and Birchwood, M. (1987) 'Specific and non-specific effects of educational intervention with families living with a schizophrenic relative', *British Journal of Psychiatry* 150: 645–52.

Sokolovsky, J., Cohen, C., Berger, D. and Geiger, J. (1978) 'Personal networks in ex-mental patients in a Manhattan SRO hotel', *Human Organisation* 37: 5–15.

Solomon, P. (1992) 'The closing of a state hospital: what is the quality of patients' lives one year post-release?', *Psychiatric Quarterly* 63(3): 279–96.

Spiers, M. (1976) *Victoria Park Manchester: A nineteenth-century suburb in its social and administrative context*, Manchester: Manchester University Press.

Spitzer, W.O. and Dobson, A.J. (1981) 'Measuring the quality of life of cancer patients', *Journal of Chronic Diseases* 34: 585–97.

Stahl, S.M. and Wets, K.M. (1988) 'Clinical pharmacology of schizophrenia', in P. Bebbington and P. McGuffin (eds) *Schizophrenia: The Major Issues*, London: Heinmann Medical Books.

Stein, L. (1990) 'Comments by Len Stein', *Hospital and Community Psychiatry* 41: 649–51.

Stein, L.I. and Test, M.A. (1978) 'Training in community living: research design and results.' in L.I. Stein, and M.A. Test (eds) *Alternatives to Mental Hospital Treatment*, New York: Plenum Press.

—— (1980) 'Alternatives to mental hospital treatment: I: conceptual model, treatment program, and clinical evaluation', *Archives of General Psychiatry* 37: 392–7.

Stewart, A.L., Greenfield, A., Hays, R.D., Wells, K., Rogers, W.H., Berry, S.D., McGlynn, E.A. and Ware, J.E., Jr (1989) 'Functional status and well-being of patients with chronic conditions: results from the Medical Outcomes Study', *Journal of the American Medical Association* 262(7): 907–13.

Stich, T.F. and Senior, N. (1984) 'Adventure therapy: an innovative treatment for psychiatric patients', in B. Pepper and H. Ryglewicz (eds) *Advances in Treating the Young Adult Chronic Patient*, San Francisco: Jossey-Bass.

Stock, W.A., Okun, M.A., Haring, M.J. and Witter, R.A. (1983) 'Age and subjective well-being: a meta-analysis', in R.J. Light (ed.) *Evaluation Studies: Review Annual* (8: 279–302), Beverley Hills: Sage.

Stone, M.E. and Nelson, G.L. (1979) 'Coordinated treatment for long term psychiatric patients', *Social Work* 460–510.

Strack, F., Argyle, J. and Schwarz, N. (eds) (1991) *Subjective Well-Being – An Interdisciplinary Approach*, Oxford: German Press.

Strathdee, G. and Williams, P. (1985) 'Patterns of collaboration', in P. Williams, G. Wilkinson and M. Shepherd (eds) *Mental Illness in Primary Care Settings*, London: Tavistock.

Strauss, J.S. and Carpenter, W.T. (1972) 'The prediction of outcome in schizophrenia', *Archives of General Psychiatry* 27: 739–46.

—— (1977) 'Prediction of outcome in schizophrenia. III: 5-year outcome and its prediction', *Archives of General Psychiatry* 34: 159–63.

Stroul, B.A. (1989) 'The community support system concept', *Psychosocial Rehabilitation Journal* 12: 5–8.

Sturt, E., Wykes, T. and Creer, C. (1982) 'A survey of long-term users of the community psychiatric services in Camberwell', *Psychological Medicine. Monographs and Supplements* 2: 3–35.

Tan, K.H. (1993) 'Mental health services in Singapore', *Singapore Medical Journal* 34(3): 259–61.

Tannahill, M., Wilkinson, G. and Higson, P. (1990) 'Beyond mental hospital sites', *Psychiatric Bulletin* 14: 399–401.

Tantam, D. (1988) 'Review article: quality of life and the chronically mentally ill', *The International Journal of Social Psychiatry* 34(4): 243–7.

Tarrier, N., Beckett, R., Harwood, S., Baker, A., Yusuposs, L. and Ugarteburu, I. (1993a) 'A trial of two cognitive behavioural methods of treating drug-resistant residual psychotic symptoms in schizophrenic patients: 1: outcome', *British Journal of Psychiatry*, 162: 524–32.

—— (1993b) 'A trial of two cognitive behavioural methods of treating drug-resistant residual psychotic symptoms in schizophrenic patients. II: treatment specific changes in coping and problem-solving skills', *Social Psychiatry and Psychiatric Epidemiology* 28: 5–10.

Tarter, R.E., Hegedus, A.M. and Van Thiel, D.H. (1984) 'Neuropsychiatric sequelae of portal-systemic encephalopathy: a review', *International Journal of Neuroscience* 24(3–4): 203–16.

Taube, C.A., Goldman, H.H., Burns, B.J. and Kessler, G. (1988) 'High users of outpatient services. I: definition and characteristics', *American Journal of Psychiatry* 145: 19–28.

Tessler, R.C. and Manderscheid, R.W. (1982) 'Factors affecting adjustment of community living', *Hospital Community Psychiatry* 33(3): 203–7.

Thapa, K. and Rowland, L.A., (1989) 'Quality of life perspectives in long-term care: Staff and patient perceptions', *Acta Psychiatrica Scandinavica* 80: 267–71.

Thompson, K.S., Griffith, E.E.H. and Leaf, P.J. (1990) 'A historical review of the Madison model of community care', *Hospital and Community Psychiatry* 41: 625–34.

Tolsdorf, C.C. (1976) 'Social networks, support and coping: an exploratory study', *Family Process* 15: 407–17.

Torrance, G.W. (1987) 'Utility approach to measuring health-related quality of life', *Journal of Chronic Diseases* 40(6).

Torrey, E.F., Bigelow, D.A. and Sladen-Dew, N. (1993) 'Quality and cost of services for seriously mentally ill individuals in British Columbia and the United States', *Hospital and Community Psychiatry* 44, 10: 943–50.

Townsend, P. (1979) *Poverty in the United Kingdom*, Harmondsworth: Penguin.

Townsend, P., Phillmore, P. and Beattie, A. (1988) *Health and Deprivation: Inequality and the North*, Kent: Croom Helm.

Tsuang, M. (1978) 'Suicide in schizophrenics, manics, depressives and surgical controls: a comparison with general population suicide mortality', *Archives of General Psychiatry* 35: 153–5.

Turk, D.C., Flor, H. and Rudy T.E. (1987) 'Pain and families: etiology, maintenance, and psychosocial impact', *Pain* 30(1): 3–27.

USDEHW (United States Department of Health Education and Welfare) (1969) *Toward a Social Report*, Washington, D.C.: U.S. Government Printing Office.

Vitello, S.J. (1986) 'Deinstitutionalisation progress in the United States', *Medical Law (Germany)* 5(4): 273–8.

Wadsworth, W.V., Wells, B.W.P. and Scott, R.F. (1962) 'A comparative study of fatiguability of a group of chronic schizophrenics and a group of hospitalised non-psychotic depressives', *Journal of Mental Science* 108: 304–8.

Walker, L.G. (1979) 'The effect of some incentives on the work performance of psychiatric patients at a rehabilitation workshop', *British Journal of Psychiatry* 134: 427–35.

Wallot, H. (1985) 'La deinstitutionalisation. 1re partie' ['Deinstitutionalisation. Part 1'], *Union of Medicine, Canada* 114(7): 584–5.

Waltz, M. (1986) 'Marital context and post-infarction quality of life: is it social support or something more?', *Social Science of Medicine* 22(8): 791–805.

Ware, J.E. (1984) 'Methodology in behavioural and psychological cancer research: conceptualizing disease impact and treatment outcomes', *Cancer* 53 (10th supplement): 2316–26.

Warner, R. (1985) *Recovery from Schizophrenia: Psychiatry and Political Economy*, London: Routledge & Kegan Paul.

Warner, R. and Huxley, P.J. (1993) 'Psychopathology and quality of life among mentally ill patients in the community: British and US samples compared', *British Journal of Psychiatry* 163: 505–9.

Warr, P. (1987) *Work, Unemployment and Mental Health*, Oxford: Clarendon Press.

Wasylenki, D.A., Goering, P.N., Lemire, D., Lindsey, S. and Lancee, W. (1993) 'The hostel outreach program: assertive case management for homeless mentally ill persons', *Hospital and Community Psychiatry* 44(9): 848–53.

Waterman, A.S. (1984) *The Psychology of Individualism*, New York: Praeger.

Waters, B. (1992) 'The work unit: the heart of the clubhouse', *Psychosocial Rehabilitation Journal* 16(2): 41–8.

Watts, F. and Bennett, D. (1983) 'Management of the staff team', in F.N. Watts and D.H. Bennett (eds) *Theory and Practice of Psychiatric Rehabilitation*, London: John Wiley & Sons Ltd.

Wehman, P., Kregel, J. and Shafer, M.S. (1989) *Emerging Trends in the National Supported Employment Initiative: A Preliminary Analysis of Twenty-Seven States*, Richmond, VA: Virginia Commonwealth University, Rehabilitation Research and Training Center.

Weinman, B. and Kleiner, R.J. (1978) 'The impact of community living and community member intervention on the adjustment of the chronically psychotic psychiatric patient' in L.I. Stein and M.A. Test (eds) *Alternatives to Mental Hospital Treatment*, New York: Plenum Press.

Weiss, R.S. (1974) 'The provisions of social relationships', in Z. Rubin (ed.) *Doing unto Others*, N.J.: Prentice-Hall.

Weller, M.P. and Jauhar, P. (1987) 'Wandering at Heathrow Airport by the mentally unwell', *Medicine, Science and Law* 27(1): 37–9.

Weller, B.G., Weller, M.P., Coker, E. and Mahomed, S. (1987) 'Crisis at Christmas 1986' (published eratum appears in *Lancet* 1[8533]: 642 [14 March 1987], *Lancet* 1 (8532): 553–4.

Wells, E. and Marwell, G. (1976) *Self-esteem*, Beverly Hills: Sage Publications.

Welsh Office (1989) *The All Wales Strategy Mental Illness*, Cardiff: Welsh Office.

Wessely, S., David, A., Butler, S. and Chalder, T. (1989) 'The management of post-viral fatigue syndrome', *British Journal of General Practice*, 40(331): 82–3.

WHO (1988) 'Chapter 5: mental, behavioural and developmental disorders', in *International Classification of Disease*, Geneva: World Health Organisation.

—— (1991) *Assessment of Quality of Life in Health Care: A working party report*, Geneva: World Health Organisation.

—— (1993) *WHOQOL: Study Protocol: Division of Mental Health*, Geneva: World Health Organisation.

Widlak, P.A., Greenley, J.R. and McKee, D. (1992) 'Validity of case manager reports of clients' functioning in the community: independent living, income, employment, family contact, and problem behaviours', *Community Mental Health Journal* 28(6): 505–17.

Wiersma, D., DeJong, A. and Ormel, J. (1989) 'The Groningen social disabilities schedule: development, relationship with ICIDH and psychometric properties', *International Journal of Rehabilitation Research* (forthcoming).

Wiersma, D., Giel, R., De Jong, A. and Slooff, C.J. (1983) 'Social class and schizophrenia in a Dutch cohort', *Psychology of Medicine* 13(1): 141–50.

Wilkinson, G., Tannahill, M.M. and Higson, P. (1990) 'Beyond mental hospital sites' (letter), *Psychiatric Bulletin* 15: 41.

Wilkinson, W.H. (1992) 'New Day, Inc. of Spartanburg: hospitalisation study', *Psychosocial Rehabilitation Journal* 16(2): 163–8.

Wing, J.K. (1978a) *Schizophrenia: Towards a New Synthesis*, London: Academic Press.

—— (1978b) 'Planning and evaluating services for chronically handicapped psychiatric patients in the United Kingdom', in L.I. Stein and M.A. Test (eds), *Alternatives to Mental Hospital Treatment*, New York: Plenum Press.

—— (1983) 'Schizophrenia' in F.N. Watts and D.H. Bennett (eds) *Theory and Practice of Psychiatric Rehabilitation*, London: John Wiley & Sons Ltd.

Wing, J.K. (1986) 'Psychosocial factors affecting the long-term course of schizophrenia', in J.S. Strauss, W. Boker and H.D. Brenner (eds) *Psychosocial Treatment of Schizophrenia*, London: Hans Huber Publishers.

—— (1990) 'The functions of asylum', *British Journal of Psychiatry* 157: 822–7.

Wing, J.K. and Brown, G.W. (1970) *Institutionalism and Schizophrenia*, Cambridge: Cambridge University Press.

Wing, J.K. and Freudenberg, R.K. (1961) 'The response of severely ill chronic psychotic patients to social stimulation', *American Journal of Psychiatry* 118: 311–22.

Wing, J.K. and Furlong, R. (1986) 'A haven for the severely disabled within the context of a comprehensive psychiatric community service', *British Journal of Psychiatry* 149: 449–57.

Wright, R.G., Heiman, J.R., Shupe, J. and Olvera, G. (1989) 'Defining and measuring stabilisation of patients during four years of intensive community support', *American Journal of Psychiatry* 146(10): 1293–8.

Wykes, T. (1982) 'A hostel-ward for "new long-stay" patients', in J.K. Wing (ed.) *Long-term community care: Experience in a London Borough, Psychological Medicine*, supplement 2: 41–55.

Wykes, T. and Sturt, E. (1986) 'The measurement of social behaviour in psychiatric patients: an assessment of the reliability and validity of the SBS schedule', *British Journal of Psychiatry* 148: 1–11.

Wykes, T. and Wing, J.K. (1982) 'A ward in a house: accommodation for "new" long-stay patients', *Acta Psychiatrica Scandinavica* 65: 315–30.

—— (1991) 'New long-stay patients: The nature and size of the problem' in R. Young (ed.) *Residential Needs for Severely Disabled Psychiatric Patients: The Case for Hospital Hostels*, London: HMSO.

Wykes, T., Creer, C. and Sturt, E. (1982) 'Needs and the deployment of services', in J.K. Wing (ed.) *Long-term Community Care: Experience in a London Borough, Psychological Medicine Monograph*, supplement 2: 41–55.

Young, R. (ed.) (1991) *Residential Needs of Severely Disabled Psychiatric Patients: The Case for Hospital Hostels*, London: HMSO.

Zautra, A. and Goodheart, D. (1979) 'Quality of life indicators: a review of the literature', *Community Mental Health Review* 4(1): 2–10.

Zautra, A. and Simons, L.S. (1978) 'An assessment of a community's mental health needs', *American Journal of Community Psychology* 6: 551–62.

Name index

Subject index